OLMEC ARCHAEOLOGY AND EARLY MESOAMERICA

The foundations for the Maya and other civilizations of ancient Mesoamerica were laid down over 2,400 years ago during the early and middle phases of the Formative period. The most elaborate of these formative Mesoamerican societies are represented by the archaeological culture called Olmec, which merged some 3,500 years ago in the tropical lowlands of southern Veracruz and Tebasco, Mexico. Flourishing over the next 1,000 years, the Olmec created the most complex social and political hierarchies of their time on the North American continent. Olmec rulers expressed their material and religious power in the first monumental stone art of Mesoamerica, remarkable for its sophistication and naturalism, as well as through massive buried offerings of wealth obtained from great distances. *Olmec Archaeology and Early Mesoamerica* offers the most thorough and up-to-date book-length treatment of Olmec society and culture available.

Christopher A. Pool is associate professor of anthropology at the University of Kentucky. He has conducted archaeological fieldwork in southern Veracruz state, Mexico, and in the eastern United States.

CAMBRIDGE WORLD ARCHAEOLOGY

The *Cambridge World Archaeology* series is addressed to students and professional archaeologists, and to academics in related disciplines. Most volumes present a survey of the archaeology of a region of the world, providing an up-to-date account of research and integrating recent findings with new concerns of interpretation. While the focus is on a specific region, broader cultural trends are discussed and the implications of regional findings for cross-cultural interpretations considered. The authors also bring anthropological and historical expertise to bear on archaeological problems and show how both new data and changing intellectual trends in archaeology shape inferences about the past. More recently, the series has expanded to include thematic volumes.

BOOKS IN THE SERIES

A.F. HARDING, *European Societies in the Bronze Age*
RAYMOND ALLCHIN AND BRIDGET ALLCHIN, *The Rise of Civilization in India and Pakistan*
CLIVE GAMBLE, *The Palaeolithic Settlement of Europe*
CHARLES HIGHAM, *Archaeology of Mainland South East Asia*
DAVID PHILLIPSON, *African Archaeology* (second revised edition)
OLIVER DICKINSON, *The Aegean Bronze Age*
KAREN OLSEN BRUHNS, *Ancient South America*
ALASDAIR WHITTLE, *Europe in the Neolithic*
CHARLES HIGHAM, *The Bronze Age of Southeast Asia*
CLIVE GAMBLE, *The Palaeolithic Societies of Europe*
DAN POTTS, *The Archaeology of Elam*
NICHOLAS DAVID AND CAROL KRAMER, *Ethnoarchaeology in Action*
CATHERINE PERLÈS, *The Early Neolithic in Greece*
JAMES WHITLEY, *The Archaeology of Ancient Greece*
PETER MITCHELL, *The Archaeology of Southern Africa*
HIMANSHU PRABHA RAY, *The Archaeology of Sea-Faring in Ancient South Asia*
TIMOTHY INSOLL, *The Archaeology of Islam in Sub-Saharan Africa*
PETER M. M. G. AKKERMANSA AND GLENN M. SCHWARTZ, *The Archaeology of Syria*
PAUL RAINBIRD, *The Archaeology of Micronesia*

CAMBRIDGE WORLD ARCHAEOLOGY

OLMEC ARCHAEOLOGY AND EARLY MESOAMERICA

CHRISTOPHER A. POOL

University of Kentucky

CAMBRIDGE
UNIVERSITY PRESS

CAMBRIDGE UNIVERSITY PRESS
Cambridge, New York, Melbourne, Madrid, Cape Town, Singapore, São Paulo

Cambridge University Press
32 Avenue of the Americas, New York, NY 10013-2473, USA

www.cambridge.org
Information on this title: www.cambridge.org/9780521783125

First published 2007

Printed in the United States of America

A catalog record for this publication is available from the British Library.

Library of Congress Cataloging in Publication Data

Pool, Christopher A.
Olmec archaeology and early Mesoamerica / Christopher A. Pool.
    p.   cm. – (Cambridge world archaeology)
Includes bibliographical references and index.
ISBN-13: 978-0-521-78312-5 (hardback)
ISBN-10: 0-521-78312-7 (hardback)
ISBN-13: 978-0-521-78882-3 (pbk.)
ISBN-10: 0-521-78882-X (pbk.)
    1. Olmecs – Antiquities.   2. Olmec sculpture.   3. Olmecs – Social life and customs.
4. Excavations (Archaeology) – Mexico – Veracruz-Llave (State)   5. Veracruz-Llave
(Mexico : State) – Antiquities.   I. Title.   II. Series.
F1219.8.O56P66   2007
980′.012 – dc22   2006015899

ISBN 978-0-521-78312-5 hardback
ISBN 978-0-521-78882-3 paperback

For Margaret B. Pool and Jack E. Pool

CONTENTS

LIST OF ILLUSTRATIONS

LIST OF TABLES

ACKNOWLEDGMENTS

As I have written this book my thoughts have often turned to Philip Drucker, who began his pioneering work in Olmec studies at Tres Zapotes, where I have directed recent fieldwork, and who ended his career in the Department of Anthropology at the University of Kentucky, where I teach. Following thus in Drucker's footsteps, I am made keenly aware of the debt we all owe to the scholars, past and present, who make up the fractious community of *olmequistas*. I cannot recognize each of these people individually in these brief acknowledgments, but their work is highlighted in Chapter 2 and throughout the volume.

This book owes its existence to Tom Dillehay. It was at his suggestion that I proposed the volume to Cambridge University Press, and his encouragement sustained me as I wrote it. Norman Yoffee, the series editor, likewise offered support leavened with great patience as I wrote and revised the manuscript. I am also deeply grateful to Cambridge Managing editor Jessica Kuper and her successor, Simon Whitmore, for their equally patient assistance in the completion of the book project. I especially thank Peter Katsirubas for his gentle but persistent guidance through the final stages of production and Kathleen Paparchontis for her wonderfully thorough job preparing the index.

The thoughtful reviews of David Grove, John Clark, and Norman Yoffee improved the original text considerably. John Clark deserves special recognition for the thoroughness of his critique and for his generous provision of unpublished papers, published reprints, and New World Archaeological Foundation reports. Others who provided me with access to unpublished information and commentary on specific points in the text include Philip J. Arnold, III, David Cheetham, Robert Cobean, Travis Doering, Michael Glascock, John Hodgson, Rebecca González, Hector Neff, Ponciano Ortiz, Carmen Rodríguez, Christopher von Nagy, and Carl Wendt. I thank all of these people for enlightening me on various aspects of Formative period archaeology, but I alone am responsible for any and all errors of fact and interpretation in the text.

David Cheetham, Robert Cobean, John Hodgson, Ponciano Ortiz, and Carmen Rodríguez supplied original photographs and drawings reproduced in this book. I thank them for their generosity as I do Jorge Angulo, John Clark, Michael Coe, Richard Diehl, David Grove, Rebecca González, Joyce Marcus, Guadalupe Martínez Donjuan, Ponciano Ortíz Ceballos, María del Carmen Rodríguez, George Stuart, Karl Taube, and Princeton University Press, who gave permission to reproduce illustrations from previously published works. Olaf Jaime Riverón provided valuable assistance in preparing illustrations and tracking down references.

I would also like to thank those who guided me on my winding course to Olman. My parents, Margaret and Jack Pool, who encouraged my interest in archaeology from the beginning; Will Andrews, who taught me my first course in Olmec and Maya archaeology at Tulane; Dan Healan, who taught the archaeology of Highland Mexico at Tulane and who directed my dissertation; Robert Santley, who invited me to work in southern Veracruz on his Matacapan project; and Ponciano Ortiz, who co-directed the Matacapan project, and who has been a constant source of help and advice ever since. Philip Arnold, Richard Diehl, and Barbara Stark also deserve special recognition for their years of friendly encouragement and constructive criticism. The continued mentoring and friendship of all these people has sustained me throughout this project and my career. Financial and institutional support for the research presented in this book that I have conducted at Tres Zapotes and in the Tuxtla Mountains was provided by the National Science Foundation, the University of Kentucky, Ithaca College, the Universidad Veracruzana, the Instituto de Investigaciones Antropológicas at the Universidad Nacional Autónoma de México, and the Instituto Nacional de Antropología e Historia of Mexico.

Finally, my deepest gratitude goes to my wife, Kathleen Pool, and our daughters, Caroline and Maggie, whose contribution is measured in the nights, weekends, and vacations when I was too occupied with "that book" to join them in the celebration of their amazing lives.

CHAPTER I

INTRODUCTION

One day in the late 1850s (the precise year is not recorded) a farm worker was clearing a cornfield on the Hacienda Hueyapan in southern Veracruz state, Mexico. As he hacked at the forest, he came upon what he thought was the bottom of an overturned cauldron, partly buried in the ground. Ordered by the hacienda owner to retrieve the cauldron, he returned and began to dig. To his surprise, his labors were rewarded not by the rim of an iron vessel, but by the baleful stare of a great head carved in dark volcanic stone (Melgar 1869: 292) (Fig. 1.1).

Today we recognize the "*cabeza colosal de Hueyapan*" as one of the master-works of the earliest tradition of monumental sculpture on the North American continent. Modern scholars have given the name "Olmec" to this artistic tradition, the archaeological culture of which it was the most spectacular expression, and the people who created it. Beginning about 1400 B.C. in the tropical low-lands of Mexico's southern Gulf Coast, the Olmecs achieved an unprecedented level of social and political complexity. From the early Olmec capital at San Lorenzo, and later ones at La Venta, Laguna de los Cerros, and Tres Zapotes, paramount rulers wielded their power and influence over subordinate local leaders and thousands of subjects in surrounding towns, villages, and hamlets. At San Lorenzo, at least ten rulers were memorialized between 1400 and 1000 B.C. with colossal stone portrait heads such as the one from Hueyapan. The hard basalt stone used to fashion these heads, along with the multi-ton table-top thrones and over a hundred sculptures of humans and supernatural beings were brought from volcanic slopes 60 km away. The inhabitants of San Lorenzo reshaped the plateau on which the capital rose with extensive terraces and built causeways across the swampy lowlands to river ports. Later, between 1000 and 400 B.C., the rulers of La Venta constructed a carefully planned civic and ceremonial precinct with over 30 earthen mounds, the largest rising 30 m above the grand plaza below. These La Venta rulers were laid to rest in elaborate tombs, and they imported thousands of tons of serpentine, which they buried in massive offerings, along with hundreds of jade ornaments and figurines. Like their counterparts at San Lorenzo, early rulers of La Venta celebrated their might and prestige with the creation of colossal heads and table-top thrones, but their successors commemorated diplomatic encounters and the divine sources of their power with low-relief carvings on slab-like stelae. A column of symbols on a late monument at La Venta, and symbols on a cylinder seal and fragments of a stone plaque from nearby San Andrés, also suggest the Olmecs made early steps toward writing (Pohl et al. 2002).

Monumental artwork and public works, a complex social hierarchy, and writing are all traits that V. Gordon Childe famously included in his definition of civilization, and some have described Olmec culture as "America's first civilization" (Coe 1968a; Diehl 2004). Like much about the Olmecs, this claim has provoked considerable controversy. "Civilization" implies the highly stratified political organization of the state, and modern scholars disagree strongly over whether state institutions existed among the Olmecs. They also argue vehemently over the significance of Olmec contributions to later civilizations in Mexico and Central America. At its extremes, this debate pits those who view the Olmecs as the "Mother Culture" of Mesoamerica, vastly superior to their contemporaries and responsible for the major ideas and institutions that laid the foundation for all subsequent Mesoamerican civilizations, against those who argue the Olmecs were on a par with their contemporaries, who contributed equally to the development of Mesoamerican civilization. Like many, perhaps most, current Olmec scholars, I see the truth as lying between these extremes (for a particularly cogent discussion see Lesure 2004). The Olmecs of San Lorenzo were one of only a handful of societies in the Americas that had achieved a comparable degree of social and political integration by the end of the second millenium B.C. On the other hand, sociopolitical complexity varied among the Olmec societies within the Gulf Coast region, the intensity and effects of interaction with the Olmecs varied across Mesoamerica, and other Formative societies made significant contributions to the development of a distinctively Mesoamerican civilizational tradition. Consequently, much of this book focuses on how leaders among the Olmecs and other Formative societies used local and external sources of power as they created the early complex polities and societies of Mesoamerica.

THE GEOGRAPHICAL SETTING

The modern countries of Central America and Mexico define the geographical area known as Middle America. A land of exceptional natural variation, the environments of Middle America range from deserts in the north to tropical rainforests in the south and from hot coastal lowlands to snow-covered mountain peaks, with cool highland slopes, plateaus, and valleys in between.

The early inhabitants of Middle America shared a hunting-gathering way of life and also styles of chipped stone projectile points with other societies

Figure 1.1. The *cabeza colosal de Hueyapan*, Tres Zapotes Monument A, during re-excavation by Matthew Stirling in 1939 (from Stirling 1943: Plate 4a).

in North and South America. Between 2000 and 1500 B.C., however, in the central portion of Middle America, there began to emerge a distinctive cultural pattern that would define the culture area of Mesoamerica. Early elements of this pattern included permanent settlements, manufacture of pottery, and subsistence based on cultivation of domesticated maize, beans, and squash (cf. Clark and Cheetham 2002). Over the next 2000 years social hierarchies, centralized governments, and specific religious concepts and practices emerged in various societies, including the Olmecs, and were adopted by their neighbors.

At their maximum geographical distribution in the sixteenth century A.D., societies that participated in the Mesoamerican cultural tradition extended from the edge of the northern Mexican desert through the rainforests of northern Central America (Fig. 1.2). These boundaries fluctuated, however, with shifting patterns of cultural interaction and climatic changes that affected the northern range of maize agriculture (Braniff 1989). Neither did the spread of characteristic Mesoamerican traits obliterate cultural difference. Rather, the area encompassed an astounding variety of regional traditions and ethnicities. By some estimates, more than 200 languages were spoken in Mesoamerica when Cortes landed on its shores in 1519.

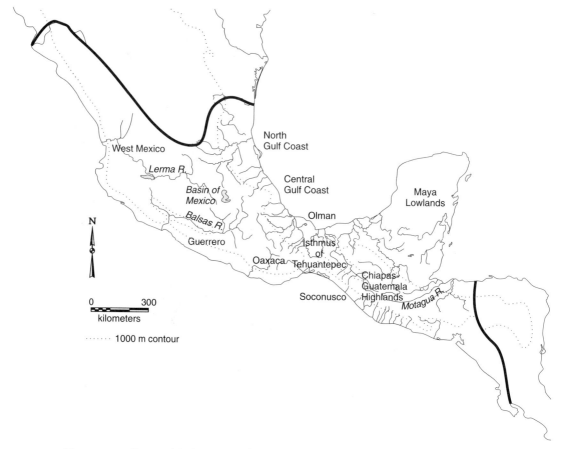

Figure 1.2. Geographical regions of Mesoamerica.

Muriel Porter Weaver (1993: 5) aptly describes the map of Mesoamerica as a lopsided bow, its knot formed by the Isthmus of Tehuantepec, which separates the Gulf of Mexico to the north from the Pacific Ocean to the south. The Olmecs resided on the north side of the Isthmus amid the tropical rain forests, swamps, and savannahs in the hot, humid, southern Gulf lowlands of southern Veracruz and western Tabasco (Fig. 1.3). There, the broad rivers of the Papaloapan, Coatazacoalcos, Tonalá, and Mezcalapa-Grijalva systems meander across the coastal plain, which is broken by the low volcanic massif of the Tuxtla Mountains. The four major sites of Tres Zapotes, Laguna de los Cerros, San Lorenzo Tenochtitlán, and La Venta form a rough semicircle running from west to east from the Papaloapan to the Tonalá drainage, and hundreds of smaller sites dot the coastal plain and mountain slopes between them.

Archaeologists have labeled this region the "Olmec heartland" and the "Olmec Metropolitan Zone." These terms recognize the southern Gulf lowlands as the homeland of the Olmecs, but they also controversially cast the rest of Formative period Mesoamerica in the role of an exploited hinterland. The

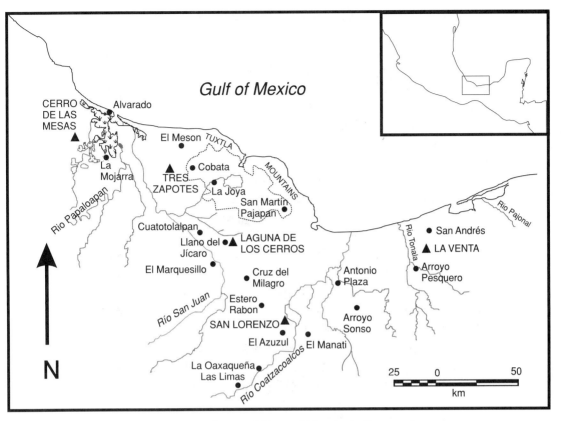

Figure 1.3. Formative period sites of Olman. Triangles indicate major centers.

Aztecs, however, have given us an alternative name that avoids presupposing Olmec dominance. They christened the Gulf lowlands of southern Veracruz and Tabasco *Olman* (or *Ulman*), meaning "Land of Rubber" in their Nahuatl language, evoking an economically and spiritually important resource as well as the tropical nature of the region (Diehl 1996: 29).

The Aztecs referred to the people who inhabited Olman as the *Olmeca* (also rendered as *Ulmeca*). Modern scholars have adopted the Nahuatl name for the archaeological culture representative of a group of closely interacting societies that flourished in the region more than 18 centuries before the Aztecs forged their empire, as well as for the associated art style, elements of which were shared widely across Mesoamerica between 1400 and 400 B.C.

This book is about Olmec societies as they adapted to the specific challenges and opportunities of Olman and the broader sociopolitical context of Formative Mesoamerica. Throughout the volume I use the terms "society" and "culture" advisedly. By "society" I mean a group of people united in regular interactions by a set of relationships and institutions. These social relationships and institutions include those of kinship, sodality, occupation, rank or class, and political administration. By "culture" I refer to the system of learned behaviors, beliefs, and ideals shared to a greater or lesser extent by individuals as members of a society and expressed in their art, architecture, and crafts. Admittedly, this common anthropological distinction is more analytical than real. Social (including political and economic) institutions are supported by cultural beliefs and ideals, and individuals and groups within a society vary in the degree to which they share cultural precepts and behaviors.

Like many early complex societies of the Americas, the Olmecs relied upon domesticated crops and animals as well as wild foods they obtained by hunting, fishing, and gathering. With these they provided for their individual needs and produced the surpluses of food that supported the construction of large public works and the emergence of social and political hierarchies that integrated many formerly autonomous communities. As all societies must, the Olmecs adapted their subsistence practices and social institutions to the specific challenges, resources, and opportunities afforded by their land's ecology and geographical setting.

The linguistic affiliation of these people remains a matter of debate, with some arguing they spoke a Mayan language. The evidence of later inscriptions and studies of loan words into other Mesoamerican languages, however, suggest the Olmecs spoke an ancestor of the Mije-Sokean languages still spoken in parts of the southern Gulf lowlands and adjacent regions parts of Chiapas and Oaxaca (Campbell and Kaufman 1976; Justeson and Kaufman 1993, 1997).

CHRONOLOGY

A handful of scattered archaeological sites and skeletal remains suggest that humans may have entered Middle America between 35,000 and 14,000 years ago, initiating the Paleoindian period. Around 8000 B.C., the advent of modern climates and the extinction of many Pleistocene species caused hunter-gatherers throughout the Americas to adopt new adaptations and technologies that characterize the Archaic period. The remaining pre-conquest history of the developing culture area of Mesoamerica is roughly divided into the Preclassic or Formative period (ca. 2000 B.C. – A.D. 300), the Classic period, (ca. A.D. 300–900), and the Postclassic period (ca. A.D. 900–1521), although the precise divisions between these periods vary from region to region (all dates are in calendar years as opposed to uncalibrated radiocarbon years)[1] (Fig. 1.4). The Olmec culture flourished during the Early Formative period and the Middle Formative period (ca. 1500–400 B.C.). Subsequently, in the Late Formative period (ca. 400 B.C.–A.D. 100), the Olmec culture evolved into the epi-Olmec culture, continuing and transforming many earlier practices.

One of the persistent difficulties for students of Mesoamerica has been the conflation of chronological periods and developmental stages under the same names. Mesoamerican studies are not unique in this regard, but the problem in this field is particularly acute, because "Mesoamerica" encompassed many

C14. Date	Cal. Date	General Periods	San Lorenzo	Western Tabasco	Tres Zapotes	Central Tuxtlas	Soconusco	Oaxaca	Morelos	Basin of Mexico
200	300	Terminal Formative	hiatus	hiatus	Nextepetl	Late Bezuapan	Istapa	Monte Albán IIIa	Terminal Formative	Miccaotli
	200									
50	100									Tzacualli
50	A.D. / B.C.	Late Formative		hiatus		Hato	Monte Albán II			
150	100				Hueyapan	Early Bezuapan	Guillén			Patlachique
200	200		Remplás						Late Formative	
300	300							Monte Albán I		Ticoman
400	400		hiatus	Late Franco			Francesa			
	500								Late Cantera	
550	600	Middle Formative	Palangana	Early Franco	Tres Zapotes	Gordita	Escalón	Rosario	Early Cantera	Zacatenco
	700			Late Puente						
650	800		hiatus				Duende	Guadalupe	Late Barranca	
800	900		Nacaste	Early Puente			Conchas		Middle Barranca	Tetelpan
900	1000									Manantial
950	1100			Palacios	Arroyo		Jocotal		Early Barranca	
	1200	Early Formative	San Lorenzo	. . . .		Coyame		San José		Ayotla
1050	1300						Cuadros		Late Amate	
1150	1400		Chicharras	Molina			Cherla			
1250			Bajio	. . . .		Tulipan	Ocos	Tierras Largas	Early Amate	Nevada
1300	1500									
	1600		Ojochi	Pellicer	"Ocos"		Locona			
1400	1700	Initial Formative								
1500	1800						Barra	Espiridión		
1600	1900									
1700	2000									

Figure 1.4. Formative period chronology of Mesoamerica. See note 1 on cultivation and text for discussion of specific sequences.

distinct cultural traditions that experienced different tempos of change during particular spans of their histories. Technically, periods refer to blocks of time, with precise, if somewhat arbitrary, beginning and ending dates. Thus for the southern Maya lowlands we can refer to a Classic period between A.D. 250 and A.D. 900, roughly bracketed by the earliest and latest calendrical dates in the Long Count system inscribed on stone monuments. In contrast, developmental stages are defined by cultural characteristics, such as urbanism, state organization, agriculture, technological innovations, and so on. Of course, it is the aim of most archaeological periodizations to identify when or in what sequence such developments occur. The conflation of periods and stages presents few problems when consideration is confined to a particular region, or when the lack of chronometric dates forces archaeologists to rely on relative chronology, as was the case for most of Mesoamerica before the development of radiocarbon dating. Stages, however, are usually time-transgressive; that is, they begin and end at different points in the history of different regions. When absolute dating methods reveal these differences in timing, then the use of the same terms for periods and stages over an entire culture area such as Mesoamerica can create considerable confusion.

Stage schemes have a long history in Mesoamerican archaeology; Pedro Armillas (1948) introduced such a scheme with similar developments occurring at different times in different parts of the culture area (Willey and Sabloff 1993: 207). Likewise, the early use of the term "Archaic" (Vaillant 1941) for what is now called the Formative or Preclassic had stage-like implications. Use of the term "Formative" became widespread in the Mesoamerican literature as the result of the evolutionary scheme for the entire New World developed by Gordon Willey and Philip Phillips (1955, 1958), where it indicated the "village agricultural threshhold and/or sedentary life" (Willey and Sabloff 1993: 207). For those who are uncomfortable with the evolutionary implications of the term "Formative," "Preclassic" exists as an alternative, but Preclassic is still identified by the same set of cultural traits, particularly the appearance of pottery. The compromise has been to use Formative and Preclassic interchangeably, to refer to them as a period, and to recognize that the period begins and ends at different times in different parts of Mesoamerica.

An additional complication is that, historically, some authors who used the term Formative in their writing divided the period between 2000 B.C. and A.D. 300 differently from those who used the term "Preclassic" (Grove 1981a: 374). The "Middle Preclassic" was usually defined as corresponding to the period of Olmec culture between about 1500 and 400 or 500 B.C. The "Middle Formative," however, typically referred to the time span between about 1000 and 500 B.C., which accords better with cultural changes widespread throughout Mesoamerica (Grove 1981a: 374). I follow Grove's suggestion and use "Formative period" to reflect the way the period is subdivided in this book.

CULTURAL DEVELOPMENTS OF THE FORMATIVE PERIOD

The Formative period saw the most fundamental changes in the prehispanic history of Middle America. Before 2000 B.C., most inhabitants of the region lived in small, seasonally mobile, hunting-gathering bands; by A.D. 300, large urban centers were common features of the landscape. This remarkable transformation occurred through a complex set of interrelated processes. Over the preceding five millenia, small hunting-gathering bands had gradually become less mobile, staying in larger base camps for longer periods of the year. In many highland valleys of Mexico this was made possible through greater use of storage facilities and an increasing reliance on domesticated crops. In a few favored locales, such as along the estuaries on the Pacific coast of Chiapas, abundant wild resources made year-round occupation possible without cultivating domestic plants. In the Initial Formative period (2000–1500 B.C.) (see Evans 2004), the processes of domestication and sedentarization combined to foster the spread of settled farming villages over much of the area that was becoming Mesoamerica.

Significant changes in technology accompanied the transition to the Formative period, the most ubiquitous of which was the creation of pottery vessels.

Pottery appears between 1900 and 1750 B.C. on the Pacific coast of Chiapas, in the valleys of highland Mexico, and on the Gulf coast of northern Veracruz (Clark and Cheetham 2002; Clark and Gosser 1995), expanding over the rest of Mesoamerica after 1750 B.C. Differences in form and amount of decoration among these early ceramic complexes suggest that the initial functions of pottery differed regionally, with more utilitarian uses favored in the highlands and forms of social display emphasized in some lowland complexes (Clark and Gosser 1995: 216–217). After about 1400 B.C., widespread sharing of ceramic motifs and long-distance exchange of obsidian, shell, serpentine, jade, and artifacts shaped from iron ore indicate increasingly intensive interaction among different regions in Mesoamerica.

Over the course of the Initial and Early Formative periods, ranked social statuses emerged in several Mesoamerican regions. In the Mazatán region on the Pacific coast of Chiapas, settlement patterns during the Locona phase indicate a two-tiered settlement hierarchy of small centers and villages (Clark and Blake 1994). At the largest site, Paso de la Amada, a large rectangular structure with rounded ends was built, measuring 21 m by 10 m. Different authors disagree as to whether this apsidal structure constituted public architecture (Marcus and Flannery 1996: 90) or served primarily as the residence of a high-ranking household (Clark 1994b: 339–362; Love 1999: 362).

In the Valley of Oaxaca, during the Tierras Largas phase (ca. 1650–1400 B.C.) small public buildings were constructed by egalitarian village inhabitants. These buildings had plastered walls and plastered floors set into low platforms of crushed rock, in contrast to the dirt floors and unplastered walls of residences (Flannery and Marcus 1994: 31–33). Other distinctive features included a central pit filled with powdered lime and a low step or altar at the center of the back wall. Rank society (*sensu* Fried 1967: 110) appears to have emerged in the succeeding San José phase (ca. 1400–1000 B.C.) (Marcus 1999). A two-tiered settlement hierarchy was established in the northwestern Etla arm of the valley, as San José Mogote expanded to a 70 ha center (Blanton et al. 1993: 60). San José Mogote also boasted a large nondomestic structure built in several tiers of stone and adobe, on which were placed stone carvings of a jaguar head and a raptorial bird (Blanton et al. 1993: 60). Social differentiation also is evident in the varying sizes of residential buildings, differences in their associated artifact assemblages, and in contrasting amounts and quality of grave goods (Blanton et al. 1993: 61). Horizontal social distinctions are suggested by differential distributions of ceramic motifs that may reflect the kin-based division of San José Mogote into residential wards.

Similar developments are seen after 1450 B.C. in the Valley of Mexico (Niederberger 2000). In the Ayotla phase (1450–1000 B.C.), Tlapacoya, Tlatilco, and Coapexco served as regional centers. Grave goods in burials at these sites also suggest the emergence of ranked social statuses and the use of specific pottery styles to distinguish kin and residence groups (Tolstoy 1989a).

None of these developments was uniform throughout Early Formative Mesoamerica. Differing degrees of reliance on domesticated crops, sedentism, and social complexity are all documented in diverse areas. In particular, hierarchical social differentiation is not strongly marked in most of the Maya lowlands until after 400 B.C., and even later in the northwestern and northeastern frontiers of Mesoamerica.

OLMEC CULTURE AND SOCIETY

Among the Early and Middle Formative cultures of Mesoamerica, the Olmecs of the Gulf Coast are exceptional in several respects. Their most obvious accomplishments were in monumental stone sculpture. Although stone sculptures appear at least as early on the Pacific slope of Guatemala, at sites such as Takalik Abaj[2] and Monte Alto, no other contemporaneous culture matches the Olmecs for the sophistication, size, and number of their stone monuments. Indeed, it is precisely the concentration of Olmec-style monuments in southern Veracruz and Tabasco that most clearly distinguishes Olman as a cultural region (Grove 1997: 51–53). Although Olmec sculptors expressed several themes, and sculptural styles do vary in time and space throughout Olman, consistencies in representation, subject, and symbolic expression define a coherent Olmec sculptural tradition spanning the period from 1400 to 400 B.C. These include a focus on humans and composite supernatural beings depicted with harmonious flowing lines and swelling volumes and a standard set of symbols representing cosmological concepts and natural forces.

One of the prominent themes in Olmec sculpture is rulership. The distinctive colossal heads are believed to be portraits of rulers, who also appear carved in the round in niches on the fronts of massive table-top thrones and in low relief on later stelae. The largest of these sculptures weigh up to 40 tons and the stones were transported as much as 90 km from their sources across swamps and rivers. The sheer labor requirements involved in these operations attest to the exceptional power of the rulers who commissioned them (Clark 1997: 218–219; Drucker 1981: 32–33). At San Lorenzo, elites also used basalt for carved columns, drains, and other embellishments in large houses, the earthen walls and floors of which were colored red with hematite-stained sand (Cyphers 1997a, 1997e, 1997f). Graves of the elite from the Early Formative period have not yet been recovered from Olman, but the later tombs of individuals buried in a ceremonial precinct at La Venta are the most elaborate discovered for the Middle Formative period in Mesoamerica.

The Olmecs also participated to an unusual degree in the exchange of prestige goods. Literally tons of iron ore in the form of perforated iron cubes and polished mirrors were imported from Chiapas and Oaxaca to San Lorenzo (Agrinnier 1984; Coe and Diehl 1980a; Cyphers and DiCastro 1996; Pires-Ferreira 1976b), and iron ore mirrors later were interred with high-ranking individuals at La Venta (Drucker et al. 1959). Imported jade and serpentine from sources in the Guatemalan and perhaps Mexican highlands were deposited as offerings in Laguna Manatí before 1500 B.C (Ortiz and Rodríguez 2000). The display of such exotic greenstones reached an extravagant level in Middle Formative La Venta, where thousands of tons of serpentine blocks were buried in massive offerings (Drucker et al. 1959).

Although social ranking developed earlier in the Mokaya tradition of coastal Chiapas, and rank societies appeared in highland Mexico after 1400 B.C., the Early Formative Olmecs of San Lorenzo achieved a degree of sociopolitical hierarchy unprecedented in Mesoamerica. Settlement patterns in the San Lorenzo region provide one set of evidence for political hierarchy. The ceremonial precinct of San Lorenzo rests on the 52 ha summit of a plateau. Early Formative residential occupation is distributed on the terraced slopes of the plateau, expanding the site to an area currently estimated at 500 ha, more than seven times the size of its largest contemporary in Mesoamerica (Clark 1997: 224; Symonds et al. 2002: 66–68). A settlement pattern survey of a 400 sq. km. area of the site's hinterland further demonstrates that San Lorenzo stood at the apex of a three-or four-tiered settlement hierarchy, which included subordinate centers, villages, and special-purpose sites (Symonds et al. 2002).

To summarize, the Early and Middle Formative periods witnessed profound changes in Mesomerican subsistence, technology, art, and sociopolitical organization, which laid the foundation for the urban civilizations of the Classic period. The Olmecs developed the most elaborate of the complex societies to emerge in this time span. Understanding their role in this grand transformation is therefore a critical issue for Mesoamericanists, and it remains one of the most hotly debated topics in the field.

ISSUES AND CONTROVERSIES

The Olmecs merit study in their own right as one of the earliest hierarchical societies in their part of the world, in the same way as do the Preceramic societies of the Peruvian coast, the Predynastic societies of Egypt, the 'Ubaid societies of Mesopotamia, and the Longshan societies of China. Mesoamerican scholars, however, have focused more heavily on the interaction between the Olmecs and their contemporaries and the significance of Olmec contributions to later civilizations. The resulting debate has shed much light on Formative Mesoamerica – and it has generated considerable heat as well. It nevertheless must seem a highly parochial dispute to readers whose primary interests lie outside Mesoamerica. Moreover, lack of agreement on matters as basic as the definition of Olmec, the origins of Olmec culture, and the degree of Olmec sociopolitical integration may have contributed to the fact that Olmec society now often receives only passing mention in comparative studies of the emergence of social differentiation. Be that as it may, this controversy is central to current conceptions of the Olmec in the sense that it touches on matters of origins, economy, sociopolitical organization, ideology, and their ultimate legacy.

WHAT IS "OLMEC?"

To embark on a study of the Olmecs is to be tossed immediately on a sea of conflicting definitions and interpretations. The very word "Olmec," as we have seen, comes from the Aztec name for the people who inhabited the southern coast of the Gulf of Mexico in the fifteenth and sixteenth centuries. But these historic "Olmeca" and the semi-legendary Olmeca-Xicallanca of the Mexican altiplano, held only the most tenuous descent from the people that occupied the southern Gulf lowlands nearly two thousand years earlier. The chronological error in ascribing this name to the ancient inhabitants of southern Veracruz and western Tabasco, and to the art they produced in precious jade and massive basalt, was evident by the watershed meeting of the second Roundtable of the Mexican Anthropological Society in 1942. The name was already entrenched in the literature, however, and so it has remained to the present.

In modern times, the term Olmec was first used to refer to an art style, rendered most conspicuously in jade artifacts and stone monuments, which employed a distinctive set of motifs and representational conventions. By the late 1920s, it was becoming evident that the geographic center of this style, known mainly from pieces in private collections, lay within the southern Gulf lowlands. The antiquity of the style was not yet appreciated, however, and so Hermann Beyer (1927) and Marshall Saville (1929a; 1929b) referred to them as Olmec, in reference to the ethnohistoric occupants of the region. As Olmec studies progressed, the term not only became attached to the early Olmec culture of the Gulf coast, but also to ceramic and figurine styles associated with it. In a figurative sense, Olmec became "The Culture that Ate the For-mative." Regardless of where they occurred, all objects bearing motifs also found in Gulf Olmec contexts, and even objects of distinctive styles found in association with them, were attributed to contact with or inspiration from the Gulf Coast. This terminological imperialism has had unfortunate effects, for as David Grove has repeatedly argued, "it preordains an interpretation that [the artifacts'] importance was somehow linked to the Gulf Coast Olmec" (Grove 1989b: 10; see also Grove 1974; 1997).

Today, different authors use the term "Olmec" in very different ways (Clark and Pye 2000b: 217–218; Grove 1997: 55). The most restrictive definition bounds Olmec in time and space as the archaeological culture of the southern Gulf Coast that existed from about 1500 to 400 B.C. As employed in this defi-nition, "archaeological culture" refers to "a characteristic set or assemblage of artifacts that occur repeatedly within a specific geographic area" (Grove 1993: 84, paraphrasing Childe 1950: 2). Often this usage carries an ethnolinguistic connotation, distinguishing the Olmec from groups such as the Zapotec or the Maya (e.g., Flannery and Marcus 2000, see discussion in Clark and Pye 2000b: 217–218). The most liberal definition uses the term for both the archaeological culture and the style, and applies it to artifact categories and sites within and outside of the Gulf Coast "heartland" of Olman. Many archaeologists using "Olmec" in this traditional manner nevertheless recognize the archaeological culture and the style as distinct and separate entities (e.g., Paradis 1990; Niederberger 1996), whereas others expressly associate the origins of the style with the Olmec culture of the Gulf Coast (e.g. Coe 1965c; Diehl and Coe 1995; Tolstoy 1989b) (Grove 1997: 55).

John Clark and Mary Pye (2000b: 217–218) have recently argued for a definition of Olmec that focuses on the cultural practices of which Olmec-style art and artifacts are the material representations (Clark and Hansen [2001] later extended the suite of representations to architectural layouts). In Clark and Pye's view, Olmec properly refers to a historical phenomenon with a specific distribution in time and space that reflects a "cultural and/or poltical commitment to certain beliefs, practices and material representations" (Clark and Pye 2000b: 218). Following this prespective, and recognizing that the most prominent themes in Olmec art concern rulership, ritual, and religious concepts, they argue for Olmec as "a politicoreligious entity (or several) of societies and peoples with deeply shared cultural practices" (Clark and Pye 2000b: 218).

Clark and Pye's emphasis on cultural practice has the advantage of separating Olmec from an essentialist notion of ethnicity. As Clark and Pye observe, the problem with viewing Olmec as a people, who presumably had ancestors and descendants, is that it makes little sense to say that Olmec culture began about 1500 B.C. and ended about 400 B.C. Clark and Pye's usage also opens up the possibility that Olmec culture was practiced by people of varied ethnicities and languages. This is a necessary assumption for their contention that non-Olmec people of the Chiapas coast became Olmec through the adoption of Olmec practices and representations (see also Clark 1990b, 1997), but it also allows for a multilingual Olman. In the end, Clark and Pye's use of Olmec is not so much non-ethnic as it is one that employs a constructivist view in which people create, define, and express their ethnic affiliation through practice (see Jones 1998 for a thorough discussion of approaches to ethnicity).

More problematic is Clark and Pye's 2000b: 218) identification of Olmec as "a politicoreligious entity (or several) of societies and peoples with deeply shared cultural practices." To be sure, this definition correctly identifies rulership, ritual, and religion as prominent themes in Olmec representation. Clark and Pye do not explicitly state the nature of the "politico-religious entity" they have in mind, but the examples they give of similar phenomena, "Victorian, Carthaginian, Roman, or Byzantine," are suggestive. All invoke cultural patterns that were spread by empires. Clark views the Olmecs as an expansionary state rather than an empire per se (personal communication 2005), but the evocation of imperial styles coincides with Clark's emphasis on political practice based on social stratification and an inherited right to rulership (Clark and Pye 2000b: 244–245; see also Clark 1997). From the perspective of this volume, this is problematic in that it would exclude some manifestations of Olmec culture in Olman that appear to reflect non-stratified social organization (see especially Chapter 4 below). A separate issue is how deeply (and broadly) shared were the cultural practices in question. That is, to what degree did the adoption of Olmec forms of representation reflect a commitment to (Gulf) Olmec practices versus a reinterpretation of Olmec representation in terms of local practices and precepts, and to what extent were Olmec practices pursued by different elements in the affected societies? Such questions do not undermine the notion of Olmec as a politicoreligious entity (certainly populations in the provinces of the Roman Empire and the colonies of Victorian England varied in their acceptance of the imperial mantle), but they do suggest that "deeply shared" cultural practices are not essential to Clark and Pye's definition.

Clark and Pye (2000b: 218) observe that, "Identification of such entities is based upon the homogeneity of material culture that resulted from a consistency of practices," and I substantially agree. Operationally, however, this is no different from defining archaeological cultures. Such definition is a process of discrimination that hinges on the selection of criteria for distinguishing among phenomena of a similar kind at a similar level of specificity. Although the criteria should be objective in the sense that they are reproducible and consistently observable, the selection of the criteria is ultimately subjective and determined by the theoretical perspective and practical aims of the study. Criteria may be selected to define the phenomenon broadly or narrowly, and different sets of criteria may divide the field of interest in substantially different, overlapping ways. Furthermore, cultural phenomena, including archaeological cultures, are best conceived of as polythetic sets, with membership determined by possession of most, but not all, of the defining traits. Sites, or components of sites, are unlikely to express all the characteristics selected as criteria for discriminating the archaeogical culture to which they are assigned, and the possession of a few of the criteria may not be sufficient to establish membership. This is simply a consequence of the fact that material culture is an expression of the practices of the people who produced it, and members of a society are not homogeneous in their practices.

This volume is a study of the historical development of the Formative societies of Olman and their interaction with other societies in the emerging culture area of Mesoamerica, as reflected in the archaeological record. The definition of "Olmec" that best suits these purposes is as an archaeological culture defined by characteristics of material culture that co-occur most consistently in Olman between 1500 and 400 B.C. The underlying premise, similar to that of Clark and Pye, is that these characteristics are the material expression of a coherent set of cultural practices shared (to a greater or lesser degree) by the members of a closely interacting set of societies. I acknowledge that my use of a narrow definition of Olmec reflects a personal bias toward "splitting" as opposed to "lumping." That preference, however, is based in a conviction that by isolating the components of a system (such as the interaction sphere of Formative Mesoamerica) we may better discern and characterize their interaction. By defining Olmec in a way that restricts it narrowly in space and time I believe we can better trace variable patterns of interaction among Formative societies, including those of Olman, than if all those exhibiting "Olmec" traits are subsumed under the same label.

A preponderance of monumental stone sculpture in Olmec style is an important characteristic of the Olmec (archaeological) culture so defined, as may be particular motifs and modes of representation in "fancy" pottery and figurines. However, there is no necessary reason to privilege these elements over more mundane artifacts, as long as the latter effectively distinguish one archaeological culture from others. In fact, recent research suggests that "technological styles," including those embodied in utilitarian or common artifacts, may be particularly indicative of social boundaries, because they tend to be embedded in social practice and learning networks (e.g., papers in Stark 1998). Therefore, I include among the defining characteristics of Olmec culture specific styles of common storage, cooking, and serving vessels found in conjunction with fancier carved and incised vessels and figurine styles also found in centers in Olman that contain examples of Olmec-style monumental art.

I refer to the people whose practices produced these cultural expressions as the Olmecs. The populations of people who shared these practices and who were linked by regular and frequent interactions constitute Olmec societies; the set of behaviors, beliefs, and ideals they shared and the material objects through which they expressed them constitute Olmec culture. Where necessary for clarity in discussing the positions of others, I add the modifier "Gulf" to distinguish the people, societies, and culture of Olman from phenomena described as "Olmec" in other regions. I use "Olmec style" to refer only to those objects that adhere to the artistic canons of the Olmec culture, wherever they appear and whose occurrence can be attributed beyond a reasonable doubt to creation by or contact with the inhabitants of Olman. None of this precludes the likelihood that Olmecs ventured beyond Olman or the possibility that they settled in distant lands individually or as enclaves or even overlords among local populations. In fact, my contention is that only by using a restricted definition of Olmec that associates the phenomenon with a specific region can the patterns of interregional interaction be discerned and their form inferred.

ONE MOTHER CULTURE OR MANY SISTER CULTURES?

The "Olmec Problem," as it has been called, reflects two opposed paradigms for the evolution of civilizations. One sees civilizations as originating in a small

number of societies whose unique circumstances propel them toward a state
level of sociopolitical integration and that serve as the sources for the diffusion
of complex institutions to less advanced societies. The other views the evolution of civilizations primarily as the result of broader processes affecting the
development of multiple interacting societies in a region. The former paradigm
is manifested by the "Olmec-centric" school (Grove 1997), which identifies
the Gulf Olmecs as the precocious "Mother Culture" that created a set of
advanced institutions, practices, and symbols, which they transmitted to their
less advanced neighbors, who in turn passed them on to their successors (e.g.,
Clark 1990b, 1997; Diehl and Coe 1995; Tolstoy 1989b). Proponents of the
Mother Culture model emphasize evidence for greater sociopolitical complexity among the Gulf Olmecs as compared to their contemporaries. They also
claim temporal priority in Olman of a range of Mesoamerican traits and practices. As enumerated by Diehl and Coe (1995: 23) these include monumental
stone sculpture, including ruler portraits; site layouts that reproduce cosmological concepts; sacred ritual locales at springs, mountaintops, and caves; sacrifice
of infants in water-related rituals; ritual use of rubber; particularly for balls used
in the sacred ballgame; and a sophisticated system of conventionalized symbols
and symbol complexes (Diehl and Coe 1995: 23). Mother Culture adherents
attribute the wide distribution of these symbols as motifs on Early Formative
ceramics to dissemination by and emulation of the Gulf Olmecs.

The identification of the Olmecs as "*la cultura madre*" of Mesoamerica dates
back to the early 1940s (Caso 1942; Stirling 1940: 333). The premise that
Mesoamerican civilizations derived from a single progenitor was rooted in the
diffusionist tenets of historical particularism, which dominated Americanist
anthropology in the early twentieth century. In the late 1930s and early 1940s
the question was not whether there had been a Mother Culture, but which
archaeological culture had played that role. After radiocarbon dating confirmed
the antiquity of the Olmec phenomenon in the 1950s (Drucker et al. 1959), its
identification as the Mother Culture appeared secure, and this idea dominated
discussions for the next three decades. David Grove (1997: 53) therefore identifies adherents of the Mother Culture scenario as "traditionalists," although
some ground their arguments in contemporary theory, as in John Clark's (1997,
2000) discussions of governmentality and agency.

The alternative, "nontraditionalist" position is championed mainly by
archaeologists who have conducted fieldwork since 1970 in areas outside of
Olman and who challenge the identification of much Early Formative iconography as specifically Gulf Coast Olmec (Grove 1997: 53). Instead, they see the
Formative societies of Mesoamerica as an evolving co-tradition whose members drew upon ancient, widely shared symbolic themes and who influenced
and interacted with one another in a more balanced fashion (e.g., Demarest
1989; Flannery and Marcus 2000; Graham 1989; Grove 1981a, 1989b, 1997).
Nontraditionalists tend to view the Olmec as a "sister culture" (*cultura hermana*)

to other Formative complex societies, or at best the *primus inter pares* (first among equals) (Diehl and Coe 1995; Hammond 1989). In support of their position they point to the traditional ambiguity in the definition of Olmec as both an art style and a culture (e.g., Grove 1989b; 1993), and question the temporal priority of many symbols and practices in Olman (e.g., Flannery and Marcus 1994; 2000). Further, they observe that, in those cases where societies did borrow specifically Olmec motifs, the process of emulation requires that donor and recipient societies occupy a similar level of sociopolitical development (e.g., Flannery and Marcus 1994: 389; 2000).

The Mother Culture/Sister Culture debate has been the touchstone for a great deal of important research on Formative Mesoamerica, but the polarizing rhetoric of the more vehement participants dichotomizes what is actually a continuum of opinion. Some sympathetic to the Mother Culture position nevertheless acknowledge that the degree to which the Olmecs influenced their contemporaries varied (e.g., Clark 1997: 230), and even the most vociferous antagonists concede that "the Olmec look impressive relative to their contemporaries (Flannery and Marcus 2000: 6) and protest that they "would not describe the Olmec as 'no more advanced' or 'contributing little'" (Flannery and Marcus 2000: 2). My own reading of the evidence, shared with Richard Lesure (2004: 79), is that both sides of the debate are partly right: social stratification and a pronounced political hierarchy appeared first in Olman; Olmec societies influenced some of their neighbors and interacted with others to different degrees and in diverse ways; and many Early and Middle Formative societies, including the Olmecs, contributed significantly to the development of later Mesoamerican civilizations. In short, the "Olmec Problem," as I see it, is better cast as a "Formative Problem" that concerns how the internal processes and external interactions of Formative societies produced the beliefs, practices, and institutions of Classic Mesomerica.

OLMEC ORIGINS

Disagreements over what is Olmec obviously impact the question of where and when Olmec culture originated. Initially, the search for Olmec origins was a search for the hearth of the art style (Diehl 1989: 20), and it remains so for those who see Olmec culture and the Olmec art style as coterminous. Since the early 1940s, the southern Gulf lowland region of Olmec florescence has been most often identified as the heartland of the culture and the art style. Before Michael Coe (1968b, 1970b; Coe and Diehl 1980a) excavated at San Lorenzo in the 1960s, though, the lack of a pre-Olmec cultural sequence in Olman, coupled with the widespread distribution of purportedly Olmec ceramic motifs left open the possibility of a heartland in some other part of Mesoamerica. Moreover, though Coe now appears to favor an autochthonous origin for Olmec culture (Diehl and Coe 1995: 150), he long held that true Olmec traits appeared at San Lorenzo rather suddenly during the Chicharras phase (ca. 1450–1400 B.C.) (Coe 1970a: 25, 32; Coe and Diehl 1980a: 150). Thus, Miguel Covarrubias (1957: 76), Carlo Gay (1973), and Gillett Griffin (1981: 222) argued for Guerrero as the heartland of the Olmec style; Charles Wicke (1971: 161–162) suggested Oaxaca; and Roman Piña Chan (1955: 10–107) favored Morelos. Others have argued that the antecedents of Olmec sculpture lie in the Pacific coasts and piedmonts of Chiapas and Guatemala (Girard 1968; Graham 1981, 1989), and John Clark once argued that the intrusion of Mije-Soke speakers from the Chiapas coast contributed to the development of Gulf Olmec culture (Clark and Blake 1989b: 390), though he soon altered his position in favor of emulation of Mokaya practices by Gulf Olmec societies (Clark 1990b: 49).

Most arguments for an external origin of Olmec culture either select one trait as essential to the definition of Olmec (e.g., monumental sculpture, Graham 1981) or see culture as diffusing in coherent packages, which include artistic canons, motifs, and techniques. The former view may be rejected as overly simplistic and reductionist. The latter is challenged by the "nontraditionalist" position, that distinguishes between Olmec culture and widespread Formative ceramic motifs and which posits a fluid, multicentric, process in which different elements may have diverse origins, and be accepted or rejected within local social contexts (e.g., Demarest 1989). This model resembles later patterns of diffusion for traits associated with Central Mexico, the Gulf Coast, and the Maya region in the Classic, Epiclassic, and Early Postclassic periods. The synchretic melding of traits by indigenous populations in the Colonial period offers another parallel.

Recent archaeological fieldwork in Olman also has uncovered evidence for a continuous sequence of social and ceremonial development stretching back as far as 1700 B.C. (Ortiz et al. 1997; Rodríguez and Ortiz 1997; Rust and Sharer 1988). Therefore, there remains little doubt that the emergence of Olmec culture was primarily a local phenomenon. Even from such early times there is ample evidence for widespread sharing of ceramic technology and acquisition of exotic materials, thus influences from other areas are not ruled out. Such interaction, however, should not be seen as "causing" Olmec culture any more or less than it "caused" any other Mesoamerican culture.

SOCIOPOLITICAL ORGANIZATION

Scholars have debated the complexity of Olmec political organization for more than three decades without arriving at a consensus (Grove 1997: 74). The issue is usually framed in terms of whether in their most elaborate manifestations the Olmecs crossed the boundary from "chiefdom" to "state" or "civilization." Individual scholars differ in their applications of these labels but, for most, "chiefdom" refers to a hierarchically organized society in which social rank is inherited (Sahlins 1958; Service 1962; cf. Carneiro 1998: 20). Political authority is vested in the office of chief, which is held by a single person; other members of the society are ranked in terms of their relationship to the chief (Service 1971: 146). Frequently, a distinction is made between "simple chiefdoms" with populations of a few thousand and one level of political administration above the local community and "complex chiefdoms" with populations in the tens of thousands and two levels of political administration (e.g, Earle 1991: 3; Wright 1984; cf. Carneiro 1981: 47, who distinguishes minimal, typical, and maximal chiefdoms).

In an evolutionary sense, chiefdoms are viewed as an intermediary stage between egalitarian tribes and states (Carneiro 1981; Service 1962; Sanders and Price 1968). "State" also refers to a hierarchically organized society, but social divisions are more rigidly stratified into (generally endogamous) classes, governmental institutions are specialized, and the government is able to enforce its decisions with a degree of coercive force not available to chiefs. "Civilization" is a broader term referring to a combination of social, political, cultural, and aesthetic characteristics, usually associated with states, but sometimes extended to complex chiefdoms (Coe and Koontz 2002: 61; Diehl and Coe 1995; Smith 2004: 87). In common usage and the older anthropological literature, it also carries unfortunate connotations of moral superiority in opposition to "barbarism" (Smith 2004: 87–88). Nevertheless, the term is useful – in the restricted technical sense I employ in this book – as the cultural matrix that supports and reproduces the state through its economic and social institutions and its artistic conventions (Sanders and Price 1968: 45; see also Yoffee 2005: 17).

In his alternative classification of societies with respect to political organization, Morton Fried (1960, 1967) interposed stratified societies lacking developed state political institutions between rank societies and states. The key distinction between Fried's rank and stratified societies is that in the latter, "members of the same sex and equivalent age status do not have equal access to the basic resources that sustain life" (Fried 1967: 186). Because their criteria differ, the categories proposed by Fried and by Sahlins and Service do not align precisely. However, simple chiefdoms generally exhibit non-stratified ranking, whereas ranks in complex chiefdoms tend to be stratified (Earle 1991: 3; Wasson 1996: 45).

Individuals differ in their view of the evolutionary position of stratified societies. Fried (1967) proposed stratified societies as a brief evolutionary stage between rank and state societies. Kristian Kristiansen (1991: 18–23) sees stratified societies (including both "decentralized stratified societies" and centralized "archaic states") in a similar way, as a stage between "chiefdoms" (with ranking based on kinship) and "full-fledged" states with developed bureaucracies. In contrast, Sanders and Webster (1978) see stratified society as an alternative to chiefdom organization (that they likewise restrict to rank societies) in evolutionary trajectories.

The question of Olmec sociopolitical complexity is relevant not only to the evolution of Olmec culture itself but to the nature of its interactions with other societies in terms of the Mother Culture debate. The implication is that if Olmec sociopolitical organization was markedly more complex than that of its contemporaries, then the Olmecs would have been in a better position to influence them, either through political and economic domination or as a source of prestige through elite marriage, exchange, and symbolic emulation. Thus, most (though not all) of those who favor the Mother Culture argument emphasize a high degree of sociopolitical complexity and *primus inter pares* advocates downplay the contrast between the Olmecs and their contemporaries.

Before 1968, few questioned that the Olmecs had achieved a state level of organization. Rather, debate revolved around the specific organization of the political system and the extent of its domination. Heizer (1960) characterized the Olmecs as a "theocratic state" ruled by a small priesthood. Although it is widely accepted today that Olmec rulers wielded religious as well as secular authority, most see the ultimate base of their power as resting in the control of material resources, and others question the ability to identify a theocracy with archaeological data alone (e.g. Diehl 1989: 28).

Alfonso Caso (1965) and Ignacio Bernal (1969: 188–189) believed the Olmec controlled an extensive empire, exerting political, economic, and military domination over local leaders (Diehl 1989: 27). The idea of an Olmec empire seems implausible on several grounds. First, it is unlikely that populations in Olman were large enough to provide an army of sufficient size to control such an extensive territory, even if the empire were organized in a "hegemonic" fashion like that of the Aztecs (Hassig 1985, 1988) to control tribute flows rather than territory. Second, it is unlikely that any one Olmec capital controlled the entirety of Olman, much less extensive territories beyond its boundaries (Drucker 1981: 43). Third, there is little evidence for Olmec military and political domination of foreign polities, either in the art of Olman or in the archaeological record of other regions (cf. Clark 1997). John Clark (1997), however, has suggested that reorganization of Mokaya settlement patterns resulted from political domination by the Olmec, and David Cheetham (2005) has reported evidence for an Olmec enclave in the region at Cantón Corralito. If Clark is correct, his formulation of the "Olmecization" of the Mokaya would support the idea of a limited Olmec empire or at least an expansionist state, as he prefers to characterize it (personal communication, 2004).

William Sanders and Barbara Price (1968: 126–128) first advanced the idea that Olmec polities were organized as chiefdoms, arguing that the scale of their constructions and monuments fell within the range of ethnographically documented chiefdoms in Polynesia and elsewhere, and that they differed quantitatively and qualitatively from later states in Mesoamerica. Their position has been widely accepted by opponents of the Mother Culture hypothesis (e.g. Flannery 1998: 55–57; Flannery and Marcus 1994: 385–390; Sharer 1989b: 4–5), as well as some Olmec-centrists, most notably Richard Diehl (1973, 1989: 29; Coe and Diehl 1980b: 147; cf. Diehl 2004:95). One measure of the broad acceptance of the chiefdom concept for the Olmecs is that most historic and ethnographic analogues for Olmec society have been sought among societies classified as chiefdoms, (Stark 2000: 35).

Michael Coe has been the most persistent advocate of state-level political organization among the Olmecs (1968b: 60; Coe and Diehl 1980b: 147; cf. Diehl and Coe 1995: 12), identifying their culture as Mesoamerica's first "civilization" (e.g., Coe 1968a; 1981: 16, 18–19; 1994: 60). In Coe's view, only the rulers of a state would have possessed the authority and power to organize the labor required to drag multi-ton stones over 60 km from the Tuxtla Mountains to San Lorenzo or to have constructed the San Lorenzo plateau, which he saw as an artificial effigy mound. Coe also places considerable emphasis on the Olmec sculptural style, which he views as indicative of a state religion and an essential hallmark of civilization (e.g., Coe 1994: 59–60). In considering the scope and amount of power apparently exercised by Olmec leaders, Haas (1982: 184–192) likewise concluded that the Olmec achieved a state level of organization.

The question of state vs. chiefdom levels of sociopolitical integration is by no means simple; indeed, Coe and his coauthor, Richard Diehl (1980b: 147; Diehl 1989: 29; see also Grove 1997: 75), came to different conclusions, despite working with the same data from San Lorenzo. One problem is semantic and definitional; where does one draw the boundary and on the basis of what criteria? The term "civilization" is particularly ambiguous in this regard, and different authors apply the term in very different ways (e.g., Coe 1994: 59–60; Niederberger 2000: 169; see also Service 1975: 178; Grove 1997: 74). The distinction between states and chiefdoms is not much clearer. For example, Drucker (1981: 30–31) defines the "primitive state" as "an entity in which there is a highly centralized control over a population of about 5,000 to 20,000 souls with a single major center and various dependent hamlets. . . . The control structure would center on one individual, scion of a royal lineage, whose immediate subordinates would be a hierarchy of hereditary nobles. . . . Some occupational specialization would be expectable in the lower class . . . [Economic functions] would include collecting and redistributing surpluses. . . . " Each of these criteria, however, can be matched in Sanders and Price's (1968: 42–44, 85) definition of chiefdoms! In fact the only substantive difference between Drucker's definition of the primitive state and Sanders and Price's of the chiefdom is that, "The breakdown of kinship ties and kinship-guided behavior would occur between the elite (royal, noble) sector and the mass of commoners (Drucker 1981: 31). On this point Sanders and Price (1968: 115–116) note, "Although ranking differs in principle from stratification, the distinction is often difficult to infer reliably from archaeological evidence. Empirically, the appearance is, in fact, quantitative rather than qualitative with relatively complex chiefdoms located along a continuum in close proximity to the position of relatively simple states."

Archaeologists cannot observe the actual operation of the societies they study but must rely on patterns in the material remains preserved in the archaeological record to infer sociopolitical organization. One frequently used archaeological criterion for distinguishing chiefdoms and states is the number of levels in the settlement hierarchy (Wright and Johnson 1975). This criterion derives from the expectations of Central Place Theory, which was developed to account for the emergence of market centers in Europe (Christaller 1966) and has since been applied worldwide by economic geographers. Archaeologists have further extended Central Place Theory to non-market economies. As applied to ancient political systems, the reasoning is that the political, economic, and religious institutions that unite the society will be concentrated in the community of the ruler, which will also tend to be larger than subordinate communities. Administrators of local political units may reside in subsidiary centers. The number of tiers in the settlement hierarchy therefore provides a rough, relative measure of the number of administrative levels in the political hierarchy. Chiefdoms are expected to have two or three levels in the settlement hierarchy, corresponding to chiefly centers and villages. States, due to the greater vertical differentiation of political statuses, are expected to have four or more levels (primary centers or cities, regional centers or towns, large villages, and small villages (Flannery 1998: 16; Wright and Johnson 1975; cf. Carneiro 1981: 44).

The degree of differentiation in settlement hierarchies is one useful measure for comparing sociopolitical complexity among archaeologically documented societies, but these data should be interpreted with caution. As a practical matter, determining the number of tiers in the hierarchy is not always straightforward; rankings based on different criteria, for example, site area versus volume of civic-ceremonial construction, often do not coincide neatly, and variation along these dimensions is often continuous, particularly toward the lower end, leading to arbitrary decisions about where or indeed whether to split the distribution into tiers. Furthermore, as August Lösch (1954) observed, market, administrative, and religious hierarchies can be nested differently within the same system. In her critique of locational models in archaeology, including Central Place Theory, Carol Crumley (1979; 1995) makes the more general point that settlements may be ranked differently with respect to administrative, economic, or religious functions, one of two characteristics (the other being lack of ranking), either of which characterize systems she describes as heterarchical. Most recently, Adam T. Smith (2004: 36–45) has criticized Central Place Theory for employing a "mechanical spatial ontology" that posits a universal relationship between the geometry of spatial patterns and evolutionary processes, leaving little room for analysis of the contingent social relationships that generate spatial patterns among settlements.

In a recent article, Flannery (1998) has used settlement hierarchies in combination with other settlement pattern criteria to distinguish archaic states from chiefdoms. The other criteria he proposes for identifying archaic states are rulers' residences (palaces) that are larger, more complex, and better constructed than those of other members of the society, standardized temples and priests' residences, and royal tombs. Applying these criteria to the archaeological record of Olmec-period San Lorenzo, he argues that the site so far lacks evidence for "a real Mesoamerican palace," "standardized two-room temples so typical of Mesomerican states," or residences for full-time priests. He also notes that the failure of Coe and Diehl to find burials precludes debating whether they are chiefly or royal, and that recent evidence for an administrative settlement hierarchy is inconclusive (Flannery 1998: 56; cf. Symonds et al. 2002). Flannery therefore concludes that Olmec San Lorenzo was probably "the paramount center of a maximal chiefdom rather than an archaic state." (Flannery 1998: 57).

We can argue interminably over issues such as whether elite residences at San Lorenzo constituted real palaces. For example, though they differ in form and size from later Mesoamerican palaces, the apparent use of a four-meter tall column carved from stone imported from over 60 km away to support the roof of one structure suggests San Lorenzo's rulers exerted some control over non-kin labor to construct their residences.[3] More importantly, Flannery's exercise, and the debate over Olmec political organization in general, provides an excellent illustration of how the assignment of a society to any particular category is dependent on the selection of the defining criteria and how the selection of those criteria may be manipulated to favor one position over another. In other words, one can identify a particular Olmec society as a chiefdom or a state simply by shifting the boundary between the two. Adding qualifiers such as "primitive state" (Drucker 1981: 30–31) or "incipient state" (Cyphers 1997c: 273) does little to clarify the issue. John Clark (1997: 215) has sought to avoid the controversy by using the term "kingdom" to refer to stratified societies ruled by a leader ("king") who "embodies the body politic and is its principal political force." Such societies may be either complex chiefdoms or states. Clark really has only substituted one category for another, but for the Olmec at least, his redefinition of the sociopolitical category to which they belong focuses attention on variation within the category rather than between categories. The term, "complex polity," as used by de Montmollin (1989) and Adam T. Smith (2004), encompasses a similar range of political complexity as Clark's "kingdom," but without specifying kingship as the particular form of ruling authority.

The more basic problem with the chiefdom vs. state debate in archaeology is not definitional, however; it is epistemological. The typologizing of societies was already being criticized in cultural anthropology by David Easton in 1959, even as cultural evolutionists such as Sahlins (1958), and Fried (1960) were formalizing their band–tribe–chiefdom–state and egalitarian–rank–stratified-state classifications. More recently, the typological approach has come under fire from archaeologists writing from a variety of theoretical perspectives ranging from more traditional processualism (e.g., Blanton et al.; 1993; de Montmollin 1989) to selectionist evolution (Drennan 1991: 114; Dunnell 1980; O'Brien 1996) and practice theory (e.g. Brumfiel 1992; Cowgill 1993; Drennan 2000; Marcus and Flannery 1996; Smith 2004; Spencer 1993). The continuance of the chiefdom vs. state debate in Olmec archaeology therefore seems anachronistic in the context of contemporary anthropological and archaeological theory. As Adam T. Smith (2004: 96) puts it in his thorough critique of the concept of the State, "Classification of polities as Chiefdom or State is singularly uninteresting because it speaks only to failures in our typological imagination, telling us little about the nature of politics in the past."

Whatever value societal typologies may have for specifying the objects of cross-cultural comparison or for selecting ethnographic analogs for archaeological phenomena, they have significant drawbacks for archaeologists interested in the processes of change within individual traditions (Yoffee 1993). The most obvious drawback is that the thousands of societies documented ethnographically and archaeologically clearly encompass much greater variation than can be captured by forcing them into three or four pigeonholes (Easton 1959; Blanton et al. 1993: 19; de Montmollin 1989: 12). Thus, there will always be some societies, such as the Olmec, that lie at the margins of the types. Increasing the number of pigeonholes with such types as simple chiefdoms, complex chiefdoms, and archaic states captures more of this variation, but does not eliminate the problem. A further consequence of such categorization, again well-demonstrated in the Olmec case, is that research may focus on identifying the type to which the society belongs as an end in itself, rather than as a first step towards more penetrating analysis. As Philip Arnold (2000: 121) has suggested, (paraphrasing Nelson 1995), perhaps we should frame the question not as "how complex were the Gulf Olmecs," but as "how were the Gulf Olmecs complex?"

There are also more subtle difficulties with societal typologies. One is that they foster categorizational thinking and discourage the recognition of more continuous forms of variation (de Montmollin 1989: 13). For example, the term "chiefdom" encompasses societies whose populations vary from a few hundred to a hundred thousand individuals, and whose territorial areas range from tens to tens of thousands of square kilometers.

A related problem is that societal types, when defined by multiple variables relating to political, economic, social, and/or ideological traits imply that such traits covary closely with one another (Blanton et al. 1993: 19; de Montmollin 1989: 14). This may be more or less true statistically, but it is inappropriate to extrapolate such generalized statistical correlations to specific societies, just as it is inappropriate to argue that higher crime rates in one segment of society proves that a particular defendant is guilty. In archaeology, the problem is particularly acute when the cross-cultural generalizations subsumed in the type definitions are used to extrapolate from known traits to unknown traits. An example would be if one were to argue that because the Olmec possessed monumental art, and because monumental art is characteristic of early states, that Olmec rulers also wielded a monopoly on coercive force over their subjects.

Additional problems arise when societal types are arranged in a temporal sequence as evolutionary stages (e.g., Yoffee 1993). One is that the stage concept promotes a picture of cultural evolution as a sequence of transformations between static types, rather than as a process of continuous change (O'Brien 1996; Rambo 1991). Investigation of differences in the tempo of change in different institutions also is discouraged by the assumption that they evolve together in tightly covarying ways (Blanton et al. 1993: 19). Furthermore, when, as is often the case, societies are reified as monolithic wholes, then the potential role of individuals and factions in promoting change is obscured (de Montmollin 1989: 13). In general, then, strict adherence to a stage concept makes it difficult to answer or even to ask many interesting evolutionary questions.

The Olmec case highlights some of these problems with the stage concept. First, the disagreement over whether the most elaborate Olmec societies were organized as chiefdoms or states likely reflects their position in the gray area between these categories. Second, there is good reason to doubt that all contemporaneous Olmec societies in Olman were organized in the same way during any particular point in their history. In fact, taken as a whole, Olmec polities of each period appear to have straddled multiple forms of sociopolitical organization.

One way to avoid these problems is to characterize societies along multiple dimensions of variation, rather than to classify them into bounded, essentialist categories. For example, Richard Blanton and his associates (1993) have characterized societies in the Basin of Mexico, the Valley of Oaxaca, and the Maya lowlands in terms of their scale, integration, complexity, and boundedness. In this volume I adopt this perspective, if not the specific terminology, to highlight variation and change among Formative period political, economic, and social systems in Mesoamerica generally and within Olman specifically.

EXPLAINING OLMEC SOCIOPOLITICAL EVOLUTION

If one accepts a local origin for Olmec society, as most scholars now do, then the question of origins becomes one of explaining how the complex, hierarchical, institutions of Olmec society developed. The several explanations that have been offered give different weight to ecological processes, warfare, economic exchange, and the political strategies of leaders and their followers.

Environment, Population Growth, and Conflict

Most of the explanations advanced to date seek causality in the ecological relationship between the Olmecs and their lowland environment. William Sanders and Barbara Price (1968: 131,134), for example, argued that the precocious development of Olmec chiefdoms was a response to the organizational stresses of rapid population growth made possible by the high productivity of swidden farming in the southern Gulf lowlands.

Sanders and David Webster (1978: 288–291) further developed this ecological argument, proposing more specifically that low agricultural risk attracted relatively dense populations to the southern Gulf lowlands, especially to highly productive riverine environments. According to Sanders and Webster, the redistributive functions often attributed to chiefs would not have been necessary in Olman because low environmental diversity and generally high productivity meant all segments of the population could supply their own subsistence needs. Rather, rapid population growth resulted in competition for resources, which in turn promoted the development of a chiefdom form of hierarchical organization based on ranking of social statuses. Levee lands along the rivers generated large per capita agricultural surpluses, which, combined with smaller per capita surpluses from areas of swidden cultivation, supported the hierarchical sociopolitical structure and funded the impressive displays of imported prestige goods, mound building, and elaborate burials of leaders. On the other hand, the lowland environment did not encourage agricultural intensification or expansion of the managerial functions of the political hierarchy, and there was little economic incentive to expand political-military authority. As a result, the Olmec chiefdoms did not develop into states with stratified social structures and governmental monopolies on the use of coercive force.

Michael D. Coe (1981, Coe and Diehl 1980b: 151–152) proposed a hypothesis that also sees population pressure and competition over productive levee lands as the principal factors in the origins of Olmec hierarchy, but which accords a greater role to warfare. In developing his model, Coe drew upon Robert Carneiro's (1970) theory that complex chiefdoms and states arise from competition and coercion in areas where agricultural land is highly circumscribed, either environmentally or by the presence of surrounding populations (i.e., socially). As populations increase, they seek to ameliorate resource stresses by subjugating surrounding polities. Successful war leaders thereby become the leaders of the society, with a ready source of coercive power in their armies. Carneiro extended this model from the desert valleys of Peru that inspired it to the Amazon basin, where concentrations of resources along the Amazon and its tributaries amounts to a kind of circumscription. Coe sees the

Olmec environment as similar to the Amazon case, and observes that modern community leaders (*caciques*) use control over the most productive lands along the Coatzacoalcos River as one strategy for increasing and maintaining their authority.

The generation of food surpluses is necessary for the development of social and political hierarchies, and there is no doubt that high agricultural productivity, combined with the natural abundance of aquatic foods in the Gulf lowlands, supported their development among the Olmecs. Nevertheless, there are some weak points to the preceding arguments. Barbara Stark (2000: 38–39), for example, questions whether population levels in the relatively open, poorly circumscribed landscape of Olman would have been high enough to generate widespread competition over agricultural land leading to warfare and conquest. On the other hand, Stark points out that Sanders and Webster downplay environmental risks due to flooding and changing river courses, and that these may have contributed to the rise of central authority to adjudicate land disputes as well as the development of cross-cutting cooperative institutions. Furthermore, although the southern Gulf lowlands do not match the highlands in their environmental diversity, they are more heterogeneous in geology, climate, and agricultural productivity than Sanders and Webster imply (see Chapter 3).

With respect to Coe's hypothesis, evidence for Olmec warfare is scarce or ambiguous. Some sculptures show that the Olmecs did possess weapons, and some figures are reasonably interpretable as captives, although other interpretations are possible (Grove 1981b). In any event, warfare was not a common theme in Olmec art. The frequent mutilation of Olmec sculptures can be interpreted as defeat by an external enemy, internal revolt, or ceremonial "killing" of the monuments upon the death of a ruler, and possibly cannibalized human remains that Coe interprets as evidence of warfare include women and children, who are unlikely to have been combatants (Coe 1981: 19; Coe and Diehl 1980a: 392; Grove 1981b; Wing 1980: 386).

Exchange Models

Other explanations have emphasized the evident need or desire to acquire specific goods from distant places as a cause for the development of Olmec sociopolitical hierarchies. One hypothesis, offered by William Rathje (1972), proposes that Olmec societies developed a complex hierarchical structure to ensure a regular supply of subsistence-related materials lacking in the "core area" of the Coatzacoalcos and Tonalá drainages. These utilitarian necessities included salt, hard stone for grinding implements, and obsidian for cutting implements. According to Rathje, the Olmecs would have had to compete for these materials with communities nearer their sources, particularly those in an ecologically similar "buffer zone" on the margins of the core area. The development of hierarchical political institutions gave the Olmecs a competitive advantage over less complex societies in organizing trade and the production of finished products for export, such as ceremonial paraphernalia and status symbols (Rathje 1972: 373). By controlling basic resources needed by all households, the Olmec organizers of long-distance trade became "integrative nuclei" to scattered household populations (Rathje 1972: 391).

Despite the logical appeal of Rathje's model, salt sources are more common in the Gulf lowlands than he recognized, and many Mesoamerican societies without hierarchical social organization acquired obsidian from distant sources (Stark 2000: note 7). Further, recent settlement studies suggest that Early Formative occupation was light around the edges of the Tuxtla Mountains. Thus the Olmecs of the Coatzacoalcos and Tonalá basins would have seen little competition for basalt from these relatively close sources.

In contrast, David Grove (1994: 151–154; 1997: 75–76) has drawn attention to the complementary distributions of resources within the southern Gulf lowlands, which he sees as conditioning the distribution of major Olmec centers. Timothy Earle (1976: 218) and Fred Bove (1978: 40) argued that the more-or-less even spacing between the major centers at Tres Zapotes, Laguna de los Cerros, San Lorenzo, and La Venta suggested mutual antagonism and intersite competition, provided that the sites were contemporaneous. Such antagonism would lend some support to Coe's application of Carneiro's coercive theory for the origins of Olmec civilization. Grove however, notes that each center (excluding Tres Zapotes, which reached its height later than the others), lay in a different ecological zone with a distinct suite of economic resources. He therefore suggests that cooperative exchange, as opposed to competition, may have characterized their interaction. Although Grove does not explicitly address the origins of Olmec social complexity, his suggestion does have important implications for political and economic processes in the region.

Other trade hypotheses have focused more on the long-distance exchange of prestige goods in Formative Mesoamerica, including jade, serpentine, and polished iron ore objects. In an influential article, Kent V. Flannery (1968b) presented an elegant argument that populations with emerging social ranking in the Valley of Oaxaca provided the elites of more sophisticated Gulf Olmec societies with iron ore mirrors to acquire exotic mussel shell, to ensure a secure food supply in times of need, and to enhance their own positions through prestigious marriage alliances.[4] For their part, the Olmec elites used the imported goods in displays that reinforced commitment to their own social and religious system, and maintained the flow by burying the goods and taking them out of circulation. Although Flannery's model did not directly address the origins of Olmec hierarchies, it did shift attention to the social and political uses of exotic goods by Olmec elites.

Barbara Stark (2000) has built on Flannery's (1968b) model, combining it with Mary Helms's (1993) insights regarding the rationale for acquiring exotic prestige goods. Helms argues convincingly that the widespread, cross-cultural, practice of acquiring rare and exotic goods results from common associations of distant lands with primordial origins, ancestors, and the sacred realm. Finely crafted items often hold similar associations, as crafting skill and knowledge also are seen as originating in the cosmological or ancestral realm, beyond the bounds of normal society. Access to either exotic rarities or finely crafted objects can be restricted, providing a basis for socio-economic differentiation, and the symbolic associations of the objects can be manipulated to validate and enhance social status and political power. In Early and Middle Formative Mesoamerica, emerging and established elites were mutually involved in acquiring exotic goods and fostering fine crafting, but the Olmecs were particularly successful, and their art style became a focus for emulation.

Political Models

Stark's essay reflects a general trend in archaeology toward according greater weight in explanations of political change to the strategies of individual actors, factions, and other social groups pursuing their specific agendas. Elements of this "political," "agency," "practice," or "actor-based" perspective are presaged in the arguments of Flannery (1968b), Rathje (1972), and Coe and Diehl (1980b:139–152), insomuch as they frame their discussions in terms of the activities and goals of aspiring elites. Recent discussions, however, are more explicit with regard to how multiple sources of power may have been manipulated to establish and maintain permanent positions of authority. These power sources may be economic, military, social, or ideological (e.g., Earle 1997: 4–10; Blanton et al. 1996; cf. Blanton 1998; Hirth 1996). Jonathan Haas (1982: 184–192) was one of the first to explicitly analyze sources of power within Olman, concluding that the leaders of Olmec states exerted coercive power, probably based in their economic control over trade and productive levee lands, as well as physical military coercion. Haas saw the development of an economic base for political power as a necessary prerequisite for exercising physical power, but the scarcity of data on early phases of development prevented him from explicitly testing the hypothesis for the Olmecs.

Working outside Olman, John Clark and Michael Blake (1994) argue that rank societies emerged from egalitarian ones in coastal Chiapas as the unintended consequence of competition among individuals to enhance their prestige and influence. They posit the existence in all societies of such "aggrandizers," who seek to attract loyal followers to their faction by providing physical, social, and/or spiritual benefits, often formalized as gifts and feasts. Such competitive generosity can only flourish in intensifiable environments with relatively high and reliable productivity. Establishing trade relations with distant partners further enhances the ability of aggrandizers to compete in their home communities. The inability of some recipients to reciprocate disbursements creates debt obligations, which place the successful aggrandizer in a socially superior position. When these inequalities are sustained across generations they may become institutionalized as social ranking. Clark and Blake's model offers considerable promise for understanding the emergence of ranking in the intensifiable environments of lowland Olman, although local geographic conditions are somewhat different, and data for pre-Olmec periods are still sparse.

The practices of the aggrandizers postulated in Clark and Blake's model bear much in common with the "network" or "exclusionary" politico-economic strategy discussed by Richard Blanton and his associates (1996). According to Blanton et al., (1996: 4–5), leaders pursuing an exclusionary strategy build alliances by distributing gifts to followers, exchanging prestige goods to peers, and forging advantageous marriage ties. Therefore, they will try to monopolize these material and social sources of power through methods that may include establishing exclusive exchange networks beyond the local group and patronizing specialists who produce prestige items. They also may seek to monopolize ideological sources of power by controlling symbolic systems that glorify themselves, emphasize their descent from exalted ancestors and their intercession with supernatural entities, and reflect their interaction with distant lands. In these ways they discourage followers from abandoning them for competing leaders, legitimate their own appropriation of resources, and restrict the ability to forge prestigious marriage ties. Because the exclusionary strategy is centered on an individual, successful manipulation of material and ideological sources of power results in a highly centralized political economy.

Building on Renfrew's (1974) distinction between "individualizing" and "group-oriented" chiefdoms, Blanton et al. (1996: 5–7) contrast the exclusionary strategy with a "corporate" or communal strategy that promotes the sharing of power among multiple segments of society. The role of individual leaders is de-emphasized and their ability to monopolize sources of power or to exercise power is restricted. As a consequence, assembly government, which represents a society's constituent groups, is a common element of the corporate strategy (Blanton 1998: 154–155). Communal solidarity and interdependence also are supported by a cognitive code that emphasizes collective themes such as fertility and renewal of society and the cosmos (Blanton et al., 1996: 6).

The value of Blanton et al.'s corporate-exclusionary distinction is that it recognizes patterns of political practice that coexist to some degree in all societies, and which therefore cross-cut variation in hierarchical differentiation. Their application of the framework to Mesoamerican societies, however, tends to classify them as either exclusionary or corporate (Blanton et al. 1996: 8–12). Although acknowledging that "elements of both approaches . . . may be employed in certain complex cases,"[5] they justify their dichotomization of Mesoamerican societies with the statement that corporate and exclusionary strategies result in antagonistic political economies that are likely to be separated in time and space (Blanton et a. 1996: 7). This assumption bears closer examination, however. With particular reference to the subject of this volume, Blanton et al. (1996: 8) identify Olmec societies as pursuing an exclusionary network strategy. On the other hand, Barbara Stark (2000: 36–37), although acknowledging an exclusionary emphasis in many aspects of Olmec art and society, also identifies other elements of Olmec art and public architecture as reflecting more communal themes.[6] I would argue that leaders may simultaneously employ more exclusionary or more corporate strategies in their interactions at different levels of integration, as with followers within their factions, with leaders of other factions within their polity, and with leaders of other polities.

PERSPECTIVE AND ORGANIZATION OF THE BOOK

The perspective adopted in this book presents sociopolitical evolution as a historical process that results from the pursuit of self-interest by individuals acting alone and with others in the context of specific ecological and social conditions. In other words, it is a perspective strongly allied with the political models described above, but which also recognizes the importance of local environmental settings in shaping the tempo of evolution and the specific cultural forms it produces.

We begin in Chapter 2 with an overview of the history of Olmec studies. Lively debate has characterized Olmec research from the first hyperdiffusionist explanations for the origins of the Olmecs and their art style, to current disputes over the evolution of Olmec society and its historical role in the development of Mesoamerican civilizations. The history of Olmec studies constitutes a fascinating case study in shifting intellectual paradigms, as well as the triumph of scholarship and "dirt archaeology" over speculation.

An important theme of this volume is the diversity of the Olmecs' landscape and their social, political, and economic adaptations to it. Archaeologists working in many parts of the world are coming to appreciate that the tropical lowlands contain greater natural variation than was long assumed. This is especially true for the southern Gulf lowlands, where meandering rivers, active volcanoes, and the restless sea create a tremendously dynamic landscape. The cultural effects of this natural dynamism are becoming evident as archaeologists increasingly incorporate geomorphological studies in their research and as they expand their investigation beyond the riverine centers that have dominated interpretations of Olmec society for half a century. Consequently, Chapter 3 offers a detailed examination of the natural environment of Olman.

Another theme of this book is the interplay of continuity and change in successive manifestations of Olmec culture. A lack of information on periods before the early Olmec florescence at San Lorenzo has long hampered understanding of the earliest stages of Olmec history, giving rise to arguments that Olmec culture developed elsewhere before it intruded into the Gulf lowlands.

Recent research, however, has begun to reveal a continuous sequence of cultural development within Olman starting centuries earlier in the late Archaic period. Furthermore, Olmec culture and society were not static entities, but experienced significant change over the Early and Middle Formative periods. Chapter 4 traces the development of Olmec culture from its roots in the processes of plant domestication and sedentism during the Archaic period through the collapse of the San Lorenzo polity at the close of the Early Formative period. Chapter 5 continues the story by examining the critical transformations in Olmec culture and society during the Middle Formative period. Both chapters emphasize that Olmec society was not monolithic throughout Olman, but varied significantly from place to place in accord with environmental conditions and the specific histories of Olmec communities.

Social and cultural changes within Olman were partly a consequence and partly a cause of changes in the forms of interaction among the Olmecs and their contemporaries in Mesoamerica. In order to highlight these diachronic processes, I defer consideration of the controversial issue of Early and Middle Formative interaction until Chapter 6, placing emphasis on local histories and processes of sociopolitical evolution and their implications for how and why interregional networks developed.

Just as the Olmecs were once seen as arriving abruptly in the Gulf lowlands, so have they often been characterized as experiencing a cultural and sociopolitical collapse with the abandonment of major centers in eastern Olman in the fifth century B.C. However, ongoing research in western Olman at Tres Zapotes and other sites reveals the continuous evolution of Olmec culture into the Late Formative culture we now know as epi-Olmec. Over the next centuries, epi-Olmec societies flourished and built on their Olmec heritage, creating new forms of sociopolitical organization and making far-reaching advances in writing and calendars. These developments of epi-Olmec culture and its interaction with the emerging Izapan, Mayan, and Zapotec civilizations are investigated in Chapter 7.

The final chapter offers a synthesis of Olmec social and cultural evolution and evaluates the evidence for an Olmec legacy to later Mesoamerican civilizations. The first part of the chapter highlights the implications of sociopolitical variation in Olman for understanding processes of social change. I argue that ecological processes operating at local and subregional scales cannot be generalized as causes for the development of Olmec society as a whole. Rather, the pursuit of political strategies by individual leaders provides a better framework for understanding the varying forms and histories of sociopolitical organization across Olman, and one which more successfully integrates the effects of environmental, economic, and political factors. The second part of the chapter concludes that the Olmecs did contribute significantly to succeeding civilizations, but that they were not unique in that regard. Rather, their influence on their contemporaries was variable, with different consequences for the prevalence of an Olmec legacy in different parts of Mesoamerica. The history of the Olmecs and the complex dynamism of interactions among the Formative period societies of Mesoamerica constitute the plot of a fascinating epic, which is still being written. I invite the reader to trace that story in the pages that follow, beginning with the contributions of the many scholars who are its modern authors.

CHAPTER 2

"GREAT STONE FACES
OF THE MEXICAN JUNGLE"

The rediscovery of the Olmecs is one of the great sagas of archaeology. Set in a romantic locale and populated by intriguing characters who clash in grand academic battles, the historical account of Olmec research reads like a novel. No one appreciates this more than Michael D. Coe, whose popular 1968 book on the Olmecs is as much about the individuals who rediscovered the Olmecs as it is about the ancient culture itself. Tracing the paths of our disciplinary forebears through the physical and intellectual swamps of Olman also provides perspective on contemporary issues in Olmec scholarship. As Richard Diehl, paraphrasing Glyn Daniel, observed, "The present and future states of archaeology cannot be divorced from its past state" (1989: 18). This truth applies especially to Olmec studies, in which old debates seem to renew themselves in the manner of the inevitable cycles of ancient Mesoamerican calendars (Diehl and Coe 1995: 11).

This chapter recounts the story of research in Olman in the context of investigations elsewhere in Mesoamerica and broader trends in archaeological theory. The history of Olmec archaeology parallels that of archaeology in the New World generally, in progressing from rampant speculation to concerns of definition and classification to reconstruction of culture history to investigations of functional integration and causal processes. This progression reflects shifts in the dominant paradigms in Americanist archaeology (Willey and Sabloff 1993), although new problem orientations in archaeological research on the Gulf Coast have often lagged behind their initial applications elsewhere in Mesoamerica. That time lag continues in the relative scarcity of Olmec archaeological studies that incorporate postprocessual approaches to interpreting meaning and meaningful practice, though such approaches have had greater influence in art history and in archaeological investigations of Olmec-related phenomena beyond the Gulf Coast (e.g. Clark and Blake 1994; Love 1999; Tate 1999).

Though this chapter focuses on archaeological investigations, one long-standing feature of Olmec research has been a productive interplay between archaeology and art history. This is by no means rare in the study of Mesoamerica's pre-Columbian cultures, which produced some of the world's great artistic traditions, but it has particularly affected the course of Olmec investigations. Disciplinary boundaries blur here, with archaeologists frequently contributing definitions of the Olmec art style and interpretations of its iconography (e.g. Clewlow 1974, Clewlow et al. 1967; Coe 1965c, 1989; Cyphers 1997b; Drucker 1952a; Grove 1981b; Stirling 1965). This interplay is exemplified and has been encouraged by the continuing support of the Dumbarton Oaks Research Library and Collections, which has hosted a series of important conferences on the Olmecs since 1967 (Benson 1968, 1981; Grove and Joyce 1999).

EARLY RESEARCH

José María Melgar y Serrano published the first in situ discovery of what we now recognize as a product of Olmec culture in his 1869 and 1871 accounts of the colossal head of Hueyapan (Tres Zapotes Monument A) (Fig. 1.1). Melgar also holds the dubious distinction of being the first to claim an African source for the physiognomy of Olmec sculptures, writing, "that which most impressed me was the Ethiopic type which it represents; I reflected that indubitably there had been negroes in this land..." (1869: 292, translation by author). The rest of Melgar's article, which he reproduced with some modifications in his 1871 work, is a confused defense of this thesis, citing others' interpretations of Chiapanec legends, false cognate words in Hebrew and Chiapanec, and Plato's account of Atlantis.

Melgar's speculations were very much a product of his times. The origins of Native American societies had fascinated European and American intellectuals and armchair enthusiasts for centuries, with Atlanteans, the Lost Tribes of Israel, Scandinavians, Scythians, and Hindus all mentioned as possible founders of New World populations (Willey and Sabloff 1993: 16). In the 1860s, archaeology was not yet a professional discipline in the Americas, and the recording of archaeological data was still in its infancy. Faced with a unique monument, and immersed in the racialist intellectual climate of his time, Melgar can be excused his earnest fancies. Today, however, more than a century of archaeological fieldwork on the Gulf Coast of Mesoamerica has failed to uncover any convincing evidence for ancient transoceanic contacts.

No other large Olmec monuments turned up for over sixty years, but smaller artworks in the Olmec style were making their way into private collections and museums with increasing frequency. The first of these was an incised celt, which Alexander von Humboldt brought back to Berlin from his travels in Mexico in the early nineteenth century (Humboldt 1810: pl. 28). Alfredo Chavero also published a large votive axe with carved features in 1888 (Fig. 2.1). He compared it to the Tres Zapotes head and, following Melgar, concluded that

Figure 2.1. Carved stone votive axe as published by Chavero (1888: 64).

it, too, expressed an African racial type. In 1890, George Kunz described the similar jade axe that bears his name, comparing it to Chavero's specimen and a green quartz axe from Oaxaca in the British Museum's Christy Collection. Ten years later, Marshall Saville (1900) published the first illustration of the Kunz axe, noting its feline features, and compared it with still other related objects. Thus, by the turn of the last century, scholars were beginning to recognize that these axes represented a distinctive art style. Progress on the archaeology of the Olmec heartland, however, proceeded much more slowly.

Eduard Seler and his wife, Caecilie Seler-Sachs, toured the Sierra de los Tuxtlas in 1905, visiting Tres Zapotes, where they photographed the colossal head and Monument C, an elaborately carved stone box of a later period (Seler-Sachs 1922). Serious archaeological investigation of the southern Gulf Coast did not begin until 1925, however, when Franz Blom and Oliver La Farge (1926) mounted an expedition sponsored by Tulane University's Middle American Research Institute. Born in Denmark in 1898, Blom had become fascinated with the ancient ruins of the Mexican Gulf lowlands while working as an employee of one of the foreign companies drilling in the newly discovered oil fields of the region (Coe 1968a: 40). Enlisting the services of young La Farge, Blom set off from New Orleans in February to explore the still-wild lands of southern Mexico and Guatemala. Written as much for a general audience as

Figure 2.2. The San Martín Pajapan monument.

for a scholarly one, *Tribes and Temples* combines travelogue with archaeological report and ethnography, much in the tradition of John L. Stephens' *Incidents of Travel in Central America, Chiapas and Yucatan* (1841) and *Incidents of Travel in Yucatan* (1843). Blom wrote the archaeological and geographical sections of the book with entertaining flair, while La Farge penned the ethnographic chapters in a more scholarly tone that reflected the greater sophistication of Mesoamerican ethnography at the time.

Among their discoveries were several Olmec monuments, the first identified since Melgar's visit to Tres Zapotes sixty-three years before. Atop the extinct San Martín Pajapan volcano in the Tuxtla Mountains, they located a crouched stone figure wearing a headdress adorned with a feline visage, which had been found in 1897 by the Mexican surveyor, Ismael Loya (Fig. 2.2).

Remarkable as it was, this discovery was surpassed when local guides took them to the site of La Venta on the Río Tonalá in the swamps of western Tabasco. In a single day they recorded eight monuments, including two stelae, four altars, a large sandstone block, a long row of small basalt columns, and most spectacular of all, a colossal head in the same style as that reported by Melgar at Tres Zapotes. They also reported two monuments that had been removed from La Venta to Villahermosa and sketched the principal mound of the site, which they idealized as a stepped pyramid. Others quickly appreciated the implications of Blom and La Farge's discoveries as the geographical center of the art style Saville and others had begun to recognize. In his 1927 review of *Tribes and Temples*, Hermann Beyer noted the similarities between the headdress of the San Martin Pajapan monument and the face on a votive axe in the National Museum of Mexico. Unlike the axes, which could have been exchanged over hundreds of kilometers, and which were only poorly provenienced, Loya had found the much less portable Pajapan monument in situ and associated with jade offerings (Benson 1996: 18). The Gulf Coast provenience of the monument prompted Beyer to attribute the being represented on its headdress and on the votive axe to "the Olmecan or Totonacan civilization." As early as 1892, Francisco del Paso y Troncoso (1892) had used the phrase "Olmec type" to describe ceramic figurines found in Morelos and Guerrero (Piña Chan 1989: 25), but Beyer's attribution was the first supported by in situ data from the Gulf Coast, and it achieved wider dissemination.

The "Olmec" designation for the art style spread rapidly thereafter. In 1929, Saville expanded his 1900 article on votive axes for the Heye foundation series, *Indian Notes*, and referred to them as Olmec. Three years later, George Vaillant (1932) published a description of a pre-Columbian jade figurine from Necaxa, Puebla. Arguing from the geographical distribution of similar artifacts, and citing Saville in support, Vaillant suggested that the "'tiger-face' and 'baby-face'" sculptures should be assigned to the Olmecs identified in the Aztec chronicles. The appearance of this article in the popular journal, *Natural History*, firmly established Olmec as the label for this style.

Late in 1925, as Blom and La Farge were making their trek, Albert C. Weyerstall was sent to Tlacotalpan, Veracruz "to plant bananas" (Weyerstall 1932). Over the next two years he visited several sites in the lower Papaloapan Basin, including Tres Zapotes, which he called the Hueyapam [sic] Group. Guided by an elderly resident of the village, Weyerstall recorded and photographed five monuments, including the colossal head previously reported by Melgar and the Selers. Weyerstall (1932: 32) was the first to report the presence of large mounds and regular courts at Tres Zapotes, and Matthew Stirling (1943: 7) acknowledges him as the first to sense the genuine archaeological importance of the site.

Thus, by 1935, a distinctive Olmec art style had been identified, named, and associated with the Gulf Coast region. The age of the style and its associated culture, however, remained a matter of pure speculation. In fact, regional chronologies of Mesoamerica had only begun to be synthesized, and the great antiquity of the area's cultures was just beginning to dawn on archaeologists. Until radiocarbon dating burst on the scene in the 1950s, the only absolute chronology in all of the New World was that worked out from calendrical inscriptions in the Maya region. Even this was only a "floating chronology" of about 600 years duration, for the Maya had ceased to employ their Long Count calendar at the end of the Classic period, substituting the Short Count, which only placed dates within 400 year cycles. Correlating the Long Count with the Christian calendar was therefore a difficult task, and two major correlations with a 260-year difference competed with one another for acceptance. Ceramic chronologies for Maya sites, including the Carnegie Institution's excavations of the 1920s at Uaxactun, which were among the first to recognize a Preclassic horizon, were only beginning to appear in print (e.g., Ricketson and Ricketson 1937; Smith 1936a, 1936b), and at the opening of the decade, Herbert Spinden's (1928) evolutionary seriation of Mesoamerican art was the best area-wide synthesis for Mesoamerica, despite its several misconceptions.

Elsewhere in Mesoamerica, scholars looked to native chronicles and the relative dating methods of archaeologists for clues to culture history. At the time, the most detailed stratigraphic sequence outside the Mayan region was that of the Valley of Mexico. In 1910, Manuel Gamio dug a 7 m deep stratigraphic test pit into refuse deposits at Azcapotzalco. With this single pit, Gamio pierced the veils of time and opened archaeologist's eyes to an ancient culture preceding those of Teotihuacan and the Aztecs (Gamio 1913). George Vaillant (1930, 1931) continued Gamio's stratigraphic work in the Valley with important excavations at Zacatenco and Ticoman, which supported Gamio's stratigraphy and Spinden's concept of a very early "Archaic" period. Vaillant (1941) later renamed this period the "Middle Cultures," correctly guessing they were not the earliest in the area; today we call them Formative or Preclassic.

Despite these pioneering investigations in Central Mexico and Oaxaca, in the 1930s no other part of Mesoamerica could match the Maya region for chronological control or sheer volume of research. Spinden's great synthesis, *Ancient Civilizations of Mexico and Central America*, employed his correlation of the Long Count, which placed Mayan dates 260 years earlier relative to the Christian calendar than the now more widely accepted Goodman-Martínez-Thompson correlation. Furthermore, he argued that the Classic Maya preceded the civilizations of Teotihuacan and Monte Alban, which are now known to have been their contemporaries. Meanwhile, archaeologists relying on ethno-historic sources and relative chronologies elsewhere in Mesoamerica tended to underestimate ages at the early end of their chronologies. As a result of these temporal discrepancies and the splendor of Maya civilization, it was widely assumed that if any culture could be viewed as the mother of Mesoamerican civilization it was the Maya or their ancestors. The Olmec style was gener-ally viewed as a later, or at best contemporary, offshoot of Maya art (Morley 1946; Thompson 1941). Thus the stage was set for a debate that, in modi-fied form, continues to dominate discussion of the Olmecs over sixty years later.

OLMEC ARCHAEOLOGY: THE BEGINNINGS

In the mid-1930s, a few scholars were beginning to doubt this picture of Mesoamerican prehistory. Vaillant's excavations in the Valley of Mexico soon convinced him of the contemporaneity of the Maya and Teotihuacan (Vaillant 1935), and Alfonso Caso (1938) was coming to similar conclusions from his investigations of Monte Alban. Matthew W. Stirling was another who doubted the common wisdom of the time, with particular respect to the Olmec.

Stirling's fascination with things Olmec was sparked by the power and beauty of a single object, a "crying baby" jade maskette, which he first saw illustrated in 1918 and viewed in person at the Berlin Museum in 1920 (Stirling 1968: 3). Over the next decade, as he served on the staff of the Smithsonian Institution, his interest was reinforced by objects he found in the collections of the National Museum and by the publications he read by Blom and La Farge (1926), Beyer (1927), Saville (1929), and especially Weyerstall (1932). Vaillant's (1930; Vaillant and Vaillant 1934) discovery of jades and Olmec-style ceramic artifacts in the lower levels of his excavations in Central Mexico suggested to Stirling a great antiquity for the style, as did the inscription on the Tuxtla Statuette (Stirling 1968: 3). This small greenstone figure, found in the Tuxtla Mountains of southern Veracruz, bore the earliest Long Count date known at the time (8.6.2.4.17, A.D. 162).[1]

In 1932 Stirling, who had been appointed director of the Bureau of American Ethnology, launched a program to investigate the eastern and western margins of the Maya region with the hope of clarifying the temporal and cultural relationships between the Maya and their neighbors. William Duncan Strong attacked the eastern margin in 1932–1936, where he discovered the Preclassic

Playa de los Muertos culture and the Yojoa monochrome ceramic complex in Honduras (Stirling 1968: 3).

For himself Stirling took the western margin, the presumed heartland of the Olmec culture, which had intrigued him for so long. Inspired by Weyerstall's report, Stirling began his reconnaissance in 1938, focusing on Tres Zapotes and the surrounding area between the Tuxtla Mountains and the Papaloapan River. Upon his return, with photographs of the monuments and mounds of Tres Zapotes in hand, he appealed to the officials at the National Geographic Society for financial support. The Society enthusiastically agreed to the request, financing two seasons of fieldwork at Tres Zapotes, in 1938–1939 and 1939–1940.

In 1938 Tres Zapotes was a village of about 200 people living in palm-thatched houses, reached only after a day of travel by launch and horseback from the river town of Tlacotalpan. Before the Mexican revolution of 1910, the area had supported immense herds of cattle and broad fields of sugar cane. By the time of Stirling's arrival, tropical forest had reclaimed much of the old Hacienda Hueyapan, which the people of Tres Zapotes were clearing for pasture and *milpas* (maize fields) on their recently granted communal *ejido* lands. In this setting, the logistics of hiring and training workers and building and maintaining a field camp were particularly challenging. As housekeeper, bookkeeper, and supervisor of artifact preparation in the field laboratory, Marion Stirling was an indespensable member of her husband's team at Tres Zapotes and in his subsequent projects. Her accounts (Stirling 1941; Pugh 1981) add a human dimension to the dry academic descriptions of the early Olmec expeditions.

In the first season of excavation at Tres Zapotes, Stirling and his assistant, Clarence W. Weiant, focused on finding additional stone monuments and trenching mounds. The most exciting of the season's discoveries was Stela C (Fig. 2.3). The upper and lower ends of the stela had been broken off in antiquity, and the middle portion was reset on its side at the base of the principal structure in the northernmost mound group of the site. On one face was carved in low relief a stylized supernatural face, which resembled mask panels on early Maya stelae and the façade of Pyramid E-VII-sub at Uaxactun. Stirling (1940: 5–8) also noted its similarity to the "jaguar" faces on some Olmec jades and ceramics, but closer parallels on Olmec stone monuments from La Venta had not yet been discovered.

The opposite face of Stela C bore an even more astounding feature, two columns of glyphs, which, though badly eroded, still preserved the distinctive bar-and-dot numerals of a date in the Long Count calendar used by the Maya. The crucial first coefficient had been broken off with the upper fragment of the stela, but below the column of numerals appeared the date 6 Etznab in the 260-day sacred almanac, or *tzolkin*, which intermeshes with the 365-day *haab*, or "vague year" to produce the 52-year Calendar Round of Mesoamerica. The preservation of the tzolkin glyph allowed Marion Stirling to reconstruct the entire date as (7).16.6.16.18 6 Etznab (1 Uo), corresponding

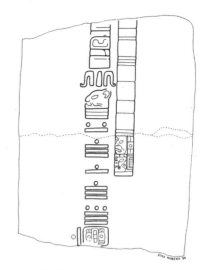

Figure 2.3. Tres Zapotes Stela C; Stirling discovered the lower portion in 1939; the upper portion was found 30 years later (adapted from Clark and Pye 2000: 136, chapter frontispiece) (drawing by Ajax Moreno, courtesy of John E. Clark, New World Archaeological Foundation).

to 32 B.C. in the Goodman-Martinez-Thompson correlation. Interestingly, Stirling declined to correlate the date to the Christian calendar in his technical report of 1940, but in his 1939 popular article for National Geographic magazine, he assigned it a date of 291 B.C. using Spinden's correlation. Regardless of the correlation used, the date on Stela C was sixty-nine years earlier than the oldest Long Count date then known, which was carved on a stela found at El Baul in the highlands of Guatemala. It also predated the beginning of the Maya Classic period by more than 300 years! For Stirling, the clear implication was that the Olmecs were not only older than the Maya, but that they had invented the calendrical system that was the paragon of Maya intellectual achievement.

That conclusion did not sit well with the leading Mayanists of the time. In a 1941 article with the understated title, "Dating of Certain Inscriptions of Non-Maya Origin," Sir J. Eric S. Thompson attacked the early correlations for the dates on Stela C and the Tuxtla Statuette, and argued that the archaeological Olmecs were contemporaries of the Postclassic Toltec. Shortly thereafter, Sylvanus G. Morley (1946) expressed similar objections in his widely read book *The Ancient Maya*. Nevertheless, the Stirlings' reconstruction of the date on Stela C helped convince many archaeologists of the great antiquity of the Olmec. The Stirlings were vindicated when the upper fragment of the stela was found in 1970 bearing the expected coefficient of 7, but by then radiocarbon dating had already shown Stela C to be younger than the Olmec culture by several centuries (Porter 1989: 41; Pugh 1981: 6).

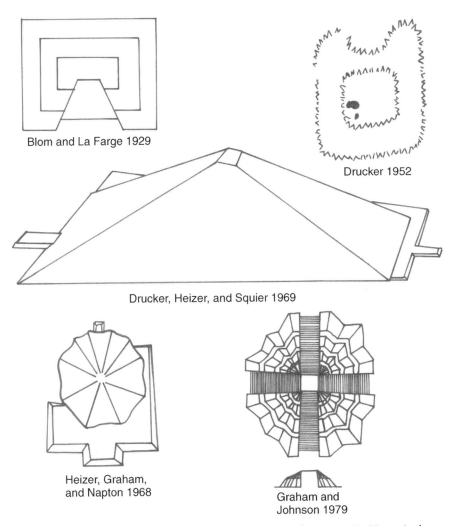

Blom and La Farge 1929

Drucker 1952

Drucker, Heizer, and Squier 1969

Heizer, Graham,
and Napton 1968

Graham and
Johnson 1979

Figure 2.4. Changing conceptions of the Great Mound, C-1, at La Venta (redrawn after González 1997: Fig. 1).

Philip Drucker, Stirling's assistant in the second season, followed up the exploratory work of the previous year by trenching additional mounds and digging test pits in several parts of the site to identify promising areas for the five stratigraphic excavations he conducted. Weiant and Drucker published separate reports of the ceramics from the 1938–1939 and 1939–1940 field seasons with brief descriptions of the excavations. Weiant was more familiar with Mesoamerican ceramics, and his typological comparisons were the more extensive of the two. Drucker, however, had the advantage of his stratigraphic excavations, which had tapped the earlier levels of occupation, and his ceramic sequence long stood as the basic one for the southern Gulf Coast. Unfortunately, the simultaneous publication of Weiant's and Drucker's Tres Zapotes reports in 1943 (a banner year, which also saw the publication of Drucker's

Ceramic Stratigraphy of Cerro de las Mesas and Stirling's *Stone Monuments of Southern Mexico*) led to considerable confusion and resulted in a rancorous exchange between the ceramicists (Wauchope 1950; Drucker 1952b; Weiant 1952).

With Drucker directing excavations in 1940, Stirling (1940; 1943) found time to visit La Venta, Tabasco, and Cerro de las Mesas, Veracruz. At La Venta, he exposed 12 Olmec monuments in 10 days, and in a mere two days at Cerro de las Mesas he recorded over 20 carved stone monuments of the Classic period. Of course, such rapid "excavations" precluded detailed recording of archaeological context or stratigraphy, but that was not Stirling's aim. Rather, these brief visits were conducted to reconnoiter the sites for future fieldwork and to obtain the spectacular photographs that would ensure continued funding from the National Geographic Society. To that end, Stirling was accompanied by the National Geographic staff photographer, Richard Stewart, whose photographs appeared in Stirling's article, "Great Stone Faces of the Mexican Jungle," in the September, 1940 issue of the magazine.

Stirling and Drucker excavated at Cerro de las Mesas in 1941, dividing their labors as they had at Tres Zapotes, with Stirling directing the clearing of monuments and excavating structures and Drucker concentrating on stratigraphic excavations in refuse deposits to reconstruct a ceramic chronology. Although a cache of 782 carved jade pieces contained a few Olmec-style heirlooms, the cache itself was evidently buried over a millennium later, and the site was primarily occupied from the Late Formative through the Postclassic periods.

The excavations at Cerro de las Mesas were important for the information they yielded on Classic period art and ceramic chronology, but it was Stirling's investigation at La Venta that thrust the Olmecs into the limelight of scholarly and public fascination. The archaeological site of La Venta occupies a low "island" of eroded Pleistocene deposits amid the swamps of northeastern Tabasco (Jiménez 1990: 7). A huge earthen mound, 30 m high, rests on a massive platform 150 m across (Fig. 2.4). Over thirty other mounds aligned to an axis oriented 8° west of true north extend to the north and south of the great mound. Drucker directed most of the three months of fieldwork at La Venta in 1942. Employing a small crew of local workers, he tested eight areas of sherd concentrations with forty non-stratigraphic pits. Using this information, he selected three areas for stratigraphic excavation. The entrance of the United States into World War II forced the investigators to shorten their field season, and it was only in the last three weeks that Drucker turned his attention to "structural investigations" in Complex A, a ceremonial precinct to the north of the "Great Pyramid." Stirling arrived in time to take part in this final phase of the field season. Trenching mound A-2 at the north end of the complex, Drucker and Stirling soon uncovered three spectacular features arrayed along the center line of the mound. The first was a massive sandstone coffer carved in the form of a saurian supernatural, which the excavators misidentified as a jaguar. The coffer was filled with red clay and contained six greenstone objects, including two earspools, arrayed as if to accompany a human body, whose bones had long-since disintegrated in the acid soil. To the north, a pile of basalt columns covered 108 objects in cinnabar-stained soil. Mainly of jade, the objects were again arranged as if to accompany a burial. North of this "Tomb E" an enclosure walled and roofed with basalt columns formed "Tomb A." It contained the remains of two or three juvenile bundle burials, stained with cinnabar, and accompanied by jade, obsidian, and polished hematite artifacts.

THE *MESA REDONDA*

As Drucker and Stirling were completing their first season at La Venta, the age and significance of Olmec culture was still very much at issue. By this time, the Mexican scholars Alfonso Caso and Miguel Covarrubias were heralding the Olmecs as the "Mother Culture" from which the great Mesoamerican civilizations had sprung. Just the previous year, however, Thompson had published his elegant paper refuting that idea (Thompson 1941; Coe 1968a: 60). George Vaillant was among the very few North American archaeologists who supported the Mexican position, because "Olmec"-type figurines appeared in the lowest levels of his Central Mexican excavations.

The "Olmec problem" came to a head in late April of 1942, when the Sociedad Mexicana de Antropología convened its Second Roundtable on Anthropological Problems of Mexico and Central America. The organizing committee, consisting of Alfonso Caso, Miguel Covarrubias, Wigberto Jiménez Moreno, Paul Kirchoff, Enrique Juan Palacios, Jorge A. Vivó, and J. Eric S. Thompson had invited a star-studded cast of ethnographers, ethnohistorians, linguists, physical anthropologists, and archaeologists to debate the topic over five days in Tuxtla Gutierrez, Chiapas. Thompson, however, was notably absent when the roundtable met (Sociedad Mexicana de Antropología 1942).

Wigberto Jiménez Moreno opened the first session by reviewing the sources recording the historic Olmecs of Postclassic times, concluding that Olmec referred properly to diverse cultures whose origin lay in the southern Gulf Coast, and relating La Venta to the earliest culture of this region. Two days later, Caso, Covarrubias, Vaillant, and Eduardo Noguera each argued strongly for the affiliation of the prehistoric Olmecs with the Formative period (then called the "Archaic Horizon"), based on stylistic considerations and stratigraphic associations outside the Gulf lowlands. The next day, Stirling, fresh from the field, described the finds at La Venta and displayed several of the jades that had been found there only a few days before (Stirling 1968: 5; Sociedad Mexicana de Antropología 1942: 8). Caso (1943: 46) issued the definitive statement of the conference, "This great culture, which we encounter in ancient levels, is without doubt the mother of other cultures, such as the Maya, the Teotihuacan, the Zapotec, that of El Tajín, and others" (translation by author). The Mexicans' arguments won the day; the conferees concluded

that Olmec was indeed aligned to the "Archaic" culture, and that it be designated "the La Venta culture." Only the great art historian, Herbert Spinden,
demurred, noting "the La Venta culture constitutes a special case, and it cannot
be placed as antecedent to all other cultures of America" (Sociedad Mexicana
de Antropología 1942: 75, translation by the author).

FURTHER INVESTIGATIONS

Despite the confident conclusions of the roundtable, far more research was
required to securely establish the age of the Olmec. In 1942, Covarrubias
began excavations with Hugo Moedano Koer at Tlatilco, on the outskirts of
Mexico City. Covarrubias had been buying figurines and other objects from
workers digging for clay in the brickyards at the site since 1936. Digging in
arbitrary levels of 20 cm, Covarrubias and Koer were able to align the site with
two early horizons of Vaillant's "Archaic" period. In 1947 Daniel Rubín de la
Bobolla and Covarrubias expanded the excavations. The presence of Olmec-
style figurines and other materials associated with some of the burials reinforced
Covarrubias's contention that Olmec culture was very early.

Stirling returned to La Venta in 1943 with Waldo Wedel replacing Drucker,
who had been called to military service. Stirling and Wedel again focused
their attention on Complex A, conducting other structural excavations that
identified layers of colored clay and adobe blocks, as well as two large buried
mosaic pavements of serpentine in the form of great supernatural masks. A
National Geographic article by Matthew and Marion Stirling (1942) described
the finds of the 1942 season, but a detailed report had to await Drucker's return
from the military. Drucker published an interim report in 1947, in which he
erroneously cross-dated the La Venta pottery with the Early Classic period of
the Maya area. The final report by Drucker, which contained a contribution
by Wedel on the 1943 excavations and a technological analysis of the ceramics
by Anna Shepard, was not published until 1952.

In 1945 Stirling (1947, 1955) investigated the Olmec monuments of San
Lorenzo, Río Chiquito (Tenochtitlán), and Potrero Nuevo, three remote
sites with Olmec monuments located up the Coatzacoalcos river in southern
Veracruz. Among the monuments Stirling recorded was "El Rey," another
colossal head like those he had uncovered at Tres Zapotes and La Venta. He
returned with Drucker in 1946 to excavate at San Lorenzo, but a detailed
report of those excavations never appeared.

It is difficult to overstate the impact of Stirling's investigations on the early
history of Olmec studies. He not only initiated modern archaeological research
in Olman, but in eight years and seven field seasons he revealed to the world
the sophistication and opulence of Olmec culture in its heartland. Indeed, the
revelations of the 1942 and 1943 seasons at La Venta defined Olmec culture
for a generation of scholars and lay people. Focusing on monuments and jade

caches, and with little concern for stratigraphic excavation methods, Stirling's own publications in the *National Geographic Magazine* and the bulletins of the Bureau of American Ethnology hark back to a 19th century fascination with the spectacular, much as Blom and La Farge's (1926) *Tribes and Temples* evoked Stephens's *Incidents of Travel*. Stirling should not be judged too harshly in this regard, however. With his uncanny sense of where to look for offerings and carvings, he ensured the continued funding of his pioneering work. Neither did he ignore the more scientific aspects archaeological research. In his support of Weiant, Wedel, and particularly Drucker, he saw to the establishment of the first regional ceramic chronologies published for southern Mexico (Ekholm 1945).

THE 1950s

As the decade of the 1950s opened, the chronological placement of La Venta remained a critical issue for Olmec studies. Despite the Roundtable's promotion of La Venta as the seat of the Olmec "Mother Culture," Philip Drucker remained unconvinced. In the 1942 field season at La Venta, he had attempted to employ the same field and analytical methods that had worked so well for him at Tres Zapotes and Cerro de las Mesas. Unlike those sites, where marked stratigraphic changes in frequencies of ceramic wares defined sequential phases, the two stratigraphic tests at La Venta that contained adequate materials for analysis showed only subtle changes in ceramic frequencies. Drucker (1952a: 130) concluded, "It seems clear then that we are dealing with ceramics all belonging to a single pattern, and so far as one can see, to the same general horizon within that tradition." Drucker apparently formed this quite reasonable opinion during the course of his excavations, as it was echoed by Stirling (1942: 57) at the Roundtable in Tuxtla Gutierrez. In contrast to Caso, Covarrubias, and Vaillant, however, Drucker aligned the La Venta horizon temporally to the Early Classic Tzakol horizon of the Maya lowlands. His reasoning was thus: the stratigraphic excavations at La Venta produced substantial quantities of "Fine Paste wares," which Drucker linked to the fine paste wares at Tres Zapotes that he had misleadingly dubbed "Polychrome." At Tres Zapotes, these fine paste ceramics showed a marked increase in levels assigned to the transitional Middle Tres Zapotes phase. The earlier Lower Tres Zapotes ceramics showed some similarities to Preclassic Mamom and Chicanel ceramics of the Maya lowlands, whereas Upper Tres Zapotes included several Teotihuacan elements, then thought to belong to the Late Classic period (Drucker 1943a: 122). Consequently, Middle Tres Zapotes must have lain within the time span of the "Old Empire" (Early Classic) Tzakol phase of the Maya lowlands, despite the fact that "nothing referable to the Tzakol phase appears at our site" (Drucker 1943a: 120). Thus Drucker's (1952a: 150) assignment of La Venta to the Early Classic was strongly influenced by the appearance of Fine Paste ceramics at that site, although in the same report, Anna Shepard's (1952) technological analysis indicated that they differed markedly from those at Tres Zapotes in that they were tempered with a very fine volcanic ash.

Drucker's (1947) interim report on the La Venta ceramics had linked them to the Tres Zapotes sequence. It was therefore with amazement that he read Robert Wauchope's 1950 synthesis assigning Middle Tres Zapotes to the Pre-classic period. Drucker (1952b) placed the blame for this "misunderstand-ing" squarely on Weiant's (1943) Tres Zapotes report, which he thought had improperly divided Middle Tres Zapotes into sequential A and B subphases. Weiant (1952) responded that he had never intended to imply a cultural break between Middle Tres Zapotes A and B, and that Drucker had misrepresented the evidence on the basis of which he had proposed the division. Such was the intensity of the heat generated by the "Olmec question" in the 1950s; the exchange did little to shed light on the problem, however.

Stirling and Wedel's excavations in Complex A of La Venta had indicated the complexity of its construction, but lacking the time and resources to excavate most of their trenches to culturally sterile levels, they were unable to confi-dently relate one series of construction phases to another. Consequently, in 1955, Drucker returned with Robert F. Heizer, Robert J. Squier, Eduardo Contreras, and "a labor force adequate to move enough dirt to yield some conclusive results" (Drucker et al. 1959: 1). The toughness of the clays used in the construction of the complex forced Drucker's crews to use picks and shovels for most of the excavation; a bulldozer loaned by Petroleos Mexi-canos (PEMEX) also was employed to strip off postoccupational "drift sands," remove backdirt, and to cut a section from the centerline through the eastern edge of the ceremonial court. The excavations revealed sequences of colored clay floors, adobe block constructions, and burial offerings, which Drucker et al. (1959: 121–127) synthesized into four general construction phases, labeled I through IV, from earliest to latest. Most spectacular of their finds were three massive buried offerings containing courses of serpentine blocks. One of these was estimated to contain an astounding 1,000 tons of serpentine, covered by a serpentine mosaic pavement similar to those Stirling and Wedel had found in 1943 (Fig. 2.5).

Most importantly, charcoal recovered from the 1955 excavations produced the first radiocarbon dates from a Gulf Olmec site. On the basis of the nine dates, which ranged from 3110 ± 300 B.P. to 2130 ± 300 B.P., Drucker et al. (1957; 1959: 263–265) concluded that Complex A was built and utilized between 800 and 400 b.c. (in uncalibrated radiocarbon years, or ca. 900–400 B.C.) These determinations appeared to correspond reasonably well with radiocarbon dates that were becoming available for Preclassic levels at the Maya site of Kaminaljuyu, Guatemala, the Zapotec site of Monte Alban, Oaxaca, and most significantly, Tlatilco, thought to be a locus of Olmec interaction in Valley of Mexico. For most archaeologists, the dates from La Venta and Tlatilco sounded the death knell for the "Classic Olmec" position.

Figure 2.5. Mosaic pavement covering a massive offering of serpentine at La Venta (Drucker et al. 1959: Plate 15).

Still, not everyone was convinced. For example, Alfonso Medellín Zenil of the Universidad Veracruzana had found Classic period pottery below Olmec monuments at Laguna de los Cerros, Veracruz, and he held until his death in 1986 that the colossal heads and tabletop altars were Classic period carvings. William Coe and Robert Stuckenrath (1964) published a long and scathing review of Drucker et al.'s 1959 report, which questioned the stratigraphy and dating of the Complex A phases. Responses by Heizer (1964) and by Drucker and Heizer (1965), however, countered Coe and Stuckenrath's charges to the satisfaction of most archaeologists.

In the 1950s the title of foremost *olmequista* passed from the bold Stirling to the more reserved Drucker, who deserves much of the credit for the maturation of Olmec archaeology on the Gulf Coast. In the 1940s, as Stirling focused on the spectacular monuments and offerings that would ensure the funding of the projects he organized, Drucker shouldered the responsibility for the more scientific aspects of the investigations. In his application of stratigraphic methods to the construction of ceramic chronology, he can be said to have introduced problem-oriented research to the Gulf Coast. Unfortunately, Drucker never revised his ceramic chronology for La Venta, and his original stratigraphic tests, excavated outside Complex A, cannot be meaningfully related to the series of construction phases in the ceremonial court (Grove 1997: 62). This oversight, though frustrating to the current generation of archaeologists, is understandable in terms of Drucker's methods and objectives. Drucker's aim in 1955 was to establish the sequence of construction phases in Complex A. For establishing ceramic chronologies, however, Drucker preferred stratified refuse deposits to construction fill, because the latter frequently incorporated materials from earlier deposits. Confident in his previous ceramic chronology, he therefore was less concerned with collecting the materials that would have tied it directly to the construction sequence, and, in any event, sherds were notably scarce in the Complex A deposits. Moreover, in the flush of excitement over the advent of radiocarbon dating, Drucker may have felt, as did the sociocultural anthropologist Fredrik Barth (1950), that the new technique would free archaeologists from concentrating on matters of chronology (Willey and Sabloff 1993: 182).

The tedium of sorting potsherds and writing reports, however, were not entirely to the liking of this former cowboy and rodeo rider. Following the La Venta project, he retired for a decade to ranching in southern Veracruz. This period of his life is described in a fascinating, somewhat fictionalized, "ethnographic sketch" he published under the pseudonym of Paul Record (the last name being a near reversal of his own). In the introduction to *Tropical Frontier*, he lays out the reasons for his change of occupation as a mathematical postulate, one term of which is "*Let*: destiny lead this country boy, as he grew older, to the city, finally to a stultifying desk job where he seemed fated to bore his life away" (Record 1969: xii). The resolution was to walk away from his desk job, marry his Mexican love, and settle on a tributary of the Coatzacoalcos River.

FUNCTION, ECOLOGY, AND EVOLUTION

Through the 1950s, the central questions of Americanist archaeology were definitional, geographical, and, above all, chronological (Willey and Sabloff 1993). These concerns are particularly well illustrated in Olmec studies, which had focused almost exclusively on defining the Olmec style, documenting its distribution, and dating its age, first in relative terms, then through chronometric methods. Moreover, the "Olmec problem" had been conceived in a diffusionist climate, and diffusionist principles continued to color its interpretations for decades. Simply stated, the Olmec art style was among the most sophisticated and widespread known from Mesoamerica. If it also was the earliest, and if it could be tied to a specific region, then by default the Olmec became the mother that had given birth to later Mesoamerican civilizations. With this problem apparently resolved by the radiocarbon dating of La Venta, Olmec archaeology could turn to other problems.

Since 1940, Mesoamericanists (and particularly Mayanists) had been encouraged to concentrate on functionalist concerns regarding past lifeways, most vociferously by the ethnologist Clyde Kluckhohn (1940) and his student, the archaeologist Walter W. Taylor (1948). Meanwhile the study of human adaptation to the environment was gaining ground in sociocultural anthropology in the form of Julian Steward's cultural ecology (e.g. Steward 1949), and Leslie White was encouraging a more unilineal brand of evolutionism. These functionalist and evolutionary concerns began to make inroads in Mesoamerican archaeology in the 1950s and early 1960s through the research of a few archaeologists, including William T. Sanders (1953, 1956, 1965) Gordon Willey (Willey et al. 1965), Richard S. MacNeish (1958, 1967), and Kent V. Flannery (1968a; Coe and Flannery 1964; 1967).

Drucker was one of the first working on the southern Gulf Coast to incorporate an environmental perspective in his writing. In 1953, he and Eduardo Conteras conducted a reconnaissance to establish the southern and western boundaries of Olmec territory (Drucker and Contreras 1953). Focusing mainly on river courses, but with brief forays into the interfluves, Drucker and Contreras identified 80 sites and suggested that Olmec expansion had been impeded by zones of savannahs between the middle courses of the Zanapa and Uxpanapa rivers. Drucker also published studies of the milpa agricultural system in the La Venta area, drawing on ethnographic interviews and his own intimate experience living in the Gulf lowlands (Drucker and Heizer 1960; Drucker 1961).

Michael D. Coe had been influenced by Flannery's ecological perspective when they collaborated at the site of Salinas la Blanca in coastal Guatemala (Coe and Diehl 1980a: 3; Coe and Flannery 1967). Thus, in the mid-1960s, when Coe initiated a major interdisciplinary project at San Lorenzo Tenochtitlán, he incorporated a "human ecology" component based on photogrametric analysis, soil and biological studies, and interviews with the local inhabitants (Coe 1968b; 1974; Coe and Diehl 1980a: 3, 1980b). The excavations at San Lorenzo, however, were directed toward the project's more central aims of seeking the origins of Olmec culture and establishing a datable archaeological sequence for the numerous monuments present there (Coe 1968b: 44) (Fig. 2.6).

Coe began the San Lorenzo project in 1966 with Richard A. Diehl as his field assistant, just a year after Alfonso Medellín Zenil and Román Piña Chan had confirmed rumors of a second colossal head at the site and removed it for an exhibition in Houston, to the consternation of the local inhabitants (Coe and Diehl 1980a: 4; Wicke 1971: 50). In three seasons of excavation, Coe pushed the beginnings of Olmec culture back well before La Venta's Complex A, demonstrating that San Lorenzo had achieved its apogee between 1150 and 900 b.c. (ca. 1400–1000 B.C.), and documenting a long sequence of earlier cultural development. Coe defined seven Formative period ceramic phases, which stretched from 1500 to 100 b.c. (ca. 1750–50 B.C.) and were anchored in time by radiocarbon dates from the Early Formative deposits; this sequence, with minor modifications, continues to form the backbone of Formative period chronology in the Gulf lowlands (Coe et al. 1967a, b; Coe and Diehl 1980a: 395–396; Grove 1997: 65; Symonds et al. 2002).

The excavations also recovered some traces of Olmec architecture, as well as extensive drain systems made of basalt troughs layed end-to-end and covered with basalt slabs (Coe 1968a: 86–87; Coe and Diehl 1980a: 118–126). Thirty-five new stone monuments were recorded at San Lorenzo, raising the total to fifty-two. Although many of the monuments lacked good archaeological contexts, some were clearly associated with deposits of the San Lorenzo phase, and one fragment, argued to be detached from a colossal head, was associated with the preceding Chicharras phase (Coe 1968b: 47–52; Coe and Diehl 1980a: 103–104, 114–118, 246, 294; cf. Graham 1989). Coe's project also introduced the innovation of using a cesium magnetometer to detect buried monuments, locating four. As a result, the Instituto Nacional de Antropología and the University of Pennsylvania's Museum Applied Science Center for Archaeology (MASCA) conducted a large-scale magnetometer survey in 1969 and 1970, finding another fourteen monuments, including two colossal heads (Beverido 1970; Brüggemann and Harris 1970; Brüggemann and Hers 1970; Coe and Diehl 1980a: 9; Grove 1997: 66).

Back at La Venta, a series of smaller investigations followed Drucker's massive excavations of 1955. Even in the 1950s, it was becoming evident that the infrastructure PEMEX was building for oil exploration was increasingly threatening the archaeological site. The Tabascan poet, Carlos Pellicer, began to negotiate for the transfer of most of La Venta's monuments to the state capital in Villahermosa. In 1957 he began the massive task of hauling the monuments, each of which weighed up to thirty-eight tons, over poor roads and ferrying them across bridgeless rivers (González 1996: 148). In 1958 the La Venta Archaeological Park of Villahermosa was inaugurated with 22 sculptures and two mosaics from the massive offerings. With concern for the destruction of the site mounting, Román Piña Chan and Roberto Gallegos conducted a general reconnaissance of the site, excavated some stratigraphic pits, and did more extensive work on the basal platform of the main pyramid (Grove 1997: 62; Heizer 1968: 28; Piña Chan and Covarrubias 1964; cf. González 1996: 146). The following year, PEMEX widened an airstrip they had constructed in 1954 and 1955, destroying parts of the Ceremonial Court and Mound A-2 to secure fill (Heizer 1968: 13).

Prompted by the early radiocarbon dates from San Lorenzo, Heizer had the remaining portions of the original samples from La Venta reanalyzed in 1967, along with two additional samples that Robert Squier had in 1974 obtained from outside the ceremonial complex. Applying the more accurate figure of 5,730 years for the half-life of Carbon 14, Heizer and his associates concluded that the floruit of La Venta lay between 1000 and 600 b.c.[2], some 200 years earlier than the previous estimate, and overlapping the San Lorenzo phase at San Lorenzo (Berger et al. 1967: 6). In 1967 Drucker, Heizer, and John Graham (1968b) collected another 32 radiocarbon samples from a series of pits in Complex A and two stratigraphic tests west of the "Great Pyramid."

Figure 2.6. Michael D. Coe excavating Monument 34 at San Lorenzo (from Coe and Diehl 1980a: unnumbered plate) (courtesy of Michael D. Coe)).

Although only one of the six samples submitted for analysis produced a date considered acceptable, the excavators concluded that it substantiated the 1967 redating (Heizer 1968: 13–14). That redating is questionable however, because the La Venta Complex A ceramics are most similar to those of the Palangana phase (600–400 b.c., ca. 780–400 cal. B.C.) at San Lorenzo (Coe and Diehl 1980a: 200–208; Grove 1997: 67).

Drucker, Heizer, and Graham's 1967 visit also led to a revised interpretation of the great mound, C-1. Having been cleared of some of its dense covering vegetation, the mound now appeared to have the form of a fluted cone, rather than the rectangular pyramid that had been assumed (Drucker et al. 1959: 11, Fig. 5; Heizer 1968: 18–20). Topographic mapping of the mound in 1968 confirmed this observation, and the investigators suggested the mound had been constructed intentionally to resemble a volcano (Heizer 1968; Heizer and Drucker 1968; Heizer et al. 1968b). This interpretation of the original form of the mound has only recently been overturned by excavations on its south face, which show it had the form of a stepped pyramid (González 1997). Drucker and Heizer also mapped Complex B to the south of mound C-1 and excavated on a massive platform, the "Stirling Acropolis." The excavations revealed stone drains similar to those at San Lorenzo, but radiocarbon dates from the excavations were inconclusive. In 1969, Frank Morrison (1971; Morrison et al. 1971) conducted a magnetometer survey of mound C-1, identifying a large anomaly, which remains unexcavated.

Systematic fieldwork at major sites greatly expanded the known corpus of Olmec art from the 1940s onward, but more often than not, it was chance finds by local inhabitants that lured archaeologists to sites like Tres Zapotes, La Venta, and San Lorenzo in the first place. Serendipity struck again on July 16, 1965 as two children cracked palm nuts on a round green stone in the village of Las Limas near Jesús Carranza, Veracruz. Deciding to take the stone home, Rosa and Severiano Salazar dug the earth from around it, revealing a beautifully carved figure seated cross-legged and holding a supernatural infant in its arms (Wicke 1971: 49–50) (Fig. 2.7). The Salazar family set the sculpture in an elaborate altar in their home, dressing it in a silk cape and setting paper flowers and candles before it until it was taken to the Jalapa Museum of Anthropology. Subsequent studies of the incised designs that grace the face, shoulders, and knees of the main figure and the torso of the infant significantly advanced the study of Olmec iconography (Joralemon 1971, 1976; Coe 1989).

Another important accidental discovery of the 1960s was made at Río (or Arroyo) Pésquero, Veracruz. Local fishers discovered a large cache of about 25 life-sized stone masks, hundreds of jade and serpentine celts, and other jade items. Archaeologists from the Instituto de Antropología at the Universidad Veracruzana salvaged a few pieces from the river bottom, but most of the items were sold on the international art market. Looting of the cache destroyed its original context, so it remains unknown if the locality represented an isolated ceremonial shrine or was part of a larger Olmec settlement (Benson 1996: 21; Diehl and Coe 1995: 19).

Other examples of Olmec-style art had been turning up in places as far away as the Pacific coast of Guatemala (Shook 1956), El Salvador (Boggs 1950), and Costa Rica (Balser 1959). During the 1960s, finds in Western Mexico further expanded the geographical range and the media of Olmec style art. Painted murals of Olmec-like personages were discovered in Juxtlahuaca Cave, Guerrero, in 1966, and in the nearby cave of Oxtotitlán in 1968, pushing back the age of Mesoamerican mural painting several centuries (Gay 1967; Grove 1969, 1970a).

The archaeological study of the Formative period elsewhere in Mesoameica advanced considerably in the 1960s, with important consequences for understanding interaction between the Olmecs and their neighbors. In the Valley of Mexico, Arturo Romano (1962, 1963, 1967) continued excavations at Tlatilco,

Figure 2.7. The Las Limas figure. Note carved profile heads of supernaturals on the shoulders and knees (de la Fuente 1994: Fig 13.2) (courtesy of John E. Clark).

which led to a refined understanding of the context of the "Olmec" ceramics and figurines in the burials there (Tolstoy and Paradis 1970), and Christine Neiderberger (1976) documented several millenia of occupation at Tlapacoya-Zohapilco, which emerged as a regional center with some Olmec-style elements in the Early Formative period. William Sanders's systematic survey of the Valley of Mexico, which continued from 1960–1975, placed these and other sites in a broad regional context of changing settlement patters and adaptations (Sanders et al. 1979).

Kent V. Flannery inititated a long-term study of "The Prehistory and Human Ecology of the Valley of Oaxaca" in 1965, which included excavations at the Formative sites of San José Mogote and Tierras Largas, and extended the chronology of the valley several millenia beyond the beginnings of Monte

Albán. San José Mogote, in particular, exhibited pottery then generally considered to be Olmec in style, as well as workshops for producing iron ore mirrors similar to examples found at San Lorenzo (Flannery 1968b).

In Chiapas, the New World Archaeological Foundation pursued its long-term program of excavation and survey, which began in the late 1950s and continues today. The Formative period was explored intensively on the Pacific Coast and piedmont at Altamira (Ekholm-Miller 1969; Lowe 1975) and Izapa, the latter possessing carvings in Olmec style and a later style apparently derived from Olmec (Green and Lowe 1967). The NWAF also collaborated with INAH in the massive salvage project for the Nezahualcoyotl (Malpaso) dam on the middle Grijalva River in west-central Chiapas. Gareth Lowe's (1998) resulting excavations at San Isidro revealed a long sequence of occupation with close contacts to Olman in the Early and Middle Formative periods, the latter with impressive greenstone celt offerings similar to those at La Venta.

A landmark conference on the Olmecs was held at Dumbarton Oaks in 1967, 25 years after the Roundtable in Tuxtla Gutierrez (Benson 1968). Stirling gave a highly personal overview of the history of the "Olmec problem." Heizer and Coe presented the results of their fieldwork at La Venta and San Lorenzo, respectively, and David C. Grove contributed a chapter on site distributions in Morelos, which was added after the conference. Ignacio Bernal discussed his conception of an Olmec world consisting of metropolitan Olmec, Olmecoid, and colonial Olmec societies and hinted at an "Olmec empire," ideas he would soon expand upon in his important book, *El Mundo Olmeca* (Bernal 1968a). Olmec art and iconography were highlighted in Tatiana Proskouriakoff's discussion of the stylistic relations of Olmec and Maya art and Peter Furst's interpretation of shamanic "were-jaguar" imagery based in ethnographic analogies. Without doubt, however, the most influential of the papers was Kent Flannery's, which employed ethnographic analogies to develop an elegant model of interaction between the Olmec of the Gulf Coast and the Valley of Oaxaca. Such was the persuasiveness of his argument that the model continues to be widely employed, despite its recent rejection by Flannery himself (Flannery and Marcus 1994: 385–390).

The 1970s began auspiciously with the first systematic regional surveys in the southern Gulf lowlands. Sisson (1970, 1976) reconnoitered the Chontalpa region of Tabasco, east of La Venta and Olman proper. He located over 200 sites, a tenth of which related to the Early and Middle Formative periods (Grove 1997: 68). At the other end of Olman, Robert Squier began a survey of the western Sierra de los Tuxtlas in 1970 in collaboration with Francisco Beverido Pereau of the Universidad Veracruzana. The reconnaissance discovered a colossal head unusual for its enormous 40-ton size and remote location on the Cerro el Vigía volcano. Test pits excavated at Matacapan, El Picayo, and Tres Zapotes helped refine the regional ceramic sequence, especially in the important Formative levels of the latter site (Ortiz 1975). The project ended abruptly before the planned 1972 field season, however, and the survey results remain unpublished (Beverido 1987: 189–190; Ortiz 1988: 406–407).

Ill will engendered by the abortive Tuxtlas survey may have contributed to a hiatus in North American involvement in field research in the southern Gulf lowlands following 1972. More generally, Mexican archaeologists increasingly expressed dissatisfaction with the research agendas of North American archaeologists (e.g. Lorenzo 1976, 1981; Arnold 1994: 217). A climate of increased nationalism led to the passage of a law in 1972 requiring review of projects and imposing a fee on foreign fieldwork grants to underwrite curation of materials and protection of sites and monuments. In addition, promotion of the tourist market tended to divert scarce national resources toward more impressive sites with masonry architecture lacking in the southern Gulf lowlands (Arnold 1994: 217). Despite economic constraints, Mexican archaeologists continued to conduct significant fieldwork. For example, Yadéun (1983) carried out a project of mapping and excavation at Las Limas in 1977 and 1978, and salvage work associated with the construction of an oil and gas pipeline identified many new sites and turned up a basalt column enclosure at Tres Zapotes similar to that of La Venta (Millet 1979).

As fieldwork waned on the Gulf Coast during the 1970s, projects in other parts of Mesoamerica continued to produce new finds, which ultimately revolutionized perspectives on patterns of Formative interregional interaction. In 1972 David Grove (1987a) initiated a ten-year multidisciplinary study of the important site of Chalcatzingo, Morelos, whose Olmec-style relief carvings in living rock had been reported by Eulalia Guzmán in 1934. In addition to finding additional carvings and working out a detailed ceramic chronology, Grove found a composite table-top altar or throne, the only such monument known outside Olman.

Research in Guerrero identified several sites with Olmec-related remains, including figurines and ceramics at Xochipala (Gay 1972) and Atopula (Henderson 1979), and rock-carving at San Miguel Amuco (Grove and Paradis 1971). The finds at Xochipala prompted Gay (1972) to suggest that the Olmec style originated in Guerrero, a position proposed earlier by Piña Chan (1955: 106) and Covarrubias (1957: 76) but now widely regarded as untenable (Henderson 1979: 58). In Chiapas, the New World Archaeological Foundation reported impressive Olmec-style rock carvings from Xoc, Pijijiapan, and Tzutzuculli, among others (Ekholm-Miller 1973; McDonald 1977; Navarrete 1974). John Graham of the University of California at Berkeley began fieldwork on the Pacific slope of Guatemala at Takalik Abaj, which contains several Olmec style carvings among its 170 monuments. Among these is what appears to be the only colossal head known from outside Olman, recarved to depict a figure seated in a niche (Graham 1981: Figs. 1 and 2).[3]

The Yucatan peninsula is notable for its relative paucity of Olmec-style objects. Scattered finds have been reported from Kabah, Mayapan, and Dzibalchen (Joesink-Mandeville and Méluzin 1976), Cozumel (Rathje,

Sabloff, and Gregory 1973), and Chichén Itzá (Proskouriakoff 1974), although most of these probably represent curated heirlooms deposited and perhaps acquired long after the Middle Formative period. Nevertheless, a Middle Formative cruciform cache of jade celts, a bloodletter, and ceramic jars at Seibal and jade clamshell pendants from Chacsinkin reflect some participation of lowland Maya in the trade network that included the Olmecs (Willey 1978: 88–89, Figs. 90,91; Andrews 1986: 27, 29–30).

New analytical techniques for sourcing materials complemented stylistic evidence for widespread contacts and the materialist perspective of the New Archaeology, resulting in several studies on Formative period economic exchange. Howel Williams and Robert Heizer (1965) conducted an early petrographic study that identified the Tuxtla mountains as the source of the volcanic stone for many Olmec monuments, and petrographic analysis was later extended to groundstone artifacts at San Lorenzo with similar results (Coe and Diehl 1980a: 397–404). Obsidian proved to be an excellent material for documenting exchange systems in Mesoamerica due to its widespread use for cutting implements, its limited number of chemically distinct sources, and the ability of techniques such as X-ray fluorescence and neutron activation analysis to discriminate those sources (Cobean et al. 1971; Hester, Heizer and Jack 1971; Hester, Jack and Heizer 1971; Pires-Ferreira 1975, 1976a). Exchange of iron ore and shell also received attention (Pires-Ferreira 1976b). William Rathje (1971, 1972), in particular, incorporated exchange of hard stone, obsidian, and salt in his influential model for the emergence of complex society among the Olmecs and the Maya.

Through the 1960s the apparently ubiquitous "were-jaguar" motif dominated interpretations of Olmec iconography. Saville (1929a, b) first called attention to the were-jaguar motif in his study of votive axes, and suggested they represented a forerunner to the Aztec god, Tezcatlipoca. Covarrubias (1957) also posited continuity between Olmec and later deities, arguing that the Olmec were-jaguar underlay all later images of rain gods in Mesoamerica. Stirling (1955) advanced the hypothesis that were-jaguars represented an Olmec origin myth most explicitly depicted in sculptures from the San Lorenzo area that seemed to show a jaguar copulating with a human female. In 1968, Furst presented a sophisticated and convincing analysis, arguing that were-jaguars in Olmec art represented the transformation of human shamans into jaguars or vice-versa, by analogy to contemporary beliefs of indigenous cultures in tropical America. Despite these various interpretations, however, the idea that Olmec iconography centered on a "jaguar cult" predominated, and all representations that included any traits referable to the were-jaguar were interpreted as depicting this central supernatural.

The discovery of the Las Limas figure opened the first breach in this monolithic view of Olmec religious thought. Coe (1968a) postulated that the four incised heads on the figure and the infant in the figure's arms represented

different deities, suggesting a more complex Olmec pantheon than that conceived by Saville or Covarrubias. He concurred with Saville and Covarrubias,
however, on the basic premise of continuity between Olmec and later deity
representations, relating the Las Limas heads to specific Aztec gods. David
Joralemon's (1971, 1976) studies of Olmec iconography in light of the Las
Limas figure further refined the identification of Olmec deities in a struc-
tured series of god complexes, depicted iconographically by combining traits
from different animals to create biologically impossible mythological creatures,
including an "Olmec Dragon" that combines avian and crocodilian traits.

By demonstrating that not every image with a cleft head or downturned
mouth was a were-jaguar, Joralemon's studies opened the door to a minor
genre of studies that seek to identify other creatures as important in Olmec
iconography. Luckert (1976), for example emphasizes rattlesnake symbolism,
Stocker et al. (1980) identify the cayman or crocodile as the central being,
and Furst (1981) argued for the importance of toad imagery (Coe 1989: 73).
More recent interpretations, inspired by Furst's (1968) ethnographic argument
and recent studies of Mayan iconography and writing, tend to emphasize the
shamanistic elements in Olmec art over deistic ones (e.g. Reilly 1995; Schele
1995; Taube 1995). A third trend in Olmec art historical studies, elaborated
most thoroughly in the writings of Beatriz de la Fuente (1977; 1981; 1996)
identifies the representation of the human figure and its relation to the natural
and supernatural worlds as central to Olmec artistic conceptions.

The continued expansion of the known corpus of Olmec monumental art
and Coe's demonstration of an early Olmec horizon at San Lorenzo prompted
significant efforts in the 1960s and 1970s to catalogue Olmec sculpture (de
la Fuente 1973) and to order the sculptures chronologically (Clewlow 1974,
Clewlow et al. 1967; Milbrath 1979). Owing to the lack of stratigraphic context for many sculptures, and the probable resetting of many others in later
times, attempts at sculptural chronologies have necessarily relied on stylistic
assessments, with ambiguous results.

NEW PERSPECTIVES FROM ABROAD, NEW DATA FROM OLMAN

As information on regions outside Olman grew, so did dissatisfaction with
the Olmec-centric view of Formative period Mesoamerica (e.g. Grove 1974,
1981a). The battle lines were clearly drawn in Santa Fe, New Mexico, at the
1983 School of American Research Advanced Seminar, "Regional Perspectives
on the Olmec" (Sharer and Grove 1989). Just over 40 years after the Sociedad
Mexicana de Antropología had given its *imprimatur* to the *Cultura Madre*, the
participants in the S.A.R. seminar again debated the role of the Olmecs in
founding Mesoamerican civilization. The question was no longer the age of
Olmec culture but the nature of interaction among the developing societies

of Formative Mesoamerica. Coe, Diehl, Lee, Tolstoy, and Lowe sided with the traditional view, while Sharer, Grove, Marcus, Graham, and Demarest supported versions of a multi-centric "lattice" model of social, political, and economic interaction. Although the participants disagreed on the nature of Olmec interaction, one point that emerged with absolute clarity was the critical need for more information from the Gulf Coast (Diehl 1989). Sharer (1989b: 4) summed up the state of affairs most eloquently, "It is perhaps ironic that . . . we now know relatively more about the origins and development of complex societies in a number of regions outside the Gulf coast than we know about the Olmec civilization itself."

The S.A.R. seminar helped spark a rennaissance in Gulf Coast archaeology that was already underway by the time the seminar proceedings were published in 1989. At the eastern margin of Olman, the continued destruction of parts of La Venta due to oil exploration, refining operations, and the encroachment of the expanding town inspired Rebecca González Lauck, in 1984, to initiate a program of protection, reconstruction, and research, which continues today (González 1988, 1996, 1998).

In the swamps east of the Coatzacoalcos River, local residents digging a spring-fed fish pond at the base of Cerro Manatí uncovered 3,000 year-old carved wooden busts in 1987 (Fig. 2.8). This exceptional discovery of perishable art launched a salvage project by Ponciano Ortiz and María del Carmen Rodríguez, which has expanded with the support of INAH and the National Geographic Society into a long-term investigation of Manatí and other rural Olmec sites in the area (Ortiz et al. 1997; Ortiz and Rodríguez 2000; Rodríguez and Ortiz 1997, 2000).

In the Tuxtla Mountains, Robert Santley and Ortiz directed fieldwork at the site of Matacapan from 1982–1984 (Santley et al 1984, 1985, 1987). Their investigations focused on the Classic period occupation of the site, but also found remains of small, scattered, Olmec farming settlements and agricultural surfaces preserved beneath volcanic ash (Santley 1992). Farther to the west, beyond the Papaloapan River and the limits of Olman proper, Barbara Stark (1991; Stark and Curet 1994) conducted a settlement survey of Cerro de las Mesas and the surrounding Mixtequilla region, recovering evidence of Middle and Late Formative occupations preceding the region's Classic period florescence.

As productive as the projects of the 1980s were in their own right, the seeds they planted bore yet more bounteous fruits in the 1990s, as long-term projects expanded their scopes and students moved on to direct their own projects in the southern Gulf lowlands. Personnel originally associated with the Matacapan project have continued to focus their attentions on the Tuxtlas region. Santley, Philip J. Arnold III, and Ronald Kneebone conducted a regional survey of the central Sierra de los Tuxtlas in 1991 and 1992 (Santley and Arnold 1996; Santley et al. 1997), which led directly to Arnold's (2000) excavations at the Olmec site of La Joya. I excavated the Late Formative site of Bezuapan on the outskirts

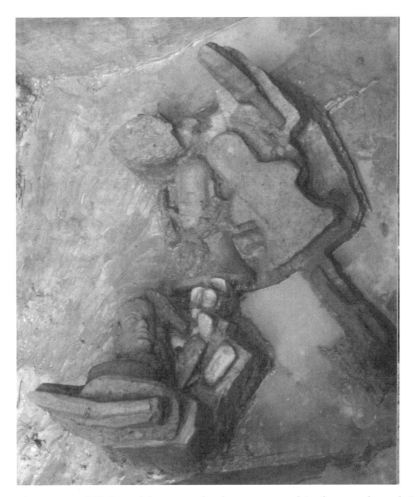

Figure 2.8. Offering of three wooden busts excavated in the waterlogged site of El Manati accompanied by wooden batons, earspools, pectorals, greenstone celts, and cinnnabar (photograph courtesy of Ponciano Ortiz Ceballos and María del Carmen Rodríguez).

of the Matacapan archaeological zone in 1992 (Pool 1997b; Pool and Britt 2000; Pool et al. 1993), then initiated an intensive survey of Tres Zapotes in 1995 (Pool 2000; Pool 2003b). Another Matacapan alumnus, Thomas Killion, began a regional survey in the Hueyapan de Ocampo region on the southern Tuxtlas piedmont in 1995 with Javier Urcid (Killion and Urcid 2001). Although not associated with the Matacapan project, David Grove and Susan Gillespie investigated the Olmec site of La Isla and a monument workshop at Llano del Jícaro, also on the southern margin of the Tuxtlas (Gillespie 1994; Grove 1994; Grove et al. 1993).

After halting the destruction of La Venta with the help of Mexico's Instituto Nacional de Antropología e Historia and the state of Tabasco, González Lauck established a museum and research facility there. Research by González

Lauck and her associates in and around the site center has clarified architectural
sequences, uncovered new monuments, revealed residential occupation, and
provided new information on the site's lithic industry and subsistence practices
(González Lauck 1988, 1996a, 1997; Gallegos Gómora 1990; Rojas Chávez
1990; Rust and Leyden 1994). Reconnaissance in the site's hinterland has
identified several Early to Middle Formative sites on levees along an ancient
channel called the Río Barí or Río Palma (Rust 1992; Rust and Sharer 1988).
Test excavations and deep sediment cores at the hinterland site of San Andrés
have documented the cultivation of domestic maize as early as 5000 B.C. (Pope
et al. 2001; Rust and Leyden 1994). Test pits at Isla Alor uncovered late Early
Formative and Middle Formative residential occupations with evidence for a
mixed subsistence pattern of horticulture and fishing (Raab et al. 2000). East of
La Venta, Christopher von Nagy (1997, 2003) conducted a study of settlement
and geomorphology in the Grijalva Delta on the eastern fringe of Olman.

Knowledge of Olmec occupations in the Coatzacoalcos basin also expanded
greatly in the 1990s. Ortiz and Rodríguez continued their work at El Manatí,
revealing deposits of an Olmec shrine where offerings of wooden busts and
implements, rubber balls, and plants were preserved by anaerobic conditions
along with greenstone celts and votive axes. They also expanded their investigations to nearby rural settlements at Macayal and La Merced. Between El
Manatí and the Río Coatzacoalcos, Robert Kruger (1996) conducted a settlement survey of 25 sq. km along an ancient river channel, where he found little
support for elite control of levee lands.

The most ambitious project of the 1990s in the Coatzacoalcos basin was
that of Ann Cyphers at San Lorenzo (Cyphers 1996; 1997g). Begun in 1990 to
excavate domestic contexts, the continuing project has expanded into a multidisciplinary investigation of San Lorenzo and its hinterland (Grove 1997: 70).
Settlement survey of some 400 sq. km surrounding San Lorenzo revealed a
complex site hierarchy with major sites distributed to take advantage of riverine trade (Symonds and Lunagómez 1996a, 1997b). In addition, surface survey
on the San Lorenzo plateau suggests the site covered nearly ten times the
52 ha previously believed (Symonds et al. 2002: 66–68; cf. Cyphers 1996:
67; Lunagómez 1995). Although excavations conducted on the San Lorenzo
plateau have shown that many of the low mounds formerly believed to be Early
Formative residences are recent agricultural features, they also have demonstrated the construction of residential terraces on the slopes of the plateau,
indicating a more substantial population (Cyphers 1997a: 102).

Other excavations by Cyphers at San Lorenzo have revealed an elite residential complex with an attached workshop for recycling stone monuments, as
well as massive deposits of enigmatic "multiperforate ilmenite cubes." imported
from Chiapas and argued to have been used in some form of craft production
(Cyphers 1996: 66; Di Castro Stringher 1997) or as prestige goods (Clark 1996)
or ornaments (Coe and Diehl 1980a: 324–326). Magnetometer survey identified several new monuments, raising the total known from the site to more

than 80 (Grove 1997: 71).[4] Excavations of these and monuments at the hinterland site of El Azuzul, along with re-excavation of the locations of previously recovered monuments provide new information on their archaeological and sociopolitical contexts (Cyphers 1997b, 1999).

In general, the fieldwork conducted in southern Veracruz and western Tabasco over the last two decades has built upon the processualist paradigm established in the 1960s. Nevertheless, recent field projects tend to share several characteristics and interrelated themes, which distinguish them from earlier efforts. Underlying much of the recent work is a greater concern with the local geographical and historical contexts of economic and political developments. This shift in emphasis is most evident in the proliferation of settlement studies at scales ranging from individual households to regions of several hundred square kilometers (see, e.g., papers in Stark and Arnold 1997b). At the smaller scales, Formative household contexts have been excavated at La Joya, Bezuapan, and Matacapan in the Sierra de los Tuxtlas (Arnold 1999, 2000; Pool 1997b; Santley 1992), at La Venta (González 1996a: 80; Rust 1992; Rust and Leyden 1994), at San Lorenzo (Cyphers Guillén 1990; Cyphers 1996, 1997b, 1997c) and at rural settlements in the Coatzacoalcos basin (Kruger 1999; Wendt 2003). Ethnoarchaeological research by Killion (1987; 1990) on houselot organization in the Tuxtlas has informed household archaeology there (Pool 1997b; Santley 1992). At the community level, reinvestigations of Tres Zapotes (Pool 2003b), San Lorenzo (Cyphers 1996; 1997b; 1997c; Lunagómez 1995), and La Venta (González 1996) have provided new information on the organization of these major Olmec centers. At regional or subregional levels, settlement surveys in the hinterlands of La Venta (Rust and Sharer 1988), San Lorenzo (Symonds et al. 2002) and Laguna de los Cerros (Borstein 2001) have provided new information on the settlement hierarchies dominated by these major centers, and regional surveys in the Mixtequilla (Stark and Curet 1994; Stark and Heller 1991), the Sierra de los Tuxtlas (Santley and Arnold 1996; Santley et al. 1997), the San Juan Basin (Borstein 2001), and the Grijalva basin (von Nagy 1997) have documented changing settlement patterns in more rural settings.

Recent ecologically oriented studies exhibit an increased concern with the effects of a dynamic landscape on ancient settlement patterns. This is reflected by the increasing implementation of geomorphological studies in research designs, particularly in the riverine settings of eastern Olman (Jiménez Salas 1990; Ortiz and Cyphers 1997; Symonds et al. 2002). Detailed geomorphological studies have not implemented in the Sierra de los Tuxtlas, but volcanic eruptions detected in excavations are thought to have had a profound effect on Formative and later settlement patterns there (Pool and Britt 2000; Santley et al. 1997; Santley et al. 2000).

Subsistence activities bridge the ecological and economic realms. It has long been assumed on the basis of indirect evidence that maize was the staple of the Olmec diet, and one theory for the development of political hierarchy among the Olmecs posits control over the best lands for maize cultivation.

Direct information on Olmec subsistence has been elusive, but it is beginning to accumulate rapidly. Recent archaeobotanical studies show that maize
was introduced to the Tabasco lowlands in late Archaic times, and by the end
of the Early Formative period it was an important staple throughout Olman,
even in the Tuxtla Mountains, where populations were still relatively mobile
(Arnold 1999, 2000; Cyphers 1996: 66; Pope et al. 2001; Rust and Leyden
1994; VanDerwarker 2003; Zurita Noguera 1997). Beans, avocados, zapotes,
and palm fruits have also been identified as staples in Early Formative and later
contexts (Cyphers 1996: 66; VanDerwarker 2003). In addition, Middle Formative agricultural fields with small parallel ridges have been detected below volcanic ash in the Tuxtlas (Arnold 2000; Pool 1997b: 54; Santley 1992). Equally
significant, however, is the clear evidence from these studies that the Olmecs
practiced a mixed subsistence economy that also incorporated a variety of wild
resources.

The economic emphasis in recent studies also extends to craft production and
local exchange, in addition to the more traditional concern with long-distance
exchange. Recent studies concerning Olmec craft production and exchange
include an analysis of the lithic industry at La Venta, which employed both
chert and obsidan (Rojas Chávez 1990), and the Formative obsidian industry
of the Sierra de los Tuxtlas (Santley et al. 2001). In addition, chemical studies
of pottery from La Venta and San Lorenzo have identified local clay sources
and interregional exchange patterns (Methner 2000; Neff and Glascock 2002).
Igneous stone, particularly basalt, was widely used by the Olmecs for grinding
implements. Excavation of one workshop attached to an elite residence at San
Lorenzo suggests that monuments were recycled for this purpose, reflecting
elite control over this locally scarce material (Cyphers 1996: 66). Basalt working
also has been studied at the monument carving workshop of Llano del Jícaro
(Gillespie 1994), and some basalt working has been noted at La Venta (González
1996a: 80). In addition to these production oriented investigations, Symonds'
analysis highlights the intraregional importance of river-borne trade in siting
Olmec communities around San Lorenzo.

The political organization of Olmec society is a long-standing concern, but
until recently interpretations have rested mainly on the spectacular discoveries
from two major centers, La Venta and San Lorenzo (Drucker 1981). Although a
concensus has yet to emerge, the projects of the last two decades have provided
archaeologists with a wealth of new data to consider. Most important in this
regard are the results of the settlement pattern studies. On the one hand,
they have documented the existence of multi-tiered settlement hierarchies in
the hinterlands of San Lorenzo, La Venta, and Laguna de los Cerros (Borstein
2001; Rust and Sharer 1988; Symonds et al. 2002). On the other hand, regional
settlement surveys in the Tuxtlas (Santley et al. 1997) and the Grijalva delta (von
Nagy 1997), as well as survey of the Tres Zapotes archaeological zone (Pool
2003b), suggest considerable variability in Olmec political systems. Variation

in political economies also is suggested by varying degrees of elite control over the production of obsidian, basalt, and other craft items (Cyphers 1996: 66; Knight 1999; Rojas Chávez 1990; Santley et al. 2001). In addition, the political perspective has had a significant influence on recent interpretations of Olmec art and iconography, which today are often seen as functioning to express and legitimize ruling authority (e.g. Cyphers 1997b; 1999; Reilly 1995).

Outside of Olman, the 1980s and 1990s revealed important new information about Early and Middle Formative interaction. Settlement surveys and excavations in the Mazatán region of coastal Chiapas revealed the emergence of Mesoamerica's first rank societies and intensive interactions with Olman in the Early Formative period, interpreted by Clark (e.g., 1990b; 1997; Clark and Blake 1989b) as evidence of a political takeover by Olmecs. Excavations at Etlatongo in Oaxaca's Nochixtlán Valley yielded unexpected evidence for interaction between the Mixteca Alta and other regions of Mesoamerica, including Olman (Blomster 1998, 2004). Yet more spectacular was the discovery in 1983 in Guerrero of the major Middle Formative center of Teopantecuanitlan (Tlacozoltiltan) and its four Olmec-style monster faces carved on stones incorporated into the walls of a sunken court (Martínez Donjuan 1994; Niederberger 1996). As discussed at length in Chapter 6, these and other significant recent discoveries document the variation in interregional interactions with Olman through space and time.

CONCLUSION

The path to understanding Olmec culture has been a long and winding one, marked by spectacular finds, and directed by the shifting theoretical concerns of the wider archaeological discipline. More than a decade ago Richard Diehl (1989: 19) remarked that all of the archaeologists who had actually dirtied their hands in Olmec soil would "fit very comfortably on the dance floor of the Club Kon Tiki in Coatzacoalcos." Today that dance floor would be crowded with a new generation of scholars. Spectacular finds still await them in the great centers and isolated shrines of Olman, but it is their investigations into the more mundane realms of geomorphology, subsistence, and settlement patterns that are opening new vistas on the Olmec landscape, the lives of its inhabitants, and the organization of their institutions.

CHAPTER 3

OLMAN, THE LAND OF THE OLMECS

> As we chugged between mangrove-covered banks, close on our left hand
> rose the great sand hills which lie behind the sea-coast . . . Our hearts beat
> a little faster when we first distinguished to the eastward the hazy volcanic
> peaks of the Tuxtla mountains . . . As we approached the higher land toward
> the foot of the mountains, the vegetation became more dense and tropical
> in appearance. Groups of parrots flew noisily over head and now and then
> we spotted a big iguana, looking like some prehistoric monster, sunning
> itself on the vine-covered jungle wall bordering the stream.
>
> (Stirling 1939: 192–194)

Thus did Matthew Stirling describe his entrance into the land of the Olmecs over 60 years ago. This and other descriptions by Stirling in the pages of *National Geographic* captured the tropical romance of the southern Gulf lowlands for a generation of archaeologists and aficionados, emphasizing the area's rivers, swamps, and rain forests. As Stirling appreciated, forest had reclaimed much of a region that the Spanish had converted to sugar cane plantations and cattle ranches, giving him a glimpse of the landscape much as the Olmecs may have known it. Today, cattle, cane, oil exploration, and urban growth have pushed the forests into remnants along stream banks and the upper slopes of the Sierra de los Tuxtlas.

The southern Gulf lowlands extend some 200 km from the Papaloapan River to the Chontalpa lowlands at the edge of the Maya region. Here the narrow coastal strip widens as it merges with the low uplands of the Isthmus of Tehuantepec, which form a gap between the higher Sierra Madre del Sur of Oaxaca and the Sierra de Chiapas (Coe and Diehl 1980a: 11). This southern region, covering some 11,000 sq km, constitutes Olman, the land of the Olmecs. The natural environment of the southern Gulf lowlands strongly influenced the development of Olmec culture, and its imprint is manifest in the Olmecs' economy, sociopolitical institutions, and art.

Two broad geological structures dominate most of Olman (Fig. 1.3). Most of the low, eastern two-thirds of the region lie within the Isthmian Saline Basin, one of the "Tertiary Basins of the Southeast" that form the coastal plain of southern Veracruz and Tabasco (Coe and Diehl 1980a: 11; Jiménez Salas 1990: 6–7). The basin is filled with Mesozoic and Cenozoic sediments, mainly sands, marls, and clays, which become progressively younger as one moves from the edge of the Isthmian uplands northward toward the Gulf of Mexico. Pressure from these overlying sediments has forced salt deposits laid down in the Jurassic period to flow upward through weaker zones, forming the salt domes that give the basin its name. Sulfur deposits associated with the salt domes and oil trapped in the upwarped sediments along their margins have both contributed to the modern prosperity of the region. In the distant past, the Olmecs extracted hematite from the redbed caprock that covers some of the domes and salt from the saline springs that flow from them (Coe and Diehl 1980a: 16–18). The Olmecs also obtained asphalt from the numerous natural petroleum seeps that dot the landscape, using it for knife handles and possibly to waterproof canoes, baskets, and pottery vessels (Coe and Diehl 1980a: 17; Ortiz et al. 1997: 90; Wendt and Lu 2006).

The second major geological structure is the volcanic massif of the Tuxtla Mountains. Broad, shield-like volcanoes, with peaks that rise over 1,600 m above sea level and hundreds of parasitic cinder cones, separate the Isthmian Saline Basin from the Papaloapan River Basin to the west. Most of the rocks erupted from the Tuxtlas volcanoes are alkali basalts, chemically and mineralogically different from the calc-alkaline rocks typical of other volcanoes in the Mexican Volcanic Belt (Thorpe 1977). Occasional andesites and basaltic andesites have also been reported in the eastern part of the range (Ríos Macbeth 1952: 365). Volcanism in the Tuxtlas area began more then twenty-six million years ago during the Oligocene epoch, when the sea covered what would become the southern Gulf lowlands (Martin-Del Pozzo 1997: 28–29). The oldest exposed volcanic rocks date to the Pliocene and early Pleistocene epochs. They occur mainly in the eastern Tuxtla Mountains, particularly on the north slope of the Santa Marta volcano, and around Cerro Cintepec, extending southward to Llano del Jícaro on the coastal plain. They also form the eroded cone of Cerro el Vigía on the western margin of the massif near the site of Tres Zapotes. These coarsely porphyritic basalts, with their large olivine and augite crystals, provided much of the material for Olmec monuments (Williams and Heizer 1965). Over the last million years, since the late Pleistocene epoch, a more fine-grained basalt has been erupted, forming the peaks of El Pelón, San Martín Pajapan, Santa Marta, and San Martín Tuxtla. More than 200 small cinder cones dot the western Tuxtlas. These have erupted at a rate of about one every 250 years over the past 50,000 years (Reinhardt 1991: 124). The last recorded eruption was that of San Martín Tuxtla in 1793 (Moziño 1870), and this still-active volcano continues to emit steam and gases from fumaroles. Natural columns from basalt flows belonging to the later volcanic series were used for enclosures and set alone at the Olmec sites of La Venta and Tres Zapotes. As the Tuxtla Mountains rose, they lifted up the sediments deposited by the Tertiary period seas, exposing on their flanks sands and fine koalin clays, which humans came to use for their pottery, particularly in the Classic period.

The differing geological histories of the eastern and western parts of Olman have created marked differences in their physiography and hydrology. In the east, broad, meandering rivers flow northward across the lowlands of the Isthmian Saline Basin. The largest of these are the Grijalva-Mezcalapa, the Tonalá, and the Coatzacoalcos. Sloughs and oxbow lakes form in their abandoned channels, and annual floods fill broad marshes and backswamps, making parts of the region impassable in the rainy season except by boat. The same floods deposit large quantities of silt and sand, raising natural levees along the river banks. Near the mouths of the rivers tidal influences create brackish estuaries lined with mangrove swamps. Farther upstream, the wandering rivers have isolated small mesas and broad islands that sometimes rise over 40 m above the surrounding plain. To the west, beyond the Tuxtla Mountains, the lower Papaloapan River basin presents a similarly waterlogged landscape, though historically its floods were more erratic and more violent (Siemens 1998: 33, 105).

Western Olman has a more upland character than eastern Olman, owing to the presence of the Tuxtla Mountains. The peaks of the highest volcanoes, San Martín Tuxtla and Santa Marta, rise more than 1600 m above sea level. Between them Lake Catemaco, the third largest natural lake in Mexico, sparkles like a jewel in a jade-green setting. Though superficially resembling a caldera, Lake Catemaco was formed when volcanoes emerged on its northern side, damming a stream that formerly flowed to the sea through the Lake Sontecomoapan estuary (Martín-Del Pozzo 1997: 34). The older volcanoes to the east of the lakes have been heavily dissected, creating a rugged, sparsely inhabited landscape. The western half has a more gentle topography and supports several modern towns. On the north slope, lava flows run down to the sea, forming rocky headlands and isolated beaches. On the southern and western sides tectonic uplift has raised older sedimentary formations to the surface, creating a low piedmont. Small streams tumble from the mountains and cut through this piedmont in deeply incised valleys. Many of them flow into the broader valley of the San Juan River, which circles the southern and western sides of the uplift before disappearing into the swamps and marshes of the lower Papaloapan basin.

The climate of Olman is generally hot and humid (Vivó Escoto 1964: 213, Fig. 14) (Fig. 3.1). Annual rainfall surpasses 1,500 mm over most of the area, and varies seasonally, with most of the rain falling between June and November (Vivó Escoto 1964: 213). Even during the nominally dry season, cold, wet *nortes* commonly sweep down the coast (Coe and Diehl 1980a: 19). Most of the region lies below the 200 m contour, placing it well within the "hot land," or *tierra caliente*, which extends up to 1,000 m. Mean annual temperatures generally exceed 25° C (77° F), and frosts are unknown except on the highest peaks of the Tuxtla Mountains (Gómez-Pompa 1973: Figs. 3 and 5). Even during the coldest months of December and January, temperatures rarely drop below 16° C (61° F) (Soto and Gama 1997: Fig. 1.7). The region warms through the drier months, reaching a maximum in April and May, when temperatures may soar to over 45° C (113° F) on the coastal plain (Soto and Gama 1997: Table 1.4). With relatively warm temperatures year round, and beneficial rains from dry season *nortes*, two crops can be grown each year in most of the region.

The topographic contrasts between the eastern and western portions of Olman, however, create greater climatic variation than this generalized description captures. The Tuxtla Mountains not only create an altitudinal gradient in temperatures, they also block the moist winds from the Gulf, producing an orographic rainfall pattern. The higher seaward slopes of the mountains receive more than 4,000 mm of rain per year, whereas parts of their inland rain shadow receive less than 1,500 mm (Fig. 3.1). Rain also tends to be more markedly seasonal to the south of the Tuxtla Mountains, with less than 5% falling in the winter months (Gómez-Pompa 1973: Fig. 7). By contrast, more than 2,000 mm of rain fall each year on the coastal plain of eastern Olman, and precipitation is more evenly distributed through the year (Gómez-Pompa 1973: Figs. 6 and 7).

Variation in source rocks, climate, and hydrographic regimes combine to create considerable diversity in soil types throughout Olman (Fig. 3.2). Their effects are particularly well demonstrated in the soils of the Tuxtla Mountains, which are neatly divided into four quadrants centered on Lake Catemaco. Rich andosols have developed on volcanic ash deposits erupted by the young volcanoes of the northwestern Tuxtlas. Torrential rains on the older northeastern volcanoes have produced a zone of heavily weathered and leached acrisols. Similar rocks in the drier, leeward quadrant of the southeastern Tuxtlas produce less developed luvisols due to rapid deposition of sediments eroded from the volcanoes. In the southwestern quadrant, the combination of volcanic ash mixed with ancient marine sediments and moderate rainfall creates large pockets of phaeozem "prairie soils." Level, fertile, and easily worked, today these are the most prized agricultural lands in the Tuxtla Mountains and they support the heaviest modern population densities, as they did in the pre-Columbian past. Circling the southern margin of the Tuxtlas, the clays of the same sedimentary formations produce yellow and red vertisols with a high content of montmorillonite clay that swells and shrinks with the coming and departure of the rains. Less productive than the phaeozems, they nevertheless are suitable for maize cultivation with adequate fallowing, and supported impressive Classic period populations.

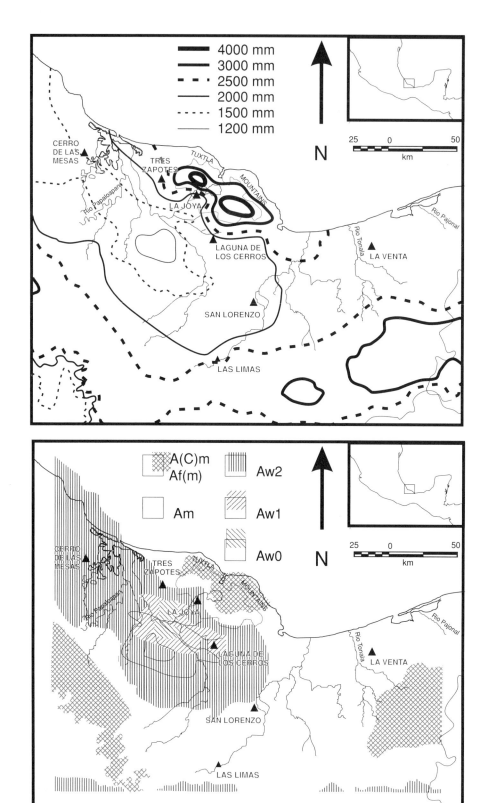

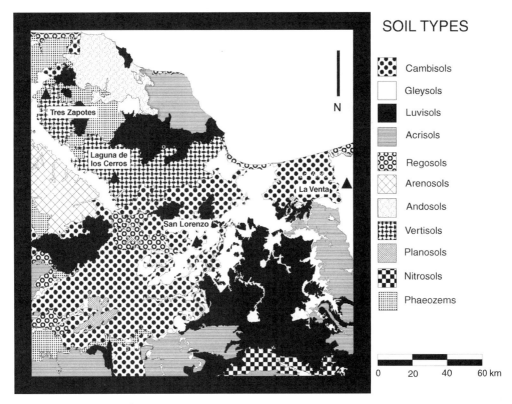

Figure 3.2. Distribution of soil types in Olman (redrawn after INEGI soil map, 1984).

On the coastal plain, wet, clayey gleysols, difficult to cultivate with traditional methods, form in the backswamps and marshes of the great rivers. Heavy rainfall weathers the soils of the higher land in the Coatzacoalcos and Tonalá valleys, producing extensive areas of cambisols, considered to be the best upland soils by local farmers (Rodriguez et al. 1997: 59). Between them in a broad zone along the Uspanapa river and in pockets along their margins, particularly rapid alluvial deposition creates poorly developed luvisols. Higher ground between the major river valleys exhibits more heavily leached acrisols, particularly between the Tonalá and Uspanapa rivers and well-drained arenosols,

←—————————————————————————————————

Figure 3.1. Upper: map of average annual rainfall in Olman. Lower: climates in Olman in the Koeppens system as modified by Garcia (1970). Awo, hot subhumid with summer rains regime, precipitation/temperature < 43.2; Aw1, hot subhumid with summer rains regime, P/T 43.2–55.3; Aw2 hot, humid with summer rains regime, P/T > 55.3; Am, hot humid with summer rains with monsoon influence; Af(m), hot humid with percentage of winter rains higher than 18% and monsoon influence. A(C)f(m), hot temperate with summer rains regime, winter rains higher than 10.2% and monsoon influence (redrawn after INEGI online state climate maps and Gómez-Pompa 1973: Fig. 2).

depending on variation in source materials and rainfall. The unconsolidated sands eroded from the arenosols and occuring in the coastal dunes constitute regosols with weakly developed soil horizons.

Soils, climate, and groundwater are not only closely interrelated, but directly affect patterns of natural vegetation and modern land use. The tropical rain-forests (known more formally as high evergreen *selvas*) emphasized in much of the literature did cover much of the lowlands and lower slopes of the Tuxtla mountains, and they are still widespread on the steep lower slopes of the Sierra Madre (Gómez-Pompa 1973; Ibarra-Manríquez et al. 1997). Nevertheless, microtopographic variation in the lowlands creates a complex patchwork of riparian forests, upland high evergreen *selvas* and oak forests, grassy marshes and savannas, and isolated palm stands (Gómez-Pompa 1973). Dune vegetation and mangrove swamps occur along the coast and around brackish estuaries. In addition, the Tuxtla Mountains contain patches of pine forest, oak forest, and liquidambar (gum) forests, as well as a low evergreen *selva* or "elfin woodland" on the foggy summit of San Martín Tuxtla.

Modern land use has greatly altered the natural vegetation. In 1997, Guillermo Ibarra-Manríquez et al. (1997: 77), for example, calculated an annual rate of deforestation in the western Tuxtla Mountains of 4.3% per year, and estimated that only 9% of the original forest would be left by 2000. Much of the forest has been cut for cattle ranching, and vast areas of the poorer low-land soils and those frequently flooded have been converted to pasture. On the coastal plain adjacent to the western Tuxtla mountains, rich phaeozem soils support vast sugar cane fields. Sugar cane also is grown on the poorer soils of the Tuxtlas piedmont and along the Papaloapan river. Higher in the Tuxtlas, near San Andrés Tuxtla, phaeozems and andosols produce tobacco for fine cigars as well as orchards of mangoes, avocadoes, and other tropical fruits. Small *milpa* plots of maize and beans are planted throughout Olman for household use and for sale in the markets (INEGI 1984a, 1984b).

In southern Mexico the ranges of animal species native to North and South America overlap, yielding an impressively diverse fauna. For the Tuxtla Mountains alone, recent studies list 129 species of mammals, 561 species of birds, 116 species of reptiles, 43 species of amphibians, and 109 species of freshwater and estuarine fish (Fuentes and Espinosa 1997: Apéndice 5.1; Martínez-Gallardo and Sánchez-Cordero 1997: Apéndice 5.7; Ramírez-Bautista and Nieto-Montes de Oca 1997: 523; Schaldack et al. 1997: Apéndice 5.6; Winker 1997: 535, Cuadro 5.6). Among the forest animals that held economic or symbolic importance to the Olmecs were tapirs, white-lipped peccaries, spider monkeys, howler monkeys, jaguars, ocelots, and other small cats. Hunting and habitat destruction have drastically reduced the range of these species. Deer, rabbits, collared peccaries, and *pacas* or *tepescuintles* (large rodents) adapt better to secondary forest growth but are affected by overhunting. Turtles, crocodiles, caymans, freshwater and saltwater fish, crayfish, shrimp, crabs, and various molluscs abounded in the lakes, rivers, swamps, and estuaries of the region. These environments also provided food and shelter for many waterfowl, including large flocks of migratory ducks and geese.

OLMEC SUBSISTENCE AND RESOURCE USE

Of course, the mere fact that a particular species was available is no guarantee it was eaten. For that we must turn to the archaeological record. Unfortunately, moisture, heat, and acid soils extract a heavy toll from plant and animal remains in the humid tropical lowlands. Even bone is often rotted away, leaving only stone and pottery grave goods in many Olmec burials. As a result, inferences about Olmec diet have long been based on the few scraps of bone and shell that remain and indirect evidence such as *mano* and *metate* grinding stones. Nevertheless, in recent years excavation techniques designed to recover carbonized plant remains, pollen, and phytoliths (microscopic silica inclusions in plants) have begun to provide direct evidence about Olmec plant use (Table 3.1).

Maize (*Zea mays*), beans, and squash were domesticated in highland Mesoamerica before the close of the Archaic period, and they became the staples that fueled later civilizations. The earliest direct evidence for domesticated maize in Olman comes from San Andrés, a small site north of La Venta on the levee of the river called the Barí or Palma (Pope et al. 2001). Pollen cores indicate cultivation of a wild ancestor of maize (probably teosinte, *Zea mexicana*) at 5100 B.C., and pollen of domesticated maize appears by about 5000 B.C., growing in importance thereafter. Pollen of *Poaceae* grasses increases greatly in these early levels, indicating clearing of the river margin forests. In the Tuxtla Mountains, pollen from Laguna Pompal also documents the appearance of *Zea* and field clearing by about 2880 B.C. (Goman 1992: 33; Goman and Byrne 1998: 85). Charred maize remains now have also been reported for Early Formative contexts after about 1400 B.C. at San Lorenzo, La Venta, and the Tuxtlas site of La Joya (Cyphers 1996: 66; Rust and Leyden 1994; Vanderwarker 2003). Thus cultivation of domestic maize appears to have been widespread among the Olmec and to be of considerable antiquity, although its importance relative to other foods remains to be assessed (Arnold 2000).

Beans complement the amino acids provided by maize to form a complete protein for human metabolism. Consequently, they were and still are a vital component of most Mesoamerican diets, which tend to be deficient in animal protein. Beans appeared at San Lorenzo between 1450 and 1000 B.C. (Cyphers 1996: 66) and may have been present in the La Venta area before 1750 B.C. (Rust and Leyden 1994: 188; Rust and Sharer 1988). The abundance of aquatic protein sources and heavy consumption of dogs (Wing 1981) may have reduced the importance of beans in the Olmec diet, however. Rounding out the trinity of Mesoamerican staples, carbonized squash remains at San Andrés have been dated directly through atomic mass spectometry to 2465 B.C., and they appear

TABLE 3.1. *Some plants utilized in Olman*

Plant	Site	Date of first appearance	Comment
Crops			
Zea sp. (wild)	San Andrés	5100 B.C.	Pollen
maize (dom.)	San Andrés	5000 B.C.	Pollen
	Río Barí sites	2250?–1750 B.C.	charred remains
	Laguna. Pompal	2880 B.C.	Pollen
	San Lorenzo	1450–1000 B.C.	charred remains, phytoliths
	La Joya	1500–1000 B.C.	charred remains
beans	San Lorenzo	1400–1000 B.C.	charred remains
	Río Barí sites	2250?–1750 B.C.	charred remains
	La Joya	1500–1000 B.C.	charred remains
squash (wild)	San Andrés	2465 B.C.	charred remains, AMS date
squash	San Lorenzo	1400–1000 B.C.	charred remains
manioc	San Andrés	4600 B.C.	Pollen
sunflower	San Andrés	2667 B.C.	charred remains, AMS date
cotton	San Andrés	ca. 2500 B.C.	Pollen
Wild Plants and Tree Crops			
avocado	La Joya	1500–1000 B.C.	charred remains
zapote	La Joya	1500–1000 B.C.	charred remains
palm fronds and wood	San Lorenzo	1450–1000 B.C.	Phytoliths
palm nuts (*coyol*)	Río Barí sties	2250?–1750 B.C.	charred remains
	La Joya	1500–1000 B.C.	charred remains
hog plum (*jobo*)	El Manatí	1700–1500 B.C.	uncharred remains
false bamboo (*otate*)	El Manatí	1700–1500 B.C.	uncharred remains
copal resin	El Manatí	1700–1500 B.C.	uncharred remains
rubber	El Manatí	1700–1500 B.C.	uncharred remains
trianthema (condiment)	La Joya	1500–1000 B.C.	charred remains

Sources: San Andrés: Pope et al. 2001.
Río Barí sites: Rust and Leyden 1994.
Laguna Pompal: Goman 1992: 33.
San Lorenzo charred remains: Cyphers 1996, 1997d.
San Lorenzo phytoliths: Zurita 1997.
La Joya: VanDerwarker 2006: Table 4.3.
El Manatí: Ortíz and Rodriguez 2000, 2005.

later at San Lorenzo (Pope et al. 2001: 1372, Table 1; Cyphers 1996: 66). Pope *et al.* (2001: 1372, Table 1) also report the discovery of a domesticated sunflower seed and sunflower fruit dated to 2667 B.C. and 2548 B.C., respectively. This find is surprising because it is earlier than dated remains from eastern North America, where the sunflower is generally believed to have been domesticated, and sunflower is not a common component of Mesoamerican diets.

Much speculation has surrounded the use of root crops by the Olmecs. Manioc, in particular, is an important source of carbohydrates in many lowland South American societies, and it thrives in lowland Mesoamerica. Other root crops consumed today in the southern Gulf lowlands include sweet potato (*camote*), *malanga*, and *ñame* (Coe and Diehl 1980b: 85; Cyphers 1996: 66). Unfortunately tubers rarely survive in the archaeological record, and to date the direct evidence for their ancient consumption in Olman rests on a single domesticated manioc pollen grain from San Andrés in deposits dated about 4600 B.C. (Pope et al. 2001: 1372).

Tree fruits have been reported from Early and Middle Formative deposits in Olmec sites. At La Joya, avocado was particularly important, followed by oil-rich *coyol* palm fruits (*Acrocomia mexicana*) and *zapote mamey* (*Pouteria sapote*) a fleshy, salmon-colored fruit with a sweet, pumpkin-like flavor (VanDerwarker 2006: 87–88, Table 4.3). Palm fruits of a different species (*corozo, Orbignya cohune*) were exploited at San Andrés (Rust and Leyden 1994: 188). The avocados, the palm fruits, which resemble small coconuts, and the seeds of the zapote may have been particularly sought for their fats and oils, which are scarce in the lean meats of wild game. In addition, fruit pits of the *jobo* or hog plum (*Spondias mombin*) were found in a ritual offering dating between about 1700 and 1500 B.C. at the waterlogged site of El Manatí (Ortiz and Rodríguez 2000: Fig. 11). Whether any of these tree fruits were domesticated is uncertain. They may have been cultivated in their wild state, protected during forest clearance, or collected from forest trees.

There is little doubt the Olmecs also exploited a variety of other wild plants for foods and medicines, as people throughout the southern Gulf lowlands do today (Coe and Diehl 1980b). Unless they beome charred or are deposited in very dry or permanently wet and anoxic conditions, the leaves, roots, and fruits of wild plants rarely survive. Nevertheless, evidence for Olmec utilization of wild plants has been recovered from El Manatí. For example, the offering with the jobo pits mentioned previously also contained several unidentified seeds, fragments of *otate* ("false bamboo"), and pieces of *copal*, an aromatic tree resin widely used for incense in Mesoamerica (Ortiz and Rodríguez 2000: Figs. 10–13). Other offerings at El Manatí contained rubber balls, providing the earliest evidence for the exploitation of this material in Mesoamerica.

As Table 3.2 indicates, the Olmecs also consumed domesticated dogs and a diverse array of wild animal species (VanDerwarker 2003: 197–203; Wing 1980, 1981). Dog remains were so prevalent in middens at San Lorenzo that Elizabeth Wing (1981) concluded they were as important a protein source as beef was for Medieval Europeans. Other wild mammals identified at San Lorenzo included white-tailed deer, rabbit, raccoon, and white-lipped peccary. Manatee were not present in the San Lorenzo assemblage, but Pope et al. (2001: 1373) interpret manatee bones recovered from a core at San Andrés as food remains.

TABLE 3.2. *Some animals exploited by the Olmecs*

Scientific name	Common name	Site(s)
MOLLUSCS		
Rangia cuneata	marsh clam	San Andrés
Ostrea sp.	oyster	San Andrés
FISH		
Megalops atlanticus	Atlantic tarpon	San Lorenzo
Pimelodidae	catfish family	La Joya
Arius cf. *A. melanops*	sea catfish	San Lorenzo
Rhumdia guatamalensis	neotropical catfish	San Lorenzo
Centropomus sp.	snook (*robalo*)	San Lorenzo
Lutjanus sp.	snapper	San Lorenzo
		San Andrés
		La Joya
Caranx sp.	jack	San Lorenzo
		La Joya
Chichlasoma sp.	mojarra	San Lorenzo
		San Andrés
		La Joya
Lepisosteus spp.	gar	San Andrés
Catostomidae	sucker family	La Joya
REPTILES		
Dermatemys mawii	river turtle (*concha blanca*)	San Lorenzo
Chelydra serpentina	snapping turtle	San Lorenzo
Claudius angustatus	mud turtle	San Lorenzo
Kinosternon cf. *K. Leucostomum*	mud turlte (*pochitoca*)	San Lorenzo
Staurotypus triporcatus	Mexican giant musk turtle (*galápago*)	San Lorenzo
Rhinoclemmys cf. *R. aureolata*	terrestrial turtle	San Lorenzo
Chrysemys scripta	pond turle	San Lorenzo
unspecified	crocodilians	Río Barí sites
Iguana iguana	green iguana	La Joya
AMPHIBIANS		
Bufo sp.	toad	La Joya
Bufo marinus	marine toad	San Lorenzo
Rana sp.	frog	La Joya
BIRDS		
Anatidae	duck	La Joya
Anas carolinensis	green-winged teal	San Lorenzo
Anas clypeata	shoveler	San Lorenzo
Arythra affinis	lesser scaup	San Lorenzo
Buteo sp.	hawk	La Joya
Buteogallus anthracinus	black hawk	San Lorenzo
Falconidae	falcon family	La Joya
Meleagris gallpano	wild turkey	La Joya
Sphyrapicus varius	yellowbellied sapsucker	La Joya

Scientific name	Common name	Site(s)
MAMMALS		
Didelphis sp.	opossum	La Joya
Sciurius sp.	squirrel	La Joya
Odocoileus virginianus	white-tailed deer	San Lorenzo
Mazama americana	red brocket deer	La Joya
Tayassu tajacu	collared peccary	La Joya
Tayassu pecari	white-lipped peccary	San Lorenzo
Procyon lotor	raccoon	San Lorenzo
Canis familiaris	dog	San Lorenzo La Joya
Orthogeomys hispidus	hispid pocket gopher	San Lorenzo La Joya
Oryzomys couesi	Coues's rice rat	La Joya
Sigmodon hispidus	hispid cotton rat	La Joya
Peromyscus sp.	mouse	La Joya
Sylvilagus sp.	rabbit	San Lorenzo La Joya
Leopardus pardalis	ocelot	La Joya
Homo sapiens	human	San Lorenzo

Sources: San Lorenzo: Wing 1980.
La Joya: VanDerwarker 2006.
San Andrés: Pope et al. 2001; Rust and Leyden 1994.

Ducks, turtles, and fish were important components of the Olmecs' diet as well (Wing 1980; VanDerwarker 2006). At San Lorenzo, the most important fish was snook (*robalo*), an estuarine species, which comes upriver to spawn. Freshwater catfish and cichlids (*mojarra*) were caught as well, and the Olmecs occasionally took marine species such as tarpon, snapper, jack, and sea catfish, which come up the Coatzacoalcos from the coast during periods of high water. Gar, oyster, and clams were apparently taken from the estuary near San Andrés (Pope et al. 2001: 1373), and crocodilian bones appear in excavations in some levee sites in the area (Rust and Leyden 1994: 200). Interestingly, inland in the Tuxtla Mountains, the Olmecs at La Joya obtained non-local snook, jack, and snapper (VanDerwarker 2006: Tables 5.2 and 5.3).

Humans sweat profusely in the humid tropics, making mineral salt another likely component of the Olmec diet. Because salt dissolves readily in the humid Olmec environment, it is rarely preserved. Nevertheless, Olmec salt production has been documented at a saline spring in the Tuxtla Mountains (Ceja 1982, 1998; Santley 2004), and other potential sources exist along the seacoast and in the springs flowing from salt domes on the coastal plain.

The Olmecs made extensive use of the other mineral resources their environment offered them. Local clays provided the raw material for pottery, figurines, and other small artifacts, and colored clays were selected for building platforms, plastering walls, and making adobe blocks. At San Lorenzo, blocks of bentonite, a clay derived from weathered volcanic ash, were used to pave floors (Cyphers 1996). The Olmecs shaped their impressive monuments as well as their grinding stones, stone bowls, celts, and other utilitarian artifacts, from basalt they obtained mainly from the Tuxtla Mountains. Fine cutting instruments, however, frequently were made from obsidian, volcanic glass, which does not occur naturally in Olman, and had to be obtained from over 200 km away at sources that included Pico de Orizaba, Veracruz; Otumba, in the state of Mexico; and El Chayal, Guatemala. Other materials available within Olman included hematite, used as a pigment, and natural asphalt (bitumen) from tar seeps. Though its entire range of uses is unknown, at El Manatí asphalt was used to form the handles of ritual knives tipped with shark teeth (Ortiz et al. 1997: Photo 36). Wooden busts and batons preserved in the mud of this water-logged site likewise document the Olmecs skill in carving this material.

In summary, the Olmecs exploited a variety of mineral and organic resources for their artifacts and architecture. Some of these, like pottery clays and wood, are widely distributed in Olman. Others, however, such as salt, asphalt, hematite, and basalt, occur only within restricted zones or at specific points on the landscape. To ensure a supply of such restricted materials, Olmecs in areas that lacked them would have had to travel to the source or trade for them with other groups. Growing archaeological evidence also indicates that the Olmecs practiced a mixed subsistence economy, which included domesticated annual crops (maize, beans, squash, and possibly manioc) and dogs, as well as wild plants and a wide variety of terrestrial and aquatic sources of animal protein. Most terrestrial animals had a wide distribution and most areas had access to fish, shellfish, and waterfowl of one sort or another, but we can expect variation in the mix of estuarine and freshwater species and in their importance relative to land animals. Likewise, the documented crops of the Olmecs can be grown throughout the region, but variations in soil, rainfall, and hydrography would have required different agricultural practices, with varying yields and risks, in different parts of Olman. The following discussion of three specific parts of Olman highlights the subtle variation in resources and land use that characterize the region today, and which have significant implications for the Olmec economy.

THE LOWER COATZACOALCOS RIVER BASIN

The earliest major center of Olmec culture, San Lorenzo, lies at the upper end of the lower Coatzacoalcos River basin, about 60 km south of the river's mouth. A short distance upstream from San Lorenzo, a geological fault at Peña Blanca separates dissected upland hills and mesas from the deltaic lowlands to the north. The change in river gradient here causes the river to slow, dropping its load of mud and sand and splitting into distributary channels that reunite farther

Figure 3.3. Floodplain of the Coatzacoalcos river, planted in sorghum. The San Lorenzo plateau appears as a low rise in the distance.

downriver (Ortiz-Pérez and Cyphers 1997: 34–35). Sandy sediments build up into natural levees along the river banks, whereas fine-grained muds deposited away from the channel compact and subside, producing low, seasonally flooded marshes and permanent swamps. The meandering river channels migrate laterally as they cut away at the outer side of the bends and deposit sand bars on the inner side. The traces of this action can be seen in the meander scars of the lowlands, sloughs separated by slightly higher ribbons of ancient levees. As the river cuts away the banks, the bends slowly approach one another, and eventually the river breaks through, forming oxbow lakes. On occasion the river will cut a new channel, abandoning its old course. The abandoned course slowly fills with sediments, creating long, sinuous sloughs, or *esteros*, which wander across the flood plain. Over the course of time, the lateral erosion of the river has isolated low islands and flat-topped mesas composed of ancient Tertiary and Pleistocene sediments. These plateaus and the salt domes emerging from the swamps provided important areas of high land for settlements, including San Lorenzo itself (Fig. 3.3).

The rhythm of the river dominates life along the Coatzacoalcos. During the rainy season, from June to October, the river overflows its banks and floods the low plains, or *potreros*. As the waters rise, the levees become a string of low islands before they disappear below the flood. In normal years, the floods rise to the level of the 24 m contour, about 6.4 m above the river's dry season level, and the potreros remain flooded until November (Coe 1981: 16). At these times, humans and land animals retreat to higher land, and boats provide the main means of transportation. Exceptional floods, occurring about once in 50 years, create a vast sheet of water broken only by the mesas and salt domes (Ortiz-Pérez and Cyphers 1997: 39). These greater floods define the edge of the high floodplain, a narrow band of flat land between the low flood-plains and the uplands. In all, Ortiz-Pérez and Cyphers (1997: 39) define seven distinctive geomorphological units in the San Lorenzo area: 1) the erosive-denuded terraces (including the summit of the San Lorenzo plateau); 2) the accumulative colluvial ramp at the base of the terraces; 3) the infrequently sub-merged high floodplain; 4) the frequently submerged low floodplain; 5) the overflow flatland on the backslopes of the levees; 6) the elevated levees; and 7) the ordinary river course. As will be discussed later, vegetation and land use respond to the varying soils and water tables of these geomorphological units.

We in the industrialized world are prone to think of flooding as invariably destructive, washing away homes and wreaking havoc on agricultural fields. That is mainly a result of our often ill-advised uses of the land. Behind the precarious protection of artificial levees we build cheap housing and extend the growing season of chemically fertilized crops on the floodplain. Meanwhile, the rivers, raised above their natural flood stages, flood more catastrophically when, inevitably, they breach their banks.

To a people more attuned to their natural environment, like the inhabi-tants of the lower Coatzacoalcos basin, the predictable annual floods bestow great benefits. Fresh sediment and organic material deposited on low-lying croplands renew their fertility, reducing the need for fallowing, or in mod-ern times, application of chemical fertilizers. The rising waters also clean the stagnant oxbow ponds and swamps and revitalize their ecosystems, restocking them with fish and other organisms (Ortiz-Pérez and Cyphers 1997: 36). As the waters recede, fish, turtles, shrimp, crayfish, and crabs can easily be net-ted, trapped, or caught by hand in the shallowing lakes and the rivulets that flow back towards the river courses (Coe 1981: 17; Coe and Diehl 1980b: 107–123).

Michael Coe and Richard Diehl conducted a particularly thorough study of the relationship among agricultural practices, river stages, climate, and soils in the San Lorenzo area (Coe 1974; Coe and Diehl 1980b; cf. Rodríguez et al. 1997). They distinguish four soil series in the area. The Coatzacoalcos series corresponds to the silty and sandy soils on the natural levees and their backslopes along the west bank of the Coatzacalcos and Chiquito Rivers. Their distribution parallels that of gleyic cambisols and gleyic fluvisols on official soil maps (INEGI 1993; cf. Rodríguez et al. 1997: 59). Each year, silt-laden floodwaters renew the fertility of these soils, which remain well-watered through the dry season. Because of their high productivity, the locals identify them as *tierra de primera* or soils of the first class. The Tenochtitlán series consists of clays, sands, and tuffs on the hilly lower slopes of the San Lorenzo

Plateau, where it generally corresponds to vertic cambisols and vertic luvisols (Rodríguez et al. 1997: 59). They are identified locally as *tierra barreal* or *tierra de segunda clase*, and are considered the best agricultural soils of the uplands or *lomería*. The soils of the San Lorenzo series are similar to the Tenochtitlán series, but are sandier and contain gravel. Known as *tierra de grava*, they occur only on the San Lorenzo plateau, and are used mainly for pasture. The fluvial clays of the Tatagapa series are the most extensive soils in the area, occuring on floodplain savannas around the San Lorenzo plateau. They correspond in most part to mollic gleysols, which due to their dense clays and long period of annual flooding are traditionally classified as *tierra de potrero*, unsuitable except for pasture without modern machinery. Nevertheless, in the 1990s they have been extensively planted with sorghum in the dry season.

The relative productivity of these soils is a matter of considerable theoretical importance to the evolution of Olmec political hierarchies. As Coe and Diehl conducted their study, a group of politically powerful brothers who managed the largest store in the village of Tenochtitlán expanded their income and power by gaining control over much of the levee lands, consisting of Coatza-coalcos series soils. Derogatorily called *caciques* (chiefs) by the villagers, these brothers' activities inspired Coe (1981 18–19; Coe and Diehl 1980b: 149–152) to propose his coercive model for the rise of Olmec sociopolitical hierarchy based on the control of the levees (see Chapter 1). Sanders and Webster (1978) likewise emphasized the contrast between the productivity of the levee lands and unflooded land away from the river. These differences in productivity are strongly conditioned by contrasting agricultural practices, particularly as regards the necessity of fallowing fields and the potential for growing multiple crops in a single year.

Agricultural practices vary with the susceptibility to flooding, the fertility, and the natural vegetation among these soil types (Coe and Diehl 1980b: 69). As many as four maize crops are possible in the hot, humid climate of the lower Coatzacoalcos basin. The two major crops are called the *temporal* and the *tapachol*. The *temporal*, also known as the *cosecha grande,* is the principal rainy season crop and adheres to the typical slash-and-burn fallow system. The fields are prepared by cutting and burning the primary forest or secondary growth in April. The maize is planted in late May or early June, and the crop is harvested by November. The tapachol is a dry season crop planted in December or January. The harvest begins in February, though crops planted later may be harvested as late as May or early June. Due to the occurrence of wet winter *nortes*, the fields cannot be burned, and the vegetation is left to cover the fields as a mulch. The same *nortes* may damage the crop with high winds.

A few farmers also plant fields during the short *chamil* and *tonamil* seasons (Coe and Diehl 1980b: 69). The *chamil* crop is planted late in the dry season in March and harvested in late May or early June, but may be destroyed by too little rain or early floods. It is generally planted on low-lying Coatzacoalcos series soils and "sandy ridge tops" (possibly referring to old silted-in levees on the flood plain) (Coe and Diehl 1980b: 69). Therefore, this crop may be seen as a form of "fugitive agriculture" or "flood-recessional agriculture" (Siemens 1998: 41–42) in which surfaces exposed by low water are planted with fast-maturing cultigens. Though risky, such phased cropping along the gentle slope bordering wetlands can significantly increase production.

The *tonamil* is a mulch crop planted on well-drained soils during the rainy season in August and harvested in November. It also is known as the *aventurero* or "risk-taker" crop because of the likelihood of damage from insects, worms, and rot. It is typically harvested fresh, rather than allowing the ears to fully mature and dry.

Lying above normal flood stage, the Tenochtitlán series soils can be cultivated at any time of the year, and are commonly planted both in the *tapachol* and the *temporal* seasons (Coe and Diehl 1980b: 143). After five crops, or two-and-a-half years, however, invasion of grasses and competition with other weeds force the farmers to fallow the fields, usually for five years. In contrast, the Coatzacoalcos soils along the river levees can only be cultivated with dry season crops, principally the *tapachol,* but with the floods replenishing their fertility they can be planted year in and year out without fallowing. Tapachol crops planted in the Coatzacoalcos series soils also can produce about 56% higher yields per hectare than the Tenochtitlán series soils, although this figure can vary considerably from year to year (Coe and Diehl 1980b: 142–143; Rodríguez et al. 1997: 68). Calculated over the 7.5 year cropping-and-fallow cycle for the upland soils, Coe and Diehl (1980b: 143) estimate the Coatzacoalcos series can produce twice as much shelled corn.

For their estimates of crop yields, Coe and Diehl relied on the reports of only three informants. Recently Rodríguez et al. (1997) conducted a more quantita-tive study of the relative productivity of the upland (*lomerío*) and Coatzacoalcos series (*tierra de vega* or *tierra de primera*) soils, basing their estimates on counts of plants along transects in 172 fields. Although Rodríguez et al. only collected data for two successive years, their results suggest that crop yields varied less from year to year in the upland soils than on the river levees. They also found that yields for individual crops were greater than Coe and Diehl estimated and that annual production in the uplands exceeds that on the levees due to the planting of a second crop. On the other hand, Rodríguez et al. did not take into consideration the necessity of fallowing the upland soils. When their figures for crop yields are adjusted for the 7.5 year crop-and-fallow cycle suggested by Coe and Diehl, then the average yearly production for a hectare of levee land is 185% that of the uplands, close to the estimate derived from Coe and Diehl's figures for crop yields (Table 3.3). Therefore, although the greater stability and annual productivity of the upland crops may have made them more important for Olmec subsistence than Coe and Diehl suggest, Rodríguez et al.'s figures confirm that the levee lands were substantially more productive over the long term.

TABLE 3.3. *Comparison of maize productivity for soils in the San Lorenzo area*

Soil series	Average tapachol yield in kg/ha	Average temporal yield in kg/ha	Tapachol yield in one fallow cycle (three crops)	Temporal yield in one fallow cycle (two crops)	Total crop yield for 7.5 year fallow cycle	Average per year
Rodríguez et al. 1997						
Tenochtitlán (lomerío)	2874	3718	8622	7436	16058	2141
Coatzacoalcos (vega)	3965	0	no fallow	no fallow	27755	3965
vega/lomerío						185%
Coe and Diehl 1980b						
Tenochtitlán (lomerío)	2250	2750	6750	6250	12250	1633
Coatzacoalcos (vega)	3500	0	no fallow	no fallow	24500	3500
vega/lomerío						214%

THE WESTERN TABASCO PLAIN

Near the coast, a zone of low hills in heavily weathered Tertiary period strata separates the mouths of the Coatzacoalcos and Tonalá rivers. Eastward stretch the marshy deltas of the vast Tabasco plain (Fig. 3.4). Here the second of the

Figure 3.4. The western Tabasco plain, looking northwest from Mound C-1 at La Venta. Note oil refinery on the right.

great Olmec centers, La Venta, rose on an island formed by the remnant of a Pleistocene terrace underlain by a salt dome. Other Olmec sites have been found as far eastward as the Chontalpa, a large area of former distributaries between the Mezcalapa and Grijalva rivers.

Examples of all the major environments of the Tabasco plain can be found within about 30 km of La Venta. The island rises from the marshes of the recent fluvial plain, and the Tertiary hills lie about 5 km away on the opposite bank of the Tonalá river. During the Formative period, the western distributaries of the Mezcalapa river emptied into the Tonalá, and their abandoned channels and levees can still be seen cutting through the marsh around La Venta (Jiménez Salas 1990; West et al. 1969: 42). The beach ridges and dunes of the coast lie less than 15 km to the north today, though the coast was much nearer in Olmec times (Jiménez Salas 1990; Pope et al. 2001). About 25 km to the southeast begins a series of intensely weathered, heavily dissected Pleistocene terraces that extend eastward behind the recent deltas. The levees of the delta channels have dammed older streams that flowed off these terraces, creating a string of small freshwater lakes at the terrace margins (West et al. 1969: 22).

Proximity to the coast and differences in sediment load create a complex hydrographic setting on the western Tabasco plain. The Tonalá is a fairly typical meandering stream, but the muddy Mezcalapa river forms braided channels. During the dry season, saltwater invades the rivers close to the coast, and wedges of saltwater creep up the bottoms of the channels as far as 30 km inland. Conversely, late summer and autumn floods freshen the lower river courses and the coastal lagoons. In the winter, the *nortes* fill the dry mangrove swamps and saltwater persists only in the deepest river pools (West et al. 1969: 30–31).

Variation in soils, salinity, and topography create a wide diversity of natural vegetation (West et al. 1969: 59–74). Originally, tropical rainforests covered most of the Tertiary hills, the Pleistocene terraces, and the better drained parts of the fluvial plain; a lower riparian forest lay on the river levees. Of course, as long as people have practiced slash-and-burn agriculture, the rainforests have included patches of secondary growth in fallowing fields, or *acahuales*. Today, the Pleistocene terraces are covered by a nearly continuous savanna of grasses and sedges with a scattering of low trees, shrubs, and palms. This formation was already widespread by the Spanish conquest, and deforestation for cattle ranching has extended it greatly since then.

Two vegetational formations characterize the vast marshes. The *popalería* is an herbaceous marsh with many aquatic plants, whereas the *mucalería* consists of dense stands of small shrubs and palms (West et al. 1969: 74). Mangrove forests line the coastal estuaries and lagoons. Salt-tolerant grasses, sedges, legumes, and weeds, including amaranth and morning glory, constitute the beach formation. A semideciduous forest once grew in the sandy ridges and dunes behind the beaches, but since the 1940s it has been replaced by coconut plantations (West et al. 1969: 67).

The forest and freshwater marshland fauna of the La Venta area are generally similar to those of the Coatzacoalcos basin. Marine and estuarine species assume greater importance, however. Today commercial fishermen take mullett, snapper, snook, sea mojarras, tarpon, and pompano in the coastal lagoons. Oyster beds form near the river mouths and along submerged levees in the lagoons, where grazing sea turtles and manatees were once numerous (West et al. 1969: 86–87). Four common species of crab live in the mangrove forest, including the large and tasty giant land crab. Oysters, mussels, and marine snails attach themselves to the stilt-like roots, and clams burrow into the muddy bottom. Farmers frequently hunt iguanas in the mangroves and collect honey and wax from the hives of stingless bees in hollow trees. Mammals are uncommon, but howler monkeys find refuge in the canopy (West et al. 1969: 85–86).

Because they are so extensive, the upland savannas to the southeast of La Venta merit additional comment. White-tailed deer, cottontail rabbits, and bobwhite quail frequent their margins, where both food and forest cover are abundant. West et al. (1969: 83) speculate that these were important prehispanic hunting grounds, which may have been burned to drive animals and maintain the habitat.

In modern times, maize, beans, sweet potatoes, manioc, and squash, in that order, have been the most important native subsistence crops in the Tabasco lowlands. When West et al. (1969: 146) visited the area, slash-and-burn agriculture was most commonly practiced in the uplands and permanent fields were maintained on the levee systems of the Chontalpa, paralleling the practice in the San Lorenzo area. Two crops are commonly planted each year. The *milpa de año* is the local equivalent of the *tapachol* dry season crop. The forest is cut in January or February and burned beginning in March. Planting continues through May, and the harvest occurs from September to November. Beans are planted among the maize plants after they reach 30 cm, and squash may be sown after the harvest. Robert Heizer (1960: 217) reports that a family of five living at La Venta could produce 150 bushels of maize in one crop, but consumed only 100 bushels, resulting in a substantial surplus. In addition, the wet season *tonamil* crop is often planted in the same fields between December and February. Traditionally, the fields were allowed to lie fallow for ten to twelve years after two to three years of cultivation, but West et al. (1969: 148) report that increasing population had begun in the 1960s to force the shortening of the fallow season.

Another Tabascan crop of particular significance is cacao. In Aztec times, the beans of the cacao were used as a medium of exchange and ground to produce the sacred drink, *chocolatl*. In early colonial times the river levees of the Chontalpa region produced the bulk of cacao for the Tabasco province (West et al. 1969: 116). Cacao also was grown in the Ahualulco region in western Tabasco, which included the La Venta area and which gave its cacao tribute to the *encomenderos* of the town of Coatzacoalcos.

THE TUXTLAS REGION

The Tuxtlas region comprises the volcanic sierra of that name and the sedimentary piedmont that fringes its southern edge (Fig. 3.5). The valley of the meandering San Juan River and the Papaloapan delta define the southern and western edges of the uplift, respectively. Although small Olmec sites and shrines have been reported from the Tuxtla Mountains proper, population was more heavily concentrated around the edges of the Tuxtlas region. The Olmec center of Laguna de los Cerros lies in the lower piedmont on a tributary that joins the San Juan River. A short distance to the west is Llano del Jícaro, a monument workshop on the toe of a basalt flow that crosses the piedmont. About 50 km away, Tres Zapotes occupies the eastern tip of the piedmont and the valley of the Arroyo Hueyapan.

Chief among the mineral resources of this land are its hard volcanic stone and thick deposits of kaolinitic clays that accumulated on ancient sea bottoms. The latter occur in the Concepción formation, which dips away from the center of the Tuxtlas beneath later sands of the Filisola formation. They are mainly exposed in the west-central area around the towns of San Andrés Tuxtla and Santiago Tuxtla (Pool 1990; Pool and Santley 1992; Ríos Macbeth 1952). In addition, a salt spring emerging from the Concepción formation at El Salado was exploited in Olmec times (Ceja Tenorio 1981; Santley 2004). It or similar springs may be the source of the salt recorded as tribute from the town of Tuxtla (now Santiago Tuxtla) and its dependent settlements in early colonial sources (cf. Stark 1974). Colonial Tuxtla headed a diversified tribute economy with subject towns specializing in salt, staple foods, cotton, or fishing, depending on their environmental setting (Stark 1974: 219, Table 10.1).

In contrast to the coastal plain, the orographic rainfall pattern of the Tuxtlas exerts considerable influence on modern agricultural practices (Killion 1987: 117–190). On the southern edge of the Tuxtlas around the small modern town of Cuatotolapan, where annual rainfall is less than 1,500 mm, the dry season *tapachol* crop is less important than the wet season *temporal*. At the community of Colonia Ruíz Cortinez on the northern slope of the San Martín Tuxtla volcano, however, the situation is reversed. Annual rainfall exceeds 3,500 mm, and torrential summer rains force the pioneering farmers clearing the rainforest to harvest only a dry season crop, which they call the *tonamil*. Between these two areas, in the upper valley of the Río Grande de Catemaco and on the southern flanks of San Martín Tuxtla, annual rainfall is about 2,000 mm and more evenly distributed throughout the year. Consequently, farmers in Matacapan and Santa Rosa Abata commonly plant both crops.

Figure 3.5. Lake Catemaco and volcanoes in the central Tuxtla Mountains.

Today the central zone is the most densely populated in the Tuxtlas, with sizeable towns at Santiago Tuxtla, San Andrés Tuxtla, and Catemaco. Large, private tobacco plantations occupy the most productive land and provide wage labor to the inhabitants. These economic and demographic factors have strongly influenced subsistence agricultural practices (Killion 1987: 144–157). Modern farmers rely on readily available chemical fertilizers to cultivate their more marginal plots, which are rarely fallowed for more than one year. Nevertheless, high yields were probably achievable on the rich volcanic soils in *milpas* cut from the high evergreen rainforest that formerly covered the region.

Located on the edge of the southern piedmont near the San Juan River, Cuatotolapan provides an environmental parallel to the Olmec centers of Laguna de los Cerros and Tres Zapotes (Killion 1987: 118–126). Here as elsewhere in the Tuxtlas, farmers maintain two kinds of fields in addition to house lot gardens. Infields are located around the edges of Cuatotolapan within a ten minute walk of the residence, and are planted once or twice a year with maize, beans, or tomatoes. The risk of drought during the dry season discourages planting of a *tapachol* crop on these upland soils. Use of chemical fertilizer, though expensive, allows a short fallow of two years after two to three plantings, but more distant fields are usually allowed to fallow for up to five years. Outfields are located over one hour's walk from the edge of town on the seasonally flooded levees of the Río San Juan. Sugar cane and pineapple now are often planted as cash crops on the higher parts of the levees, whereas maize, beans, squash, and root crops are grown on the lower portions of the levee fields. As in the Coatzacoalcos drainage, the latter crops are planted during the dry *tapachol* season when floods have receded and require no fallow period.

During times when less labor is required in the fields, farmers take fish and shellfish from the San Juan River for household consumption or sale. House lot gardens supplement the staple diet with fruits and condiments and provide medicinal herbs and timber. Excavations in the central Tuxtlas have revealed the ridged surfaces of Formative period gardens preserved under volcanic ash, attesting to their antiquity in the region as well as the risks of volcanic hazards for agricultural production (Arnold 2000: 126; Pool 1997b: 54; Santley 1992).

Over the past 50,000 years, the Tuxtla volcanoes have erupted about once every 250 years, on average (Reinhardt 1991). Most of these have been of the Strombolian type, which produces large amounts of ash and modest lava flow, usually from cinder cones. Phreatic and phreatomagmatic eruptions also have occurred in the Tuxtlas as the result of heating of groundwater by magma or direct interaction of magma with groundwater. The resulting steam explosion blows out a crater, known as a maar, which often forms a small crater lake. Though more violent than Strombolian eruptions, the phreatic and phreatomagmatic eruptions typically affect a smaller area. Flows of ash and mud, called lahars, are another volcanic hazard documented within the Tuxtlas.

The most recent eruptions occurred in A.D. 1664 and A.D. 1793 (Friedlander and Sonder 1923; Moziño 1869). The 1793 Strombolian eruption lasted for nearly nine months, producing a 5 km long lava flow, dumping volcanic ash on the town of San Andrés Tuxtla, blocking roads, and starting a fire on the slopes of the San Martín volcano. The vegetable crop was destroyed, but cotton was harvested early enough to save the crop (Moziño 1869). Similar effects would have accompanied the pre-Hispanic eruptions, nine of which are documented between 3350 B.C. and A.D. 650 (Reinhardt 1991; Santley et al. 2000). It is important to recognize, however, that the Strombolian eruptions produced by relatively small cinder cones like those typical of the Tuxtlas are not very extensive, usually depositing significant amounts of ash only 10 to 20 km from the vent. The actual area affected also depends heavily on wind direction and velocity. For example, one of the major prehistoric eruptions documented in the Tuxtlas, the Middle Classic eruption of Cerro Puntiagudo, deposited ash a meter or more deep over an area more than 10 km by 6 km extending westward from the volcano (Reinhardt 1991: 61; Santley et al 2000: Fig. 6.3). Earlier eruptions of similar scale affected settlements in the Rio Grande de Catemaco valley. One of these, around 1000 B.C. was probably responsible for the abandonment of Olmec villages around Matacapan (Santley et al. 2000). As the account of the 1793 eruption indicates, the timing of eruptions with respect to the agricultural cycle also is important: an eruption late in the growing season may be devastating, whereas one that occurs after the harvest will have little effect.

DIVERSITY, DYNAMISM, AND RISK IN OLMAN

Olman does not exhibit the close juxtaposition of contrasting environments seen in much of highland Mesoamerica. On the other hand, as this review of selected areas demonstrates, Olman is not the homogeneous, marginal environment that has sometimes been depicted (e.g., Blanton et al. 1996: 8; Rathje 1972: 365; Sanders and Webster 1978: 288–289). Moreover, environmental variation extends beyond local microenvironmental variation, such as the widely recognized differences between river levees and floodplains, to broad regional differences in topography, geology, and climate. It is neither distributed evenly throughout Olman in mosaic-like fashion, nor is it repeated in a redundant series of parallel river basins. Instead, discrete environmental zones with variant ecological processes, agricultural productivity, and resources occupy different parts of Olman (Grove 1994). Furthermore, the environment of Olman is and was a dynamic one, shaped by changing river courses, migrating coastlines, and erupting volcanoes.

The environment of Olman offered exceptional subsistence opportunities to foragers, fishers, and farmers with its many wetlands, streams, lakes, and estuaries, its extensive forests and savannas, and its generally ample rainfall and freedom from frost. The mixed subsistence economy documented archaeologically would have insulated the Olmec populace from hunger and was capable of generating substantial surpluses.

On the other hand, Olman was not a risk-free tropical paradise (cf. Sanders and Webster 1978). Floods were the most obvious risk in the river basins. Annual flooding created great benefits by maintaining fertility, watering higher areas, and restocking lakes and sloughs with fish, but major floods could interfere with planting schedules, erode levees, and alter river courses, changing the distribution of desirable lands and transportation nodes. Year-to-year variation in the timing and amount of rainfall also created risks. An early onset of rains could catch farmers unaware before they had burned their fields, and too long a rainy season could promote fungal infections in crops. On the other hand, a prolonged dry season could shorten growing seasons in uplands, particularly in the rainshadow south of the the Tuxtla Mountains. Too much or too little rain could also invite infestations by particular species of insects and rodents, depending on their specific life cycles and food requirements. In and around the Tuxtla Mountains, volcanic eruptions presented another source of risk, which could have devastating effects, but which occurred on a longer time scale and affected smaller areas.

Most variations in productivity appear to have affected the production of surpluses more than basic subsistence. Furthermore, there was little the Olmecs could do to ameliorate the risks in their environment, other than adopting a flexible subsistence strategy and establishing alliances beyond their local area. These conditions would have favored the establishment of networks to support political ends to a greater extent than they would have encouraged the rise of a managerial elite. Political leaders, however, may have handled disputes over lands affected by changing river courses, further contributing to their political power (Stark 2000: 39).

The nature of variation in the distributions of mineral resources within Olman is often underappreciated as well. Volcanic uplands and sedimentary lowlands constituted one important and widely acknowledged axis of con-trast, but it was not the only one, and within these broad zones particular resources exhibited different patterns of occurrence. Basalt stone, for example, is restricted to the Tuxtla Mountains and piedmont, but within the Tuxtlas it is ubiquitous. In contrast, tar seeps occur as discrete points in the sedimentary lowlands. Salt sources are more widely distributed than was once thought, and they included relatively broad coastal zones, as well as the discrete salt domes of the Isthmian Saline Basin and the salt springs of the Tuxtlas.

Salt, basalt, and probably asphalt may be considered to have served both subsistence (or utilitarian) and ceremonial functions. Certainly both types of use are documented for basalt, used to make implements for grinding maize and to carve monuments. Asphalt was used in making ceremonial items and may have been employed to waterproof boats, baskets, and water jars. Salt was a vital subsistence item, and may have been offered in rituals. Importantly, however, although each Olmec center was located near the sources of one or two of these materials, no Olmec center had direct local access to all three. Similar observations may be made with respect to materials used primarily for ritual and/or social display, among them red ochre (hematite) and cinnabar for pigments and burial ceremony, kaolin for fine vessels, stingray spines for blood-letting implements, and marine shell for ornaments. All were widely utilized in Olman, but none were naturally available everywhere. Thus, to obtain materi-als for display items and the full suite of utilitarian manufacturing materials, as well as to ensure a secure supply of staple surpluses, Olmec communities would have needed to establish intraregional networks through alliance, colonization, or conquest.

A final point to be made about the Olmec environment is that it is not quite true that "Such raw materials as were *necessary* for status differentiation were imported from elsewhere" (Sanders and Webster 1978: 289, emphasis added). Other societies around the world, such as Polynesia and the Northwest Coast of North America, have managed quite well with local materials in crafting material symbols of social rank, such as brightly colored feathered cloaks, beautifully woven textiles, or exquisitely carved objects of wood, bone, antler, or ivory. The Olmecs, too, could have used the feathers, pelts, wood, antler, clay, and stone of Olman to craft such symbols. The fact that, from early times, they imported iron ore artifacts and greenstone from distant lands has far more to do with the symbolic, cosmological significance of such exotica than with necessity born of environmental deprivation.

CHAPTER 4

OLMEC BEGINNINGS

People have wondered about the origin of the Olmecs since José Melgar (1869) first speculated on the "Ethiopian" appearance of the "colossal head of Hueyapan." The question of Olmec origins is really three questions: where did the Olmec people originate; how and where did the distinctive Olmec art style crystallize; and how did the complex institutions of Olmec society arise? In the beginning days of Olmec archaeology, researchers favoring a late date for Olmec culture argued it derived from the Maya. After radiocarbon dating proved La Venta predated Classic Maya civilization, Olmec culture still seemed as if it had sprung fully developed from the Tabasco swamps. This (apparently) sudden appearance gave rise to speculation that the Olmecs migrated from a yet earlier homeland (e.g., Covarrubias 1957: 76, 101; Piña Chán 1955: 106–107). The eminent archaeologist Gordon Ekholm (1964) went so far as to suggest that elements of the Olmec art style might have originated in Bronze Age China. Even after excavations at San Lorenzo pushed back the origins of the Olmec art style and revealed yet earlier cultural phases, a perceived discontinuity in the ceramic sequence (Coe and Diehl 1980a: 150) kept alive the idea of a homeland outside the Gulf Coast (e.g., Gay 1973; Wicke 1971: 161–162; Graham 1989). Today, however, evidence accumulating in Olman is documenting the in situ development of Olmec cultural practices and social institutions, without discounting the possibility of external influences over the course of Olmec history.

ARCHAIC ROOTS

The ultimate origins of the Olmec people lie among those bands of hunter-gatherers who entered North America from Asia during the last Ice Age of the Pleistocene epoch. The date of the first entry of humans into the area that would become Mesoamerica is unknown, but chronometric ages of greater than 20,000 years have been reported for materials associated with artifacts at Tlapacoya, Mexico, and Cualapan Puebla. Even earlier dates of more than

30,000 years ago are reported for an occupation at El Cedral, San Luis Potosi, and a for a human skeleton from Chimalhuacán, Mexico (Mirambell 2000; Pompa y Padilla and Serrano 2001). Though still controversial, the early dates of these "Archaeolithic" sites now seem more reasonable in light of Tom Dillehay's (1989) demonstration that humans had reached southern Chile as of 13,000 years ago.

Beginning sometime after 14,000 years ago, Paleoindian groups roamed Mexico and Central America, hunting now-extinct mammoths and camelids in addition to small game and gathering wild plants. Their characteristic lance-olate spear points included North American fluted Clovis points and South American fish-tailed points, as well as regional styles such as the thick, unfluted Lerma point.

Over the course of the Archaic period (ca. 8000–2000 B.C.) mobile bands of hunter-gatherers pursuing their seasonal rounds began to rely increasingly on plant foods, ultimately domesticating maize, beans, squash, chiles, avocados, and other plants in the Mesoamerican cornucopia (Flannery 1986; Smith 1997, 2000). In recent years, direct dating of maize cobs from dry caves in the Tehuacan Valley of Puebla has generated a heated debate over when this staple food was first domesticated, but it remains clear that this and other basic components of the Mesoamerican agricultural complex were being grown before the close of the Archaic period. As populations grew and reliance on cultivation increased, groups also became more sedentary, slowly spending greater and greater portions of the year in the same location (MacNeish 1971; Flannery 1986; Stark 1981). In particularly favorable environments, such as coastal estuaries and the shores of highland lakes, sedentism may have preceded the adoption of cultivars, although the evidence remains equivocal (Clark 1994b: 194; Niederberger 1976, 1987, 2000; Stark 1981; Voorhies 1976, 1996; Voorhies and Kennet 1995; Wilkerson 1981). In any event, by the beginning of the Formative period, around 2000 B.C., the essential elements of a farming life were in place and settled villages supported by varying mixes of agricultural products and wild resources sprang up across Mesoamerica over the succeeding millenium. These developments established the basis on which the Olmecs and later civilizations would raise their monuments and form complex social and political institutions, culminating in the rise of stratified societies and states.

EARLY CULTURES OF OLMAN

Until recently, the Archaic and Initial Formative cultures of Olman have been largely invisible to archaeology, though the existence of such early populations long has been suspected. Taking the period from ca. 1450 B.C. to 400 B.C. as "Olmec," these early cultures are usually described as "pre-Olmec," though current evidence for continuity supports the interpretation that they were direct progenitors of the Olmec culture.[1] Often covered by deep alluvium and obscured by later occupations, pre-Olmec remains usually have been ignored by archaeologists focused on more spectacular later developments. Nevertheless, investigations at a handful of sites have begun to open small windows on the early cultures of Olman.

San Andrés

Pollen from deep sediment cores at San Andrés, about 7 km northeast of La Venta, indicate human occupation of the Tabasco coast by about 5100 B.C. (Pope et al. 2001) (Fig. 1.2). At that time, an ancient coastal lagoon occupied the area, and the beach ridge stood just north of San Andrés. Archaic hunter-gatherers probably were drawn to the rich aquatic resources of this lagoon. They evidently supplemented their diet with cultivated crops, because pollen from these early levels includes that of a wild ancestor of maize (*Zea* sp.) and domesticated maize pollen appears about 100 years later. *Zea* is not native to the lowlands of Mesoamerica, and could only have been introduced by humans. An increase in grass pollens during the same period further indicates that fields were being cleared in the area. The Archaic inhabitants also may have cultivated domesticated manioc around the lagoon. The coast slowly migrated northward and, between about 3400 B.C. and 2400 B.C., the lagoon filled with the sands, silts, and clays of the levee of a distributary estuary. The inhabitants of the levee at San Andrés took oysters, clams, gar, and manatee from the brackish estuary, kept domesticated dogs, and added wild squash and domesticated cotton and sunflowers to their suite of cultivated plants (Pope et al. 2001: 1373).

    Reliance on a mix of domesticated crops and estuarine resources continued during the Initial Formative period. Basalt grinding stones also were introduced, and the evidence of the frequency of their use increased over time, which suggests the growing importance of maize in the diet (Rust and Leyden 1994). Pottery has been recovered from levels dated to before 1750 B.C. at San Andrés (Rust and Sharer 1988; Rust and Leyden 1994), although typologically they appear to be younger, and they may have been introduced into earlier levels by burrowing crabs (von Nagy 2003: 759–760; see also Raab et al. 2000). At present it is difficult to say if these ceramics represent the beginning of a long cultural tradition or post-depositional mixing of stratigraphic levels.

The Tuxtla Mountains

Pollen also provides the earliest evidence for human occupation in the Tuxtla Mountains. At Laguna Pompal, a small lake east of Laguna Catemaco on the flank of Santa Marta volcano, an 8.3 m deep sediment core yielded maize pollen, charcoal, and the pollen of other plants indicative of agricultural disturbance in sediments radiocarbon dated to 2880 B.C. (Goman and Byrne 1998: 85). Because these were in the lowest level of the 8.3 m core, maize must have been introduced to the region even earlier.

Charred remains of maize and other crops are present in pre-Olmec deposits at La Joya, a small site in the west-central Tuxtlas on the Río Grande de Catemaco (Tulipan phase, ca. 1500–1400 B.C. (Arnold 2003: 31; VanDerwarker 2006). At this time, occupation appears to have been seasonal, but the inhabitants did use pottery, consisting mainly of tecomates, bowls, beakers, and plates similar to contemporaneous Ojochí and Bajío phase pottery from San Lorenzo. Philip Arnold's (2003) analysis of the Initial and Early Formative pottery from La Joya demonstrates considerable continuity in vessel forms and surface treatments with gradual changes in pastes from pre-Olmec to Olmec times. This conclusion contrasts markedly with that of the excavators of San Lorenzo, who reported a dramatic change in ceramic types and argued on this basis for a foreign incursion of Olmecs into Olman (Coe and Diehl 1980a: 150).

El Manatí

Spectacular evidence for Initial Formative occupation also has been found at the water-logged site of El Manatí, located on a hill rising from a swamp east of the Coatzacoalcos River (Ortiz and Rodríguez 1989, 1997, 2000; Ortiz et al. 1989; Rodríguez and Ortiz 1997). In 1988, local farmers digging a fish tank next to a spring at the base of Cerro Manatí uncovered three wooden busts preserved in the muck. With foresight worthy of professional conservators, the discoverers bound the busts with cloth, submerged them in water to prevent their drying out, and contacted the regional center of the National Institute of Anthropology and History in Veracruz. Since then, an archaeological team directed by Ponciano Ortiz and María del Cármen Rodríguez have excavated a fascinating sequence of ritual offerings dating from about 1700 B.C to 1200 B.C., and they have extended their investigations to the nearby sites of El Macayal, La Merced, and El Paraíso. In addition to the wooden busts, which now number 20, the anaerobic conditions in the mud preserved a remarkable suite of wooden artifacts, plant remains, and 14 rubber balls, the earliest known from Mesoamerica.

The offerings at El Manatí were deposited in three phases, Manatí A (ca. 1700–1500 B.C.), Manatí B (ca. 1500–1400 B.C.), and Macayal A (ca. 1400–1200 B.C.) (Ortiz and Rodríguez 2000: 75, 79, 83; Rodríguez and Ortiz 2005 and personal communication). During the Manatí A phase, the bottom of the spring was lined with sandstone rocks and boulders, some of which bore V-shaped cuts and shallow depressions similar to marks on later monuments at San Lorenzo and La Venta. The sandy sediments surrounding and covering the sandstone rocks contained fragments of pots that had been flung into the spring, many polished greenstone axes and beads, stone mortars, and nine rubber balls, all about 15 cm in diameter. Most of these items had been deposited haphazardly or in loose concentrations, but one of the rubber balls was found associated with 40 fine stone axes and seeds of hog plum, fragments of *otate* (false bamboo), and a piece of copal resin. The pottery, which resembles ceramics from contemporary phases at San Lorenzo and the Chiapas coast, included flat-bottomed bowls, globular tecomates, and other neckless jars. Many of the vessels were covered with polished slips in cream, red, or dark reddish-brown, and some were decorated by brushing, grooving, fluting, rocker-stamping, or incising. In addition, some of the tecomates were sealed with bitumen, and many of the vessels had soot adhering to them, suggesting they had been used in cooking.

A layer of peat sealed these offerings below the silts and clays of the Manatí B phase (ca. 1500–1400 B.C.). During the course of the Manatí B phase, the offerings became more formalized, presaging later offerings of greenstone celts at the nearby site of La Merced and at La Venta, Tabasco, as well as sites outside of Olman such as San Isidro, Chiapas (Lowe 1981, 1998; Ortiz and Rodríguez 2000: 79, 83). Polished stone axes were placed in rows running north and south, or in bundles of three to twelve. Other arrangements include a circle of five axes arranged like the petals of a flower with the bits pointing up and outward and another group of five axes arranged in a quincunx with four axes at the corners and a fifth in the center (Ortiz and Rodríguez 1997: 236). Rubber balls continued to be deposited, but now they were larger, about 20 cm in diameter.

Rubber held an important place in later Mesoamerican cultures. In addition to balls, it was formed into figurines, burned in ritual offerings, used in medicinal preparations, and formed into bands for hafting stone axes (Hosler et al. 1999: 1988). Its most important use, however, was for the ball game played in formal courts of various dimensions. For many Mesoamerican peoples, the movement of the ball was a metaphor for the transit of the sun and, among the Maya, the game recapitulated the victory of mythic hero twins over the Lords of the Underworld. In addition to these religious associations, this ball game served as a means of mediating political disputes and was played as a sporting event accompanied by gambling by both participants and onlookers (Miller and Taube 1993: 43). Olman, of course, was a major source of rubber, which gave the land its name. When dry, however, natural latex is brittle and does not bounce; to retain its elastic properties it must be chemically altered. Spanish chroniclers reported that this was done by mixing latex with the sap of morning glories, a practice still used in Chiapas. Analysis of one of the rubber balls from El Manatí suggests that this method was used by the Olmecs before 1500 B.C. (Hosler et al. 1999).

After the last of the Manatí B offerings was laid in the spring, two to four meters of silt and clay accumulated over them. Ritual use of the spring resumed in the Macayal A phase (ca. 1400–1200 B.C.). The wooden busts that first brought attention to El Manatí were laid singly or in groups of two or three with wooden staffs and wood-handled knives, bundles of plants, mats, and red balls of hematite (Ortiz and Rodríguez 1997: 237–242). The sculptures exhibit the typical cylindrical head deformation and down-turned mouths of Olmec figurines. Ear pendants, ear spools, and pectorals adorn some of the sculptures, and some displayed red and black paint around their mouths. Polished greenstone axes and rubber balls also were offered, reflecting continuity in this ritual practice from the Manatí phase. Human infants were apparently offered at the spring as well, for their skeletons, some complete, others dismembered, and one fitted with a cord through holes drilled in the skull, occur among the wooden busts. Such infant sacrifice foreshadows the Aztecs' offerings of children to Tlaloc and Chalchiutlicue, gods associated with rain and water.

Another impressive find dating to the Macayal phase was discovered at La Merced, on a small island in the swamp about 4 km northeast of El Manatí (Rodríguez and Ortiz 2000). Here, over six hundred ceremonial axes, or celts, mainly of serpentine, were placed in three separate events, the earliest two of which are associated with radiocarbon dates of 1510–1380 and 1410–1200 B.C. (cal. 2σ), respectively (Ortiz and Rodríguez, 2005 personal communication). The celts in the earliest set of offerings also were the best finished, and some were accompanied by polished iron ore fragments. The second and third sets of offerings were dominated by unfinished celt performs, or "pseudocelts," in various stages of production (Jaime-Riverón 2003: 253–255). Among the most interesting elements in the second set of offerings is an anthropomorphic axe, christened "El Bebé," representing an infant with feline features, which itself holds an axe on its chest. Similar to the anthropomorphic axes that helped to originally define the Olmec style, this is the first found in stratigraphic context, and it is earlier than the Middle Formative date generally assigned to such axes. Also significant is a square stone slab carved in low relief with the face of a feline – or "Olmec dragon" – with a cleft head and four rectangular cleft elements at the corners. This piece was found in the latest Macayal phase offering and bears some resemblances to Middle Formative Olmec sculpture.

Macayal phase ceramics apparently exhibit considerable continuity with the Manatí phase, though new types and decorative modes were also introduced (Rodríguez and Ortiz 1997: 78–83). Of particular interest is a differentially fired black-and-white sherd with a diagonally carved motif similar to the "fire-serpent" motif common at the same time in Oaxaca (Flannery and Marcus 1994: 136–137, Figs. 12.5 and 12.6; Rodríguez and Ortiz 1997: Fig. 3.6). Most of the new ceramic types, however, are comparable to types of the San Lorenzo phase at San Lorenzo (Rodríguez and Ortiz 1997: 78–82) (Fig. 4.1).

The sequence of offerings at El Manatí document the consistent, if intermittent, use of this sacred space over a period of some 600 years, stretching back well into "pre-Olmec" times and anticipating later Olmec ritual practices. Changes occurred in the arrangements of offerings, and new elements were added in the last phase of the spring's use, but offerings of polished greenstone axes and rubber balls persisted throughout the use of the spring. Likewise, the ceramic assemblage suggests gradual, in situ development, prompting the excavators to reject the notion of an arrival of foreign groups in southern Veracruz around 1450 B.C. and to conclude, "It is no longer appropriate to view the earliest phases defined at San Lorenzo as 'pre-Olmec' (Rodríguez and Ortiz 1997: 83; cf. Coe and Diehl 1980a: 150; Lowe 1989)."

SAN LORENZO AND THE EARLY FORMATIVE FLORESCENCE

At the same time that ancestors of the Olmecs were offering greenstone celts and rubber balls at the Manatí spring, their contemporaries were settling villages 18 km to the northeast at San Lorenzo Tenochtitlán. Matthew Stirling (1955) gave the name San Lorenzo Tenochtitlán to a cluster of three settlements on an island in the swamps and marshes west of the Coatzacoalcos River and south of the Chiquito River, a branch of the Coatzacoalcos. San Lorenzo proper occupies the slopes and summit of a plateau that rises 50 m above the floodplain of the Coatzacoalcos River (Fig. 3.3). The archaeological site of Tenochtitlán lies within the modern village of the same name at the northern end of the island, and Potrero Nuevo occupies a hill east of the plateau. Another large site occupies the Loma del Zapote, a long ridge extending southward from the plateau, which includes the locality known as El Azuzul at its southern tip.

In the 1960s Michael Coe and Richard Diehl (1980a) conducted excavations at San Lorenzo and surrounding sites, defining eight major phases of occupation. The Ojochi (ca. 1750–1550 B.C.) and Bajío (ca. 1550–1450 B.C.) phases constitute the "pre-Olmec" Initial Formative sequence. More characteristically Olmec artifacts appear in the Early Formative Chicharras phase (ca. 1450–1400 B.C.), and San Lorenzo rose to the height of its power in the San Lorenzo phase (ca. 1400–1000 B.C.). San Lorenzo suffered a decline at the beginning of the Middle Formative period, which encompasses the Nacaste (ca. 1000–800 B.C.) and Palangana (ca. 800–400 B.C.) phases. Population declined further in the Late Formative Remplás phase (ca. 300–50 B.C.). Although recent surveys have revealed occupation in the area during the Early and Middle Classic periods, San Lorenzo itself was not reoccupied until late in the Villa Alta phase (A.D. 800–1000) (Symonds et al. 2002: 96–117).[2]

The last three millenia have seen significant changes in the landscape around San Lorenzo. During the Early Formative period, the Coatzacoalcos River

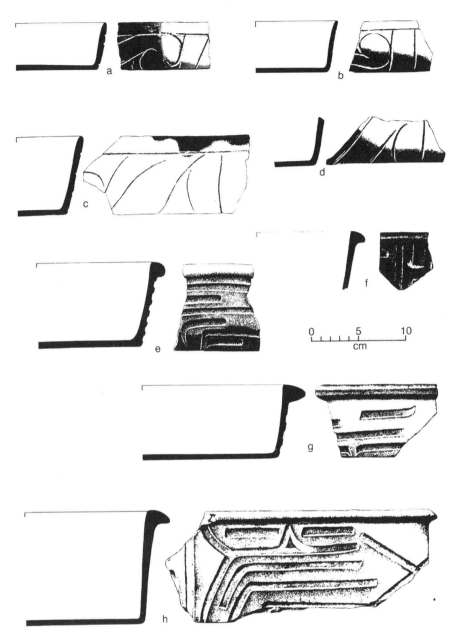

Figure 4.1. Early Formative pottery (San Lorenzo phase) from San Lorenzo. (**a–d**) Limon incised; (**e–h**) Calzadas carved (from Coe 1981: Fig. 5–8) (courtesy of Michael D. Coe).

flowed along the eastern edge of the island through the now-abandoned Azuzul-Potrero Nuevo channel. It appears to have connected to the San Antonio channel north of the Chiquito River, which probably did not then exist. South of Loma del Zapote, a branch of the Coatzacoalcos bifurcated to the west, flowing through the channel of the Tatagapa River (Ortiz-Pérez and

Cyphers 1997). Rising between these two branches of the mighty river, San Lorenzo, when it rose to prominence, would be well situated to control traffic along them.

Architecture and Landscape Modification

The broad base of the San Lorenzo plateau extends over some 700 ha, and its flat summit covers 53 ha. Deep gullies carve the north, west, and south sides of the plateau into a series of projecting ridges, which Michael Coe interpreted as the wings and tail feathers of a great bird effigy flying eastward (Coe 1989: 80; Coe and Diehl 1980a: 27–28), although recent excavations suggest they are the result of erosion that has occurred since the Early Formative period (Cyphers 1997f: 104–105) (Fig. 4.2). Likewise, most of the currently visible features on the summit of the plateau post-date the site's Early Formative apogee. At the center of the summit long, low earthen mounds flank three formal courts extending north and south from a 6 m tall conical mound, resembling, at a smaller scale, the ceremonial courts and plazas of La Venta. Adjoining the east side of the north court of this Group A complex is a fourth plaza called the Palangana. The mounds of Group A and the Palangana were first raised after ca. 800 B.C. (Palangana phase), however, and some appear to date to the Late Classic period (Diehl 1981: 70–73). Over 200 low mounds surround this formal complex, and 21 low depressions, called *lagunas* dot the plateau. With few exceptions, the low mounds appear to be recent agricultural features, and at least one of the lagunas was dug after the San Lorenzo phase (Coe and Diehl 1980a: 29; Cyphers 1997f: 102, 106–108; Symonds et al. 2002: 109).

   Nevertheless, the plateau would have been an impressive sight in Early Formative times (Cyphers 1997f). At the top of the plateau, massive thrones, colossal heads, and smaller sculptures of humans, felines, birds, and supernatural monsters, most carved from imported basalt, proclaimed the power of its rulers and its sacred source. Long lines of U-shaped drain stones directed water to the edges of the plateau, reflecting the rulers' control over this precious resource. The elites of San Lorenzo lived in large structures raised on low clay platforms amid the monuments that legitimized their authority. One such platform (D4–7) measures 50 × 75 m. Twenty post-molds on the platform mark the walls of an apsidal structure 12 m long and 9 m wide (Cyphers 1997f: 101–102). The earthen walls and floor of another elite residence, dubbed the "Red Palace," were plastered with sand stained by hematite (Cyphers 1997f: 101). Massive, 4 m tall carved basalt columns apparently supported its roof, and L-shaped basalt "benches" are thought to have been used as step coverings. Blocks of bentonite clay (a weathering product of volcanic ash) and limestone found among the collapsed debris may have been used in its walls. The 40 cm thick mud walls of several structures lack post-molds and were evidently constructed using a rammed earth technique. Others employed bentonite masonry

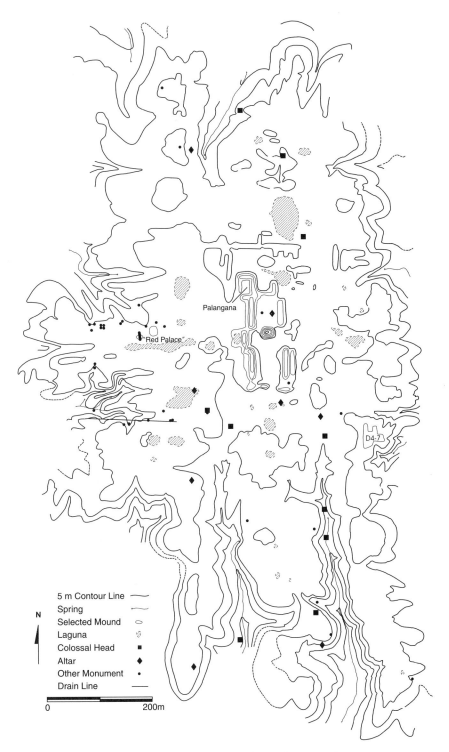

Figure 4.2. Map of San Lorenzo. Contour interval = 5 m, lowest contour = 55 m (from Coe and Diehl 1980a: Map 2) (courtesy of Michael D. Coe).

fixed with mud mortar. Floors were made of gravel or packed earth or paved with bentonite blocks (Cyphers 1997f: 99–102).

On the slopes of the plateau, stepping down to a level 40 m below the summit, broad artificial terraces supported the thatched wattle-and-daub houses of the common folk. Whether the construction of these terraces was ordered by the rulers or initiated by groups of commoners is unknown, and it should be recalled that enormous systems of agricultural terraces were built in the Andes and on the Philippines without direct elite intervention. Nevertheless, impressive amounts of labor went into building the San Lorenzo terraces, one of which was held in place by a 7 m high retaining wall.

Other modifications to the landscape around San Lorenzo include causeways or dikes. The two largest measured 750 × 60 m and 600 × 75 m and bordered ancient river courses at Potrero Nuevo and El Azuzul, respectively. Packed floors and activity areas on the Potrero Nuevo causeway show that it supported Formative period habitation. Built up more than 2 m above the floodplain, these two may have provided some measure of flood control and possibly served as wharfs for loading and unloading canoes. A third causeway found in the 1960s by Ray and Paula Krotser extends 200 m from the hills at the eastern base of the plateau toward Potrero Nuevo, and at its full extent may have connected the two sites (Coe and Diehl 1980a: 297; Cyphers 1997a: 112–113).

In sum, the Early Formative Olmecs of San Lorenzo Tenochtitlán applied a distinctive concept of architecture to their constructions. Rather than building formal courts and temple mounds as did their successors, they sculpted the natural contours of their surroundings into a cultural landscape and defined sacred areas with arrangements of stone monuments. Whether directed by elites or accomplished independently by commoners, the leveling and filling of terraces around the San Lorenzo plateau transformed the natural eminence into the largest human construction of its time in Mesoamerica, a "sacred mountain" sanctified by the monuments on its heights (Cyphers 1997e: 237).

Production and Exchange

The San Lorenzo Olmec economy was based on the mixture of agriculture, fishing, gathering, and hunting discussed in Chapter 3. The surpluses generated by these subsistence activities supported the elites and fed the artists who carved the impressive monuments as well as the crews required to haul the massive stones tens of kilometers from their sources. In addition, control over various aspects of production and exchange gave material force to the ideological underpinnings of elite governmental institutions.

Many of the materials employed by Olmecs could be procured directly from within San Lorenzo's hinterland. Wood for construction and crafts and alluvial clay for pottery were abundant in the forests and marshlands of the Coatzacoalcos basin. Finer kaolin pottery clay and bentonite occur in sedimentary formations in the hills and terraces of the region, as do isolated sources of hematite, the red ochre used to color buildings and decorate pottery. Natural petroleum seeps, located a few kilometers away and farther down the Coatza-coalcos River, provided the bitumen (asphalt) that is found widely in the San Lorenzo deposits (Wendt and Lu 2006). Salt could have been obtained from springs around salt domes and from the saline waters along the coast. The network of river channels doubtlessly facilitated the transport of these local materials as well as foodstuffs, and San Lorenzo and its subsidiary centers were located in such a way as to easily control water-borne travel (Symonds and Lunagómez 1997a, b).

By comparison, the Coatzacoalcos lowlands are poor in sources of hard stone. Sandstone outcrops on the Loma del Zapote and limestone occurs on Cerro Encantada, 7 km to the south, but these were little used for utilitarian artifacts or monument carving. Instead the Olmecs preferred the hard basalt found in the Tuxtlas some 60 km away, which they could only have obtained with a tremendous expenditure of effort. It is estimated that transporting a single colossal head would have required the labor of more than 1,500 persons over three to four months (Clark 1994c: 191–192).

Other materials came from yet more distant sources. Obsidian, the vol-canic glass used by commoners and elites alike for cutting instruments came from sources 200 to 400 km away in the Mexican and Guatemalan highlands (Cobean et al. 1991). Ilmenite, an iron ore fashioned into small cubes with mul-tiple drilled holes, most likely came from the Central depression of Chiapas. Jade, serpentine, and other greenstones are not as abundant at San Lorenzo as in the Middle Formative occupations of La Venta, but the celt offerings at El Manatí indicate that greenstone was procured and prized by the inhabi-tants of the San Lorenzo realm, who acquired them principally from sources in Guatemala (Jaime-Riveron 2003: 677). Clearly, the San Lorenzo Olmecs participated in a wide-flung network to acquire both utilitarian and prestige goods. What they exchanged in return is less clear, but some ceramic artifacts from Central Mexico, Oaxaca, and Chiapas have been chemically sourced to the San Lorenzo region (Blomster et al. 2005). Other possibilities include such perishable items as tropical feathers, pelts, rubber, and cacao, but evidence of their exchange has so far eluded archaeologists.

The degree to which craft production was specialized and the extent to which elites controlled production are important issues for assessing the degree of economic integration in Olmec society and the character of its political economy. In its broadest sense, craft specialization refers to the production of durable, alienable goods for consumption by people outside of one's own household (Clark and Parry 1990). Much specialized craft production in peas-ant and non-state societies is undertaken on a part-time basis by people who also cooperate in food production. In contrast, full-time craft specialists devote all of their productive efforts to their craft. In fact, specialization is best seen as a continuum, which ranges from sporadic, informal, part-time production (or ad hoc production, per Clark and Parry 1990: 298) to full-time production. Full-time craft production is characteristic of the greater degrees of social and economic differentiation associated with state-level societies, but it also may exist in non-state societies, especially for goods that require special knowledge or skill. Craft production also may be characterized with regard to whether it is performed on demand for an outside sponsor (e.g., a patron, a lord, or the state) (Clark and Parry 1990: 298). Such sponsorship is often called "attached" specialization, and it is distinguished from "independent" specialization in which craftspersons produce for an unspecified set of consumers (Brumfiel and Earle 1987).

The clearest evidence for Olmec craft specialization at San Lorenzo lies in the skill and effort required to carve its stone monuments. These artworks obviously were not made by all households, and the sculptors would have required years of training to perfect their craft. Other crafts that required specialized knowledge and/or long hours of effort probably included shaping and polishing stone celts, axes, and beads, building watercraft, and, possibly, making articles of ceremonial dress (Drucker 1981: 34–35) and processing rubber (Hosler et al. 1999). Importantly, all of these are articles of prestige or public display used by elites, implying some form of attached specialization, but it is more difficult to determine if the artisans and craftspersons were employed full-time.

Direct evidence for attached craft specialization comes from recent excavations by Ann Cyphers (1996: 66) on the San Lorenzo plateau. In an area about 25 m west of the "Red Palace" forty-four damaged monuments and monument fragments were found associated with stone flakes, tools, and abrasives, and another six tons of basalt and metamorphic stone fragments were discarded about 50 m east of the elite structure (Cyphers Guillén 1994: 61; Cyphers 1997b: 180–181; 1999: 166–167). Cyphers thinks the basalt monuments in this area were being recycled into preforms for metates and stone lids. In addition, a smaller area on the southwestern edge of the plateau appears to have been dedicated to recycling basalt into round plates. The identification of these basalt concentrations as "workshops" has met with some resistance. John Clark (1996: 193), for example, sees them as places where basalt was removed from circulation by burying it in caches. Though they may not have been workshops in the strict sense of places that employed full-time craft specialists, the presence of tools and abrasives for carving strengthens their identification as production areas specialized in the sense of focusing on a single activity. Regardless, the proximity of these areas to the seats of rulership bespeaks a high level of elite control over this scarce, non-local resource.

Near the second basalt recycling area were large pits containing over six metric tons of ilmenite cubes, each drilled with three perforations. Identical objects have been reported from sites in the Tuxtla Mountains (Arnold 1995: 195), Tres Zapotes (Weiant 1943: 21, Plate 76), and Las Limas (Yadeun in

Agrinier 1984: 75). Their most likely source is the Río La Venta area of western Chiapas, where one excavation at the site of Plumajillo recovered 2,131 pieces of ilmenite and magnetite, representing the entire production process from chunks of iron ore through undrilled cubes to the finished drilled cubes. Several suggestions have been offered for the function of these enigmatic objects, including net weights, beads, fire starters, tiny hammers, counterweights for spearthrowers, or amulets (Agrinier 1984: 80–81; Coe and Diehl 1980a: 242; Di Castro Stringher 1997: 156; Lowe 1989: 53). Most recently, an analysis by Anna Di Castro Stringher (1997; Cyphers and Di Castro Stringher 1996) suggests the perforations may have resulted from use as elements of a rotating instrument, perhaps as bearings for drills. If such were the case, we might expect some of the cubes to have been broken or discarded before they were exhausted, but to date all ilmenite cubes reported from Olman have three perforations. I am therefore inclined to agree with John Clark (1996: 192) that the multiperforate cubes were imported in finished form. Whether the cube-filled pits reflect the presence of a specialized craft production area nearby or the hoarding of decommissioned objects reclaimed from their users (Clark 1996: 193), they suggest elite control over access to this exotic commodity (e.g., Clark 1996: 192). However, multiperforate ilmenite cubes also have been recovered from nonelite and rural contexts in Olman (e.g., Arnold 1995: 195), indicating that elite control over their use was not absolute.

No evidence for elite control over the production of obsidian artifacts has yet been found at San Lorenzo, although prismatic blades are common there during the San Lorenzo phase and more scarce in hinterland residential sites (O'Rourke 2002: 185, 220, 225). Instead, it is has been suggested that obsidian working took place within households at San Lorenzo, and that the cores for producing the prismatic blades were shattered to make the numerous flakes used for other cutting and scraping tasks (Cyphers 1996: 66).

In sum, the Early Formative Olmec economy of San Lorenzo was a diversified one in which elites strictly controlled the procurement, conversion, and distribution of some highly prized commodities that due to their bulk, local scarcity, and/or exotic origin were difficult to obtain. They may also have controlled the import of obsidian, but apparently not its conversion into finished implements. Other commodities such as utilitarian pottery and foodstuffs doubtless circulated more freely among the commoners, although here too, control over river transport may have afforded elites opportunities to exact a tax from producers.

MONUMENTAL ART, ICONOGRAPHY, AND POWER

Monumental stone sculpture is the hallmark of Olmec culture. To be sure, stone effigy bowls were produced beginning around 1650 B.C. in coastal Chiapas (Clark 1994a: 37, personal communication 2004) and small stone carvings of ca. 1200–1000 B.C. are known from San José Mogote in Oaxaca (Flannery and Marcus 1994: 369–371, Fig. 18.9; Marcus and Flannery 1996: 109–110, Fig. 114). However, no prior or contemporaneous culture in Mesoamerica matched the Olmecs for the number, size, or sophistication of their monumental carvings. Indeed, it is the distribution of characteristically Olmec sculpture that best distinguishes the Olmec "heartland" (Grove 1997: 53). Excluding some stones whose identification as "monuments" is questionable, over 200 monumental sculptures are known from Olman, and easily a third of them come from San Lorenzo and its environs.

Within this corpus of Olmec sculpture, several classes can be distinguished. The most distinctive and most massive are the colossal heads (Fig. 4.3). Measuring from 1.47 to 3.4 m tall and weighing from 6 to 50 tons (Cyphers 1995: 45), the massive heads are all fitted with close-fitting headdresses resembling old-time football players' helmets. Each is unique, with different insignia and adornments on the headdress, a variety of ear ornaments, specific facial features, and a range of expressions from stern or placid to gently smiling. Consequently, most scholars agree with Stirling (1955: 20) that the heads are portraits of prominent individuals, most likely Olmec chiefs (Grove 1981b: 61).

Also distinctive are the massive, flat-topped rectangular sculptures commonly known as table-top altars (Fig. 4.4). Like the colossal heads, they come in a range of sizes, from 4.6 to nearly 40 tons (Williams and Heizer 1965: Appendix 1; Coe 1968b: 59). Frequently, the altars depict a human emerging from a niche on the front of the monument, with other individuals carved in low relief on its sides. Sometimes the niche, usually interpreted as a cave, is depicted as the open maw of an earth- or sky-monster. Originally considered sacrificial altars, Grove (1973) argued convincingly that they served as thrones, based on the depiction of a personage seated on just such a monument in a cave painting at Oxtotitlán, Guerrero. Gillespie (1999), however, has made an equally convincing argument, based on the contexts of the altars, their iconography, and analogy with the Classic Maya, that the table-top monuments functioned simultaneously as thrones and ancestral altars. I will use the terms altar and throne interchangeably, depending on the particular function emphasized.

The Olmecs also carved a wide variety of smaller sculptures in the round, depicting humans, animals, and fantastic composites combining the features of different animal species with one another or with humans. These sculptures often appear to represent mythic and supernatural themes or humans in ritual or symbolic postures (Figs. 2.2, 4.5).

A fourth major class of monuments, which is thought to pertain mainly to the later centuries of Olmec history, are flat stelae carved in low relief and set upright in plazas or other significant locations. They are often carved with narrative scenes depicting elaborately dressed individuals engaged in specific acts and who are sometimes watched by dwarfish supernaturals floating about them (Fig. 5.11). Other, less common or less distinctive monument types

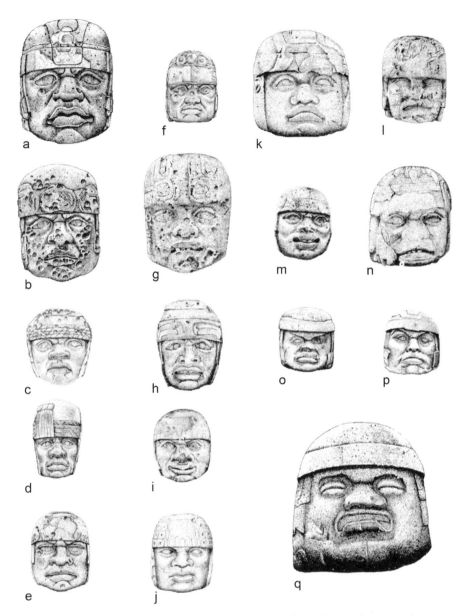

Figure 4.3. The seventeen colossal heads discovered in Olman drawn at the same scale: (**a-j**) San Lorenzo; (**k-n**) La Venta; (**o-p**) Tres Zapotes; (**q**) Cobata. Cobata head is 3.4 m tall (adapted and redrawn from *Arqueología Mexicana* Vol. 2, No. 12. (1995), insert, drawing by Magda Júarez, Ella Sánchez, and Concepción Reyes).

include circular altars, flat altars, columns, tubes, benches, basins, boxes, and sarcophagi.

Unfortunately, most Olmec sculptures lack good stratigraphic contexts that would establish a minimum age for the monuments, and many appear to have been reset long after they were carved. Attempts to order the monuments chronologically have therefore relied heavily on stylistic seriations, with variable

Figure 4.4. San Lorenzo Monument 14, a table-top altar-throne. Note mutilation, which almost completely effaces the relief figure on the side of the altar.

results (e.g., Clark and Pye 2000b; Clewlow 1974; Clewlow et al. 1967; Kubler 1962; Milbrath 1979). Nevertheless, the limited stratigraphic evidence, combined with the reasonable assumption that most of a site's monuments were carved during the period of its florescence, and cross-correlation of stylistic elements between sites, allows us to identify some general trends. Most notable of these is a greater tendency for earlier monuments to be carved in the round, and later ones to more frequently employ relief carving depicting narrative scenes (Coe 1989: 69). Several of these later narrative scenes at La Venta and Tres Zapotes appear to record the legitimizing acts of rulers as opposed to the "restful serenity" (de la Fuente 2000: 259) of earlier representations of rulers and references to mythic events. Pool (2000: 150) sees in this shift an increasing concern with historicity and propagandistic declarations culminating in the dated glyphic texts on epi-Olmec stelae at Tres Zapotes and La Mojarra.

Materials and Techniques

From the inception of their monument tradition, the Olmecs selected the hard, tough basalts of the Tuxtla mountains for the vast majority of sculptures. In this they stand in contrast to the Classic Maya, whose elaborate stelae and altars were generally carved from much softer limestone and volcanic tuffs. Local sandstone also was used for Early and Middle Formative Olmec monuments, but with much less frequency. Imported greenstones including gneiss, chlorite schist,

Figure 4.5. The twin El Azuzul monuments. Note the overhand-underhand grasp of the ceremonial bar and similar mutilation of the headdresses. Compare Fig. 2.2.

and serpentine were used for stelae and round altars, principally in the Middle Formative period, paralleling a great expansion in the use of jade and other greenstones for figurines, votive axes, celts, and other small, portable items.

The Olmecs' use of such a hard stone as basalt for their greatest monuments is all the more impressive when it is recalled that they possessed no metal tools with which to work it. Rather, they executed their carvings with stone hammers, picks, and abrasives that were little harder than the stone they were

working. The creation of an Olmec monument began with the selection of
a boulder or block of the correct general proportions for the finished item.
Excavations at the monument workshop site of Llano del Jícaro (Gillespie
1994, 2000) and basalt workshops at San Lorenzo (Cyphers 1997b: 180–184)
indicate that the monuments were roughed out by removing large chunks
and large and small flakes with direct percussion. Pecking the surface with
hammerstones refined the surfaces and sculpted the details of the carving. At
Llano del Jícaro, the hammerstones included rounded cobbles of the same
basalt as the monuments as well as some imported stones of a different material
(Gillespie 1994: 237). Abrasives found in association with monuments that were
in the process of being recycled at San Lorenzo suggest their use in grinding
and drilling fine details and finishing dressed surfaces (Cyphers 1997b: 181). In
general, the process of percussion flaking, pecking, and grinding parallels that
of contemporary makers of *manos* and *metates* in Chiapas (Hayden 1987). These
techniques were undoubtedly developed over many centuries in creating the
stone bowls and grinding implements found in the Archaic and Early Formative
periods throughout Mesoamerica. The Olmecs, though, were the first to apply
them to monumental carving on such a massive scale.

The Olmecs applied their basic repertoire of carving techniques to various
methods of representation, including three-dimensional carving in the round,
high-relief carving, low-relief carving, and engraving (Clewlow 1974; Milbrath
1979). These methods were often combined on a single monument. Details
of costume and features in full-round and relief sculptures are often shown by
incision. Combinations of high and low relief are especially common on large
table-top altar-thrones such as San Lorenzo Monument 14 (Fig. 4.4). These
monuments depict figures seated in a niche on the front of the altar in high
relief and figures on the sides of the altar in low relief. A particularly notable
example of full-round and low-relief carving is seen in San Lorenzo Monument
107 (Cyphers 1997d: 210–212, Fig. 8.10), in which a three-dimensional feline
supports a descending human figure carved in low relief. Furthermore, relief
carving on all the visible surfaces of a monument was sometimes employed
to create a three-dimensional effect, as on La Venta Monument 6, a stone
sarcophagus of the Middle Formative period carved as the crocodilian "earth-
monster," which, floating in the cosmic sea, forms the surface of the earth
(Fig. 5.9). Likewise, the colossal heads, formed from rounded boulders selected
to mimic the form of actual human heads, can be seen as all-around relief
sculptures, with the relief higher in the face than on the helmets and ear
ornaments (Tate 1995: 51). These and other monuments demonstrate that
the Olmecs employed the full range of representational methods from the
Early Formative period onward. As Clewlow (1974: 141) cogently observed
with respect to late Middle Formative relief-carved stelae at La Venta, "The
important point here . . . is that an old form was given a new task [recording
events] and not that the form itself was invented at this time."

Formal Qualities

More than the techniques of execution and representation, it is the formal qualities of Olmec art, together with the subjects and themes they embody, that define the Olmec style (Coe 1965c; de la Fuente 1981). Olmec sculptures project a monumentality that is rare in other Mesoamerican art styles. Even small figurines have a solidity and an appearance of firmly rooted mass that belies their size (Coe 1965c: 749). Of course, great physical weight is a real quality of multi-ton stone heads and thrones, but it also is enhanced in these massive sculptures and created in smaller objects by certain qualities of line and form. For example, the Olmecs often emphasized volume over flatness through true full-round sculpture as well as relief carving on the front and sides of sculptures so as to present multiple perspectives of the same subject. Another technique used to great effect is the use of swelling volumes and rounded forms to represent bodily forms of shoulders, torsos, and limbs. A contemporary parallel can be seen among automobile manufacturers in the United States, who apply similar methods to the contours of their sport-utility vehicles to convey an impression of solidity and power. In the Olmec case, rounded surfaces also serve to disguise and moderate the harshness of constituent geometric forms – cubes, rectangular prisms, and truncated pyramids – which impart an underlying sense of order to the sculptures (de la Fuente 1981: 87; 1994: 212). In relief sculptures and engravings the rounded contours are translated as curved lines, which define figures separated by broad, uncluttered zones of open space. As Coe (1965c: 748) observes, the slow rhythm of the lines and the tension between forms created by the open space separating them give three-dimensional depth and monumentality to the low reliefs. Motion is not emphasized in most Olmec sculpture. Rather, human figures, especially, tend to be posed serenely in sitting, kneeling, or standing positions. Nevertheless, motion is intimated by asymmetrical compositions, as in the magnificent Arroyo Sonso "wrestler," or the figure on the front of La Venta Altar 4 (Fig. 5.10).

Order, stability, and equilibrium also are expressed through the use of harmonic proportions in the composition of colossal heads and other early Olmec masterpieces (de la Fuente 1981: 87–88). Indeed, Beatríz de la Fuente has argued that harmonic proportion constitutes the essence of Olmec carving, and is the principal quality that gives it its vitality and strength. In her view, sculptures are less Olmec to the degree that they diverge from the idealized "golden mean" of Classical sculpture.

As many authors have noted, the preference for curved forms, simplicity, and individuality over rigid geometry, baroque detail, and conventional abstraction creates a general impression of naturalism, even in depictions of biologically impossible creatures (e.g., Coe 1965c: 748; de la Fuente 1981; 1994; Pasztory 2000). Nevertheless, Olmec artists did not attempt to recreate the natural world in slavishly realistic depictions. Rather, they subtly combined varying degrees of naturalism and abstraction in their works, idealizing forms and proportions in human and animal representations (de la Fuente 1981: 85–86; Tate 1995: 54). The use of harmonic proportions in the composition of figures is but one example of such idealization. Other examples include more abstract depiction of torsos, limbs, and extremities in human and animal sculptures and the afore-mentioned combination of full-round or high-relief carving with low relief. In fact, it is precisely the greater geometrical abstraction of forms and the flatter depiction in low relief and engraving that tends to distinguish supernatural and ideational representations from those drawn from the natural world (Tate 1995: 55). As noted above, these different realms are often thrown into sharp contrast by their juxtaposition on the same work of art, as in the monster mask carved on the upper register of La Venta Altar 4 above the naturalistic depiction of the human emerging from the cave-like niche (Fig. 5.10).

The most extreme examples of abstraction in Olmec art occur in the use of conventionalized symbols, such as the St. Andrew's cross, the "bar-and-four dots" motif, the "hand-paw-wing" motif, or the "flame eyebrow" (Fig. 4.6). Often combined on Olmec monuments in depictions of composite creatures or as elements in the headdresses and accoutrements of personages, these and other iconographic symbols also may appear individually or in novel combinations. Such *pars pro toto* ("part for the whole") representation appears frequently on Early Formative ceramics and Middle Formative jades in Olman and beyond. Indeed, it is the wide distribution of artifacts bearing such elements that has long fueled the debate over the nature of interaction between the Olmecs and their contemporaries (see Chapter 6).

Content: Subjects and Themes

Olmec artists sculpted images of humans, animals, and weird, biologically impossible composite beings that combine attributes of different species, including humans. Traditionally, it is the last group that has attracted the greatest attention, especially the snarling (or crying) were-jaguar infants, which unite anthropomorphic torsos, limbs, and eyes with snarling, down-turned mouths and cleft heads perceived as feline traits. At one time were-jaguar imagery was thought to pervade Olmec art, to the extent that it was identified as the hallmark of the style (Coe 1965c: 751). As Beatriz de la Fuente (e.g., 1977; 1981; 1996) has repeatedly observed, however, it is the human image that comprises the majority of Olmec sculptural representations, notwithstanding the frequent juxtaposition of humans with composite beings or animals. In the images themselves and through their contextual arrangements, the Olmecs expressed a variety of intertwined themes concerning the spiritual and social relations of the Olmecs to the forces of the cosmos, to their ancestors, and to one another. Especially prominent among these themes are the mythic origins of the cosmos and the Olmecs, their relation to supernatural beings and forces, and the legitimate sources of ruling authority.

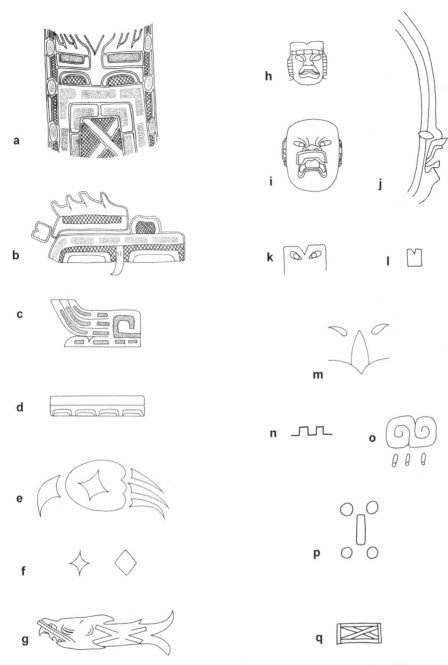

Figure 4.6. "Olmec-style" iconographic motifs of the Early (**a-g**) and Middle Formative (**h-q**) periods: (**a-b**) frontal and side views of the "earth-monster"; (**c**) hand-paw-wing; (**d**) gum bracket (compare with b); (**e**) avian talon; (**f**) diamonds; (**g**) shark with crossed bands; (**h** and **i**) were-jaguar; (**j**) profile were-jaguar; (**k-m**) cleft motifs, m has sprouting vegetation (note also cleft motifs in a, b, and h); (**n**) double merlon; (**o**) "Lazy S" or double scroll (*ilhuitl*) with raindrops; (**p**) bar-and-four-dots; (**q**) crossed bars ("St. Andrew's Cross") (adapted from Guthrie and Benson 1995: 120–122 *The Olmec World.* © 1996 by Princeton University Press. Reprinted by permission of Princeton University Press).

One intriguing set of sculptures, Potrero Nuevo Monument 3, Tenochtitlán Monument 1, and Laguna de los Cerros Monument 20, has been interpreted as depicting a central myth of Olmec descent from the sexual union of a jaguar and a human female (Stirling 1955: 19–20; Coe 1989: 71) (Fig. 4.7). Stirling presented this hypothesis as an explanation for the were-jaguar baby figures, which he perceived as the central theme in Olmec art. Although Coe (1989: 71) supports Stirling's interpreation, others have questioned the nature of the act represented in these "copulation figures" (Clewlow 1974: 84–85) and the identification of the individuals themselves (Cyphers 1997d: 216; de la Fuente 1981: 90). All three sculptures are badly mutilated, but it is evident that the upper figures on Tenochtitlán Monument 1 and Laguna de los Cerros Monument 20 are human, although the identification of the lower figure in Tenochtitlán Monument 1 as female is ambiguous at best (Clewlow 1974: 85; de la Fuente 1981: 90). Taube (1995: 100), identifies the upper figure on Tenochtitlán Monument 1 as a costumed ball player, and suggests that the sculpture represents sacrifice associated with the ballgame.

Potrero Nuevo Monument 3 (renamed Loma del Zapote Monument 3 by Cyphers [1997d: 215]) is particularly problematic as a jaguar-human copulation figure (Fig. 4.7). Although the rear paws of the upper figure are clearly feline, the identification of the lower figure as human is questionable. The lower figure, whose head is missing, has its legs flexed and upper limbs flexed and raised in an apparently defensive posture. A tail wraps around the rear of the statue, but its position does not appear to correspond anatomically to the jaguar figure. Between the hind legs of the jaguar one can see two human-like "hands" with elongated thumbs. Cyphers (1997d: 216) identifies the "hands" as those of a simian, and suggests that three individuals may be represented. The "hands," however, are correctly positioned to be the prehensile feet of the lower creature, to which the tail also would appear to belong. Therefore, de la Fuente (1981: 90) appears to be correct in identifying only two figures, an upper jaguar and a lower monkey, though why the monkey should be female is unclear.

Thus, although these three sculptures appear to share a theme of domination, their sexual content is suspect, and two of the three do not clearly refer to the participation of a jaguar. Medellín (1960) and Clewlow (1974: 85) may therefore be correct that the Tenochtitlán and Laguna de los Cerros monuments show a warrior subjugating his captive. The Potrero Nuevo monument may indeed refer to a myth of creation, but not necessarily that imagined by Stirling. Mesoamerican creation myths frequently tell of previous cycles of creation and destruction. In the Aztec myth of the Five Suns, the giants who populated the first sun, or creation, were devoured by jaguars, and the people of the second sun became monkeys when they were destroyed by great winds (Miller and Taube 1993: 70). Likewise, the *Popol Vuh* of the Quiché Maya tells of a second creation in which men formed from wood and women from rushes became

Figure 4.7. Two views of a so-called copulation figure, Potrero Nuevo Monument 3. The rear paws of the jaguar figure straddle a supine monkey, as evidenced by the latter's hand-like feet and the position of its tail.

monkeys when they were destroyed by a great flood and rain of pitch (Miller and Taube 1993: 68). It may be, then, that Potrero Nuevo Monument 3 refers to an Olmec version of an earlier destruction, in which a former people are destroyed by jaguars and become monkeys in the process.

A more common motif in Olmec sculpture is that of a human seated cross-legged and holding in his or her hands the floppy, inert, presumably dead figure of a were-jaguar baby. A particularly fine example is that of the greenstone Las Limas figure, which was probably carved in the Middle Formative period (Fig. 2.7). The image also frequently appears seated in a niche in the front of table-top altars at San Lorenzo (Monument 20), and La Venta (Altars 2 and 5), generally thought to be of Early Formative vintage. On the sides of La Venta Altar 5, pudgy were-jaguar babies struggle in the hands of human figures whose elaborate headdresses mark their high status. The contrast between the lively infants and the inert form in the central figure's hands has suggested sacrifice to some scholars. Closely related are the images on San Lorenzo Monument 14, La Venta Altars 3 and 4, and Laguna de los Cerros Monument 5 of cross-legged figures seated in niches with one hand holding a foot and the other to the side (Fig. 4.4). On La Venta Altar 4 the central figure clearly grasps a rope that wraps around the wrist of a figure on the side (Fig. 5.10). Vegetation adorns the edges of the niche, and the upper ledge of the altar bears the highly stylized image of a sky-monster (Taube 1995: 92; cf. Grove 2000: 289), whose upper jaw is directly above the niche, suggesting the niche is the mouth of the monster itself. This monument in particular suggests that the niche is intended as a mountain "cave-in-the-sky," and that particular interpretation is reinforced by later images such as the figure seated in the mouth of a serpent in a relief carved on a hill above Chalcatzingo, Morelos. There, the central figure sits at the threshhold of and appears to emerge from a portal to the underworld. Whether the scene of the human holding the infant in the cave refers to a myth of human origins, the ritual act and spiritual journey of a ruler – or both – is not clear, however.

The were-jaguar and earth-monster are two common examples of composite supernaturals. The were-jaguar (also identified as the "composite anthropo-morph" [Pohorilenko 1996] or "God IV" [Joralemon 1971, 1976]) is distin-guished by its usually toothless, down-turned mouth with everted, bow-shaped upper lip, broad nose, slanted eyes, and a headdress with a knobbed frontal band and wavy side ornaments covering the ears (Joralemon 1971: 71; Coe 1989: 75) (Figs. 2.1, 4.6). Like many other Olmec supernaturals, it sports a deep cleft in its head. Often shown as an infant with an anthropomorphic body carried in the arms of adult humans, as in the niche figures on altars, it also appears seated with knees drawn up to its chest in San Lorenzo Monument 52. It is a common theme on carved greenstone votive axes, mainly from the Middle Formative period but also including the Early Formative votive axe from La Merced (Rodríguez and Ortiz 2000).

The highly abstracted earth-monster or "Olmec Dragon" (Joralemon 1976) also has a cleft head, as well as serrated "flame eyebrows" (Fig. 4.6). When viewed from the front, its eyes are usually trough-shaped, and its mouth is represented by a rectangular bracket, often containing crossed bands. From the side, its eyes are L-shaped, and its upper jaw contains down-turned gum brackets and a projecting fang. The body, when shown, is usually that of a crocodilian, and its limbs are often depicted as the hand-paw-wing, a motif that combines human, saurian, and avian characteristics (Guthrie and Benson 1995: 120). Much discussion has surrounded the specific species abstracted and combined in the earth-monster image. Originally it was identified as a supernatural jaguar, but current opinion favors the caiman or crocodile and the harpy eagle as the dominant referents, with the feathered crest of the latter represented by the serrated brows (Joralemon 1996; Coe 1989; cf. Taube 1995).

Both the were-jaguar and the Olmec Dragon appear on the Las Limas figure, the former held in the main figure's arms, and the latter engraved in profile on its right knee (Fig. 2.7). Also engraved on the body of the main figure are the profile heads of an anthropomorphic shark or "fish monster" (left knee), an avian monster with jaguar and reptilian characteristics (left shoulder), and an enigmatic creature with a curvilinear band through its eye (right shoulder), all sporting cleft heads. In his influential studies of the iconography on the Las Limas figure and other Olmec-style sculpture from various parts of Mesoamerica, Joralemon (1971; 1976; 1996) identifies these composite beings as deities, in some cases ancestral to later Mesoamerican gods. Thus the Olmec Dragon is God I, associated with "earth, maize, agricultural fertility, clouds, rain, water, fire, and kingship" (Joralemon 1976: 58), and possibly ancestral to the reptilian high god of the Maya, Itzam-Na. The were-jaguar is God IV, the god of rain and storms, and is closely related to God II, the maize god (Joralemon 1976; 1996: 56). Like Covarrubias (1946) before him, Joralemon sees the were-jaguar as ancestral to later rain gods such as the Aztec Tlaloc and the Maya Chacs. The anthropomorphic shark is God VIII, lord of the sea and the watery underworld (Joralemon 1996: 55), and the avian monster is God III, lord of the sun and the sky associated with rulership. Although the specific associations of these beings can be debated, as can be their status as gods rather than spirits or aspects of a pervasive vital force (e.g., Marcus 1989), their identification as supernatural entities is beyond doubt. Moreover, it is clear from their depiction on thrones and their archaeological contexts that images of supernaturals were invoked to legitimize the authority of Olmec rulers from the Early Formative period onwards.

It was through the human form, however, that the Olmecs most clearly expressed the pervasive theme of rulership. During the Early Formative period, colossal heads and thrones most forcefully communicated ruling authority. The very carving and transport of these massive monuments bespoke the power of the ruler as surely as did the images themselves. Sixteen of the 17 known colossal heads come from three major Olmec centers: 10 from San Lorenzo, four from La Venta, and two from Tres Zapotes. The seventeenth is the enormous, crude, and probably unfinished Cobata head found atop a mountain ridge overlooking Tres Zapotes (Hammond 2001) (Fig. 4.3p). The strong association with San Lorenzo suggests they are principally an Early Formative sculptural type, and some authors have argued they were all produced in a timespan of perhaps 200 years (Clewlow 1974; Clewlow et al. 1967; Lowe 1989: 45; cf. de la Fuente 1977: 294, 296; Hammond 1989: 3). The lack of a large Early Formative occupation at Tres Zapotes, however, suggests that its heads were carved early in the Middle Formative period (Pool and Ohnersorgen 2003). The individualism of the heads and the specificity of their headdress regalia strongly suggest that they were intended as portraits of Olmec rulers, either then living or recently deceased (de la Fuente 1977; 1981: 93; 1996: 48). With time, they also would have become the permanent record of the ancestors of the highest ranking groups in the society. As de la Fuente (1981: 93–94; 1996: 48–49) has repeatedly emphasized, however, in their idealized proportions they represent not just illustrious individuals but also the concept of aristocracy itself.

Likewise, the figures in the niches of altar-thrones are most likely shamanic rulers, poised at the entrance to the underworld, surrounded by legitimizing supernaturals, and flanked by their subjects, conquered foes, or lineal relatives (Gillespie 1999; Grove 1981b; Reilly 1995). The central figure may be the reigning chief himself or his ancestor. In fact, James Porter (1990) has demonstrated a direct physical relationship between the thrones and the colossal heads; two of the heads at San Lorenzo bear the traces of the niches of altars from which they were recarved.

More common than heads or thrones are free standing full-round sculptures of humans, most of which are believed to date to the Early Formative period. Included among them are some of the greatest masterpieces of Olmec art, such as the twin figures of El Azuzul (Fig. 4.5). Most assume conventionalized poses, either cross-legged or half-kneeling and leaning forward, and some hold an infant in their arms. Sometimes called "priests" or "mediators" (de la Fuente 1981: 93, 1996: 46–47), in part due to their serene expressions, the headdresses on some of these figures bespeak an elite status, and the similar positions of the cross-legged figures to those on the altar-thrones suggests that they too may be related to the theme of ruling authority. Such an identification would not deny their religious connotations, and some do indeed appear to be engaged in ritual acts. For example, the San Martín Pajapan monument grasps a horizontal ceremonial bar with one hand above and one below, as if it were about to set the bar upright (Schele 1995: 108). Reilly (1991) identifies the bar as the tree that marks the central *axis mundi*. The figure also wears a headdress containing a mask of the were-jaguar supernatural, which is remarkably similar to that on the decapitated head of La Venta Monument 44 (de la Fuente 1973: 96–98; Schele 1995: 108). De la Fuente (1981: 93; 1996: 46–47) refers to these

Figure 4.8. San Lorenzo Monument 10. This human with feline features and cleft head holds cut conch shell "knuckle dusters" in its hands.

sculptures as "lords under supernatural protection," and indeed they may be images of rulers, shamans, or both engaged in the very act that establishes and defines the center of the world at the intersection of its four quarters.

Images of humans merge with those of animals and supernaturals in figures such as San Lorenzo Monuments 10 and 52, in which a were-jaguar head is attached to an anthropomorphic body (Fig. 4.8). Furthermore, sculptures clearly intended to represent felines often incorporate human characteristics in their postures and proportions, as in the swaggering stance of Monument 77 of San Lorenzo. Such figures may relate to the concept of shamanic transformation more commonly represented in portable jade figures of the Middle Formative period (Furst 1968, 1995). Drawing ethnographic analogies from South American tribes, Furst argued that these small figures, and the were-jaguar motif in general, represented a belief in the ability of shamans to transform themselves into jaguars, and conversely the idea that jaguars are really transformed human shamans. Reilly (1995) further elaborated on shamanic transformation as a legitimizing characteristic of Olmec rulership. Taken as a whole, sculptures such as the were-jaguar–masked figure of San Martín Pajapan, the were-jaguar–headed figure of San Lorenzo Monument 10, and the humanized jaguar of San Lorenzo Monument 77 reinforce the notion that shamanic transformation figured prominently in the ideological justification of ruling authority among the Early Formative Olmecs.

Monument Mutilation

An intriguing aspect of Olmec art is the frequency with which sculptures were mutilated in antiquity. Many human and animal sculptures were decapitated and dismembered. Great chunks were broken off altars, their low reliefs were effaced and rectangular gouges were carved into their surfaces. Most colossal heads are marred by circular pits or v-shaped gouges. Traditionally, these mutilations were viewed as the violent acts of an invading force or rebelling subjects, and some scholars (e.g. Clark 1997: 200; Coe and Koontz 2002: 77) continue to hold to this or related views.

David Grove (1981b) countered the hypothesis of large-scale revolt by observing that the mutilation and burial of monuments appears to have been recurring events carried out over several centuries. In its place he offered three alternative explanations: (1) mutilation was periodic and tied to ritual cycles, (2) mutilation occurred with a change of rulers or ruling dynasties at a site, and (3) mutilation occurred with the death of a ruler. Grove favored the third explanation, which is aligned to the idea that shamanism was a component of Olmec belief. In Grove's view, the mutilation and burial of monuments served to neutralize the supernatural powers controlled by the deceased ruler during his lifetime. Such a practice would parallel the customs of many tropical forest cultures in South America, which, upon the death of a shaman, destroy the possessions in which his power is thought to reside. Among groups such as the Canelos Quichua of lowland Ecuador such "power objects" include wooden stools that constitute literal and figurative "seats of power" and stone objects, which, obtained from the earth, hold connections with the underworld. In life the shaman controls the power embodied in these objects, but upon his death the power becomes uncontrolled and must be neutralized to prevent harm to the living. Thus Grove (1981b: 63–65) draws an analogy between the destruction of wooden stools and the burial of stone objects among these present-day societies and the mutilation and burial of stone thrones and other monuments by the ancient Olmec.

The principal weakness of Grove's argument is that it does not explain why some objects of power, including ruler portraits and thrones, were spared. John Clark (1997: 220–222) offers an explanation that accommodates both muti-lated and unmutilated monuments, and that expands upon Grove's suggestion that mutilation might have occurred with a change in rulership by relating monument mutilation to competition among political factions. Clark agrees with Grove that mutilation was carried out to neutralize the power of objects, but argues that the mutilation was aimed at erasing the claim to legitimacy of specific deposed rulers. Monuments associated with past rulers from whom succession was uncontested would escape mutilation. The temporal pattern (or lack thereof) in monument mutilation identified by Grove would there-fore result from recurring competition for rulership (Clark 1997: 222).

The San Lorenzo Olmecs not only mutilated, but in some instances resculp-ted, monuments into new forms (Porter 1990). Two of the colossal heads from San Lorenzo (numbers 2 and 7) bear the traces of the niches that typically grace the fronts of altar-thrones. The flattened posterior surfaces of these heads would have represented the flat bases of the thrones from which they were carved. Flattened backs occur on all but four of the other fifteen colossal heads known from the Olmec heartland; these too may have been carved from thrones (Porter 1990: 92), though the flat back also would have facilitated the transport of completed heads (Clark 2004, personal communication). In addition, some of the mutilated altar-thrones from San Lorenzo and La Venta may represent intermediate stages in the process of resculpting (Porter 1990: 94–96). Other evidence for recarving of Olmec monuments include vestiges of earlier surfaces on two large jaguar figures from El Azuzul to the south of San Lorenzo, and the previously described "monument recycling workshop" in Group D of San Lorenzo itself (Cyphers 1999: 166–168; 172).

Early Olmec Monuments in Social Context and Practice

These cases of monument mutilation and recarving remind us that the mean-ings given to art objects derive not only from their intrinsic characteristics of form, content, and material, but also from what people do to and with them. Olmec monuments had particularly dynamic histories in this regard. The ini-tial transformative act of carving, the re-transformation of monuments into new monuments, the mutilation or destruction of monuments, and the social contexts in which these acts were performed served to emphasize, expand, and modify the meanings expressed in material, form, and iconography. Simi-larly, the physical placement of monuments with respect to other monuments, to architectural spaces and edifices, and to natural features on the landscape involved the sculptures in a broader network of meaningful associations and contrasts (Cyphers 1997b, 1997e, 1999; Grove 1999).

The most extraordinary demonstration of this point was discovered at El Azuzul (León and Sánchez 1991–92). The Azuzul "acropolis" (Cyphers 1996: 68) is a culturally modified hill at the southern point of the Loma del Zapote ridge, which runs southward from San Lorenzo. The hill and the monuments on it would have been visible from the then-active Azuzul branch of the Coatzacoalcos River. On a paved surface about midway up the hillside, three sculptures had been arranged together in a profoundly evocative scene (Fig. 4.5). Though the statues had fallen over, their original settings are easily reconstructed. Two exquisitely carved life-size human figures, one behind the other, sit before the more crudely but powerfully carved figure of a feline seated on its haunches. A second, larger feline was set a few meters up the slope. Like the San Martín Pajapan monument, the nearly identical human figures each grasp a horizontal bar with the right hand underneath and the left hand on top, as if poised to set it upright as the *axis mundi* (see Schele 1995: 108). As a whole, the juxtaposition of the El Azuzul sculptures amplifies their individual meanings, evoking associations between twins and jaguars, as well as between jaguars and human authority, known from later Mesoamerican cultures (Cyphers 1999: 172).

A larger grouping of monuments within Group E, on the west side of San Lorenzo, further extends the associations expressed at El Azuzul. This area contains an aqueduct of U-shaped trough stones laid end-to-end that extends 171 m toward the edge of the San Lorenzo plateau. Clustered around the aqueduct and fallen into the adjoining ravines were found eight monuments, including a font in the shape of a duck (Monument 9), an anthropomorphized feline statue whose head is replaced with a trough (Monument 77), and a seated were-jaguar figure (Joralemon's God IV) with the back hollowed out in trough-like fashion. Monument 14, the largest altar-throne at San Lorenzo (Fig. 4.4), and Monument 61, a colossal head, were discovered about 60 to 70 m east and northeast of the aqueduct, which may have extended another 18 m to the east. In Group E, then, monumental references to rulers (the throne and head) are linked in their settings to the control of water and to felines, again amplifying the specific referents carved on the monuments themselves (Cyphers 1999: 164).

Broader distributions of altars and colossal heads at San Lorenzo suggest the existence of a grand sculptural macro-display (Cyphers 1997e: 234; Grove 1999: 276). Though many of the ten colossal heads from San Lorenzo were recovered from ravines, and so were undoubtedly displaced from their original location, they lie approximately along two parallel lines crossing the central part of the plateau from north to south (Cyphers 1997e: 234) (Fig. 4.2). Altars of rectangular and round varieties also lie near and help define these lines (Grove 1999: Fig. 12). Thus the locations of colossal heads and altars circumscribed and defined the very center of governance and sacred ritual in the San Lorenzo polity. Grove (1999: 277, 280) notes that their wide spacing would have prevented observers from seeing any one head at a time, suggesting they were intended to be viewed in a procession, moving from the portrait of one ancestral ruler to another. Such a processional arrangement also appears later at La Venta in the distribution of monuments in its more public southern sector and at the highland site of Chalcatzingo in its Olmec-style rock carvings.

Beyond San Lorenzo and the other major Olmec centers, stone monuments also communicated the political rank of subordinate sites and the sacredness of particular points on the landscape. The San Martín Pajapan monument best illustrates the latter point, although it may be of Middle Formative vintage (Blom and LaFarge 1929: 45–47; Diehl and Coe 1995: 19–20, Fig. 15) (Fig. 2.2). Placed at the summit of an isolated volcano in the eastern Tuxtla Mountains, the human figure, half-crouched and leaning forward, grasps a carved bar in an attitude similar to that of the El Azuzul twins. Its elaborate headdress bears the mask of a supernatural with cleft head, almond-shaped eyes, and snarling mouth. A mass of plumes cleft into four parts flows behind the mask, and vegetation sprouts from an element above the plumes shaped like a table-top altar, the overhanging ends of which are cleft in four parts like the plumes. The referents of this headdress appear to relate to maize and to rain, reflecting widespread Mesoamerican beliefs that place the abodes of rain gods amid clouded mountaintops (Diehl and Coe 1995: 19; Taube 2000: 305). Directing attention to the bar grasped with one hand below and the other above, Schele (1995: 108) suggested the image was poised to raise this representation of the "world tree," or *axis mundi*, at the center of creation atop this most sacred mountaintop in the Olmec landscape.

David Grove (1999: 282–284) has highlighted thematic differences between carvings in the major Olmec centers and their hinterlands. These differences, in large part, reflect the position of sites in the regional political hierarchy. With the exception of the possibly unfinished Cobata head, all colossal heads currently known are from the Olmec centers of San Lorenzo, La Venta, and Tres Zapotes. Likewise, table-top altar-thrones are scarce outside major centers (a large, recently discovered altar from El Marquesillo and the small Potrero Nuevo altar are notable exceptions). Monuments at outlying sites are fewer in number and tend to be restricted to less massive human, animal, and composite figures. Many are feline images, sometimes in aggressive postures. To Grove this suggests a thematic contrast with the San Lorenzo center, reflecting widespread Mesoamerican associations of the periphery with danger, the supernatural, and the mythological past.

To summarize, the messages of Early Formative (as well as later) Olmec art were complex, polyvalent, and dynamic. Iconographic elements drawn from myth, the natural world, and human society were combined to communicate and reaffirm the position of the Olmec people with respect to the cosmos, the past, and one another. Those meanings were elaborated and subtly altered by arranging monuments within sites and on the broader landscape, by the rituals and offerings performed before the monuments, by the transformation of old monuments into new ones, and by the mutilation of these powerful symbols. In secular terms, the monuments conveyed the authority and power of Olmec rulers. In some cases the message of authority was explicit, as in the individualized colossal head portraits of the rulers and the massive thrones on which they sat. Images on the thrones of rulers seated in openings to the underworld, often surrounded by supernatural beings and fertility symbols and, occasionally, by earthly captives or ancestors, conveyed the religious and secular sources of their power. Implicitly, the ability of rulers to commission the difficult carving of these symbols, to transport them from distant locations, and to bestow them on subordinate leaders likewise reinforced their earthly power.

EARLY FORMATIVE SETTLEMENT AND POLITICAL ORGANIZATION

Clearly, the iconography and contexts of monuments bespeak the hierarchical organization of Early Formative Olmec society. Patterns of human settlement across the landscape also provide important clues to the political and economic organization of ancient societies. The locations of sites relative to one another and to landscape features respond to considerations of resource exploitation, transportation, and integration into a broader system of economic and political interaction. Further, variations in the sizes of sites and the extent and kinds of constructions on them may indicate their positions in a hierarchy of administrative centers and rural settlements.

Though Drucker and Contreras (1953) and Sisson (1970) conducted pioneering surveys in southern Veracruz and Tabasco, detailed information on settlement patterns within and beyond the hinterlands of Olmec centers has only recently begun to be revealed by systematic archaeological surveys. Archaeologists face significant challenges to survey in the humid tropical lowlands of the Gulf Coast. Dense vegetation and swamp often obscure artifacts on the ground surface, and even whole mounds may be lost in the tangled secondary growth of the *monte*. Meandering rivers wash away many sites and cover others with deep alluvium. The continuing expansion of agricultural fields is a mixed blessing; clearing opens new areas to investigation and plowing turns up buried artifacts, but the same plowing destroys low mounds. Archaeologists must therefore attune their survey methods and interpretations to local conditions, and many elements of ancient settlement systems have undoubtedly been lost. Differences in survey methods, the extent and intensity of coverage, field conditions, and settlement classifications complicate comparison of their results, but the recent surveys clearly indicate that Early Formative Olmec political and economic organization varied significantly across Olman (Fig. 4.9).

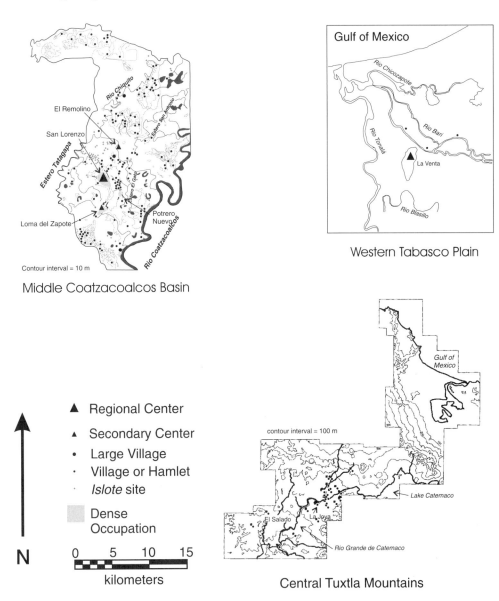

Figure 4.9. Late Early Formative settlement patterns in three regions of Olman (adapted from Rust and Sharer 1988: Fig. 1; Santley et al. 1997: Fig. 7.3; Symonds et al. 2002: Fig. 4.6).

The San Lorenzo Hinterland

Survey of some 400 sq km in the Coatzacoalcos river basin has documented population growth over the Initial and Early Formative periods (Symonds et al. 2002; see also Lunagómez 1995; Symonds 1995, 2000: 64; Symonds and Lunagómez 1997a, 1997b). One hundred five sites have been identified with occupation dating to the Ojochi and Bajío phases (ca. 1750–1450 B.C.). More than three-quarters of these Initial Formative sites are clustered within the 90 sq km "inner hinterland" surrounding San Lorenzo, which as a medium-sized village of about 20 ha was already the largest site in the survey area. About half of these early sites are low mounds (*islotes*) on the floodplains northwest of San Lorenzo. They and another 22 small hamlets situated on stream banks and on the edges of the higher ground may have been seasonally occupied to exploit crustaceans, fish, and other resources in these humid bottomlands, and to plant crops as the floodwaters receded. Other more permanently occupied sites were situated on higher ground safe from floods and, it has been suggested, from human attack (Symonds et al. 2002: 56).

As San Lorenzo grew between 1400 and 1000 B.C., so did the regional population. Survey recorded 226 sites occupied in this timespan, and the sites tend to be much larger than in previous periods. Indeed, the total area of permanent settlement is estimated to have increased tenfold, from 165 to 1627 ha (Symonds et al. 2002: Fig. 4.4) (Fig. 4.9). This density of settlement represents a peak in human occupation that would not be surpassed for nearly two millenia, until the Late Classic and Postclassic periods. As before, many *islotes* and small hamlets were placed within and adjacent to the seasonally inundated floodplains. The remaining sites tended to cling to the higher ground of remnant terraces and salt domes and the banks of then-active river courses. Differences in the size of the sites and the number and kind of artifical constructions within them define eight site types, which may be ordered into at least three levels in a regional settlement hierarchy (that is, at least two tiers of administration above the village level) (Symonds et al. 2002:39–46, 126). At the top of the hierarchy was the regional center of San Lorenzo itself, which may have sprawled across as much as 500 ha on the plateau and the terraces below. Secondary centers containing three or more levels of terraces and covering more than 30 ha included El Remolino and Loma del Zapote to the north and south of San Lorenzo, respectively. Potrero Nuevo to the east also may have served as a secondary center, if size and number of monuments are accurate indications of site rank.[3] Large villages, covering up to 25 ha, possibly represent a third level of the administrative hierarchy, though they are not regularly distributed with respect to higher order centers, as might be expected. Rather, they tend to have been placed at key transportation points where overland and riverine routes meet. At the bottom of the settlement hierarchy were numerous medium to large hamlets and small- to medium-sized villages. Linear distributions of sites along the levees of river courses reflect the advantages of these locations for agriculture and collection of fish and shellfish from the rivers and backswamps on either side. The distributions of these sites also indicate that settlement responded strongly to the transportation network formed by the rivers, with lower order sites concentrated along active stream courses and higher order sites located on high ground or at important nodes in the river system (Symonds 2000: 65).

Survey in adjacent areas of the Coatzacoalcos basin likewise indicate a strong riverine orientation to Early Formative settlement. In a 36 sq km survey to the east of the Coatzacoalcos River, it was found that rural settlement contemporaneous with the apogee of San Lorenzo eschewed higher ground for the levees of a now-abandoned river channel (Kruger 1996: 102). In the Coatzacoalcos basin west of Symonds and Lunagómez's survey area, survey in three 25 sq km blocks documents a strong preference for settlement at the interface of floodplain and upland zones, expanding into more upland areas only toward the end of the florescent San Lorenzo phase (ca. 1200–1000 B.C.) (Borstein 2001: 151, 158, 176). The important site of Estero Rabón had already achieved a prominent position before the beginning of the San Lorenzo phase at 1400 B.C., covering some 60–80 ha, and quite possibly rivaling the emerging center at San Lorenzo. During the early half of the San Lorenzo phase it continued to grow, but it failed to keep pace with its eastern competitor and apparently became a secondary center in the San Lorenzo polity, meriting a small table-top altar similar to that from Potrero Nuevo (Borstein 2001: 151, 158–162). Like other centers in the San Lorenzo hinterland, Estero Rabón lies at a node in the local transportation network, in this case a restriction in the El Juile River as it flows through a narrow pass (Borstein 2001: 160).

La Venta and the Western Tabasco Plain

On the far eastern margin of Olman, the Pajonal channel and adjacent distributaries of the Grijalva delta were a focus of occupation in the Early Formative period Palacios phase (von Nagy 2003: 1019–1024, 1080). This zone may have seen the first steps toward political complexity in far eastern Olman (von Nagy 2003: 1080), including the emergence of a two-tiered settlement hierarchy focused on the local center of Zapata (von Nagy 1997: 267).

In the La Venta area, in what is today the estuarine setting of the lower Tonalá/Mezcalapa basin, small settlements spread northward as a prograding delta changed the swampy environment from brackish to freshwater conditions (Jiménez 1990; Pope et al. 2001; Rust and Leyden 1994; von Nagy et al. 2002) (Fig. 4.9). These Initial and Early Formative settlements are best known from excavations at San Andrés, Isla Alor, and other sites on the banks of the ancient channel known today as the Río Barí or Río Palma. Like their contemporaries in the Coatzacoalcos basin, they practiced a mixed subsistence economy, focused on cultivating maize, gathering wild palm fruits and beans, and exploiting the local rivers and estuaries for molluscs, fish, and turtles (Rust and Leyden 1994; Pope et al. 2001: Raab et al. 2000).

Excavations at La Venta have recovered Early Formative ceramic sherds from four mound complexes (B, E, G, and the Stirling Acropolis) over an area of some 20 ha surrounding Mound C-1 (Hallinan et al. 1968; Lowe 1989: 50; Rust and Sharer 1988: 103).[4] La Venta also has yielded three radiocarbon dates between 1400 and 900 B.C. (Rust and Sharer 1988: 103; Squier 1968), including one stratigraphically above a deposit of Early Formative tecomates and other vessels (Hallinan et al. 1968: 164–165). Most of the other Early Formative sherds come from mound fill, and it is likely that the Early Formative component predated substantial mound construction at La Venta (it should be remembered, though, that San Lorenzo lacks evidence for substantial mound construction during its apogee). The relationship of this occupation to the stone monuments of La Venta is less certain. Several stone monuments from La Venta bear iconographic similarities with colossal heads and table-top thrones at San Lorenzo. If they are contemporaneous, it would suggest both the appearance of a regional center at La Venta by the end of the period and its interaction with its larger contemporary (Grove 1981b: 66–67). In combination with an excavated Early Formative occupation at Isla Alor (Raab et al. 2000), and surface remains from other Río Barí sites (Rust and Sharer 1988), it appears that La Venta may have dominated a two-tiered settlement hierarchy by the close of the Early Formative period.

Laguna de los Cerros and the Upper San Juan Basin

Across the divide from the Coatzacoalcos basin, the San Juan River flows westward around the southern piedmont of the Tuxtla Mountains. Rarely exceeding 6 km in width, the floodplain of the upper San Juan is much narrower than that of the Coatzacoalcos system, and the rolling hills and sloping plains that bound it rise higher than the salt domes and terraces in the Coatzacoalcos basin. The upper San Juan basin is therefore less subject to extensive flooding, but it does posses similar microenvironments of river levees, oxbow lakes, backswamps, and elevated terrain. Joshua Borstein (2001) recently conducted a survey in an 800 sq km area in the north side of the San Juan basin, extending eastward to the Estero Rabón area in the Coatzacoalcos drainage, discussed above. Borstein's survey methods differed from the full-coverage methods used by Symonds and Lunagómez in that he surveyed discontinuous blocks around known centers and systematically selected from outlying areas to proportionately represent lowland and upland zones. His sampling strategy nevertheless provides important insights into general trends in settlement patterns in this area.

Before 1400 B.C., settlement was sparse in the San Juan basin, and all seven sites in the sampled area were located at the interface of the lowland and upland zones (Borstein 2001: 155). Most of the settlement was located along the Negra River, a branch of the San Juan that probably formed the main course of the river at that time. Settlement densities increased dramatically over the Early Formative period, reaching 35 settlements by 1200 B.C. and 153 by 1000 B.C. (Borstein 2001: Figs. 5.8 and 5.9). As regional population grew, settlements expanded into upland areas, possibly reflecting the growing importance of rainfall maize agriculture to the subsistence economy, in addition to the attraction of settlement around newly founded upland centers (Borstein 2001: 185).

The growth of these centers and their surrounding sites likewise reflects the gradual development of a regional settlement hierarchy. The largest center in the upper San Juan basin was Laguna de los Cerros, which apparently was founded in the San Lorenzo A phase (ca. 1400–1200 B.C.) (Borstein 2001: 168; Bove 1978: 31). By the end of the phase the site may have covered as much as 150 ha, and formed a focus for satellite villages and hamlets. During the succeeding San Lorenzo B phase (ca. 1200–1000 B.C.) the site grew to some 300 ha, and 47 small sites with ceramics from this phase are clustered in the 25 sq km survey block around it (Borstein 2001: 168, 180). Many of the twenty-eight monuments from Laguna de los Cerros probably date to this phase. By this time, a three-tiered settlement hierarchy may have emerged, with secondary centers to the west at Cuatotolapan (Cuauhtotolapan) and to the east at or near Cruz del Milagro (Grove 1993: 94). Both of these sites have produced impressive Olmec statues. At 151 cm tall, the Cuatotolapan monument is the largest Olmec full-figure statue of a human known. Seated cross-legged and inclined forward, its resemblance to figures on altar-thrones at San Lorenzo suggests it may date to the late Early Formative period, when the density of sites around Cuatotolapan peaked (de la Fuente 1973: 129; Borstein 2001: 183). The smaller Cruz del Milagro statue known as "El Principe" assumes a similar posture, but its more sensitive carving relates it stylistically to the late Early Formative twins from El Azuzul. Archaeological investigations at Cruz del Milagro so far have failed to identify a substantial Early Formative occupation, however, and the administrative center may have been located elsewhere, perhaps amid a cluster of sites two to four km to the south (Borstein 2001: 171–172, Fig. 5.9).

One of the most remarkable sites in Olman lies a few km west of Laguna de los Cerros at Llano del Jícaro. Named for the thorny plain formed by a basalt flow emanating from the Tuxtla Mountains, Llano del Jícaro has been identified as a monument workshop (Gillespie 1994), and unfinished monuments – including an abandoned table-top altar-throne – dot its inhospitable surface. Ceramic artifacts from the site indicate it was utilized during the San Lorenzo phase (Gillespie 1994: 238). The basalt here is of the same Cerro Cintepec type from which most of the monuments at Laguna de los Cerros and San Lorenzo were carved (Coe and Diehl 1980a: 396–404; Williams and Heizer 1965). At 60 km, Llano del Jícaro is also one of the closest sources of basalt to San Lorenzo and has the added advantage of the San Juan river as a route for transporting monuments toward the Coatzacoalcos basin.

The degree to which San Lorenzo may have controlled Llano del Jícaro and Laguna de los Cerros is a matter of particular concern. Borstein (2001: 169–171) argues that San Lorenzo founded both of the latter sites in the San Lorenzo

A phase, when ceramics indicate a high degree of interaction among them. In Borstein's opinion, Laguna de los Cerros at this time was not sufficiently powerful to control the Llano del Jícaro basalt deposits on its own; rather, it was intentionally placed by San Lorenzo elites to administer the extraction and carving of the hard stone. Alternatively, Borstein suggests that San Lorenzo elites may have sent workers directly to Llano del Jícaro and that an autonomous Laguna de los Cerros benefitted from its contact with San Lorenzo and its location near the route from the workshop to the larger center. Borstein dismisses the third possibility, that independent elites at Laguna de los Cerros controlled the Llano del Jícaro workshop and that the San Lorenzo elites negotiated with them for access to this precious resource. This last scenario, however, merits further investigation, particularly given the 60 km distance between San Lorenzo and these San Juan basin sites.

Whatever the relationship between San Lorenzo and Laguna de los Cerros in the early half of the San Lorenzo phase, growing stylistic differences between ceramic artifacts from the two sites after 1200 B.C. suggest a change in, and perhaps a weakening of, interaction between the two sites. Various authors (Clewlow 1974; de la Fuente 1977, 2000; Gillespie 2000) have suggested the existence of a distinctive Laguna de los Cerros "school" of monument carving based on stylistic and iconographic differences between many of the monuments from Laguna de los Cerros and other sites, although Gillespie (2000) also identifies similarities, particular with San Lorenzo monuments. To the extent that the Laguna de los Cerros monuments are contemporaneous with late Early Formative monuments elsewhere, which is still a matter of debate, it would appear that as Laguna de los Cerros expanded it asserted its autonomous dominance in the upper San Juan basin (Drucker 1981: 47). Significantly, it is during the San Lorenzo B phase that the recycling of monuments intensified at San Lorenzo, suggesting its access to Cerro Cintepec basalt had become more tenuous. Other late developments at San Lorenzo include the first representations of weapons in monumental art and more widespread distribution of status items, suggesting the San Lorenzo elites were employing new strategies for managing an increasingly fractious populace (Borstein 2001: 188–187). If Laguna de los Cerros had previously been controlled by San Lorenzo, it would seem to have exploited troubles in that center to its own local political advantage.

The Tuxtla Mountains

In sharp contrast to the eastern and southern lowlands of Olman, an administrative hierarchy did not emerge in the central Tuxtla Mountains until the Late Formative period, after 400 B.C. (Santley et al. 1997). A survey of 400 sq km in the Tuxtlas identified 24 Early Formative sites (Santley and Arnold 1996: 228–229; Santley et al. 1997: 180–181). Characterized as hamlets and small villlages, they were mainly concentrated in the broad, fertile valley of the upper Catemaco River valley (Fig. 4.9).

Excavation of the Initial and Early Formative components at the site of La Joya provides important insights into the character of settlement in the Tuxtlas (Arnold 1999, 2000, 2003; McCormack 2002). The excavated remains here included the post-mold patterns and trampled earth floors of insubstantial structures. Oval pits containing fire-cracked rock appear to have been used only once before being abandoned, and later pits overlapped and cut into earlier ones. Absent here from the early components are the more permanent, deep bell-shaped storage pits that are associated with the site's Late Formative occupation. These features of the Early Formative archaeological record at La Joya suggest to Philip Arnold (2000: 126–128; Arnold and McCormack 2002: IV-4) that the site was occupied intermittently by small, seasonally mobile groups of people, although McCormack's (2002) auger-testing program found that certain areas of the site were occupied more consistently after 1400 B.C., suggesting decreasing mobility over the course of the Early Formative period.

The Early Formative artifact assemblage from La Joya tends to corroborate an interpretation of less permanent settlement than occurred in and around Olmec centers. Obsidian artifacts at the site consisted primarily of expediently produced flakes and chipping debris. Stone grinding tools consisted of small basalt mortars and pestles, rather than the larger, less easily transported metates and two-handed manos associated with Early Formative San Lorenzo and sites in its hinterland (O'Rourke 2002: 195; Wendt 2003: Table G.3) as well as La Joya's later occupations. In addition, the pottery, consisting mainly of tecomates, seems well-suited to serving multiple functions while representing an effective compromise among transportability, durability, and cooking effectiveness (Arnold 1999). The mixed nature of the subsistence economy at La Joya likely contributed to the high degree of residential mobility there. Archaeobotanical and faunal analysis suggests that although maize cultivation was practiced by the Early Formative inhabitants of La Joya, forest clearance increased in the Middle and Late Formative periods and reliance on wild animals and fish for food decreased as they became more committed to agricultural subsistence (VanDerwarker 2006).

Finally, though most Early Formative ceramics at La Joya correspond to general Olmec canons, some ceramics and figurines point more strongly to more westerly Mexican connections than to eastern Olman (Arnold 2003). Likewise, the obsidian assemblage at the site is heavily dominated by material from the Pico de Orizaba and Guadalupe Victoria sources to the northwest near the Veracruz-Puebla border, while the Guatemalan obsidians present at San Lorenzo are lacking from La Joya (Arnold 2003; Cobean et al. 1971, 1991; Santley et al. 2001). Together these data suggest that the inhabitants of the central Tuxtlas participated in somewhat different economic and social networks from their contemporaries in eastern Olman and were not incorporated into the political realms they dominated.

Summary

The growing volume of settlement pattern data from Olman implies considerable variation in political organization during the Early Formative period. The last centuries of the period saw the development of hierarchical political systems with two to three levels of administration in the riverine and estuarine settings of eastern Olman and the southern Tuxtlas piedmont. In the uplands of the western Tuxtla Mountains, however, communities appear to have been more mobile, and hierarchical administrative formations did not become institutionalized until much later.

PATHS TO COMPLEXITY

At the beginning of this chapter it was noted that the question of Olmec origins really encompassed three questions: one ethnic or cultural (where did the Olmec people come from?), one artistic (how and where did the Olmec art style develop?), and one sociopolitical (how did the complex institutions of Olmec society arise?). The answers to these are not simple. It now appears that people entered the southern Gulf lowlands of Mesoamerica before 5100 B.C. However, the mere fact of human occupation does not necessarily mark the beginning of a continuous, evolving cultural tradition. It is likely that many groups passed through the region, and not all may have been related culturally or linguistically. Nevertheless, there does appear to have been a gradual evolution of ecological adaptations, with humans increasing their reliance on domesticated maize and other crops as a supplement to the natural abundance of wild foods in the lowlands (Pope et al. 2001). This mixed economy proved an effective and flexible adaptation to the varied and dynamic landscape of lagoons, estuaries, swamps, rivers, and mountains along the Gulf coast. The emergence of an Olmec culture, however, is more significantly one of the formation of a coherent identity, reinforced through actions and materialized in artifacts and their attendant iconography. Neither is cultural identity a static entity, but one which is actively reproduced and renegotiated. That is, we should not expect that the expression of Olmec culture should remain monolithically homogeneous through time, any more than the expression of American, English, or Mexican identity has remained static over time. Rather, archaeologists must look for continuity between changing forms and their proportional representation in the archaeological record. From this perspective, the beginnings of a distinctive Olmec tradition are evident by 1700 B.C. in the ritual offerings of El Manati, and their link to florescent Early Formative Olmec culture is documented in the gradually changing ceramic and ritual traditions there and in the "pre-Olmec" levels of San Lorenzo, San Andrés, and other sites. In other words, there is no longer a basis for seeing Olmec culture as an intrusion from elsewhere in Mesoamerica.

Art and Iconography

Likewise, the origin of Olmec art and iconography is a complex issue, to which we will return in Chapter 6. Olmec iconography is widespread in Early Formative Mesoamerica, particularly on pottery, and it is not clear that all the elements of this symbolic complex originated or are even strongly represented in Olman (Grove 1989b; Flannery and Marcus 1994: 386–387). Hence, Grove (1989b) advocates it be designated by the neutral term "X Complex" so as not to prejudice interpretation toward a Gulf Coast origin, though the alternative designation of "Early Horizon motifs" seems to have wider acceptance (Flannery and Marcus 1994: 390). Coherence in the execution and combination of many elements, does, however, argue for a common origin of at least a portion of the X Complex, which may have been emulated, modified, and augmented with other symbols elsewhere (Blomster 2002; Stark 2000: 41). Recent chemical studies suggest that pottery vessels with Early Horizon (X Complex) iconography frequently were traded from San Lorenzo to other parts of Mesoamerica (where they also were produced locally) (Blomster et al. 2005; cf. Stoltman et al. 2005) (see Chapter 6). Given that motif styles also could have diffused without the exchange of vessels, this information supports a special, though not necessarily exclusive, role for the Gulf Olmec in the dissemination of Early Horizon iconography.

Outside of Olman the selective adoption and reinterpretation of Early Horizon iconography is associated with the emergence of hierarchical social ranking. Within Olman, however, Early Horizon motifs appear on technologically similar pottery in societies that minimally span the range from tribes to complex chiefdoms in traditional anthropological classifications of sociopolitical integration. The appearance of this set of symbols in such a variety of societies speaks not only to the degree of interaction among them, but also to the appeal and adaptability of the symbols as representations of widely held concepts about the cosmos and the forces that inhabit it.

One artistic tradition that clearly originated in Olman is the distinctive Olmec style of carving monumental sculptures in hard volcanic stone. Though diverse in theme and form (Cyphers 1996: 67; 1997d), Early Formative Olmec sculptures nevertheless possess overlapping traits that clearly distinguish them from other Mesoamerican sculptural traditions, and no other region of Mesoamerica can match the southern Gulf lowlands in quantity, size, or variety of monuments (Grove 1997: 80–81). A somewhat controversial fragment of a carved basalt monument from San Lorenzo may push the beginnings of the Olmec sculptural tradition tradition as far back as the Chicharras phase (ca. 1450–1400 B.C.) (Coe and Diehl 1980a: 246; cf. Lowe 1989; Hammond 1989). Regardless, however, recent excavations at San Lorenzo very clearly indicate that colossal heads and other monuments were being carved in the succeeding San Lorenzo phase (ca. 1400–1000 B.C.) (Cyphers 1999: 161–168). Far more than iconographic motifs on pottery, monumental stone carving in Olman is closely tied to political hierarchy in its subjects and contexts. Colossal heads and table-top altar-thrones express the power and authority of individual rulers and the contexts of these and other monuments within sites reinforce their political messages. Moreover, the vast majority of Olmec monuments are located in centers of primary or secondary rank, and the number of sculptures at these sites generally correlates with their relative sizes, tending to corroborate their inferred levels in regional administrative hierarchies (Grove 1997: 75).

Sociopolitical Evolution

Explaining the development of these hierarchical sociopolitical systems remains a contentious issue in Olmec studies; indeed, one author identifies "Olmec" specifically with the system of "governmental practices based upon social stratification and kingship" that emerged about 1400 B.C. in the southern Gulf lowlands (Clark 1997: 213). Such a definition would exclude the more simply organized Early Formative societies of the Tuxtla Mountains and the Papaloapan basin, however, unless they too were viewed as incorporated into larger, hierarchically organized polities – a view that is difficult to support with current archaeological evidence. The perspective taken in this book is that Olmec is best seen as a set of closely interacting, autonomous societies located in the southern Gulf lowlands during the Early and Middle Formative periods, which shared more similarities with one another in artifact styles and iconography than with more distant regions. From this perspective, Olmec culture and the symbolic system that identifies it were a flexible adaptation to a varied and dynamic environment, capable of encompassing a broad range of sociopolitical forms. The development of complex social ranking, then, was a prominent, but not universal, characteristic of these societies.

The foregoing review of Early Formative Olmec society strongly supports the idea that the political system that emerged at San Lorenzo was highly centralized and that authority was vested in powerful individuals. The central issue in the emergence of such centralized political systems is: why do individuals and larger groups allow their autonomy to be subjugated to the will of a central authority (Carneiro 1998: 21)? The explanations reviewed in Chapter 1 for the development of Olmec political hierarchy draw on, and in some cases combine, three perspectives on sociocultural evolution. The adapatationist perspective, most strongly associated with the paradigm of cultural ecology, views cultural change as a set of essentially voluntary solutions to problems of survival presented by the natural and social environment (e.g., Sanders and Price 1968). Frequently, these problems are seen to result from imbalances between human populations and natural resources. Centralized political systems develop to redistribute surpluses, mobilize labor for the intensification of production, and adjudicate disputes that arise from competition over scarce resources. Individuals may not like the solutions, but the majority accept them as necessary to the survival and stability of the group.

An alternative perspective grounds the emergence of political hierarchies in the application of coercive force, particularly in the form of warfare and the conquest of surrounding groups (e.g., Carneiro 1970; Coe and Diehl 1980b). As competition for land and resources increases, raiding provides a means for enhancing individual prestige and acquiring goods that can be redistributed to followers. Conquest also incorporates new lands for reallocation, and captives and tributaries may become new sources of productive labor for the victors. Furthermore, the threat of force can be used against members of one's own group. For such threats to succeed, however, conditions must preclude individuals from allying with other factions or simply "voting with their feet" and colonizing new territories.

A third view sees the initial emergence of centralized political institutions as the unanticipated result of competition among individuals and groups for prestige and the influence it engenders (Clark and Blake 1994). This perspective assumes the existence in all or most societies of some ambitious individuals ("aggrandizers") who desire greater influence, despite the effectiveness of social sanctions in moderating and channeling those desires. It also recognizes that some degree of social inequality exists even within "egalitarian" societies wherein inequality is based on age, gender, or ability (Clark and Blake 1994: 17–18). Aggrandizers acquire prestige through displays of generosity, which are made possible by drawing on a network of supporters who provide the labor necessary to produce the required surpluses of goods. Though production can be increased by increasing the size of one's household, successful aggrandizers look beyond the household for followers who form a coalition or faction. In egalitarian societies, aggrandizers cannot force others to meet their demands, rather, followers support their leaders because of the material and social benefits they realize from that association. When followers cannot reciprocate the largesse of aggrandizers, they incur social debts that may be paid by their labor in supporting future acts of generosity. Ultimately, the social superiority of successful aggrandizing individuals may become institutionalized in subsequent generations if individuals are able to confer their success on their dependents. This may be accomplished by creating opportunities for advantageous marriages, by creating heritable wealth through patronized craft production, or by monopolizing the acquisition and distribution of nonlocal resources

(Clark and Blake 1994: 20–21). Once ranking is institutionalized, leaders may draw upon various sources of power to ensure the compliance of their subjects (Earle 1997).

Circumstantial evidence points to a role for environment in the development of sociopolitical hierarchy in Olman. The settlement pattern data discussed previously indicate that Early Formative settlement hierarchies emerged first in lowland river valleys and estuarine environments and only centuries later in the mountain valleys of the Tuxtlas. Furthermore, the most vertically differentiated of these settlement hierarchies and the most pronounced expression of sociopolitical ranking developed in the San Lorenzo area of the Coatzacoalcos basin. The aggrading rivers, deltas, and estuaries of the lowlands would surely have attracted the early inhabitants of Olman, with their reliance on wild as well as cultivated resources. The abundance of fish, fowl, mussels, and crustaceans in these naturally productive environments and the annual replenishment of agricultural fertility on levees and floodplains would have allowed for substantial concentration of population and periodic accumulation of surpluses to be expended in feasts, feeding laborers, or trading for other resources. Thus the riverine and estuarine lowlands of the Coatzacoalcos, San Juan, and Tonalá/Mezcalapa drainage systems do represent the kind of intensifiable environments conducive to aggrandizing behavior, and they clearly permitted the growth of ranked societies. The same may be said, however, of the nearby Papaloapan and Usuamacinta/Grijalva river systems, which did not produce similarly complex societies as early.

Whether population pressure and competition for productive agricultural land caused the development of rank society remains an open question. Using fairly conservative values for population densities within sites, Symonds et al. (2002: Fig. 4.4) estimate that the maximum pre-Olmec population for the 400 sq km San Lorenzo survey area was 426 to 1017, or about 1 to 2.5 people per square kilometer. Even the most densely populated area, the 90 sq km inner hinterland of San Lorenzo, would have held a population density of less than 7 per sq km. By comparison, Symonds et al. estimate that maize yields from the inner hinterland alone could have supported 3,505 to 8,763 people (39–97 per sq km, which, incidentally, overlaps considerably with Coe and Diehl's estimates of 30–73 per sq km). Thus, there appears to have been little demographic pressure on land in pre-Olmec phases, although Symonds et al. (2002) invoke resource competition when they interpret the establishment of islote mounds and small, low-lying hamlets as strategies for laying claims to specialized resource areas, and when they note the defensive positioning of pre-Olmec villages on high ground (see above).

During the Chicharras and San Lorenzo phases, however (ca. 1450–1000 B.C.), population grew some 20-fold. Total population is estimated to have been between 8,554 and 18,735 (21–47 per sq km), and population in the inner hinterland was between 6,952 and 15,022 (71–167 per sq km) (Symonds et al. 2002: Figs. 4.4, 4.5). Fraught with difficulty though they are, these figures suggest there were heavy local pressures on agricultural land during the florescence of San Lorenzo, particularly given that many sites have been lost to erosion and burial. Even accepting this possibility, for several reasons it is not clear that demographic pressure caused the formation of political hierarchy. First, estimates of carrying capacity based strictly on maize production are difficult to assess because the contribution of maize to the Olmec diet relative to other crops and wild foods is unknown. Second, and countervailing the first reason, population estimates in the San Lorenzo environment are likely to be underestimates, due to destruction and burial of sites by meandering rivers. Most importantly, it is not known how rapidly population increased, that is, whether local carrying capacity was surpassed in the Chicharras phase, before San Lorenzo's florescence.

Another environmental factor that merits consideration is that of risk (Sanders and Webster 1978; Stark 2000: 39). All environments pose some risk to subsistence and human occupation, given a particular subsistence technology; what varies is the severity, geographical patterning, and temporal structure of these risks (Halstead and O'Shea 1989). In broad terms, it is easier for human groups to adapt to risks that have mild effects, are localized in space, and/or occur regularly at short intervals or, if not regularly, then frequently enough for humans to anticipate that they will occur in the future. In Olman, seasonal floods are not only predictable, but beneficial in that they replenish soil fertility, allow for "fugitive" or flood-recessional planting, and restock lakes and sloughs with fish. However, floods that come too early or too late, that last too long, or that recede too quickly, can decrease agricultural yields in low-lying lands throughout a river basin and alter the accessability and abundance of aquatic food sources. Severe floods may alter river courses, affecting the distribution of agricultural lands and access to transportation routes. Although severe drought is rare in the humid lowlands, fluctuations in the timing and amount of rainfall also can have a significant effect. For example, a decrease of 32% in the winter (*tapachol*) maize crop of the Coatzacoalcos basin was reported between 1991 and the drier year of 1992 (Rodríguez et al. 1997: 68). Increases in pest and fungal infestations related to rainfall also may affect crops adversely, as may infrequent hurricanes and, in the Tuxtla Mountains, volcanic eruptions.

From an adaptationist perspective, the need to redistribute surpluses and lands to affected households would have provided one impetus for centralized leadership. Other adaptations are possible, however. In the Tuxtla Mountains, residential mobility appears to have been one strategy for dealing with spatial and temporal fluctuations in productivity (Arnold 1999). This mobility may have taken the form of "trekking" as practiced by contemporary South American tribes in which large segments of the population leave their permanent villages for extended periods to hunt, forage, and visit distant gardens in the Amazonian rainforest (Werner 1983). Within the lowland river basins, a household could have guarded against agricultural risk by dispersing their landholdings in a variety of topographic settings (levees, floodplains, and uplands) and diversifying their subsistence strategies. Such considerations may have encouraged the Pre-San Lorenzo phase distribution of settlement at the interface of upland and lowland zones in the San Juan drainage (Borstein 2001). Because these strategies do not rely on centralized redistribution of goods, the adaptationist argument appears to work better as a justification for the continuation of existing centralized political systems rather than as a proximate cause of their origin.

A more productive approach for understanding the emergence and variation in Olmec political organization is one that considers the sources of power and prestige available to aspiring leaders and strategies for acquiring them within the environmental context of Olman (Stark 2000: 36, see also Blanton et al. 1996; Brumfiel 1994; Clark and Blake 1994; Earle 1997). The strategies that appear to have most relevance to the Olmec case are those identified as "exclusionary" or "networking" strategies wherein individuals attempt to attract supporters and expand their influence by establishing networks of social ties and reciprocal obligations outside their own group, as opposed to "corporate" strategies aimed at sharing power among diverse segments within the society (Blanton et al. 1996). Political power, "the mastery a leader exercises over others" (Earle 1997: 3) may derive from economic, military, social, and/or ideological sources (Earle 1997: 4–10).

Military might is perhaps the most obvious source of social power, and it is explicitly invoked in coercive theories of the evolution of political systems (Carneiro 1970). The coercive theory for the rise of Olmec political hierarchy (Coe and Diehl 1980b: 139–152) hinges on three issues: competition for relatively scarce, highly productive levee lands, forceful subjugation of neighboring communities, and impediments to outmigration. Warfare and raiding are common in transegalitarian societies (tribes and simple chiefdoms), and it is likely that Olmec groups fought with one another. Nevertheless, the archaeological evidence for warfare among the Olmecs is notable for its scarcity and ambiguity. Coe (1981: 19; Coe and Diehl 1980b: 152) relied on the recovery of human remains from refuse deposits at San Lorenzo to argue for cannibalism and warfare. Only one of the reported human bones exhibits cut marks that might be interpreted as evidence for butchering, however, and it is a juvenile, unlikely to have been a war captive (Coe and Diehl 1980a: 386); the remaining bones could well be redeposited from previous burials. The Olmecs probably did sacrifice humans, as the infant remains from El Manatí suggest, but again these are unlikely to have been war captives. With regard to potential weapons, projectile points are rare, and may as well have been used for hunting as for war (Lowe 1989: 49). Polished stone celts and axes, and obsidian-tipped knives, such as were deposited at El Manatí, could have served as weapons or as sacrifical instruments and ceremonial representations of land-clearing implements unrelated to war.

Military force is not a common theme in Early Formative Olmec art, and in some cases the military interpretation is open to question. For example, two of the most likely candidates for Early Formative depictions of bound captives are altar-thrones from San Lorenzo (Monument 14) and La Venta (Altar 4), but they also have been interpreted as representing genealogical ties with the ruler (Grove 1973a). A handful of other monuments (Río Chiquito Monument 1, Laguna de los Cerros Monument 20, and Potrero Nuevo Monument 3), showing a person or feline above a supine figure more likely relate to mythical themes than earthly domination (cf. Drucker 1981: 45). Convincing Early Formative depictions of weapons are confined to four monuments from San Lorenzo. One is "Pedro Navaja," the figure on the recently discovered San Lorenzo Monument 112, who carries a curved knife in his belt (Cyphers 2004: 190–191). The others consist of bent, serrated "swords" or war clubs depicted on San Lorenzo Monuments 78, 91 and probably 83, but only in the last is the implement shown in a person's grasp (Cyphers 2004: 145–146, 149–150, 159). Ceremonial bars and scepters are represented on several Early Formative monuments, and they may be ceremonial equivalents of war clubs, but they are not shown in that use.

Additional objections to the coercive theory concern the requirements of resource pressure and circumscription. As we have seen, the differential production of levee lands may not have been as great as reported to Coe and Diehl (Rodríguez et al. 1997). Furthermore, despite apparently high populations in the inner hinterland of San Lorenzo, the site's outer hinterland evidently was more sparsely populated, as were the Tonalá and San Juan valleys preceding and during the initial emergence of the San Lorenzo polity. Thus circumscription of any kind was at best weak during the crucial initial phases of Olmec culture (Stark 2000: 39).

None of this confirms that the Olmecs did not engage in war or that Olmec rulers never coerced their subjects through force. However, intensified warfare, to the extent it is represented in Olmec art, appears to have followed the establishment of social ranking rather than to have fostered its emergence. Moreover, the use of military force by Olmec rulers against their own subjects seems to have been more an implied threat than an active strategy. This would have been wise, for military might is literally a two-edged sword. Rulers who employ warriors to enforce and extend their control also must guard against treachery (Earle 1997: 7–8), and excessive use of force provokes rebellion as often as it compels fealty.

Economic sources of power may also be applied coercively, but their manipulation lays an easier path from egalitarian to hierarchical society. The generous provision of staples and prestige items not only enhances personal and familial prestige and attracts followers, but once the sources of those goods are monopolized, bestowing and withholding them become powerful means of rewarding service and punishing resistance (Earle 1997: 6–7). Early Formative Olmec leaders had access to several economic sources of power, and demonstrably employed some of them. In large part, the potential for economic control was conditioned by the natural environment of Olman, including the distribution of resources and the structure of environmental risk. Those households that held rights to land that, by virtue of favorable topography or chance, persistently avoided crop failure, more often also would have been in a position to grant gifts of food to more severely affected households, and to use surpluses more frequently to acquire nonlocal resources to distribute to followers. In either case they would have been able to incur the social indebtedness of a larger group of households than their fellows. This argument is appealing because it holds whether crops, such as maize or cacao, were essential elements of the Olmec diet or more valued for feasting and other social exchanges (e.g., Clark and Blake 1994).

A second potentially significant element of the Gulf lowland environment is the transportation network provided by its rivers. Clark and Blake (1994: 19–20) call attention to the role of geography in providing opportunities for social interaction among communities, which aggrandizers may employ to establish broader networks of supporters and allies. In this regard, the intersecting branches of the Coatzacoalcos river system allowed for a high degree of connectivity among communities and efficient transport between them (Symonds and Lunagómez 1997b). It may be the greater potential for communication, rather than control of transportation *per se* that initially encouraged settlement at nodes in the river system. In comparison, the still-emerging delta of the Mezcalapa/Tonalá system was more attenuated in the vicinity of La Venta during the Early Formative period, and the Upper San Juan river valley was an essentially linear transportation route, linking fewer communities together directly.

Controlling access to non-local resources is another important means of acquiring power, and one that is strongly indicated for Early Formative Olman. The imported goods may include those used widely in day-to-day tasks ("utilitarian" or "subsistence" goods), or those used in more restrictive contexts of social interaction or ceremony ("prestige goods," "primitive valuables," or "preciosities"). A further distinction may be made within the class of prestige goods between "badges of office" used primarily to legitimate social status and generalized wealth that may be used and distributed in prescribed ways to establish social relationships (Hirth 1992). It is important to note that these distinctions rely on the way different materials and goods are used and perceived rather than their intrinsic properties. For example, the Olmecs used basalt as the principal material for fashioning utilitarian grinding stones but also as the prime medium for representing supernatural and human power in carved monuments. Likewise, obsidian flakes and blades sliced meat and fiber, but probably also sliced human flesh in blood offerings to supernatural beings. Nevertheless, some rare, exotic materials, because of their scarcity and the difficulty of acquiring them, are more likely to serve as prestige goods. Such materials obtained from distant, poorly known regions also often take on cognitive associations with the poorly apprehended realm of the sacred and the mythic past (Helms 1993; Stark 2000: 40). Controlling access to such materials therefore draws on ideological as well as economic sources of power. From an economic perspective, however, the political value of prestige goods lies in their use by leaders to manipulate the social relations of labor by distributing or withholding them from followers and as a medium for consolidating alliances with other leaders through gift exchanges. These interelite gift exchanges establish social networks that may be drawn upon to accumulate other goods, to acquire emergency provisions when local food supplies fail, and to provide for mutual defense and dispute resolution (Hirth 1992).

The Early Formative Olmecs acquired a variety of materials for utilitarian and nonutilitarian purposes both from within and from beyond the region of Olman. The best documented material acquired within Olman is basalt from the piedmont and slopes of the Tuxtla Mountains. For the inhabitants of the Coatzacoalcos and Tonalá/Mezcalapa basins, basalt was a non-local resource that had to be transported tens of kilometers. The early utilitarian use of basalt in these areas is documented by bowl and grinding stone fragments from before 1550 B.C. at El Manatí and San Lorenzo (Coe and Diehl 1980a: 231, 233) and somewhat later in the La Venta area (Rust and Leyden 1994: 189; Rust and Sharer 1988; von Nagy et al. 2002). By 1400 B.C. basalt also was used in and around San Lorenzo for stone monuments. Whether the early inhabitants of eastern Olman traveled directly to the basalt sources or acquired the stone through exchange is still not clear, but it is plausible that emerging leaders gradually came to monopolize its procurement and distribution by developing social ties with groups at the sources to establish rights to extract or trade for the material. Furthermore, the monument recycling workshop at San Lorenzo strongly suggests that elites eventually came to control its local distribution there.

Other materials with restricted distributions that appear to have been traded among Olmec sites, either in their raw form or as finished products, include kaolin clay, hematite, bitumen, and coastal products, including shell, stingray spines, and shark's teeth. Cacao and salt also may have been exchanged within the region, though it is difficult to recover them in archaeological contexts. With the exception of salt, these materials generally had ritual uses or were used in the production of more highly crafted ceramics and other artifacts, therefore they may have served as prestige goods. Grove (1994: 228) has suggested that the major Olmec centers were established in zones with differing access to these and other materials to facilitate cooperative exchange for the mutual benefit of the entire Olmec region. The political perspective elaborated here suggests a slightly different view, however. That is, emerging leaders were able to manipulate the differential distribution of resources in Olman to their personal benefit, by exchanging goods not found elsewhere with other leaders, in order to acquire locally unavailable utilitarian and prestige items, which they could then distribute to followers in their own political factions (cf. Rathje 1972). Moreover, aspiring leaders near the margins of the system in areas where resources replicated those of more centrally located communities would have been disadvantaged in establishing ties with complementary resource zones. This would help account for the slower development of sociopolitical hierarchy at Tres Zapotes and in the central Tuxtlas Mountains.

In terms of sheer volume, exchange within Olman appears to have out-weighed interregional exchange in the Early Formative period. Nevertheless, the Olmecs also sought utilitarian and prestige goods from distant regions. Obsidian was the most prevalent of these goods, and it was acquired from sources hundreds of kilometers away in Central Mexico and Guatemala. Like basalt, it occurs early in the archaeological records of San Lorenzo and the La Venta area. Jade, serpentine, and other greenstones were not acquired in the quantities they would be during the Middle Formative period, but they were obtained by 1700 B.C., most impressively for the ritual offerings at El Manatí. Later, during the San Lorenzo phase, iron ore mirrors and cubes, the latter in impressive quantities, were imported from Oaxaca and Chiapas. Clearly, the "pre-Olmec" groups acquired their obsidian and greenstone by means other than centralized redistribution. Nevertheless, they would have been attractive goods for emerging leaders to attempt to monopolize – obsidian as a ubiq-uitous necessity and greenstone as a ritually important prestige good. The massive deposits of ilmenite cubes found on the San Lorenzo plateau and on the heights of Loma del Zapote suggest elite control over this resource. A few ilmenite cubes also have been found in residential contexts (Di Castro Stringher 1997: 157), however, implying they also may have constituted more generalized wealth items (or "primitive money" as once suggested by Gareth Lowe, cited in Clark 1996: 193). Monopolizing the procurement, distribution, and productive context of this exotic material likely provided one more source of economic power to the established elites of San Lorenzo.

The preceding discussion highlights the importance of social relations as sources of power for political leaders. Aspiring leaders rely on the labor of their own households and relations to accumulate surpluses they need to attract other followers and to forge social ties with exchange partners and allies beyond the local group. Increasing the size of one's own household and forging advanta-geous marriage ties therefore are important strategies for ambitious individuals as they increase the pool of productive labor at their disposal. Moreover, the establishment of more extensive social networks in turn provides leaders with staple and/or prestige goods to maintain and expand their local factions (Clark and Blake 1994: 21). Thus the creation of social relations not only provides the means for conducting economic exchanges, but is the very purpose of those exchanges.

In pre-state societies kinship plays a dominant role in structuring rights and obligations among individuals and therefore also relations of authority and power (Earle 1997: 5). In chiefdoms kinship forms the basis for sociopolitical hierarchy – a person's rank in the social and political system is determined by his or her degree of relationship to the chief through genealogical ties to a presumed common ancestor (Sanders and Price 1968: 43). Consequently, the rhetoric of kinship reinforces the political hierarchy and constitutes an important component of the ideology that legitimates the power and authority of rulers in chiefdoms as well as archaic states.

Ideology refers most specifically to the "principles, philosophies, ethics, and values by which human societies are governed" (Flannery and Marcus 1993). As such it is part of the broader domain of human knowledge and belief, which also includes ideas about the supernatural (religion) and the structure and origin of the universe (cosmology). These ideas are materialized and communicated symbolically through the iconography of art and the practice of ritual. When religious, cosmological, philosophical, and ethical concepts are employed to legitimize or contest the governance of society, they constitute components of ideology themselves. These concepts, along with the iconography and ritual that manifest them, become sources of political power manipulated by leaders and their competitors.

The contexts and content of Early Formative monuments spectacularly demonstrate that Olmec leaders employed an impressive array of ideological concepts and practices to legitimize their rule. Cosmological and mythical referents were juxtaposed with pesonalized images to situate Olmec rulers at the nexus of supernatural and earthly power. Colossal portraits conveyed the individual authority of living rulers and served as enduring reminders of their genealogical ties to powerful ancestors. The power of the individuals represented in these and other images was further acknowledged in practice by mutilating the monuments, whether that mutilation was effected to neutralize the power they possessed or to express rebellion against the ruler. Seated on massive thrones above their image in the niche-cave below, Olmec rulers expressed their roles as intermediaries between the levels of the cosmos. The same concept may have been expressed by figures like the El Azuzul twins and the San Martín Pajapan monument, seemingly poised to raise a ceremonial bar as the *axis mundi* that connects the earthly plane with the realms below and above. Combinations of human, avian, feline, crocodilian, and ophidian features on individual images invoked the powers of the natural and spiritual realms, as did arraying humans, felines, and other beasts in narrative scenes.

Furthermore, the "jaguarization" of some human figures and the anthropo-morphization of some feline figures suggest the theme of human–animal spirit transformation more explicitly represented in Middle Formative jades.

Human–animal transformation, communication across cosmic planes and with ancestors, and the necessity of destroying "objects of power" are common components of a complex of ideas associated with religious specialists in many indigenous societies of the Americas, from egalitarian bands to stratified states (Furst 1968; Grove 1981b; Reilly 1995; Freidel et al. 1993). These specialists are usually called "shamans" by analogy with Siberian practitioners (Eliade 1964), although some object to this extension of the term (e.g., Klein et al. 2002). The important point here is that the Early Formative Olmecs incorporated into the ideology of rulership concepts and practices that were very likely also present among their Initial Formative ancestors. It is easy to imagine that early aspirants to leadership drew upon similar sources of ideological power and that through generations of repeated use they became essential components in the legitimation of authority throughout Olman, from the egalitarian groups of the Tuxtla Mountains to the hierarchical polities of the eastern riverine lowlands.

In brief, the evolution of sociopolitical systems in Early Formative Olman took varying paths, such that late in the period societies spanned the range from egalitarian, relatively mobile societies in the Tuxtlas to the highly centralized, stratified society of San Lorenzo, with intermediate degrees of hierarchy in the Tonalá and San Juan drainages. While each of these systems adapted effectively to its local environment, the proximate cause of this variation lies in the varied success of aspiring leaders in attracting and retaining followers, in part through extending their networks of social and economic interaction beyond their local groups. These leaders drew on economic, ideological, social, and almost cer-tainly military sources of power, but economic and ideological power appear to have been the most important in the creation of enduring political hierarchies.

CHAPTER 5

OLMEC TRANSFORMATIONS: THE MIDDLE FORMATIVE PERIOD

The Middle Formative period (ca. 1000–400 B.C.) saw important changes in Olmec culture and society. At the beginning of the period, San Lorenzo suffered a sharp decline; although people continued to occupy the San Lorenzo plateau, they virtually ceased to erect stone monuments, and many of the surrounding settlements were abandoned (Coe and Diehl 1980a: 188, 1980b: 152; Cyphers 1996: 70–71; Symonds et al. 2002: 88–90). San Lorenzo's misfortune reverberated in centers such as Laguna de los Cerros, La Oaxaqueña, and Las Limas, with which the great capital had held close ties. Other sites prospered, however. On the western frontier of Olman, Tres Zapotes emerged as a regional center. In the east, La Venta continued to expand, ultimately to become the most spectacular of Olmec capitals.

Great changes also were afoot elsewhere in Mesoamerica. Many societies continued to increase in social complexity, and ranking of social status became commonplace. Ties between regions shifted as more societies demanded greater volumes of prestige goods to support their political and religious institutions. Back in Olman, rulers adapted their strategies to the changing political and economic landscape with significant consequences for the form and content of monumental art, architecture, and ritual offerings, in addition to the new ceramic styles that mark the period (Fig. 5.1).

MAIZE AND JADE: MIDDLE FORMATIVE OLMEC SUBSISTENCE AND ECONOMY

The Olmecs of the Middle Formative period continued to rely on a mixed subsistence economy, which included wild plants and animals as well as domesticated crops. The great story of Middle Formative subsistence in Olman, however, is the growing importance of maize in the Olmec diet. This trend is demonstrated especially well by increasing frequencies of carbonized maize fragments per cubic meter of deposits excavated at La Venta and nearby sites, which reached a peak during La Venta's height in the late Middle Formative period (Rust and Leyden 1994: 192–194, Table 12.3). The La Venta Olmecs planted a small-eared, low-growing popcorn with ten to fourteen rows of kernels, which Rust and Leyden (1994: 198) suggest was better adapted to the humid soils of the area. Farmers in upland areas may have used other maize varieties, and the contribution of maize to the Olmec diet almost surely varied with local agricultural conditions and the abundance of alternative wild sources of carbohydrates and protein. Nevertheless, the importance of agriculture apparently increased in upland as well as lowland environments. In the Tuxtla Mountains, animal species associated with land clearance became more prevalent in the Middle Formative period at La Joya (VanDerwarker 2006), and ridged surfaces of Middle Formative agricultural fields were preserved below volcanic ash at Matacapan (Santley 1992: 171).

The expansion of agriculture had broad effects on Olmec economy and technology. In excavations at La Venta, the ratio of basalt manos and metates to the volume of deposits increases in tandem with the increase in maize fragments (Rust and Leyden 1994: 194, Table 12.3), indicating a growing trade in this non-local material. In the Tuxtla Mountains, where basalt was locally abundant, grinding stones show a shift from less specialized forms in the Early Formative period to more specialized forms designed for more intensive usage (McCormack 2003). Furthermore, changes in subsistence practices apparently had ideological and political as well as practical consequences for the Olmecs. As discussed below, maize symbolism became much more prevalent in the iconography of Middle Formative art and prestige objects (Taube 2000).

Other aspects of Middle Formative Olmec economy can be inferred from the materials, technology, and formal qualities of craft items and art objects. Together, these lines of evidence suggest a complex set of relationships among consumers, producers, and exchange partners that varied across Olman and with respect to particular classes of goods. Pottery, for the most part, appears to have been produced from local materials in household contexts throughout Olman (Arnold 1996: 205; Methner 2000), although some pottery at Estero Rabon is thought to be non-local (Borstein 2001: 191), and a chemically distinct group of pottery from La Venta may have been imported from eastern Tabasco or the Chiapas depression (Methner 2000; Neff and Glascock 2002: 14). At Tres Zapotes, scarce sherds tempered with pumiceous ash similar to that used at La Venta suggests the possibility of exchange between these sites around the transition from the Middle to Late Formative period (Pool et al. 2001).

As in the Early Formative period, the sources of stone for grinding implements and monuments provide some of the clearest evidence for Middle Formative resource procurement and exchange within Olman. As might be expected, sites within and adjacent to the Tuxtla Mountains obtained the bulk of their stone from local basalt sources. At Tres Zapotes, for example, almost

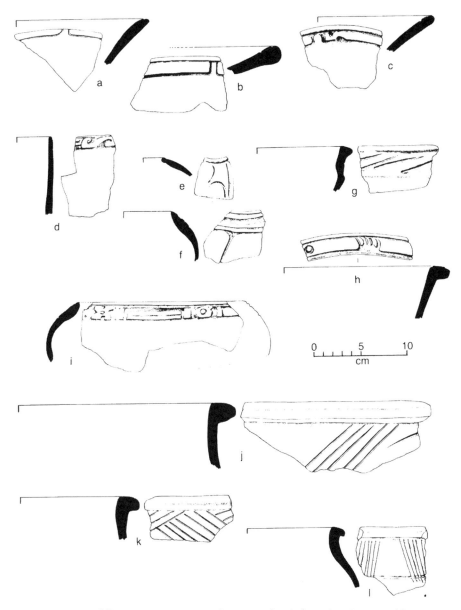

Figure 5.1. Middle Formative pottery (Nacaste phase) from San Lorenzo (Coe 1981: Fig. 5–10) (courtesy of Michael D. Coe).

all of the material for ground stone implements and monuments came from five to ten km away on the slopes of Cerro el Vigía (Kruszczynski 2001; Porter 1989; Williams and Heizer 1965: 15–16), while natural basalt columns such as those used to construct an enclosure around an altar apparently came from sources 10 to 20 km to the east (Millet 1979).

Lacking local sources of hard stone, La Venta was forced to look farther away, and its sculptural corpus includes a wider variety of stone types than was

utilized at Tres Zapotes, or earlier at San Lorenzo (Fig. 5.2 inset). The Cerro
Cintepec basalt type, which outcrops some 90 to 120 km from La Venta at
Llano del Jícaro and elsewhere in the southwestern Tuxtlas, is represented in
three of the four colossal heads and five of the six altar-thrones from La Venta
(Williams and Heizer 1965: 17). On stylistic grounds these probably date to
the end of the Early Formative period or beginning of the Middle Formative
period, and may have come from Llano del Jícaro. It is uncertain whether Llano
del Jícaro continued to supply much of this basalt into the Middle Formative
period, however. Ceramic evidence suggests the monument workshop site
was abandoned in the Middle Formative, and the nearby center of Laguna
de los Cerros suffered a significant decline in population (Borstein 2001: 195,
Fig. 5.12).

Many stylistically later basalt monuments from La Venta are distinctive
in composition and are attributed more generally to the Tuxtla Mountains
(Williams and Heizer 1965: 18–20). Among these Tuxtla basalt sources was
one that supplied La Venta with columnar basalt late in the Middle Formative period. This source tentatively has been suggested to have been Punta
Roca Partida, about 140 km up the coast (Williams and Heizer 1965: 18),
though other columnar basalt flows may have been closer. In addition, La
Venta obtained andesite for some of its monuments from La Unión volcano
(better known since its 1982 eruption as El Chichon or El Chichonal) 120 km
to the southeast in Chiapas, and sandstone possibly from the Huimanguillo area
95 km to the southeast. Metamorphic schists and gneisses used in other monuments came from more distant sources in the southern Sierra Madre and Isthmus of Tehuantepec (Curtis 1959; González 2000: 390; Williams and Heizer
1965: 12, 20–21). Notably, Williams and Heizer (1965: 8) report observing La
Unión andesite blocks in a habitation deposit containing manos and metates
exposed by a pipeline trench on the north side of La Venta. Clearly, La Venta
diversified its sources of stone for monuments and grinding implements alike,
perhaps because the political decline of San Lorenzo and Laguna de los Cerros
disrupted procurement networks.

Obsidian was the principal material used for chipped stone tools in Middle Formative Olman, although obsidian technology varied among sites and
subregions. In the central Tuxtla Mountains and at Tres Zapotes, the manufacture of obsidian flakes was a household activity (Santley et al. 1997, 2001;
McCormack 2003: 83), a pattern that continued from the Early Formative
period and also characterizes the Middle Formative obsidian industry west of
Olman in the Mixtequilla region (Stark et al. 1992: 226). At San Lorenzo, prismatic blades peaked at 73% of the assemblage in the early half of the Middle
Formative period during the Nacaste phase, then declined in the subsequent
Palangana phase (Coe and Diehl 1980a: 258–259). At La Venta, Rojas Chávez
(1990), has documented both the prevalence of prismatic blade technology in
the obsidian industry and the persistence of an earlier chert and quartzite flake

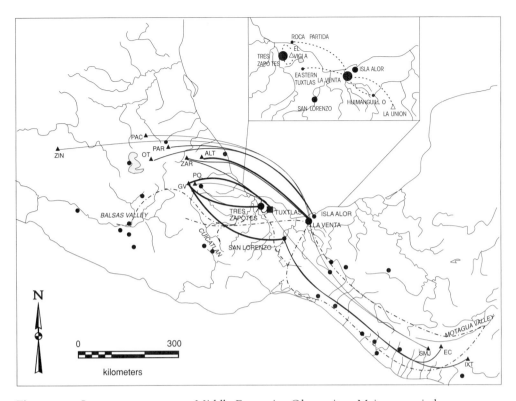

Figure 5.2. Stone procurement at Middle Formative Olmec sites. Main map: circles, sites; triangles, obsidian sources (ZIN, Zinapécuaro; PAC, Pachuca; OT, Otumba; PAR, Paredon; ZAR, Zaragoza-Oyameles; ALT, Altotonga; GV, Guadalupe Victoria; PO, Pico de Orizaba; SMJ, San Martín Jilotepeque; EC, El Chayal; IXT, Ixtepeque); solid lines, obsidian exchange (major sources indicated by thicker lines); dashed lines, iron ore; dash-and-dotted lines, greenstone (including jade from Motagua Valley, serpentine, and other stones). Inset map: stone for monuments, see text for explanation.

industry. Following Clark (1987), Rojas Chávez suggests the prismatic blade technology reflects elite control over the production of obsidian, and argues that La Venta supplied the surrounding area with blades.

Obsidian sourcing indicates the existence of multiple, overlapping exchange networks in Middle Formative Olman (Fig. 5.2). The Olmecs obtained their obsidian from diverse sources in Mexico and Guatemala at distances ranging from 200 km to more than 500 km, but sites and subregions differ markedly in the proportions of different sources. Chemical analyses of obsidian from La Venta and the nearby site of San Andrés identify San Martín Jilotepeque as the most important Guatemalan source at these sites. Paredón, Puebla was the most common Mexican source at San Andrés and one of the most important at La Venta (Doering 2002, González personal communication 2005; Hester et al. 1971; cf. Nelson and Clark 1998).[1] Pachuca, Otumba, and Zaragoza also were significant sources for La Venta and its hinterland (Doering 2002; González, personal communication 2005; Stokes 1999). In contrast, Guadalupe Victoria, Puebla is the dominant Middle Formative source at San Lorenzo, followed by the Guatemalan sources at El Chayal and Ixtepeque(Cobean et al. 1971, 1991). Guadalupe Victoria obsidian also predominates in the Middle Formative assemblage at Tres Zapotes (followed by Pico de Orizaba and minor amounts of Zaragoza) (Knight 1999, 2003), and in the central Tuxtla Mountains, where obsidian from Zaragoza, Pico de Orizaba, and San Martín Jilotepeque appear in lesser amounts (Santley et al. 2001).

The Middle Formative period in Olman is notable for the amount of stone imported for prestige items. These included iron ores for concave mirrors as well as jade, serpentine, and other greenstones used for a vast variety of objects, such as figurines, ornaments, ceremonial celts and axes, masks, and monuments, and shaped blocks of serpentine that were buried in massive offerings at La Venta. The sources for these primarily metamorphic rocks likely lie in the southern Sierra Madre of Puebla and Oaxaca and the highlands of Chiapas and Guatemala (Fig. 5.2). The production of such artifacts was probably in the hands of skilled specialists, although production contexts are elusive in the archaeological record. One good candidate was uncovered in Complex E at La Venta (Rust and Sharer 1988: 242), which, although primarily domestic in character, is close enough to the central ceremonial zone of the site to have been controlled by its rulers.

Because of their beauty, their obvious ideological and political importance, and their greatly expanded use in the Middle Formative period, jade artifacts have attracted a great deal of attention from Olmec scholars. The term jade, as it has been used by Mesoamerican archaeologists, actually covers a wide variety of relatively hard, usually green, metamorphic and igneous rocks and minerals, including albitite, chloromelanite, chrysoprase, omphacite, metaba-site, and quartzite, in addition to jadeite (Harlow 1993, 1995). There is some cultural justification for lumping together these very different geological products, because the stones were used in similar ways by ancient Mesoamericans. Hence, they are sometimes referred to together as "cultural jade." As we have seen, the Olmecs and other Mesoamerican peoples also utilized softer stones such as serpentine and soapstone for figurines, celts, and ornaments. These are often lumped with the harder "jades" as "greenstones," a term which, like jade, also has a more restricted geological meaning. As a lapidary term, jade is mainly restricted to two mineral varieties, nephrite and jadeite. Nephrite, the apple-green jade so prized in east Asia, is composed of intergrown crystals of the amphibole minerals tremolite and actinolite, and is not found in Mesoamerica, either naturally or as artifacts. Instead, the Olmecs and other Mesoamerican cultures employed the hard rock known geologically as jadeitite, which is composed mainly of the pyroxene mineral jadeite. Jadeite may range in color from white, through emerald green, to blue-green. To date, the only docu-mented source of jadeite in Mesoamerica lies in the Motagua valley region of Guatemala, some 600 km southeast of La Venta. For many years it had been suggested that there might be another source in the Balsas River valley of Guerrero state in western Mexico, because the source of the "Olmec blue" jade had not been identified and many jadeite artifacts had been recovered from the region. In 1998, however, a hurricane exposed an enormous blue jadeite source, tumbling boulders the size of busses into the ravines of a valley near the Motagua (Seitz et al. 2001).

Jadeite was not only difficult to acquire, but owing to its hardness, which is greater than steel, it also was difficult to shape with the tools available to the Olmecs. Forming even a single jade bead would require many hours of sawing, drilling, grinding, and polishing with quartz sand or another hard abrasive. That Olmec artisans and their contemporaries were able to achieve the aesthetic heights of their finest jade figurines represents a triumph of patience, skill, and vision. Moreover, the long treks into strange lands to obtain the material, the technical skill required to execute the carvings, the esoteric knowledge embodied in their iconography, and the symbolic associations of their green and blue colors with water and fertility made Olmec jades the quintessential objects of status and power (Tate 1995: 50).

A DYNAMIC LANDSCAPE

The foregoing discussion of Middle Formative subsistence and economy hints at the profound changes in the political landscape of Olman, and suggests that the expansion of maize agriculture and alterations in exchange networks were partly responsible. Other factors that contributed to the rise and fall of individual Olmec polities lie in the dynamic physical landscape of Olman and the internal processes within Olmec societies.

Middle Formative Settlement Patterns

In the Middle Coatzacoalcos drainage, Symonds and Lunagómez's surveys document what can only be described as a collapse of San Lorenzo and the settlement hierarchy it headed (Symonds et al. 2002: 88–90) (Fig. 5.3). On the San Lorenzo plateau, all that remained of the great Early Formative center was a medium-size village. In the surrounding hinterland the number of occupied sites declined from 226 to 54 villages, hamlets, and *islotes*, and the estimated regional population fell by nearly 92% to 1,039. Farther upriver, the smaller, former centers at Las Limas and La Oaxaqueña show little evidence of Middle Formative occupation (Cobean 1996: 50; Gómez Rueda 1996: 74). At the same time, Estero Rabón, a secondary center on the western edge of the middle Coatzacoalcos basin, was reduced by two-thirds to 50 ha, although the presence of some possibly Middle Formative monuments and ceramic imports at the site suggests it maintained a degree of political importance (Borstein

2001: 191–195). Population loss does not appear to have been even throughout the Coatzacoalcos basin, however, for Robert Kruger (1997: 149–150)
found evidence for a local increase on hilly uplands along an abandoned river
channel just 10 km southeast of San Lorenzo. Nevertheless, the overall pattern
is one of drastic political and demographic decline.

Similarly dramatic changes characterize the Middle Formative settlement
pattern in the adjacent San Juan river basin to the west, where the number
of identified sites fell by 63% (Borstein 2001: 191). The greatest population
losses appear to have been in the western part of the zone, around Laguna de
los Cerros and Cuatotolapan. Although settlement density remained highest
around Laguna de los Cerros, there appears to have been no regional capital
within the basin. More or less permanent occupation around the monument
workshop at Llano del Jícaro disappeared, although parties still may have visited
the rocky plain to extract basalt. Elsewhere in the San Juan basin, settlement
was distributed in scattered concentrations of farmsteads forming dispersed
communities, mainly located on flat plateaus with deep, fertile soils.

The trend toward more upland settlement seen in the San Juan basin is even
more dramatically documented immediately to the north in the Hueyapan
area of the southern Tuxtlas piedmont (not to be confused with the Arroyo
Hueyapan at Tres Zapotes). In sharp contrast to the river basins of the San Juan
and Coatzacoalcos, this area shows a dramatic increase in settlement during
the Middle Formative period (Killion and Urcíd 2001). Farther north in the
central Tuxtla Mountains, population increased nearly twofold and became
more nucleated with the appearance of large villages (Santley and Arnold 1997:
187) (Fig. 5.3).

Just beyond the western edge of the Tuxtlas, at the interface of the Tuxtla
piedmont and the vast Papaloapan deltaic plain, Tres Zapotes emerged as a
regional center covering some 80 ha (Pool and Ohnersorgen 2003). The two
Olmec colossal heads from Tres Zapotes may date from early in the Middle
Formative period, since Early Formative occupation at the site appears to have
been too small to provide the labor or the political power necessary to commission the sculptures and transport them from the basalt source on Cerro el
Vigía. The 5 m tall Stela A and an altar surrounded by upright basalt columns
resemble late Middle Formative examples from La Venta. These, along with the
five to six other known Olmec monuments from Tres Zapotes further confirm
the regional importance of the center and the development of a political and
social hierarchy. Unfortunately, the settlement pattern of Tres Zapotes's hinterland is still poorly understood. The chronological distribution of settlements
around Tres Zapotes in a recent archaeological survey conducted by Ignacio
León Pérez (2003) has not been analyzed in detail, but intensive survey in the
site's immediate vicinity indicates that it was surrounded by a relatively dense
cluster of hamlets and villages covering up to 15 ha (Pool and Ohnersorgen

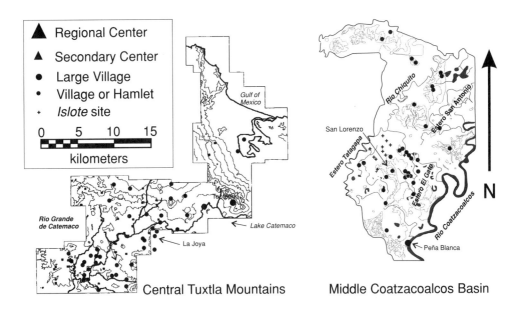

Central Tuxtla Mountains   Middle Coatzacoalcos Basin

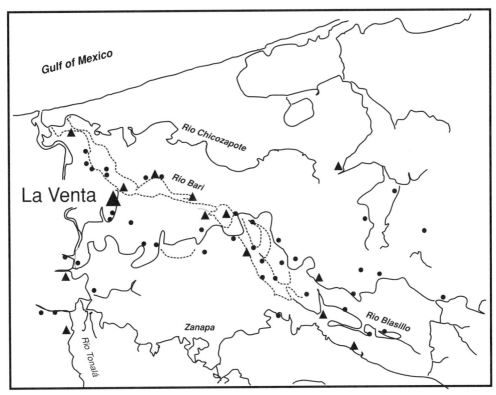

Western Tabasco Plain

Figure 5.3. Middle Formative settlement patterns in three regions of Olman (adapted from Rust and Leyden 1994: Fig. 12.1; Santley et al. 1997: Figr 7.4; Symonds et al. 2002: Fig. 4.12).

2003). In any event, it is evident that at least a two-tiered settlement hierarchy centered on Tres Zapotes emerged in the Middle Formative period, and further investigation may reveal additional administrative levels.

The greatest elaboration of Middle Formative Olmec political hierarchy developed far to the east, in the estuarine setting of the lower Tonalá river basin (Fig. 5.3). La Venta, described in detail below, continued its growth to become the preeminent Middle Formative Olmec center, although its dominion does not appear to have extended to Tres Zapotes. The surrounding population likewise reached a peak in the Middle Formative period, as new settlements sprouted along the banks of the then-active Río Barí and other distributary channels of the Mezcalapa delta. The emergence of a three-tiered settlement hierarchy is indicated by the establishment of more than a dozen secondary centers marked by central mounds, not all of which may have been active administrative centers at the same time (Rust and Leyden 1994: Fig. 12.1; Pool 2001). The extent of the realm under La Venta's direct control is uncertain. It likely included Arroyo Pesquero, a site 20 km to the south, which produced an astounding cache of finely crafted stone masks. Whether the site functioned as a shrine like El Manatí or was a center in its own right is unknown. La Venta also may have controlled the site of Arroyo Sonso about 35 km to the southeast, which was home to the exquisite "Wrestler" statue. If either of these sites or other, similarly distant sites functioned as centers under La Venta's domination, it could imply an additional administrative tier in the polity's settlement hierarchy.

To summarize, the Middle Formative period in Olman witnessed broad population shifts, with pronounced declines in the Coatzacoalcos and San Juan basins, and substantial gains in the Tabasco lowlands around La Venta, in the Tuxtla Mountains, and at Tres Zapotes (Fig. 5.3). These complementary trends suggest, if not conclusively demonstrate, a pattern of migration out of the center of Olman toward its margins. As was the case during the Early Formative period, settlement systems indicate a wide range of variation in sociopolitical organization paralleling subregional population densities, which included widely dispersed and apparently autonomous hamlets and villages in the Tuxtla Mountains and the middle Coatzacoalcos basin, and simple chiefdoms with two tiers of settlement at Estero Rabon and Laguna de los Cerros. Tres Zapotes emerged as a regional center, though it is not yet known if its settlement system included secondary administrative centers.

Environment and Ecology

Ultimately, the political fortunes of chiefdoms and stratified societies hinge on the ability of leaders to attract and retain followers by manipulating economic, social, military, and ideological sources of power. Nevertheless, changes in the natural environment and its exploitation can profoundly affect the distribution of people on the landscape and the routes of communication and exchange among them, thereby undermining or enhancing the ability of leaders to exert their authority over a region and mobilize labor for their political agendas.

Changes in subsistence practices can be expected to have affected patterns of land use and settlement, though the specific effects would have varied with local environmental conditions. In the La Venta area, Rust and Leyden (1994:) suggest a link between the growth of maize agriculture and more intensive occupation along river channels, paralleling Coe's (1981; Coe and Diehl 1980b: 151–152) arguments for the development of sociopolitical hierarchy at San Lorenzo (see Chapter 4). In other parts of Olman, the growing reliance on maize agriculture may have allowed and encouraged the expansion of population in upland areas, such as the central Tuxtla Mountains and their southern piedmont (Borstein 2001: 199; Killion and Urcid 2001; Santley et al. 1997). The substantial basalt deposits of the Tuxtlas piedmont would have provided an additional attraction for populations increasingly dependent on grinding tools to process maize (Killion and Urcíd 2001). At the same time, the extensive swidden methods of agriculture favored in upland areas would have favored the relatively dispersed pattern of hamlets and villages that characterize Middle Formative settlement in these areas and locally on hilly zones of the eastern Coatzacoalcos basin (Kruger 1996: 181–183, 1997: 150). In addition, local overexploitation of agricultural land and aquatic resources has been offered as a partial explanation of the population decline in the inner hinterland of San Lorenzo (Symonds et al. 2002: 79).

Linked geological processes also may have impacted settlement in the Tuxtla Mountains and the Coatzacoalcos basin. The southward shift of settlement in the central Tuxtlas corresponded to an eruption of Cerro Mono Blanco near the close of the Early Formative period (Reinhardt 1991: 92–95; Santley et al. 1997: 184–185; Santley et al. 2000). The reader will recall that excavations at La Joya suggested that Early Formative groups in the Tuxtlas moved their residences frequently. This residential mobility may have helped them cope with volcanic disaster, for population continued to increase in the central Tuxtlas (Santley et al. 1997: 184; 2000). If general tectonic uplift accompanied this episode of volcanic activity, then some changes also would be expected along the San Juan river, which circles the southern margin of the Tuxtlas. Quite possibly this was when the main course of the river shifted southward from the Río Negro branch to its current location, an event that might have contributed to the Middle Formative decline of Laguna de los Cerros and nearby sites (see Borstein 2001: 155, 195–196).

Farther afield, Cyphers (1996: 71), has suggested that uplift in the Tuxtlas contributed to changes in river courses around San Lorenzo. Some geomorphological and settlement studies suggest that the river channels that had previously lain close to San Lorenzo shifted farther away (Ortiz and Cyphers 1997), although a more recent settlement analysis indicates the nearby El Gato channel continued to operate (Symonds et al. 2002: 89). In any event, dramatic shifts in river courses are common in mature, meandering streams such as the Coatzacoalcos, and the rise of salt diapirs in the middle Coatzacoalcos basin has clearly help to shape local stream patterns (Ortiz and Cyphers 1997). Such shifts could well have diminished San Lorenzo's control over the local transportation network (Symonds and Lunagómez 1997a: 158–160). Combined with the posited overexploitation of the capital's inner hinterland, such local environmental changes would have reduced the ability of the San Lorenzo elite to extract surpluses and labor from its supporting population. Whether the decline of San Lorenzo contributed to the decline of Laguna de los Cerros or vice versa, the importation to San Lorenzo of basalt necessary for grinding tools and for the symbolic expression of secular and spiritual power through the carving of monuments also diminished. Obsidian exchange from the sources at Guadalupe Victoria and Pico de Orizaba to central and eastern Olman also may have been compromised by the rise of the regional center at Tres Zapotes. Together, the loss of these sources of economic power would have undermined the authority of the San Lorenzo elites. In terms proposed by Jonathan Haas (1982: 166–169, see also Earle 1991), the costs to the populace of complying with the demands of the San Lorenzo elite would have exceeded the costs of refusal, loosening the hold of the elites on their subjects and leaving them vulnerable to internal revolt and external attack. Whether the mutilation of monuments discussed in the previous chapter constitutes evidence for such aggression is not clear. Many of the former subjects of San Lorenzo may simply have "voted with their feet" and migrated to the Tuxtla hills or joined the growing numbers of followers at Tres Zapotes and La Venta.

Far to the east, the delta of the Mezcalapa river continued to expand into the Gulf of Mexico. Farmsteads, villages, and small civic-ceremonial centers grew along its distributary rivers, including the Río Barí, which by then was an active channel (Rust and Leyden 1994: 192; Pope et al. 2001). These hinterland sites undoubtedly provided the surplus that financed the programs of Olmec rulers in their marshbound island capital of La Venta, to which we now turn.

LA VENTA

The archaeological site of La Venta sits atop a low hill formed by the erosion of the ancient Pleistocene landscape, which rises more than 20 m above the surrounding wetlands (González 1996a: 74; Jiménez 1990: 7). The site is estimated to have originally covered some 200 ha, nearly half of which suffered major disturbance from urban expansion and industrial growth. At the summit of the "island" the Olmecs constructed a civic-ceremonial zone impressive both for its size and for the formal conception of its architectural program (Figs. 5.4, 5.5). Stretching for nearly 1.5 km and covering some 65 ha, it contains over 30 earthen mounds and platforms, each oriented to 8° west of north. The buildings of the central zone are grouped into four functionally distinct complexes, designated A, B, C, and D, from north to south. Two other pairs of platforms, Complexes G and H, lie on the edges of the central zone. Other groups of low mounds, the Cerro del Encanto group (Complex F) in the north and the Southern Mound Group at the south end of the island, contain much later Classic period artifacts unrelated to the Olmec occupation.

In Complex A, a series of low mounds set about the central axis of the site in perfect bilateral symmetry surround and define two courts that constituted a restricted ceremonial precinct in which were interred important individuals and sumptuous offerings. A wall of natural basalt columns set upright in the ground enclosed the northern court. A 4 m high mound (A-2) interrupts the northern line of columns, and five low mounds arranged as an irregular quincunx lie within the basalt column enclosure. The adjacent southern court is formed by two long flanking mounds with an elliptical mound between their northern extremes.

Complex C contains the "Great Pyramid" of La Venta, mound C-1. With a volume of 90,000 cu m, mound C-1 was the largest single structure of its time in Mesoamerica. Set on a 150 m wide platform (structure C-3), the pyramid rises 34 m above the plazas of Complexes A and B. From its summit, one has an unrestricted view of the surrounding wetlands, and on a clear day one can see the distant volcanoes of the Tuxtla Mountains and the Isthmus of Tehuantepec. Today, erosion has smoothed the contours of the great mound and carved shallow flutes down its flanks. This fluted cone was once interpreted as a faithful representation of a volcano, but recent excavations on the southern side of the mound show that it was built as a stepped earthen pyramid with inset corners (González 1996a: 75). Nevertheless, it is well established that pyramids symbolized sacred mountains to later Mesoamerican cultures, and they probably did to the Olmecs as well (Reilly 1999: 18).

Mound C-1 looms over the great plaza of Complex B, separating this more public space from the restricted ceremonial plazas of Complex A (Fig. 5.4). The eastern edge of the great plaza is bounded by the Stirling Acropolis, a massive platform measuring 300 × 250 m. Three smaller rectangular mounds enclose the western edge of the plaza and a fourth occupies its center. To the south, Complex D contains 20 mounds arranged in three parallel lines flanking two long avenues that open into a second large plaza on the south. Much more investigation is necessary to determine the functions of Complex D, but they may have been largely administrative (González 1996a: 75).

When the major constructions of the central civic-ceremonial zone were all that were known of La Venta, the site was thought to have been a "vacant" ceremonial center devoid of residents other than rulers, priests, and their retainers.

Figure 5.4. La Venta Mound C-1, with reproduction of Stela 2 in foreground.

Important investigations in Complexes G, E, and I have overturned this idea with evidence of residential occupation in the form of low habitational platforms, packed earth house floors, food storage pits, and high phosphate concentrations in the soil, which are commonly associated with areas where humans discard waste (Barba 1988; González 1996: 80; Rust and Sharer 1988).

Chronology

In general terms, the florescence of La Venta is dated between 1000 and 400 B.C., encompassing the Middle Formative period (Lowe 1989: 54–61). However, the details of chronology at La Venta have troubled the minds of archaeologists like few others in Mesoamerica. The basic tools of archaeological chronology are stratigraphy, the seriation and cross-dating of artifacts, and the "absolute" or chronometric methods of techniques such as radiocarbon dating. Stratigraphy, seriation, and cross-dating are relative techniques that reveal the order of events in time, and the chronometric method of radiocarbon dating assigns events to a time range in years before the "present," defined by convention as A.D. 1950. Ideally, each of these lines of evidence would complement one another, with stylistic changes in pottery tied to stratified deposits and construction sequences dated by radiocarbon or another chronometric technique. For various reasons, this has not occurred at La Venta. The early attempts to construct a ceramic chronology did not reveal a clear sequence of stylistic change, and the stratigraphic excavations that were conducted for this purpose were located outside Complex A, which provided the most detailed sequence

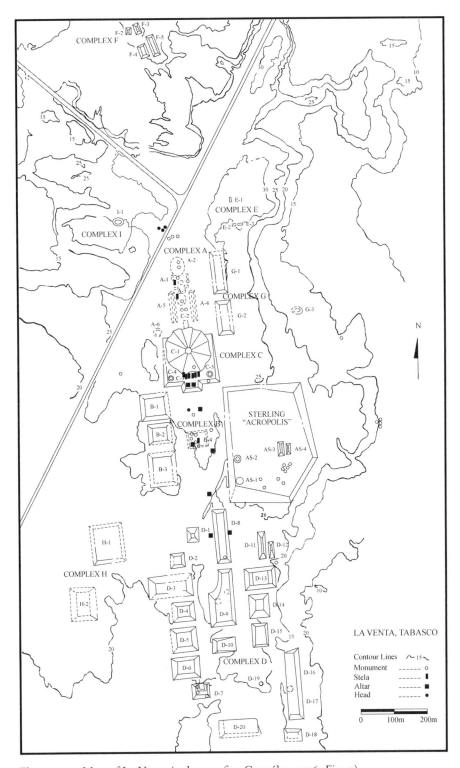

Figure 5.5. Map of La Venta (redrawn after González 1996: Fig. 1).

of construction stages (Drucker 1952a; Drucker et al. 1959). The construction stages in Complex A were dated with radiocarbon assays, but the nature of the radiocarbon calibration curve for the timespan of the Middle Formative period makes obtaining a clear sequence of radiocarbon dates and calibrating radiocarbon years with calendar years particularly difficult. This is because between about 450 and 800 B.C. (ca. 450–600 b.c. in radiocarbon years), radiocarbon years do not vary uniformly with respect to calendar years due to past variations in the concentration of carbon-14 in the atmosphere. In fact, a piece of wood cut down and burned in 750 B.C. is likely to give a radiocarbon date younger than one from 600 B.C. (Stuiver et al. 1998).

As a result of these difficulties, the details of La Venta's chronology are still vigorously debated. For example, some researchers dispute the presence of a major occupation prior to 1000 B.C. due to the absence of the diagnostic Calzadas carved and Limon carved-incised types (Clark 2001: 184; von Nagy 2003: 1081), although a handful of radiocarbon dates, recovery of other diagnostic ceramic types, and some sculptural similarities to San Lorenzo monuments suggest the presence of an Early Formative center at La Venta (González 1990: 159–167, 1996a: 73; Grove 1981b: 66; 1997: 72–73; Hallinan et al. 1968; Lowe 1989: 50). For the Middle Formative sequence, the original chronology was based on a sequence of four construction episodes in Complex A (Drucker et al. 1959; Berger et al. 1967; Heizer et al. 1968a; cf. Coe and Stuckenrath 1964). Radiocarbon dates from all of these phases overlap due to the nature of the calibration curve, but a conventional placement of phases I and II before 600 B.C. and phases III and IV afterward is consistent with medians of the probability distributions for dates from phases I and II and the recovery of Early Franco phase ceramics (ca. 700–500 B.C.) from Offering 5 in construction phase III (Drucker et al. 1959: Figure 42a; von Nagy 2003: 633, 835). Alternatively, construction phases II and III may overlap in time (Lowe 1989; Grove 1997: 72). A recently obtained radiocarbon assay from Mound C-1 suggests the mound was still in use until 400 B.C. and supports a median probability date of 646 B.C. (580 ± 302 uncalibrated B.C.) for the beginning of construction on the small platform (C-2) that projects from the north side of the mound (Berger et al. 1967: 14; Drucker et al. 1959: 120; González 1997: 93).

As noted, most of the Complex A construction phases have not been clearly related to changes in pottery styles and technology that typically form the basis for regional chronologies in archaeology. Ongoing investigations at the site should resolve this issue in the near future, but in the meantime, investigations in hinterland sites suggest an equivalence of phase I with the Late Puente phase (ca. 800–700 B.C.) of the Chontalpa region, phases II and III with the Early Franco phase (ca. 700–500 B.C.) and phase IV with the Late Franco phase (ca. 500–400 or 350 B.C. (von Nagy 2003: 835, 844; Lowe 1989: Table 4.1; Rust and Leyden 1994: Table 12.1; Sisson 1970: Fig. 10.1), generally corroborating the ages discussed above.

Tombs and Treasures

The ceremonial offerings discovered in Complex A during the 1940s and 1950s are some of the most impressive ever recovered from the Formative period in Mesoamerica. The earthen mounds and courts that form the complex are not impressive for their size, but they are notable for the care and elaborateness of their construction. Erected in four major stages and enduring numerous resurfacings over 400 years, more or less, the stepped platforms and courts were built up with carefully laid layers of red, pink, yellow, gray, and purple sands and clays (Drucker et al. 1959). Some of the platforms also incorporated adobe bricks, unusual at that early time, to fill their volumes. In the final building stage, around 400 B.C., a thick cap of red clay was laid over the entire complex.

It is the massive offerings, however, five in number and unique to La Venta, which most eloquently express the power of her rulers. Composed of cut serpentine blocks imported from highland sources in Mexico or Guatemala, they were laid in deep pits at the beginnings of major construction phases. The earliest two intact offerings were placed on either side of the center line of the complex beneath the southeast and southwest platforms of the north court (Drucker et al. 1959; Wedel 1952). They date from the beginning of phase II, perhaps around 700 B.C. In the most completely excavated example, under the southwest platform, a pit measuring 15 by 19 m and 7 m deep was filled with 1000 tons of serpentine blocks laid in 28 courses set in olive-green and blue clay (Fig 5.6).

The last course was arranged as a nearly square mosaic pavement with a cleft on its north side and fringed diamond-shaped appendages on the south (Fig. 2.5). In the middle of the pavement, open areas filled with colored sands and clays described a bar surrounded by four trilobed "dots" and a sideways E-shaped element. The pavement under the southeast platform matches this one element-for-element, while a third pavement, laid much later on the center line of the southern court, lacks only the central bar and the fringed appendages. The design of the mosaic pavements was first interpreted as a highly stylized four-eyed jaguar mask (Drucker et al. 1959: 94) and later as the Olmec Dragon (Joralemon 1976: 45–52). More recent interpretations view the pavements as representations of the multi-layered cosmos, with the central bar connecting the quadripartite earthly plain with the watery underworld below (represented by the appendages as water lilies) and the sky above (Reilly 1994), or as a kind of stylized map of La Venta at the center of the earth between the Gulf to the north and the water lily-choked swamps to the south (Tate 1999). Although they vary substantially, these interpretations are not entirely incompatible with one another, given the penchant of the Olmecs for combining multiple referents in the same polysemic design.

Two other massive offerings buried under the center line of the north court and the northernmost mound, structure A-2, contained pavements of

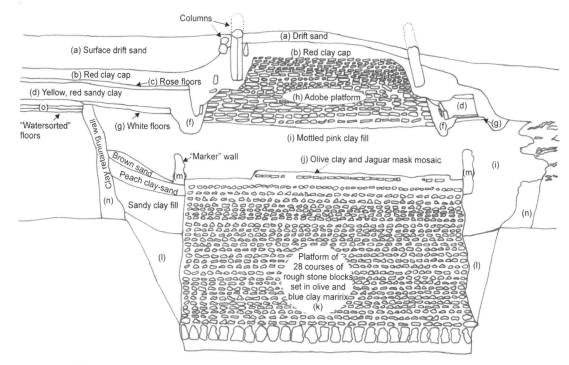

Figure 5.6. Stratigraphy of the southwest platform, Complex A, La Venta (redrawn after Drucker et al. 1959: Fig. 26).

serpentine blocks in the bottoms of deep pits, but lacked the mosaic masks (Drucker et al. 1959). The largest of these, Massive Offering 3, contained six courses of serpentine blocks laid in a pit 23.5 m square and 4 m deep dug at the beginning of phase III, around 600 B.C. Massive Offering 2, placed within structure A-2 at the beginning of phase IV contained a single course of serpentine blocks in the bottom of a pit 15 m long, 6 m wide, and 5 m deep.

Astoundingly, these opulent, labor-intensive offerings were intended to be observed only briefly, for they were almost immediately covered with more layers of clay, earth, and other materials. To describe one example, shortly after the pavement under the southwest platform was laid, it was covered with a thin cap of olive green clay and a thick layer of pink clay, and a platform of adobe bricks was raised over the offering (Drucker et al. 1959: 97). Similar treatment was given to the mosaic under the southeast platform, with the addition of an offering of 20 greenstone celts and a concave iron ore mirror arranged in the shape of a cross immediately below the platform. We cannot know how many people observed these rites in the confines of La Venta's most sacred precinct. Perhaps their numbers were limited to the toiling laborers and the nobility of La Venta. Perhaps leaders from dependent communities and more distant rivals also were invited to witness the ostentatious display and disposal of wealth. Or perhaps thousands of subjects from near and far filed before the grand offerings

Figure 5.7. La Venta Offering 4 (González 1994: Fig. 6.20) (courtesy of John E. Clark).

before they were buried from view. Whatever the audience, the simultaneously flamboyant and pious act of committing tons of exotic, symbolically charged materials to the earth undoubtedly conveyed a strong message of secular and sacred power to those in attendance.

Massive offerings of serpentine were not the only displays of wealth and power at La Venta. Forty-eight other offerings of votive celts, figurines, pottery vessels, iron ore mirrors, and other portable objects were recovered from in and around Complex A. Many of these consisted of groups of polished jade and serpentine celts, some in cruciform arrangements. They tended to be buried along the centerline of the complex, under its platforms or in association with the massive offerings. The most famous, though, is Offering 4, a scene of sixteen human figurines, one in course sandstone and the rest in jade and serpentine (Fig. 5.7). The figurines, painted red with cinnabar, were set upright

Figure 5.8. Basalt column tomb (Tomb A) from La Venta, now in the Parque La Venta, Villahermosa, Tabasco.

in red sand as if frozen in the performance of a ceremony and then covered with white sand. The lone sandstone figure stood before six celts set upright like stelae. In front of him filed four individuals, and the remaining figures stood in a semicircle to witness the event. Afterwards the entire court was covered with a series of clay floors. Many years or decades later someone dug a small pit through these floors just to the level of the figurines' heads, and then refilled the pit (Drucker et al. 1959: 154). Why, we cannot know, but the accuracy with which the pit was placed attests to the importance and long-held memory of the original offering.

Bone and dental enamel fare poorly in the acid soils of La Venta. Nevertheless, five features indicate that important individuals were accorded the honor of burial on the centerline of Complex A in the final construction phase before the site was abandoned (Drucker 1952; Drucker et al. 1959). The most elaborate of these features, appropriately designated Tomb A, was placed over Massive Offering 2 in the northernmost mound of the complex (Fig. 5.8). The tomb was walled and roofed with natural basalt columns and paved with limestone slabs. On top of the slabs were laid the bundled remains of two or three children accompanied by figurines, ornaments, and a stingray-spine effigy, all in jade, a concave hematite mirror, 2 obsidian disks, a shark tooth, and 6 natural stingray spines. Stingray spines, it should be noted, are thought to have been used to pierce the body in a ceremonial offering of blood. One exquisite figurine of a seated female bore on its breast a miniature hematite mirror (Drucker 1952a: 23–26).

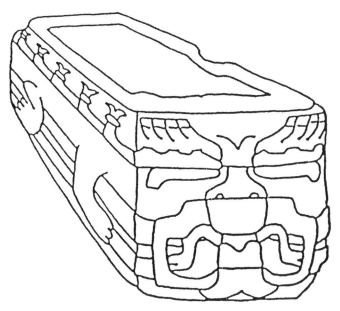

Figure 5.9. Sandstone sarcophagus (Tomb B) from La Venta, carved in the form of a crocodilian earth supernatural with vegetation sprouting from its back (Reilly 1994: Fig. 15.7) (redrawn from drawing by John E. Clark).

Tomb B, placed over the center of Massive Offering 2, took the form of a large, lidded sandstone coffer carved to represent the Olmec earth-monster floating on the primordial sea of creation (Reilly 1995: 35) (Fig 5.9). No bones were recovered from within the coffer, but items similar to those in Tomb A, including two jade earspools with pendants, a jade perforator, and a serpentine figure, suggest it too orginally held a burial (cf. Drucker 1952a: 27). Between them was a series of basalt columns laid side-by-side and covering the deposit identified as Tomb E, consisting of jade earplugs, beads, a jade disk, a broken magnetite mirror, and a tiny carved jade skull, arranged as if they adorned an interred body (Wedel 1952: 64). Two more probable burials with similarly arranged artifacts, a stone lined cyst (Tomb C), and a cinnabar-stained feature (Tomb D), were found beneath the centerline of Mound A-3 at the north end of the south court.

Stone Monuments

The sculptural corpus of about 90 monuments from La Venta is one of the largest and most diverse from Olman, exceeded in number only by that of San Lorenzo. Because the stratigraphic contexts of most of these monuments are uncertain, and many appear to have been reset long after they were carved, it is difficult to construct a completely satisfactory sculptural sequence for the site. Nevertheless, the contextual evidence we do have from La Venta, combined

with sculptural comparisons to other sites, suggests the sculptural arts at La
Venta developed over a considerable period, during which preferences shifted
from sculpture in the round to relief carving.

The earliest monuments include several full-round carvings bearing similarities to sculptures at San Lorenzo and other probably Early Formative carvings
in Olman. In addition, the site's four colossal heads were most likely carved at
the end of the Early Formative period or perhaps the beginning of the Middle
Formative period, as suggested for the colossal heads at Tres Zapotes (Fig. 4.3).
Like the San Lorenzo heads, the heads at La Venta are each unique in their
features, expressions, and regalia, implying that they were portraits of La Venta's
rulers. One (Monument 2) even sports a faint smile. Another (Monument 4)
has prominent teeth and wears the three-clawed foot of a raptorial bird in its
headdress. These features also are seen on a figure carved in low relief on the
side of San Lorenzo Monument 14, a table-top altar-throne. Though erased
by mutilation, a rope apparently bound this figure to the person seated in the
central niche on the front of the altar. Whether this rope identifies the "eagle-
foot chief" as a captive or a relative (Grove 1981b: 66–67), the similarity of the
figures suggests some form of interaction with San Lorenzo early in La Venta's
history.

Another early sculptural type is represented by five table-top altar-thrones
with frontal niche figures (de la Fuente 1973: 18–32). The largest of these, Altar
4, weighs some 40 tons and ranks among the greatest masterpieces of Olmec
art (Fig. 5.10). The central figure wears a harpy eagle headdress (Grove 1973:
130) and feather cape (Clark 2005: 214) and is seated cross-legged in a niche
framed by four stylized maize ears. He grasps in his right hand a twisted rope
that extends around the side of the throne to wrap around the wrist of a captive
or lineal relative in low relief (Grove 1981b: 61, 66). Another rope extends from
under his left knee around the opposite, effaced, side of the throne. The niche
itself suggests the maw of the supernatural earth-monster whose upper jaw
and face are carved in low relief on the projecting upper band of the throne.
Crossed bands in the supernatural's mouth identify the niche as an entrance and
geometric bands symbolizing earth and sky flank the supernatural face (Reilly
1995; Grove 2000). Thus the ruler in the niche is poised at the interface of
underworld, earth, and sky, and is framed by visual references to fertility and
to dominance over, or kinship with, other leaders in a perfect allegory of the
sources of his earthly and supernatural power.

Later sculptures at La Venta document the increasing importance of relief
carving, particularly on late Middle Formative stelae (Fig. 5.11). Three distinctive styles of stela carving can be noted. The first consists of a single example,
Stela 1, which depicts a figure in high relief standing in a niche surmounted
by a geometric band reminiscent of the bands on Altar 4. The second class
consists of six "celtiform" stelae, so-called because they resemble in form and
subject votive greenstone celts (Porter 1992). Carved in low relief, three on
greenish metamorphic stones (schist and gneiss) and three on grey volcanic

Figure 5.10. La Venta Altar 4.

stone, the six were originally placed along the southern base of Mound C-1, green to the west, gray to the east (González 1997: 91; Jaime-Riverón 2003: 645–650). Four of the stelae bear stylized supernatural masks, often interpreted as earth-monsters, which would have marked Mound C-1 as a sacred mountain similar to the pyramids of the Maya (Grove 2000: 291). The fifth (Stela 5) bears a narrative scene of three figures observed from above by a fourth "floating" figure who seems to be offering an object to the central figure below, while the sixth is plain.

The content of Stela 5 links it to the third class of stelae, which also bear narrative scenes, represented by Stelae 2 and 3 (Fig. 5.11). On Stela 2 a large central figure holds a ceremonial bar in his hands and wears a stiff cape. On his head he bears an enormous, elaborate headdress as tall as the figure itself, inset with iconographic elements, one of which recalls the headdress on the colossal head, Monument 1. Five chubby supernatural dwarf figures, three floating in the air, surround the central figure. Stela 2 contains a yet more complex scene of two figures facing one another, also surrounded by floating dwarves. Both of the principal figures wear elaborate, composite headdresses. The figure on the left wears a stiff cape and holds a bar in his right hand. The one on the right sports a pointed beard, earning him the nickname "Uncle Sam" among *olmequistas*. He stands in front of a low-relief representation of a niche bearing the diagonal lines of the sky band.

The encounters shown on the narrative scenes of Stela 3 and Stela 5 seem to reflect a growing interest among Olmec rulers in depicting historic events, albeit sanctioned and mythologized by the floating dwarves that observe the action. As we will see later, this concern with historicity reflects a trend,

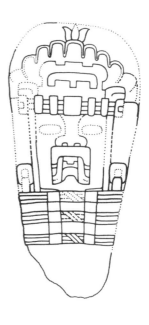

Figure 5.11. La Venta stelae: clockwise from upper left: Stela 1, Stela 2, Monument 26/27 (Taube 1996: Fig. 13d) (courtesy of Karl Taube), and Stela 3 (Bernal 1969: Plate 4).

Figure 5.12. Early steps toward writing: La Venta Monument 13 and cylinder seal from San Andres (Pohl et al. 2002: Fig. 2) (redrawn from original by Ajax Moreno).

foresaged by the relief panels on earlier thrones, that would ultimately culminate in the glyphic texts on Late and Terminal Formative Epi-Olmec stelae. With respect to the development of writing, one more monument of La Venta merits special mention. This is Monument 13, a circular "altar" found in the final construction phase at the southern foot of Structure A-2 over an earlier offering of 20 serpentine celts and the still earlier Massive Offering 3. Nicknamed "The Ambassador," this late monument shows a striding, bearded figure holding what appears to be a penant. Most extaordinary, however is a column of three glyph-like elements in front of the figure and a fourth element in the shape of a footprint behind him, similar to the footprint glyphs that denoted travel in Aztec codices (Fig. 5.12). Other glyph-like elements have been discovered recently on a cylinder seal and fragments of greenstone plaques at the nearby site of San Andrés (Pohl et al. 2002). Thus the well-documented Olmec use of symbolic elements in *pars pro toto* representation of concepts may already have crossed the line into formal writing by the end of the Middle Formative period.

Like their predecessors at San Lorenzo, the Olmecs of La Venta arranged stone monuments to demarcate important spaces and to imbue those spaces with specific meanings. We have already seen the example of the celtiform stelae associated with mound C-1, and David Grove (1999: 265–276) has identified several other significant arrangements of monuments in the sacred landscape of La Venta. One is the placement of the site's four colossal heads. Three were ultimately set facing north in a line 110 m north of Complex A, as if to mark the entrance to the site's ritual and administrative center. In combination with the fourth colossal head, located south of Mound C-1, they also serve to set off the northern sector of the site formed by Complexes A and C. As Grove points out, by the late Middle Formative period, these portraits would have been of ancestral, rather than living, rulers, consistent with the mortuary and ceremonial themes of this northern sector. In contrast, stelae and altars, many of which combine religious and monarchial themes, are concentrated in the more public venues in and around the plaza of Complex B and at the north end of Complex D. Widely spaced, they would have been viewed best in procession, in the same manner as the colossal heads of San Lorenzo. Grove (1999) also notes significant pairings of the altars, with those depicting central figures holding babies facing toward the public space of the plaza and those with central figures alone facing in the opposite direction. Finally, near the south end of the site center, on structure D-7, three massive sandstone sculptures of squatting individuals holding their outsized heads mirror the colossal heads at the opposite end of the site center.

Portable Art and Middle Formative Iconography

As awe-inspiring as are the massive offerings and stone monuments of La Venta, so too, in a more intimate way, are the numerous figurines and other small artifacts of imported stone that were interred in the burials and caches at the site. Though the Olmecs of the Middle Formative period used many exotic rocks and minerals for their portable art, they clearly preferred green and blue jades. Over 3,000 jade objects were recovered from Complex A at La Venta alone (Drucker 1981: 36), reflecting in spectacular fashion an explosion in the exchange of this precious commodity across Mesoamerica.

Although ceramic artifacts bore much of the symbolic load for Early Formative cultures, small, portable objects of jade and other stones functioned widely as components of the Middle Formative Ceremonial Complex, "the physical evidence – artifacts, symbols, motifs, and architectural groupings – for the rituals practiced by, and the ideology and political structures of" the various cultures of Middle Formative Mesoamerica (Reilly 1995: 29). Some components of this complex were already present in the Early Formative period. These continuities apparently include the concept of a multi-layered universe connected by a world tree as the *axis mundi*, the religious importance of mountains, caves and springs, and the belief in various supernatural entities such as the were-jaguar baby or dwarf, the earth-monster, and the sky-serpent. Over the course of the Middle Formative period, however, novel ways appeared of expressing these ancient concepts, new emphases emerged, and the repertoire of symbols became more systematically codified. Neither was the Middle Formative Ceremonial Complex homogeneous in its expression across Mesoamerica. Some symbols, motifs, and forms appear to be better represented outside of Olman than within it. Here caution must be exercised, because so much of our knowledge of Olmec-style iconography derives from objects in private collections with poor provenience. Nevertheless, the portable stone artifacts of La Venta and contemporary sites in the Gulf lowlands provide a good entrée into the beliefs and ceremonial practices of Middle Formative Mesoamerica.

Some of the most revealing of these artifacts are polished stone celts with finely engraved designs that were often filled with red cinnabar or hematite to bring out their details. Offering 2, a cache of 51 celts from phase III in Complex A, included four engraved examples (Fig. 5.13). One of these bears the profile head of Joralemon's God II wearing a long-lipped buccal mask with a downturned mouth that covers the lower face, a head band with two oval elements and a detached circular element with three erect plumes representing seed corn. From a cleft in the top of the head sprouts a banded projection representing maize (Joralemon 1971: 61, Schele 1995: 106). A common element in Olmec engravings, a narrow vertical band here placed at the rear of the head, repeats the long-lipped, down-turned mouth, slanted eye, and cleft of the principal figure. Similar, more crudely engraved figures are shown in full body on two other celts from the offering. A fourth celt sports the "bar-and-four-dots" motif with the upper two dots surmounted by two sideways E-shaped elements, recalling the mosaic pavements of Complex A. Three engraved celts from Offering C of the 1942 field season, also deposited in phase III of Complex A, expand on the symbolic associations of the engraved celts in Offering 2 (Drucker 1952a: Fig. 47). One shows the abstracted face of Joralemon's God II in frontal view with the banded maize motif rising from a head band with a central circular element and four oval elements, two to either side. On other Olmec-style carvings and celts, these four oval elements are shown in greater detail as sprouting cleft maize seeds (Fields 1989; 1991; Reilly 1995: 39; Schele 1995: 106). In its hands the image holds double-pointed "knuckle dusters," probably representing cut conch-shell bloodletters (Andrews 1987; Grove 1987c; Joyce et al. 1990). The bar-and-four dots motif is represented on two other celts from Offering 1942c, but on these it is infixed in the cleft-seed motif from which sprouts a three-pronged element identified by Schele and Looper (Schele 1995: 106) as a dicot sprout evocative of bean and squash plants (cf. Taube 2000: 298–303) (see Fig. 4.6 for an example).

Three jade celts said to come from Arroyo Pesquero, a site in La Venta's hinterland, combine the elements engraved on the La Venta celts in a particularly informative manner (Reilly 1995: 38–39; Schele 1995: 105–107). In each of these three celts, the image of God II becomes the central bar in the bar-and-four-dots motif and sprouting maize seeds become the dots. Upon his head, the image wears a feathered headdress from which sprouts vegetation. On two of the celts, the central figure, face in profile, holds a ceremonial bar marking him as an Olmec ruler in the costume of God II. In one, the ruler's bar takes the form of a serpent with a flame eyebrow, and his legs are replaced with the downward-facing head of the crocodilian Olmec dragon, complete with L-shaped eyes, flame eyebrows, protruding nostrils, and gum brackets (Reilly 1995: 38–39, Figs. 25 and 26). Reinterpreting the two-dimensional image on this last celt in three dimensions, Reilly (1995: 25–26) convincingly argues that it is a cosmogram of the four-quartered earth with the ruler in the center as the world-tree. Thus the ruler's roles as communicator with the layers of the cosmos, intermediary with the supernatural realm and guarantor of agricultural plenty are all implicated in and underwrite his earthly authority.

I have selected these few examples from La Venta and its environs for extended discussion because they illustrate a particularly well-documented complex of mutually reinforcing ideological, cosmological, and political referents. They also illustrate the common principal in Olmec iconography of *pars pro toto*, whereby individual elements of more complete figures, such as the bar-and-four-dots motif or the sprouting seed, may stand as abbreviations for a broader concept or set of related concepts. These examples by no means exhaust the variety of engraved Olmec symbols, any more than they exhaust the diversity of the interpretations attributed to Olmec iconography. The essential point is that the Middle Formative iconography of the Olmecs and their contemporaries was complex, multivocal, and highly codified, though the code is by no means easily accessible to modern scholars.

As noted in Chapter 4, the concepts of a multi-layered cosmos, a "world-tree" as the *axis mundi* connecting the cosmic planes, and the ability of certain individuals to communicate across the cosmic layers, thereby metaphorically becoming the world-tree, form constituents of a widely shared cosmology frequently associated with the ritual practices of shamans in the Americas (Reilly 1995: 31). The inspiration for shamanic interpretations of Olmec art derive from Peter Furst's (1968; 1995) analysis of a set of powerfully carved stone figurines, referred to as "transformation figures." Most are now, or once were, in private collections, and the provenances attributed to them are at best vague, but at least one head fragment was found by Stirling near Huimanguillo, Tabasco (Furst 1968: 150; Fig. 2), and several others are said to come from elsewhere on

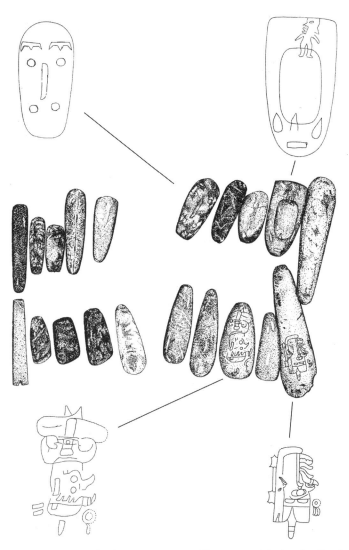

Figure 5.13. Celts from La Venta Offering 2, with detail of incised designs (adapted from Drucker et al. 1959: Figs. 34 and 35).

the Gulf Coast in Veracruz or Tabasco (Furst 1995; Guthrie and Benson 1995: Catalog Nos. 46–48). Standing with one foot slightly forward, or crouching with one knee up, the faces of the figures bear the features of a grimacing were-jaguar, with furrowed brow and crenulated designs on the forehead and pate. Rather than standing out from the face like masks, however, the features are recessed relative to the back of the head, suggesting that the skin has been peeled away to reveal "the jaguar beneath." Other Olmec and Olmec-style figurines show a human kneeling with hands on knees, in one case with were-jaguar features and in another with serene human features and the incised figure of a toad on his shaved head, recalling, though in different form, the designs on the heads of the other transformation figures. Viewed as a set, these figures evoke the transformation of South American shamans into jaguar spirits and of Mesoamerican specialists variously described as sorcerers, priests, and shamans into their *naualli*, or animal spirit companions (Furst 1968: 151).

In order to travel to the supernatural realm, the shaman enters a trance or ecstatic state through techniques ranging from meditation, drumming, and dance to sensory deprivation, pain, or the taking of hallucinogens (Eliade 1964; Reilly 1995: 30). Travel in this trance state is often described as flying between different planes of reality (Reilly 1995: 30). Small carvings of a human figure seated or lying on the back of a feline or crocodilian, including one from Arroyo Pesquero, have been argued to represent this flight (Reilly 1995: 43; Guthrie and Benson 1995: Catalog Nos. 63 and 64), as have horizontal figures holding "torch bundles" (possibly feathered maize fetishes, Taube 2000: 307) such as one carved in rock at Chalcatzingo, Morelos, and another incised on a stone celt from La Venta (Drucker et al. 1959: Fig. 40c; Guthrie and Benson 1995: Catalog No. 70; Tate 1995: 56). Reilly (1995: 39–42) also interprets the harpy-eagle headdress of the central figure at La Venta Altar 4 and the owl mask and feathered cape of a figure seated on a throne in the painted mural of Oxtotitlan Cave, Guerrero, as examples of the shamanic flight costume. Still other representations from Olman and across Mesoamerica interpreted as related to this shamanic complex include the bent-kneed figurines best represented in La Venta Offering 4, and beautifully carved polished stone masks with rapt expressions, including many from a large cache at Arroyo Pesquero (Tate 1995: 57–60).

Another class of figurines are small, usually chinless sculptures standing with deeply flexed knees (e.g. La Venta Figurines 10 and 11). Some hold their oversized heads like the large sandstone sculptures from La Venta structure D-7; others stand with arms crossed or slightly raised. Some appear to be dwarves, which also are represented on Early Formative monuments from San Lorenzo (Monument 18) and the Potrero Nuevo altar (Monument 2). Others may be deformed infants or fetuses (Tate 1995: 60–62). Though their associations are not clearly shamanic, often dwarves are shown attending rulers in later Maya carvings, and they may have held specific supernatural associations.

The shamanic interpretation of Olmec iconography and ritual is a convincing one, as is the proposed link between this ideological complex and rulership, but here we must sound a note of caution. One of the traditional distinctions between shamans and priests is that the former are part-time specialists who acquire their spiritual power from personal experiences, while the latter are full-time, formally trained specialists who acquire their spiritual power from their office (e.g., Lowie 1963). In this respect, it is important to maintain a distinction among shamanist belief, shamanic practice, and the social role of the shaman. The complex of shamanist beliefs that comprise the Middle Formative Ceremonial Complex is widespread in contemporary and historically documented societies of the Americas. Likewise, shamanic practice, involving techniques of ecstasy and rituals of transformation, is typical of these societies, and would appear to be well-illustrated in Olmec art. Nevertheless, similar beliefs were held, and ecstatic acts engaged in, by religious practitioners in societies with formalized priesthoods, including the Aztecs. Thus, the mere identification of such concepts and practices in art and iconography does not definitively identify the holders of the beliefs and the practitioners of the rites associated with them as shamans. If religious practitioners other than shamans can include in their practical and conceptual repertoire shamanic ritual and shamanist belief, then the principal distinction between shamans and priests must lie in the character of their status and the requirements for attaining it. In other words, those who hold formalized positions as religious practitioners may do and think shamanic things, but they are not shamans in terms of their social and religious roles; they are priests. It is likely that Olmec and other Middle Formative societies included informal religious specialists accurately described as shamans, but in co-opting and regularizing shamanist belief and shamanic ritual, Olmec rulers instituted a formal priesthood.

SOCIOPOLITICAL CONTINUITY AND CHANGE IN OLMAN

The development of the Middle Formative Ceremonial Complex from Early Formative antecedents is emblematic of general patterns of continuity and change in Olman. The broad principles of sociopolitical organization remained intact and leaders drew on the same basic sources of power to acquire and retain their positions. On the other hand, the balance of power and influence among Olmec centers changed dramatically and new emphases emerged, both in the specific political-economic strategies employed by leaders and in their symbolic expressions. The shifting geopolitical relationships between Olmec centers and their contemporaries in Mesoamerica were one important impetus toward change in Olman and will be treated in the next chapter. In each of the participating societies, however, these interregional ties were established for the benefit of leaders and their followers at home, and it is in that local context that they must be understood.

Despite the obvious geographic shifts in political power among Olmec centers during the Early to Middle Formative transition, the overall variation in sociopolitical organization changed little in Olman. The inhabitants of the Tuxtlas became more sedentary as they invested more heavily in agriculture. At the other end of the sociopolitical spectrum, some expansion of administrative positions may be reflected in the construction of Complex D at La Venta. Nevertheless, Olman remained divided among autonomous polities that spanned a range of organizational forms. These included egalitarian communities of hamlets and villages in the Tuxtlas and San Juan and Coatzacoacos drainages; simple, two-tiered chiefdoms such as that headed by Estero Rabon and perhaps Tres Zapotes; and the more highly stratified polity with three or more administrative levels controlled by La Venta. Like its Early Formative predecessor at San Lorenzo, whether the La Venta polity should be considered a paramount chiefdom or an archaic state is a semantic and empirical problem with no simple resolution. At present, however, La Venta appears broadly comparable to San Lorenzo in the extent and administrative organization of its realm.

The rise and fall of individual centers across Olman reflects the widely recognized process of cycling in chiefdoms and archaic states (Anderson 1994a, 1996a; Flannery and Marcus 2000; Marcus 1998; Marcus and Feinman 1998: 11). Particularly when power is organized along exclusionary principles, such political formations are rife with internal factionalism, and subordinate leaders may lay claim to their own sources of legitimation and power. Rulers must achieve a balance between the perceived costs and benefits to subjects of complying with their demands vs. the costs and benefits of refusing them (Earle 1991: 13). That balance is easily upset by abuses of power or by environmental and political events beyond their control. As a result, complex chiefdoms and archaic states tend to be highly volatile political formations. Indeed, the ability of the La Venta polity to retain its stability and preeminence for several centuries is a testimony to the political acumen of its leaders. When the most centralized Olmec centers passed away, however, they left in their wake a depleted and dispersed population of villages and hamlets, unlike many complex chiefdoms elsewhere in the world, which broke into the simple chiefdoms that comprised their constituent units (e.g., Anderson 1994b; 1996b).

Stone monuments, massive earthworks, and large volumes of imported goods indicate that Middle Formative Olmec leaders continued to rely heavily on the monopolization of ideological and economic sources of political power, manipulating similar concepts, materials, and goods as their predecessors. Advantageous marriages and other forms of alliance undoubtedly remained important strategies for securing the surplus labor and resources needed to finance their construction and sculptural programs as well as to establish the social networks through which exotic prestige and utilitarian goods flowed. Rulers and aspirants well may have had recourse to military power but, if anything, the evidence for warfare and rebellion is even less visible than in the Early Formative period.

Notwithstanding these broad continuities in political-economic principles and sociopolitical forms, the specific means of acquiring, maintaining, and expressing political power show significant changes in the Middle Formative period. One of the most interesting of these changes is the growing emphasis on the explicit representation of legitimizing acts, seen particularly in late Middle Formative bas-relief carvings. There is a narrative quality to La Venta Stelae 2 and 3 and Monument 13 (The "Ambassador") that is rare in Early Formative sculpture. It is perhaps significant that the presumably Early Formative Olmec monuments that incorporate narrative bas-relief carvings either come from La Venta (Altars 3, 4, and 5), or suggest a tie with La Venta (San Lorenzo Monument 14). Therefore, this style of representation well may have originated and have been further elaborated in the context of the particular political strategies of La Venta's elite. Be that as it may, by the close of the Middle Formative period it had spread to Tres Zapotes and beyond Olman. From the El Viejón stela on the north-central Gulf Coast and the relief carvings at Chalcatzingo, to the numerous stelae distributed through the pacific coasts of Chiapas and Guatemala, Olmec-style narrative relief sculptures provide some of the strongest evidence for Middle Formative interregional interaction. Like La Venta Stela 3, many of these carvings depict encounters between individuals that suggest the formation of political alliances. Others, such as Tres Zapotes Stela A and the carving at Tiltepec, Chiapas, show a large, elaborately garbed, central figure flanked by smaller subordinates suggesting local hierarchical relationships, and perhaps the installation of a ruler. Often accompanied by mythico-religious references, these sculptures nevertheless suggest a growing Olmec historicism and concern with the activities of rulers at home and abroad.

Another important trend was toward new forms of ostentatious display in communal and esoteric ritual. A prime example is the construction program at La Venta. The volume of filling and terracing at San Lorenzo may have been greater, but from a distance such construction was less visible than was the "Great Pyramid" rising from La Venta's core. The themes and settings of monumental sculpture helped to define ceremonial space at La Venta, as they did at San Lorenzo, but they complemented and commented upon the spaces defined by formal mound complexes. Moreover, while the layout of La Venta may have embraced communal themes of the relations of humans to the cosmos and the forces that inhabited it, these monumental constructions also proclaimed the power of the rulers who amassed the labor and materials to build them. Middle Formative Olmec rulers also displayed their elevated status in elaborate mortuary practices so far unknown in the Early Formative period. The most reasonable interpretation of the buried basalt column structure at La Venta, as well as the sandstone sarcophagus and "offerings" of earspools, beads, and other adornments of precious stones, is as elite tombs and burials.

The most ostentatious display of secular and religious power in Olman, however, was the burial of tons of imported serpentine in the massive offerings of La Venta. Together with the thousands of pieces of jade and other greenstones in La Venta's smaller offerings, they reflect the greatly expanded flow of exotic prestige goods, not only to Olman, but across the Mesoamerican landscape. Early Formative Olmec leaders had acquired such items, but their efforts were dwarfed by the volume of later imports to La Venta. In the context of broader developments in Mesoamerica, the Middle Formative acquisition of greenstones, iron ores, and other prestige goods, as well the more mundane but economically important resources such as obsidian required new political arrangements with emerging elites, partly reflected in the themes and distribution of Olmec-style monuments discussed above. It is to these relations with cultures beyond Olman that we now turn.

CHAPTER 6

THE OLMECS AND MESOAMERICA

Interpretations of the Early and Middle Formative periods in Mesoamerica have long been colored by "The Olmec Problem" (Chapter 1), a term which draws attention to the specific relations of the Gulf Olmecs with their contemporaries in Mesoamerica rather than to the full range of interactions that took place among Formative societies. Inevitably, in a book about the Olmecs, this issue will be our principal concern, but it should not detract from the recognition that each Formative society interacted with other groups, or from the critical importance of the local contexts within which interregional interactions were negotiated and employed toward particular ends. In other words, the "Olmec Problem" is important not so much for what it may say about the power and the glory of the Olmecs but for what its resolution can tell us about the causes, forms, and effects of interregional interaction among Mesoamerican societies during a crucial epoch in their development.

The evidence from Olman presented in the previous chapters leaves no doubt that the Olmecs were significant players in the web of heightened interactions that characterized segments of Early and Middle Formative history in Mesoamerica. The diversity and volume of imported materials in Olman indicate widespread and persistent contact with many far-flung regions. As this chapter will discuss in greater detail, such contacts moved not just materials, but ideas and technical knowledge, best represented in the iconography and style of ceramic artifacts and stone sculptures. At issue are the origins of the ideas and modes of expression embodied in these artifacts and the directions of influence that disseminated them. Arthur Demarest (1989) has elegantly summarized the principal models of Formative cultural influence as uni-directional (emanating exclusively from Olman), bi-directional (with the Olmecs both contributing and receiving influences from other societies, but with little additional interaction), and lattice-like (with multi-directional influences among many Formative period societies). The accumulating evidence suggests an even more complex landscape of Formative interaction, with some polities more

lattice-like in their interactions, others more constrained, and with varying
degrees of symmetry in the direction of influences. The picture becomes all
the more complicated when we consider that the forms of interaction among
Formative societies changed over time and that they varied with respect to
different materials, concepts, and social phenomena.

The models described by Demarest address primarily the directionality of
influence among societies (who received what from whom) and their boundedness (how open or resistant they were to "exchanges of energy, materials,
people, genes, and information" [Blanton et al. 1992: 18]). Inferring these and
other aspects of interaction requires attention to several additional issues, all of
which present their own problems of interpretation. The most obvious is the
temporal priority of relevant cultural elements in specific regions. Unfortunately, the blocks of time with which archaeologists work are often too gross to
unequivocally determine when and where a particular element first appeared.
This can be especially true of the relatively rapid dissemination of traits that
characterizes "horizon styles" like that of the Early Formative period.

How and to what extent these elements were elaborated once they were
acquired or invented also is a matter of interest. This is not because it informs
us of the age of a trait or style in a particular region (as is sometimes assumed,
apparently by analogy to biological populations and languages), but because
it addresses the adaptation of symbols to local circumstances. Likewise, the
particular media and styles in which interaction was expressed tells us as much
or more about the interests of the receiving groups as about the resources and
agendas of the donors.

The comparative scale, integration, and complexity of the participating societies also affect the character of interregional interaction. Too often, however,
arguments on both sides of the "Olmec Problem" seem to assume that cultural
influences inevitably flow from larger, better integrated, and more complexly
organized societies to smaller, less integrated and simpler ones. This rather
bowdlerized version of Sahlins and Service's (1960: 69–92, especially p. 77)
"Law of Cultural Dominance" underlies much of the Olmec-centric view as
well as the efforts of *primus inter pares* adherents to downplay Olmec accomplishments (compare, e.g., Diehl and Coe 1995; Flannery and Marcus 2000). A more
nuanced view, however, acknowledges that larger, more complex societies may
adopt concepts and styles from their less complexly organized neighbors, that
societies at all levels of sociopolitical integration may selectively incorporate,
ignore, or actively resist outside influences, and that the interacting societies
are not monolithic entities, but composed of groups and individuals with their
own agendas. Thus the relative size, integration, and complexity of societies
are more significant in terms of how they structure interactions beyond their
boundaries. As a result, it is vitally important to understand the local social,
political, economic, and historical contexts in which the articles and symbols
acquired from distant regions were employed.

None of these inferences is simple, and for many regions of Mesoamerica (including Olman), pertinent data are lacking, spotty, or in need of further refinement. Nevertheless, a fascinating, multi-hued tapestry of Formative interaction is beginning to emerge. We begin with the Early Formative period, which differed markedly in the character of its interactions from the Middle Formative period considered later in this chapter.

The Early Horizon

Between about 1400 and 1000 B.C. much of Mesoamerica was involved in heightened interregional interactions marked by the widespread appearance of conventional symbols rendered in carved and incised pottery and ceramic figurines as well as the exchange of iron ores, obsidian, greenstones, and other goods over great distances. Archaeologists refer to such periods of widely disseminated art and artifact styles as horizons, though horizons are usually briefer. The particular time span of concern in Mesoamerica has been called the "San Lorenzo horizon" because it coincides with the florescence of that great Olmec center, which many consider the font of the symbolic system (Coe 1977: 84; Tolstoy 1989b). Others have referred to the period as the Olmec A horizon, also emphasizing its Gulf Coast connections (Diehl and Coe 1995: 3). Still other names attributed to the time span are the Olmec Blackware horizon in contradistinction to the later Olmec Whiteware horizon, both referring to common ceramic wares (Henderson 1979), and the more neutral "X-Complex" horizon, which emphasizes its iconographic symbols (Grove 1989b). In recent years, the term "Early Horizon" proposed for the chronological sequence of the Basin of Mexico has gained wider acceptance as a culturally neutral term that does not focus on a particular class of material culture (Flannery and Marcus 1994: 390). This Early Horizon geographically and temporally is not so homogeneous as the "horizon" designation implies. As discussed in the next section, changes in the form and execution of ceramic iconography that distinguish the Manantial phase from the earlier Ayotla phase of the Early Horizon in the Basin of Mexico appear to varying degrees in other parts of the Mexican highlands and Soconusco, but they are rare or absent in Olman.

The Soconusco and Eastern Mesoamerica

Whatever it is called, and regardless of the circumstances of its origin, the hallmarks of the Early Horizon symbolic complex include the Saint Andrew's cross, the hand-paw-wing motif, and stylized zoomorphic depictions of sky (the "avian-serpent," "fire-serpent," or lightning) and earth (the "earth-monster" or "Olmec dragon"), often shown frontally or in profile, the *ilhuitl* or double scroll, and a variety of other more-or-less abstract motifs (Fig. 6.1). Often called "olmec" or "Olmec-style," these widely distributed motifs, which are typically carved and incised on black, white, or black-and-white differentially fired

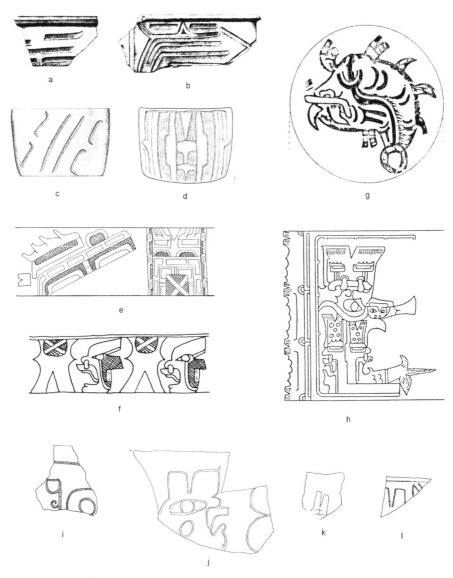

Figure 6.1. Early Horizon ceramic motifs: (**a–b**) Olman, San Lorenzo phase; (**c–d**) Valley of Oaxaca, San José phase; (**e–g**) Basin of Mexico, Ayotla phase; (**h**) Basin of Mexico, Manantial phase; (**i–l**) Soconusco, Jocotal phase (a–b from Coe 1981: Fig. 5–8; courtesy of Michael D. Coe) (c–d from Marcus and Flannery 1996: Fig. 86; courtesy of Joyce Marcus and Kent Flannery); (e–h redrawn from Niederberger 2000: Figs. 8, 9, and 10) (i–l redrawn from Clark and Pye 2000: Fig. 32).

pottery, constitute Grove's (1989) "X-Complex," They occur in early levels at Copan (Fash 1991: 69–70) and Puerto Escondido (Joyce and Henderson 2001) in eastern Honduras, and they mark the recently defined "Cunil Horizon" at Cahal Peche and ten or so other sites scattered across northern Guatemala and southern Belize (Cheetham 2005) (Fig. 6.2). The characteristic motifs are

Figure 6.2. Map of Early Formative sites mentioned in text.

notably absent, however, from the few Early Formative ceramic components known from farther north in the Yucatan peninsula.

By contrast with the sparsely populated Yucatan peninsula, the Pacific coastal lowlands and piedmont of Chiapas and Guatemala show ample evidence of participation in the Early Horizon interaction sphere. Backed by the mountains of the Sierra Madre, the narrow coastal strip is crossed by many short, more-or-less parallel rivers, which flow into lagoons behind barrier beaches or directly into the ocean. Prevailing wind patterns and differences in the height of the nearby mountains cause variable patterns of rainfall, which, in combination with high evaporation rates, create exceedingly humid zones in the southeastern piedmont and subhumid to semiarid conditions along the coast (Clark 1994b: 46–47). These differences in climate, together with the resulting variations in stream discharge, coastal salinity, and soil types, create a mosaic of forests, savannas, swamps, and coastal vegetation. Overall, the Pacific Coast of southeastern Mesoamerica is a diverse, highly productive, and intensifiable environment for fishing, gathering, hunting, and agriculture. By permitting the production of large and predictable subsistence surpluses, these characteristics contributed to precocious cultural developments in the region (Clark 1994b: 88–87).

Like the Olmecs, the Formative period inhabitants of the Soconusco are thought to have spoken an ancestral Mije-Sokean language. Therefore, John Clark and Michael Blake (1989b) dubbed them the Mokaya, a name derived from words meaning "people of maize" in modern Mije and Soke languages, recalling the myth that the gods created modern people from ground maize mixed with their divine blood. Although maize no longer appears to have been as large a component of the Mokaya diet as once thought, the name is still appropriate for these early settled villagers, who adopted maize into their mixed subsistence economy (Clark 1990a; 63–64).

The Soconusco comprises the southeastern half of the Chiapas coast and part of adjacent Guatemala. With higher humidity than the more westerly *costa seca*, it was coveted as a prime area for cacao by the Aztecs, who conquered it as the most distant tributary province in their empire. Moreover, it constituted an important route between the jade and obsidian sources of Guatemala and the isthmian and highland regions of western Mesoamerica, a fact that figured importantly in its cultural development. Currently, the most complete archaeological information for the Initial and Early Formative periods comes from the Mazatán area of the Soconusco, between the Cantileña Swamp and the Coatán River in Chiapas (Blake 1991; Blake et al. 1995; Clark 1994b; Lesure 1997, Rosenswig 2000).

Pre-Early Horizon Developments in the Soconusco

During the Barra phase (ca. 1900–1700 B.C.), population in the Mazatán area was distributed in numerous hamlets and three larger villages, the largest of which, at Paso de la Amada, covered about 10 ha (Clark 1994b: 551). The inhabitants practiced a mixed economy, cultivating domesticated crops and collecting wild foods (Blake et al. 1992). Maize was grown, but it does not appear to have been a major source of subsistence. Instead, maize may have been used to produce special foods for feasts, including drinks such as *atole,* a thin corn gruel, or *chicha*, a corn beer (Clark and Blake 1994: 28).

The Barra phase also contains some of Mesoamerica's earliest pottery, comprising mostly hard, thin-walled, neckless jars, called *tecomates*, and fewer strongly incurved bowls, both often with flat bottoms (Fig. 6.3). Ceramic slips occur in a variety of colors, with red becoming prevalent toward the end of the phase. For such an early ceramic complex, the decoration of the Barra phase pots is unexpectedly elaborate, employing black, orange, red, and white slips and paints, as well as plastic techniques like incising, zoned cross-hatching, and zoned punctuation. Fluted, gadrooned, and lobed vessels occasionally mimicked the segmented shapes of squashes (Clark 1994b: 183–186; Clark and Blake 1994: 25). Clark and his colleagues (Clark and Blake 1994; Clark and Gosser 1995) argue that this already well-developed, highly decorated ceramic technology was adopted to serve maize drinks and other valued foods in competitive feasts sponsored by individuals seeking greater prestige and influence. It is unlikely, however, that high social status was formally inherited during the Barra phase.

Settlement patterns and details of house construction document the emergence of the earliest rank society known in Mesoamerica during the succeeding

Figure 6.3. Barra (upper) and Locona (lower) phase pottery of the Soconusco (from paintings by Ajax Moreno in Clark and Pye 2000: Figs. 17 and 18) (courtesy of John E. Clark).

Locona phase (1700–1550 B.C.). The population of the Mazatán area increased
and expanded into previously unoccupied piedmont and estuary zones (Clark
1994b: 196–199). Settlements were organized into at least two distinct tiers,
with seven large sites evenly spaced through the territory. At the beginning
of the phase the largest village, still at Paso de la Amada, consisted of several
small barrios. Most of the inhabitants lived in small, wattle-and-daub houses
rounded at each end in an apsidal floor plan, but each barrio also contained
one apsidal residence that was much larger, and which may have housed the
village chief and his family. In addition, one early Locona barrio contained an
80 m long ballcourt, which served as a focus of public ritual (Hill et al. 1998).
Soon the barrios of Paso de la Amada merged to form the 37 ha core of a
civic-ceremonial center that sprawled over at least 140 ha (Clark 2004: 53–54,
60). At this time, Paso de la Amada was the largest site in the Mazatán region,
which also contained six or so large villages and dozens of smaller villages and
hamlets. Spaced about 5 km apart, it is not clear if the large villages were centers
of small, independent polities or dependencies of Paso de la Amada (Clark et
al. 2004).

As the barrios of Paso de la Amada coalesced, all but one of the large platform structures were abandoned, leaving a single impressive building located
on Mound 6, an earthen platform near the ball court, which grew through six
construction phases to a height of 2.8 m (Clark 1994b: Table 22; Clark and
Pye 2000b: 232). The largest and most elaborate of the series of apsidal buildings erected on Mound 6, Structure 4, measured 22 × 10 m, with recessed
porches and a hearth in each of its curved ends (Fig. 6.4). Broad clay footings
supported its wattle-and-daub walls, and large posts held up the massive, presumably thatched, roof. Whether this and other large platform structures in
the Mazatán area served as elite residences or had a more public, communal
function is difficult to determine (Blake 1991; Lesure 1997; Lesure and Blake
2002). Marcus and Flannery (1996: 90–91) interpret Structure 4 as a men's
house or "initiates temple," but sub-floor burials of a woman and two infants
from Mound 6 suggest their use was not so gender-specific (Lesure 2000: 227),
and patterns of artifacts and refuse on the floor of Structure 4 revealed areas of
eating, cooking, and obsidian tool manufacture common in domestic settings
(Clark 1994b: 350–362). At present, the most likely interpretation is that the
large platform structures of the Early Formative Soconusco were high-status
residences, which may also have served as foci for public ceremonies sponsored
by their inhabitants (Lesure and Blake 2002).

The ballcourt, Mound 6, and an elongated mound of unknown function
mark the northwest, southwest, and southeast edges of a plaza 173 meters on
a side, with the entire plaza complex contained within an area about 304 m
square (Clark 2004: 59). This Locona phase plaza has a reasonable claim as
the earliest formal ceremonial complex of comparable scale in Mesoamerica.
In addition, northeastward beyond the plaza and roughly aligned with it are a

Figure 6.4. Excavation of Paso de la Amada Mound 6, Structure 4 (from Clark and Pye 2000: Fig. 21) (courtesy of John E. Clark).

raised area with some low mounds and a depression, or *bajo*, each of similar dimensions to the plaza. Clark (2004: 57–59) speculates that the above areas and a fourth, to the east, were laid out as aligned modules that employed a standard indigenous unit of 1.666 m multiplied by multiples and simple fractions of the ritual numbers 13, 20, 52, 260, and 365 used in later Mesoamerican calendar counts. Thus the full length of the ballcourt, estimated by Clark at 86.63 m, would be 52 units long, the southern plaza twice that, or 104 units, and the external dimensions of the southern plaza group 182.5 units, or one-half of 365.

The pottery of the Locona phase shows a greater variety of forms than that of the Barra phase (Fig. 6.3). In addition to new round-bottomed and tripod tecomates, there was a proliferation of shallow dishes and plates and new bowl forms, including flat-bottomed cylindrical and tripod varieties. The pottery was often decorated with sparkling red bands and slips of specular hematite, some with pink iridescent stripes, and incised lattice designs. Rocker stamping, executed by moving the edge or back of a shell back and forth across the surface of the pot, and fabric- and cord-impressed designs make their first appearance (Clark 1994b: 181–183; Clark and Blake 1994: 27–28). Notably, the closest parallels to pottery of the Locona phase and the succeeding Ocos phase occur in Initial Formative phases in Olman.

In general, the elaboration of Locona phase serving vessels suggests a continued importance of feasting, but in a context where ceramics were no longer novel and were more widely used for utilitarian purposes (Clark and Blake

1994: 26–28). In addition to fancy pottery, the Locona phase contains the first indications of exotic prestige items, including pieces of greenstone and mica mirrors worn on the foreheads of buried individuals and represented on some figurines. Currently, the only evidence for production of mica mirrors comes from a large platform at the site of San Carlos (Clark 1994b: 495–496). When considered in conjunction with the variations in size and complexity of domestic architecture and the development of a site hierarchy, these prestige items suggest the emergence of social ranks (cf. Rosenswig 2000: 435–437). In addition, large, hollow ceramic statuettes are so far documented only for platform structures, and amounts of obsidian standardized by sherd weights appear higher in platforms of the Locona phase (Lesure and Blake 2002: 13, 15, 17). Nevertheless, these emerging elites do not appear to have had greater access to rare exotic items and materials such as mica, galena, quartz crystals, jade artifacts, or more common greenstone celts, than did people living off the platforms (Lesure and Blake 2002). Thus status differences appear to have been expressed more in the size and labor requirements of houses, and perhaps certain forms of ritual, than economic inequality (Lesure and Blake 2002: 20).

Little population change is indicated in the Ocos phase (ca. 1550–1450 B.C.), although population aggregated more in large villages, and intervening areas were more sparsely occupied (Clark 1994b: 199–203; Clark and Pye 2000b: 232). Furthermore, percentages of obsidian imported from three principal sources in Guatemala were more homogeneous within the large villages and their surrounding settlements than between them, suggesting that each large village was the center of its own redistribution system and, by inference, of an autonomous chiefdom (Clark and Salcedo 1989). Pottery became less elaborate than before, but a new class of figurines representing fat, seated men wearing animal masks appeared, which Clark and Pye (2000b: 232) interpret as village "shaman-chiefs."

The Barra through Ocos sequence presents a fascinating picture of the early emergence of sociopolitical hierarchy in the Mazatán area (Clark 1994b: 471–474). From relatively egalitarian Barra villages led by individuals competing for prestige, a network of simple chiefdoms arose in the early decades of the Locona phase. Before the end of the phase these "village chiefdoms" were consolidated into three or four larger polities ruled by individuals who expressed their status with large structures, probably their residences, raised on platforms. Noting the lack of clear evidence for warfare, population pressure, or subsistence specialization before the emergence of the first village chiefdoms, Clark (1994b; Clark and Blake 1994) argues that Mokaya sociopolitical hierarchies developed as the unintended consequence of competition among aggrandizing individuals.

In addition to these local processes, similarities in the pottery of the Soconusco, central Chiapas, and the Gulf Coast suggest that these regions were bound together in a sphere of interaction from very early times. This

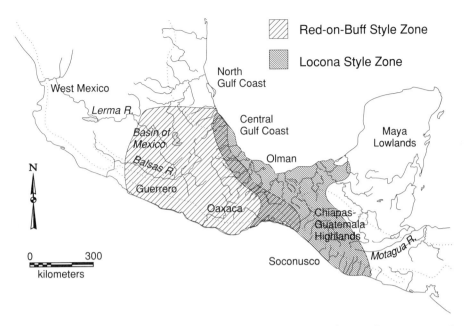

Figure 6.5. Early Formative style zones in Mesoamerica (redrawn after Marcus and Flannery 1996: Fig. 82).

"Locona-style zone" can be distinguished by its emphasis on tecomates with bichrome slips, fluting, and crosshatching from the "red-on-buff" style zone of the western Mesoamerican highlands that featured necked jars, bottles, and hemispherical bowls (Clark 1991; Flannery and Marcus 2000: 9–10) (Fig. 6.5). Clark (1993: 49; Clark and Blake 1989b: 390) once argued that an intrusion of Mixe-Zoquean speakers from the Pacific Coast was responsible for the appearance of the Locona-style zone on the Gulf Coast, the linguistic split between the main branch of Mayan languages and the Huastec speakers of the northern Gulf Coast, and the appearance of chiefdoms in Olman. Clark (1990b: 49) soon abandoned the idea of a Mokaya migration to the Gulf Coast, but continues to see Mokaya influence as a a significant stimulus in the early processes of Olmec cultural evolution (e.g., Clark and Pye 2000b: 243). The recent investigators of San Lorenzo likewise note that the specific ceramic similarities with the Barra, Locona, and Ocós phases are too few to support a hypothesis of migration, but they further argue that the settlement and political system of the contemporary Ojochi and Bajío phases were at least as differentiated as their Mokaya contemporaries (Symonds et al. 2002: 123–124). Granting that the latter argument, which is based on the number of different kinds of sites identified in the San Lorenzo area, needs further confirmation through excavation and that much more work needs to be done on the "pre-Olmec" period on the Gulf Coast in general, early interactions between Olman and the Soconusco appear to have been less direct and perhaps more symmetrical than Clark originally suggested.

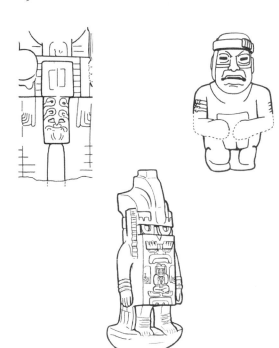

Figure 6.6. Early Olmec-style sculptures in the Soconusco. Clockwise from upper left: Alvarez Obregon, Buena Vista, and Ojo de Agua (from drawings by Ajax Moreno in Clark and Pye 2000: Figs. 4, 5, and 6) (courtesy of John E. Clark).

The Early Horizon in the Soconusco

The precocious rise of hierarchical polities during the Locona and Ocos phases provides the backdrop for important changes that took place beginning in the Cherla phase (ca. 1450–1400 B.C.). During the Cherla phase, the black-and-white pottery that is one hallmark of the Early Horizon joined the red wares of the Mokaya ceramic tradition (Clark and Cheetham 2002; Clark and Pye 2000b: 232). Most of these black-and-white vessels were local copies, but others arrived as imports from the Gulf Coast (Blomster et al. 2005; Clark and Pye 2000b: 232). "Olmec-style" slipped figurines of seated males, both hollow and solid, appeared alongside a local tradition of standing, unslipped female figurines with carefully depicted hairstyles (Clark 1994b: 424). Chemical analysis has confirmed a Gulf Coast origin for one of the hollow figurines (Blomster et al. 2005: Table S3). Items of personal adornment, including greenstone beads and small iron-ore mirrors, reached a height of popularity, and long-distance trade for these and other materials expanded (Clark and Pye 2000b: 234). Locally, the overall population within the surveyed portion of the Mazatán area dwindled, though a two-tiered hierarchy of large villages and smaller sites seems to have persisted (Rosenswig 2000: Figure 3d).

By the beginning of the Cuadros phase (ca. 1400–1150 B.C.), a regional center emerged in the middle of the Mazatán region at Cantón Corralito (Clark 1994b: 474; Clark and Pye 2000b: 236) as local consumption of obsidian in the surveyed zone diminished to less than half what it had been previously (Clark 1990b: 54). At the same time, carved and incised designs of composite

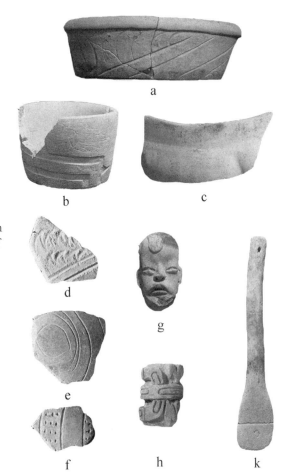

Figure 6.7. Early Horizon ceramics from Cantón Corralito (photo courtesy of David Cheetham).

zoomorphs and other Early Horizon elements appeared on pottery both local and imported, replacing an older tradition of naturalistic zoomorphic representation in figurines (Blomster et al. 2005; Clark and Pye 2000b: 236; Lesure 2000) (Fig. 6.1, i-l). Although it is true many of these motifs were widely shared in Early Formative Mesoamerica, connections appear to be strongest with the Gulf Coast. Furthermore, some of the first Olmec-style stone monuments outside the Gulf Coast appeared a short distance to the southeast at Alvaro Obregón and Buena Vista (Clark and Pye 2000b: 226–227; 236) (Fig. 6.6). Together with demonstrably imported pottery, these sculptures comprise some of the strongest evidence for specific Early Formative contacts with Olman.

Interaction with Olman was particularly strong at Cantón Corralito (Cheetham 2005) (Fig. 6.7). Located on an old channel of the Coatán River, massive floods around 1150 B.C. buried the site under thick deposits of sand, leaving only an Initial Formative mound protruding. David Cheetham's (2005a, 2005b) recent excavations distributed across the sandy plain have shown that the site covered at least 25 ha, and it may have been much larger. Olmec-style pottery is unusually common at the site, with carved sherds representing 2–3% (2.3 % overall) and incised examples 4–13 % (7.2% overall) of all classified potsherds, depending on location and context (Cheetham 2005b and personal communication). In addition, some kaolin vessels appear to have been imported from the Gulf Coast. Additionally, over 75% of all figurine heads conform to Olmec style, including specimens with closed eyes identical to San Lorenzo examples. Other artifact classes that show close similarities to those of the San Lorenzo phase include red-slipped jars and tecomates with zoned incision, roller stamps, and ceramic spatulas. Even more remarkable than these similarities in decorated pottery and special-use artifacts is Cheetham's report of close correspondences to the types, forms, and metric attributes of San Lorenzo phase pottery in common serving vessels. Although decorative techniques and motifs are readily copied, these more subtle similarities suggest broader sharing of a common ceramic tradition. That shared tradition did not extend, however, to the jars and tecomates typically used for storage and cooking, which were made in a different, local style (Cheetham 2005).

The high frequencies of Olmec-style artifacts and the presence of Olmec decorative and technological styles in several different artifact classes make Cantón Corralito the strongest candidate for an enclave of Olmecs outside of Olman, or for that matter, one of the strongest for a foreign enclave at any time in Mesoamerica's history. More difficult to answer is the question of how these Olmecs related to local populations. A woman buried late in the Cherla phase with a large flat iron-ore mirror on her chest and accompanied by an adult male and a juvenile may have held high social status, but the later burial of a 13-year-old juvenile with 15 polished stone axes and the decapitated adult laid nearby may be sacrifices (Cheetham 2005a). Determination of whether these individuals are Gulf Olmecs, local Mokaya, or both, awaits isotopic analysis of their remains. The likely presence of an enclave in what appears to be a regional capital also makes some degree of administrative control over local populations possible. Until more of the site is excavated, however, the presence of local elites cannot be ruled out.

The data from Cantón Corralito strengthen John Clark's (1990b, 1997; Clark and Blake 1989b; Clark and Pye 2000b) argument that the political and economic changes of the Early Formative period in the Soconusco were inextricably linked to interactions with Olman through a process of "olmecization." In Clark's (1997: 228) reconstruction, this process began with the importation and emulation of Olmec vessels and figurines by Mokaya leaders during the Cherla phase to enhance their local prestige. During the Cuadros phase leaders in the Mazatán area overtly signaled their connections to the rulers of Olman in a range of media, including serving vessels with Olmec motifs, figurines, grinding stones, and anthropomorphic stone statues, incorporating not only the trappings of Olmec culture, but the intertwined religious and political ideology of stratification they supported. Implementation of this ideology transcended the limitations inherent in the political strategies of village chiefs, with their emphasis on attracting followers through feasts and gifts of exotic materials. In concert with these symbolic, artistic, and artifactual changes, population in the Mazatán area fell, the head villages of simple chiefdoms were abandoned as the area was integrated under a single paramount center, and consumption of imported obsidian and prestige goods outside the center declined markedly.

With some modification to accommodate chronological revisions in the Soconusco[1], Clark's reconstruction of these events appears to be on the mark. Although some might dispute that the appearance of Early Horizon motifs in the Soconusco was exclusively the result of contacts with Olman, the Soconusco does appear to share more motifs with this region than others, it demonstrably imported Olmec vessels, and it is unique in the early appearance of Olmec-style statues outside the southern Gulf lowlands. Moreover, heightened contact with Olman appears to precede and intensify in lockstep with local political and economic developments, providing strong circumstantial evidence that these processes were linked. However, two other elements of Clark's argument are more controversial. First is his contention that in adopting Olmec political ideology, the Mokaya themselves became Olmec. Clark (1997: 213–215) argues that "Olmec" is best perceived not as a culture or ethnic group, but as a set of beliefs and practices specifically related to government. Clark's semantic (but by no means trivial) argument has considerable merit, but his use of "Olmec" differs from that employed in this book, and it would exclude certain societies in Olman, such as those of the Early Formative period in the Tuxtla Mountains or of the Middle Formative period in the Coatzacoalcos basin.

Even more provocative is Clark's (1997: 229) conclusion that the political-economic changes of the Early Horizon in the Soconusco resulted from direct intervention by the Gulf Olmecs. Clark sees this as occurring as the result of Mazatán leaders asking for help from Olmec partners in gaining power locally. Olmec elites, he argues, came into and ultimately took over the local system, incorporating parts of the Soconusco under their hegemony. The interest of the Olmecs in the Soconusco would have been to monitor transshipment of Guatemalan obsidian and jade into Olman. Control of cacao production is another possibility, although cacao also could have been grown in the Gulf lowlands.

As argued in Chapter 4, it is doubtful that the rulers of San Lorenzo subjugated much of Olman beyond the Coatzacoalcos basin, and any control they might have exerted over places like Laguna de los Cerros and the western Tabasco lowlands appears to have been at best brief and contested. It is therefore hard to imagine them extending their direct administration to distant lands if they failed to do so successfully closer to home. Clark (1997: 229) acknowledges the logistical difficulty of ruling a region 400 km away, and suggests that

Gulf Olmec control of Mazatán would have been loose, with provincial Olmec elites having considerable flexibility to rule as they saw fit.

It also is possible that an Olmec enclave in Mazatán retained its ethnic identity while severing political ties to Olman. If so, the Mazatán case would resemble models recently proposed for Matacapan, a Classic period site in the Tuxtla Mountains, which exhibits similarities to the Central Mexican city of Teotihuacan in ritual and domestic pottery (including some imports), figurines, and architecture (Pool 1992; Santley 1994; Santley et al. 1987). Matacapan was initially interpreted as a colonial enclave founded and controlled by the Teotihuacan state (Santley et al. 1987), but more recent interpretations have questioned Teotihuacan's political control over Matacapan (Arnold et al. 1993), viewing it as an enclave founded by Teotihuacanos fleeing political unrest at home (Arnold and Santley 2003), or a terminal in a trade diaspora (*sensu* Cohen 1971; Curtin 1984; see also Stein 1999), "operating outside the formal political structure of Teotihuacan while depending on a constructed Teotihuacanoid identity to maintain links between communities and access to particular resources" (Spence 1996: 349–350).

The concept of the trade diaspora may prove useful for modeling some cases of Olmec interaction (as Curtin [1984: 81–83, 85] suggested), if and where a strong case for enclave formation can be made. However, trade diasporas encompass a wide spectrum of ethnographically and historically documented arrangements (Curtin 1984: Stein 1999). They range from the sharing of an ethnic identity among groups that originate in and operate among stateless societies, like the Aro or the Nzabi of West Africa (Curtin 1984: 46–49), to colonies dominated by foreign powers. In any event, the ongoing research at Cantón Corralito will be critical for resolving the specific form of interaction between the Soconusco and Olman (Cheetham 2005).

After the flooding of Cantón Corralito, about 1150 B.C., a site on the opposite bank of the Coatán River, Ojo de Agua (El Silencio), emerged as the administrative center of a growing population supported by increased exploitation of the nearby estuaries, possibly for salt and fish products (Clark and Pye 2000b: 236–237). Recent investigations by John Hodgson and John Clark (Hodgson, personal communication, 2005) reveal that Ojo de Agua extended over at least 110 ha. At its center a 44 ha ceremonial complex constructed in the Jocotal phase (ca. 1150–1000 B.C.) consisted of a rock-lined platform and 13 mounds arranged on a consistent NNE alignment.

Reflecting the site's regional importance, a remarkable monument from Ojo de Agua continues the tradition of Olmec-derived sculpture-in-the-round seen earlier at Buena Vista and Alvaro Obregon (Clark and Pye 2000b: 221, Fig. 4) (Fig. 6.6). An elaborately attired figure with goggle eyes wears a large headdress and a box-like garment appointed with Early Horizon motifs. Carved in relief on the front of the garment, a typical "Olmec" supernatural (Joralemon's God I) sits cross-legged with hands on its chest, atop the cleft eyebrows of an underworld serpent-monster that surmount an upside-down U-shaped motif, which may denote a throne. Above the central image is a flame-eyebrowed earth-monster face suggestive of a cave entrance, and on either side hang paw-wing motifs. Consistent with its probable Jocotal phase date, these designs show strong similarities with Early Formative Olmec sculptures like Monuments 10 and 52 from San Lorenzo and the cleft eyebrows on the Phase I balustrade figure at Teopantecuanitlán (see below), as well as with widely distributed Early Horizon ceramic motifs and Middle Formative votive axes. The box-like attire and goggle eyes of the figure are unique, however, and point to a local interpretation of an Olmec heritage, both in sculptural representation and the ritual it depicts.

In other respects, interaction between the Soconusco and Olman declined during the Jocotal phase (Clark et al. 2004; cf. Love 2002: Figure 5). In general, ceramic styles reflect local continuity and are quite different from other areas of Mesoamerica (Clark and Pye 2000b: 240). The "pan-Mesoamerican" ceramic motifs that do occur, including profile faces, double-line-breaks, and clover-like elements, appear more closely linked to the Manantial phase in the Valley of Mexico and contemporaneous styles in Oaxaca, and Guerrero than to the Gulf Coast. Their execution is highly variable, though, and they appear to represent a regional variant of the "Manantial" style.

Clark and Pye (2000b: 241) formerly attributed these developments on the Chiapas coast to a power vacuum in Olman between the decline of San Lorenzo and the rise of La Venta. This proposition needs to be reevaluated in light of the revised dating of the Jocotal phase, which makes it contemporaneous with the San Lorenzo B phase in Olman. At that time San Lorenzo was still an important center, but the appearance of weapons in artwork and increased recycling of monuments suggests its rulers were experiencing challenges to their power and difficulties in acquiring important resources (Cyphers cited in Borstein 2001: 187). Challenges may have come from competition with rival centers like Laguna de los Cerros, which was then at its Formative period height (Borstein 2001: 180–181, 187), as well as from subordinate leaders. In other words, Olman in the San Lorenzo B phase suffered not from a power vacuum but from an overabundance of power centers. In any event, the growing cultural influence of the Central Mexican societies is clear, and it is entirely plausible that the rulers of the Mazatán region strengthened their economic and political contacts with the Mexican highlands to supplement or replace their earlier ties with Gulf Olmec polities.

Early Villagers in the Valley of Oaxaca

Some 400 km to the northeast of the Soconusco, amid the jagged mountains of Mexico's southern Sierra Madre, the Río Salado joins the Río Atoyac to form the three-armed Valley of Oaxaca. At an elevation of 1,550 m, this temperate, semi-arid valley is a far cry from the tropical lowlands of the Soconusco or Olman. Nevertheless, its inhabitants also participated actively in the Early Horizon interaction sphere, contributing polished iron ore mirrors and placing their own imprint on Early Horizon iconography. That said, the Valley of Oaxaca presents a rather different Early Formative trajectory from the Soconusco or Olman; one in which communal ritual seems to have played a more central role, Early Horizon motifs were more subject to local reinterpretation, and interactions with other parts of the Mexican highlands appear to have been more critical than with Olman.

Permanent settlements first appeared in the Valley of Oaxaca during the Tierras Largas phase (ca. 1650–1400 B.C.). Like their lowland contemporaries, the inhabitants of these hamlets and villages practiced a mixed economy, supplementing domestic maize, beans, squash, chiles, and avocados with wild walnuts, leguminous tree pods, hackberries, and cactus fruits. Animal protein was provided by domestic dogs as well as wild deer, peccary, rabbits, pocket gophers, quail, doves, mud turtles, and other small game (Marcus and Flannery 1996: 83).

These foods supported a population that numbered between 300 and 700 persons, most of them living in the valley bottoms on or near the best agricultural land (Marcus and Flannery 1996: 78; Kowalewski et al 1989: 56). Something over half the population was concentrated in the northwestern (Etla) arm of the valley, which had the greatest concentration of highly productive land (Nicholas 1989). The largest settlement in the Etla arm, and for that matter the entire valley, consisted of a loose aggregation of nine residential areas at San José Mogote, which formed a 7 ha village (Marcus and Flannery 1996: 78).

By and large, the inhabitants of the Tierras Largas phase settlements lived in small wattle-and-daub houses, about 6 × 4 m, each of which probably housed four or five family members (Marcus and Flannery 1996: 83) (Fig. 6.8). Some had better finished, whitewashed walls, but none were as large as the Early Formative platform structures in the Soconusco. People often were buried in the houseyard in varying positions and orientations, sometimes in bell-shaped storage pits (Marcus and Flannery 1996: 84). Some individuals were interred with grave goods – a pot here, a bead there – and a handful of older males were buried sitting upright. These variations in mortuary practice, however, appear to have reflected gender roles and achieved statuses, rather than any social ranking that was ascribed at birth (Marcus and Flannery 1996: 84–86; Rosenswig 2000: 434).

A few distinctive buildings in the larger village at San José Mogote differed from the villagers' homes (Fig. 6.8). Though of similar dimensions, they were set on low earthen platforms, their wattle-and-daub walls used more pine posts, and the floors and walls were covered with lime plaster. Notably, however, they contain little of the refuse associated with residences, or the small

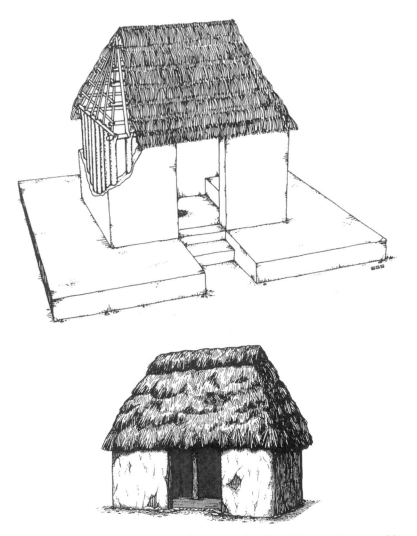

Figure 6.8. Artist's conception of structures San José Mogote. Upper, public structure ("men's house"), Tierras Largas phase: Lower, common residence, San José phase (redrawn after Marcus and Flannery 1996: Figs. 79, 102).

figurines thought to have been used by women in household rituals (Marcus 1989; Marcus and Flannery 1996: 87). In addition to the greater care given their construction, two features of these structures suggest they were built as public buildings for ceremonial functions (Marcus and Flannery 1996: 87). First, all were oriented 8° west of north, an orientation later used for ceremonial buildings in Oaxaca and Olmec La Venta. Second, a small, centrally located pit was set in the floor of several of these structures, apparently to hold powdered lime for ingestion with ritual plants like tobacco. Marcus and Flannery (1996: 87–88) therefore interpret them as a kind of "men's house," that due to their small size would necessarily have been restricted to a small group of initiates.

These "initiates' temples" are quite different in their size and contents from the proposed elite residences like Mound 6, Structure 4, at Paso de la Amada, and point to a different, more communal concern in the social organization that bound together the Oaxacan villages of the Tierras Largas phase.

San José Mogote apparently was not only a seat for certain kinds of ceremony, but its leaders also appear to have been more heavily involved in long-distance trade. Compared to households elsewhere in the Valley of Oaxaca, they received more marine shells and almost all the examples of polished black pottery made from non-local clays (Marcus and Flannery 1996: 88). All households appear to have had access to obsidian from a number of sources. The proportions of obsidian from different sources varied widely from one residence to another, implying that each household acquired its own obsidian independently. The farther a village lay from a particular obsidian source in Central Mexico, the less obsidian from that source it had, indicating that obsidian was passed "down-the-line" from one trading partner to another (Pires-Ferreira 1976a).

The archaeological record from the Tierras Largas phase shows us an egalitarian society of village farmers, some of whom may have acquired greater prestige by manipulating external trading contacts, sponsoring feasts, and attracting followers who contributed their labor to the construction of modest public buildings. Formal ranking does not appear to have been a feature of Tierras Largas societies, as it does in the contemporaneous Locona and Ocos phases of the Soconusco, but that would soon change.

The Early Horizon in the Valley of Oaxaca

The Early Horizon corresponds to the San José phase (ca. 1400–950 B.C.) in the Valley of Oaxaca. This also is the time when a clear hierarchy of social positions and settlement functions appears in the valley. The number of occupied sites doubled to about 40, and the population tripled to something over 2,000 people (Marcus and Flannery 1996: 106). Population remained concentrated in San José Mogote and surrounding villages in the Etla arm of the valley. San José Mogote now contained about 79 ha and about 1,000 people, making it more than ten times the size of the next largest village at the nearby site of Tierras Largas (Kowalewski et al. 1989: 66; Marcus and Flannery 1996: 106). Thus a two-tiered settlement hierarchy had emerged, and it was highly primate in character. Although population in the Etla subvalley and elsewhere was still concentrated on the best agricultural lands, that alone does not explain its heterogeneous distribution, for much good land in the other valley arms was unoccupied. Rather, people seem to have been attracted to the Etla arm as much for social as for environmental reasons (Marcus and Flannery 1996: 107–108).

Not only was San José the largest settlement in the Valley of Oaxaca by an order of magnitude, it also was the one settlement with a variety of public buildings that did not appear in smaller communities (Marcus and Flannery 1996: 108–110). By the end of the phase, the small, Tierras Largas phase "initiates temples" on low earthen platforms had been superseded by larger structures set on platforms up to 2.5 m high filled with earth gathered from a variety of locations. The platforms were reinforced and faced with bun-shaped adobes and stones brought in from as much as 5 km away. Structure 2 included in its facing wall two small carved stones, which represent a feline and a raptorial bird. At about 20 cm long, it may be stretching the point to call them monuments, but they are the earliest stone carvings in the region, and they owe nothing to Olmec canons. These platforms apparently elaborated on the earlier tradition of public buildings. Furthermore, their construction clearly involved the cooperation of numerous individuals, some evidently from dependent villages located at some distance from San José Mogote.

Evidence from household excavations and burials argues for an expansion in the range of social differences during the San José phase, but for the most part such distinctions remained gradational, rather than a matter of sharply segregated ranks (Marcus and Flannery 1996: 96–106; Rosenswig 2000: 436, 442). Higher-status houses were whitewashed and better built than those of lower-status households. Their residents also consumed more deer meat, had better access to imported marine shell, jade, and pottery, and were more involved in making crafts like basketry, shell ornaments, and iron ore mirrors, but the differences are a matter of degree rather than kind.

Variation in the number and diversity of grave goods is similarly gradational (Marcus and Flannery 1996: 101; Rosenswig 2000: 436). One particularly rich burial was of an old woman at the small site of Fábrica San José (Drennan 1976: 248). She was buried with a greenstone pendant, 53 greenstone beads and a brown stone bead, all in her mouth, a ceramic vessel at her feet, two at her breast, and one at her head, and she was covered with red pigment. Others had fewer grave goods, but there is no sharp break in the numbers or quality of objects to indicate the expression of social rank in death (Rosenswig 2000: 436). Burial practices suggest that individuals were increasingly treated as members of a group, as husbands and wives began to be buried together for the first time and primary burials were sometimes accompanied by the exhumed and re-interred bodies of others who had died before them (Marcus and Flannery 1996: 96).

Some evidence does point to more formalized status differences, however. In the large San José phase cemetery at Tomaltepec, six adult males out of 80 individuals were buried beneath stone slabs in a tightly flexed position that suggests they had been tightly bound and perhaps interred in a sitting position, mimicking figurines of the same period that show individuals seated in what is thought to have been a posture of authority (Marcus and Flannery 1996: 100). Most of the secondary burials in the cemetery accompanied these six individuals, and they were interred with more than half of all vessels in the cemetery carved with "fire-serpent" motifs. These more highly honored individuals are reasonably interpreted as lineage heads and leaders of the community (Marcus and Flannery 1996: 96–99).

Of all the prestige goods buried with people and recovered from residential contexts, only magnetite appears to have been subject to sumptuary rules that restricted it from some groups in the population (Marcus and Flannery 1996: 102). Small, polished quadrangular mirrors of magnetite occur as grave goods only in burials otherwise identified as of high status. Access to the raw material also seems to have been highly restricted, for one neighborhood in San José Mogote accounted for 99% of all the magnetite identified in the archaeological survey of the Valley (Marcus and Flannery 1996: 102). Furthermore, similar mirrors, evidently manufactured at San José Mogote from the same source of magnetite, appear in Olman at San Lorenzo and at Etlatongo in the Nochixtlán valley of Oaxaca (Pires-Ferreira 1975: 60).

Export of magnetite mirrors from the Valley of Oaxaca and import of jade, greenstone, marine shells, stingray spines, and some pottery in the San José phase all demonstrate the participation of the valley's inhabitants in an exchange network that stretched from Central Mexico and the Gulf Coast to Guatemala. Interaction with these areas also is seen in the use of Early Horizon symbols carved and incised on black, black-and-white, and white vessels. The Valley of Oaxaca is notable, however, for the degree to which these symbols were reinterpreted in local styles and the particular social uses to which they appear to have been put.

Nanette Pyne (1976) first called attention to the differential distribution of two motif sets in the Valley of Oaxaca. One set consists of highly stylized representations in profile of a composite zoomorphic being (Fig. 6.1c). In addition to the full profile rendering of the being's head, they include abbreviated versions, often in combination, of its flame-like eyebrows, upside-down, U-shaped gum brackets, the Saint Andrew's cross that sometimes marks its body or mouth, and broad excised bands that represent its head and eyes (Flannery and Marcus 1994: 135–149). Another set of free-standing motifs represent frontal images of a composite zoomorph. These also are highly stylized, consisting of an abstract representation of the being's cleft forehead, with lateral flanges and "music brackets" executed in fine incision and hachuring (Fig. 6.1f). Sometimes the image is reduced to a vertical bar with "music brackets" to either side or a simple incised cleft head with eye circles. The latter design is sometimes included in the "double-line-break" motif that appears around the rims of plates and other vessels, providing evidence that in Oaxaca, at least, the double-line-break derived from and is an alternate representation of the cleft-headed composite zoomorph.

Following Coe (1965b), Pyne (1976: 273) identified the profile zoomorphic images as "fire-serpents" or "sky-dragons" and the frontal zoomorphs as "were-jaguars." By analogy to spiritual concepts held by many modern speakers of Otomanguean languages, including Zapotec, Marcus (1989, 1998; Marcus and Flannery 1976, 1996: 95–96; Flannery and Marcus 1994: 136–137) regards the "fire-serpent" and "were-jaguar" images as representations of sky and earth, respectively, in their angry aspects as lightning (*Cociyo*) and earthquake (*Xòo*). Marcus's interpretation is challenged by scholars (e.g., Clark 2001; Taube 1995) who point out that, in Early Horizon pottery from the Basin of Mexico (which the Oaxacan examples resemble most closely), the "fire-serpent" motif clearly represents the profile view of the "were-jaguar" or "Olmec Dragon" (Joralemon's God I), which Taube (1995) identifies as the "Avian Serpent." In these vessels the flame eyebrows, trough-shaped eyes, gum brackets, and sometimes even the cleft, can be matched element-for-element in profile and frontal views. Moreover, both views occasionally appear on the same Ayotla and Mananatial phase vessels (e.g., Niederberger 1987: Figures 458, 514) (Fig. 6.1e).[2]

I suspect that Early Horizon Mesoamericans would have answered the question, "Do these images represent the same entity or different ones?" with an emphatic "Yes!" In ethnohistorically documented Mesoamerican religions, deities had remarkably fluid and overlapping attributes. Deities also might possess dual aspects associated with complementary oppositions such as male-female, light-dark, or sky-earth, or multiple aspects associated with directions, calendrical periods, or cosmological realms (Gossen 1996: 315–316; Nicholson 1971). In the Zapotec case this was possible because "All deities were but aspects, attributes, or refractions of a supreme force or principle, Coqui Xee" (Whitecotton 1977: 165). Related to this was the concept of *pèe*, the animating force possessed by all living things, including lightning and the quaking earth (Marcus and Flannery 1996: 19). As the angry, animated aspects of sky and earth, *Cociyo* (Lightning) and *Xòo* (Earthquake) were complementary embodiments of *Coqui Xee,* and whose underlying unity is expressed in the Zapotec phrase for thunder, *Xòo Cociyo* ("Lightning's Earthquake") (Marcus and Flannery 1996: 19). Which component of the dual nature of these forces, their unity or their opposition, was emphasized would likely have depended on the particular contexts in which they were expressed. The inhabitants of the Basin of Mexico often (though not always) emphasized their unity, while their Oaxacan contemporaries more often emphasized their distinctive, opposed, aspects.

In the Valley of Oaxaca, distributions of the composite zoomorph motif sets suggest they were incorporated into the iconography of local social distinctions. In adult burials for which sex can be determined, these motifs are associated with males, whereas different kinds of vessels, including squash-like tecomates, accompany adult females. A similar dichotomy in motifs and vessel types occurs in juvenile burials, although the sex of these individuals cannot be determined from their skeletons (Marcus and Flannery 1996: 95–96). Even more intriguing is the differential distribution of profile ("fire-serpent") and frontal ("were-jaguar") motifs in space. At a statistically significant level, households in San José Mogote tended to have one or the other motif, but not equal numbers of both (Pyne 1976). Moreover, fire-serpent motifs appeared mainly in the eastern and western residential wards, while were-jaguar motifs were more strongly associated with the southern ward (Marcus 1989: 169). Contrasting distributions of the two kinds of motifs also extended to the surrounding countryside, with fire-serpents represented at the communities of Abasolo and Tomaltepec in the Tlacolula arm of the valley and were-jaguar motifs better represented at Tierras Largas and Huitzo in the Etla arm (Marcus 1989: 170). Both kinds of motifs were rare at smaller villages in the valley.

If they are contemporaneous,[3] the significant association of either fire-serpents or were-jaguars with specific residential wards or entire sites, together with their apparently exclusive occurrence in male burials, suggests that these motifs expressed local social distinctions. Although there is a tendency for the vessels bearing them to accompany honored individuals in burial, they are not confined to wealthier burials or higher-status residences (Marcus and Flannery 1996: 105). One plausible explanation of these patterns is that the motifs communicated membership in descent groups with a male bias, if not exclusively patrilineal (Marcus 1989: 169; Pyne 1976). The idea that the "were-jaguar" (Earthquake) and "fire-serpent" (Lightning) may have represented the apical ancestors of those lines coincides with the similar role held by these forces in Zapotec descent groups of Oaxaca (Marcus 1989: 170; Marcus and Flannery 1996: 95–96). Moreover, if earthquake and lightning did represent complementary aspects of the same entity, as I argue above, they would be a powerful metaphor for the union of opposed groups in the larger society, whether those groups were strictly descent groups or more broadly conceived houses or factions.

Other differences in context and distribution suggest variable social associations of the frontal and profile views in other parts of Mesoamerica. In illustrated examples of Early Horizon pottery from the Soconusco, profile views predominate (Clark and Cheetham 2002). The same is true for Early Horizon pottery in Olman at San Lorenzo (Coe and Diehl 1980a: 159–187), where frontal views of the period are mainly confined to sculpture (Stark 2004). The profile and frontal views may be equivalent representations of the same being or concept, but in Olman, at least, there does appear to be some differentiation in representation according to the social and ceremonial contexts in which different media were employed. As described in greater detail further on, in the Basin of Mexico at Tlatilco, it is not the difference in frontal and profile views that seem to mark social segments, but the overall association of Early Horizon motifs with a subset of burials, mainly female, oriented east-west.

To summarize, the San José phase of the Valley of Oaxaca saw the emergence of a two-tiered, highly primate, settlement hierarchy suggestive of a centralized political organization. Centralized administration also is suggested by the elaboration of public architecture, which by virtue of its size and materials implies control over, or at least contribution by, populations beyond the principal village where it is found. On the other hand, grave goods, house construction, and household artifact assemblages suggest that, with the exception of magnetite for the production of mirrors, differences in access to prestige goods and preferred foods were gradational, rather than marked by sharp differences in social rank. Some male individuals received special burial treatment consistent with their inferred status as lineage patriarchs. Highly crafted objects, including mirrors and pottery vessels, were used along with exotic jade and greenstone ornaments to communicate social distinctions. Some of these distinctions appear to have been inherited as a consequence of being born into a particular lineage, but achievement during one's own lifetime also was necessary to obtain high social status.

Within this sociopolitical milieu, Early Horizon motifs underwent significant and highly particular modification in form and meaning. No similar distributions in space and burial associations have been identified from elsewhere in Mesoamerica, save the Basin of Mexico, where they appear more strongly associated with female than male burials. And though the inferred differentiation of Earth and Sky descent groups appear most clearly in San José Mogote and certain of its key dependants, the association of the motifs with kin groups (as prestigious as they may have been) as opposed to individual rank is significant and perhaps reflective of the more communal character of the Oaxacan polities than their lowland counterparts.

Exchanged materials leave no doubt that the San José phase villages were in contact with their contemporaries in Olman and the Soconusco. The origin of the Early Horizon symbols and the processes by which they came to be represented on Oaxacan pots are another matter. Kent V. Flannery (1968b) once argued that village chiefs in the Valley of Oaxaca emulated the symbols of the Gulf Olmecs to enhance their own prestige and to symbolize their specific relationship to Olmec elites, as trading and perhaps marriage partners. In return, the Olmecs obtained iron ore mirrors. In constructing his argument, Flannery observed that apparently analogous situations in Burma and northwestern North America resulted in the less sophisticated participants, the Kachin "Hill Shan" of Burma and the Athabascan "Inland Tlingit" of the American Northwest, adopting the symbols, dress, and behaviors of their more sophisticated neighbors. Importantly, in Flannery's (1968b: 106) view it was not the least developed highland societies that should emulate the Olmecs, but the most developed – those in areas of high agricultural and demographic potential in which emerging elites would have the greatest use for the symbols of the presumably more stratified Olmec leaders.

So elegant was Flannery's argument that many archaeologists (e.g., Clark 1997; Stark 2000) remain convinced of its validity, although Flannery has since revised his model (Flannery and Marcus 1994: 385–390; 2000). The revised position favors a model of "competitive interaction" among autonomous chiefdoms, which spread innovations in technology and sociopolitical strategies and accelerated sociopolitical evolution over a wide area (Flannery and Marcus 2000: 33). With respect to the Valley of Oaxaca, this proposal observes that the region's strongest interactions were not with the South Gulf Coast, but with Central Mexico. It also acknowledges the greater sociopolitical differentiation of the San Lorenzo Olmecs, at the level of a paramount chiefdom (Flannery and Marcus 2000: 8–9), but views the Valley of Oaxaca societies as similar in their degree of cultural sophistication, particularly noting their earlier use of lime plaster, adobe bricks, and stone masonry for public architecture and the earlier appearance and greater prevalence of some Early Horizon motifs in Oaxaca (Flannery and Marcus 1994: 389).

The central Valley was not the only part of Oaxaca that interacted significantly with other regions during the Early Horizon. To the northwest lies the mountainous region called the Mixteca Alta and in it the Nochixtlán Valley. During the Middle Cruz phase (ca. 1400–950 B.C.), the inhabitants of Etlatongo, the largest site in the valley at about 26 ha (Blomster 2004: 66), used pottery with Olmec motifs, making some locally and importing some from Olman (Blomster et al. 2005). Pottery from the Nochixtlán Valley also may have been traded elsewhere (Stoltman et al. 2005), though this is less certain. Especially notable is the presence at Etlatongo of vessels with the distinctive bounded scroll designs of Limón Incised pottery (Blomster 2004: Figure 6.9), which is exceedingly rare outside Olman and the Soconusco.

The recent work at Etlatongo has produced some interesting hints about the use of Early Horizon symbolism and exotic items there, although confirmation will require the investigation of a larger sample of contexts in the site and region. Some inhabitants of Etlatongo evidently lived in houses built on low platforms, stored more food in bell-shaped pits than necessary to support a nuclear family, and acquired exotic items, including imported Olmec pottery. Because the excavated sample is biased toward what are interpreted as higher-status households and public space (Blomster 2004: 74–75), however, it is not clear to what degree less fortunate households also may have employed Early Horizon symbols in domestic contexts. The differential intrasite distribution of fire-serpent and were-jaguar motifs noted for San Jose Mogote has not been identified at Etlatongo. Blomster (2004: 129) therefore rejects the notion that they represent local descent groups, but he also notes that fire-serpent motifs are more common at Etlatongo, which parallels the differential frequencies of these motifs between sites in the Valley of Oaxaca (see previous discussion). Were-jaguar motifs have not been identified on pottery from early Middle Cruz stratigraphic contexts at Etlatongo (Blomster 2004: 130), calling to mind Winter's (1994) suggestion that different motifs may have been emphasized at different times, but the reported sample of all sherds with "Olmec-style" motifs from these contexts is still too small to confirm this pattern (Blomster 2004: 124).

Chemical analyses using instrumental neutron activation analysis (INAA) indicate that the Valley of Oaxaca and the Nochixtlán Valley, like other Early Formative regions, received some ceramic vessels made in the San Lorenzo area, including white wares and carved-incised examples with Early Horizon motifs (Blomster et al. 2005). Although the chemical analysis supports the conclusion that San Lorenzo was more heavily engaged in the export of pottery than were other regions, it does not preclude the possibility of some exchange of ceramics from Oaxaca to Olman and other regions, as has been suggested by petrographic thin section analysis of the mineralogical compositions of other sherds (Neff et al. 2006a: 68, 73; Stoltman et al. 2005; cf. Neff et al. 2006b: 112–113; see also Flannery et al. 2005; Flannery and Marcus 1994: 262–263). At present it seems evident that San Lorenzo did play a significant role in disseminating the carved pottery on which Early Horizon motifs were expressed, but San Lorenzo may not have been the only exporter of such pottery, and other regions well may have contributed to the complex of motifs. Moreover, the data on exchange patterns do not address the novel ways in which the Early Horizon motifs were utilized socially and manipulated stylistically in San José Mogote, Etlatongo, and other communities across Mesoamerica.

Central Mexico

Northwest of the Valley of Oaxaca, beyond the rugged mountains and narrow valleys of the Mixteca Alta, lie the high, broad basins of Mexico's semiarid Mesa Central in the modern states of Mexico, Morelos, Puebla, Tlaxcala, and Hidalgo. At the core of the region is the Basin of Mexico, a wide valley hemmed in by snow-capped volcanic peaks. In prehispanic times the valley was occupied by five interconnected lakes. Blessed with high agricultural potential and an abundance of waterfowl, fish, and other aquatic resources, the Basin of Mexico gave birth to the powerful Classic and Postclassic states of Teotihuacan, the Toltecs and the Aztecs. In the Early Formative period, the southern basin supported a sparse but culturally vigorous population, the members of which were important participants in the Early Horizon interaction sphere (Sanders 1981: 164). Best known from burial contexts, the archaeological culture is characterized by a ceramic complex that included red-on-brown bowls and bottles, among them such exotic forms as stirrup-spouted vessels, as well as many "pretty lady" figurines with elaborate hairstyles and wide hips. These elements indicate a connection between this "Tlatilco culture" and West Mexico. In addition, it contains occasional black, gray, or differentially fired cylinder vessels and flat-bottomed bowls with carved and incised Early Horizon motifs and hollow, white-slipped "Olmec-style" figurines (Grove 1974: 3–4) (Fig. 6.1e-f). The Basin of Mexico sites represent the northern limit of the Tlatilco culture, which may have originated in the lower, warmer river valleys of Morelos, where it is more common (Grove 1996: 106).

   Three millennia of increasingly intensive occupation in the Basin of Mexico have doubtless obscured many Early Horizon sites. What is known, however, suggests that a sparse population numbering perhaps 2,000 was concentrated in the better-watered southern half of the basin (Sanders 1981: 164–165).

Settlements included several small hamlets as well as three or four nucleated villages that may have served as ceremonial and economic foci integrating small hinterlands. Excavations at three of these villages, Tlatilco, Tlapacoya, and Coapexco have provided the bulk of our information on Early Horizon society in the Basin.

Tlapacoya is located at the foot of a small, extinct volcano that formed an island or peninsula at the northern edge of Lake Chalco. Like too many Early Horizon sites in Central Mexico, Tlapacoya has suffered destruction under the wheels of progress and the shovels of looters (Niederberger 1996: 86–87). A major highway was bulldozed through the site in 1958, and quarrying of the volcano's pink andesite removed all but a handful of ancient paintings that graced its cliffs and caves. Nevertheless, archaeological excavations on the ancient lake shores at the site's Zohapilco locality have yielded an impressively long sequence of occupation stretching back to 6,000 B.C. (Niederberger 1976; 1987), and excavations in the Ayotla zone on the northwest edge of the site clarified the Basin of Mexico's Formative chronology. By ca. 1650–1450 B.C. the Nevada phase inhabitants of Tlapacoya were practicing a well-established agricultural economy whose roots lay nearly a millennium earlier.

During the Ayotla phase (ca. 1450–1150 B.C.), "Olmec-style" hollow and solid figurines of the Pilli type appeared at Tlapacoya along with burnished black and gray vessels with Early Horizon motifs. These include some of the most elegant and informative examples of Early Horizon pottery. Among the most famous is a cylinder vessel that demonstrates the equivalence of frontal and profile versions of the "Olmec dragon" or zoomorphic super-natural. Other Tlapacoya cylinder vessels of the Paloma Negativo type include some of the finest examples of Early Horizon profile heads known, incised and often enhanced with bold resist painting in dark gray and red on a white slip (Fig. 6.1f). Remains of such vessels have now been found in residential con-texts, although many of the vessels with Early Horizon motifs and figurines now in museums and private collections were apparently found in burials asso-ciated with a large earthen platform, which also contained celts, ornaments, and mirrors of imported jade, greenstone, seashell, and iron ores (Niederberger 2000: 175). Chemical analysis of ceramic pastes also indicates importation of vessels from the southern Gulf lowlands (Blomster et al. 2005), and petro-graphic analysis suggests the possibility of some importation of vessels from Oaxaca (Flannery and Marcus 1994: 259–268; Stoltman et al. 2005).

By the Manantial phase (ca. 1150–900 B.C.) Tlapacoya had grown to cover perhaps 70 ha and included stone as well as earthen structures (Niederberger 2000: 179). At this point in the site's history, the Early Horizon motifs under-went substantial development, including a great expansion of cross-hatched medallions with spiked outlines and double-line-breaks (Niederberger 1976: 182–184, 1986; 569–591; see also Tolstoy 1989a: 98). A particularly notable vessel is incised with a profile face formed by the intricate superimposition of multiple profile and frontal faces and iconographic elements (Niederberger 1986: Figure 449) (Fig. 6.1h), a style of representation that becomes prevalent in greenstone celts and figurines during the Middle Formative period.

Southeast of Tlapacoya the site of Coapexco sits at an elevation of 2,600 m on the cool upper piedmont astride a major route southward out of the Basin of Mexico towards Morelos. Inhabited for a century before it was abandoned around 1350 B.C., the densely occupied village of 44 ha contained a population estimated at 1,000 persons living in small wattle-and-daub houses (Tolstoy 1989a: 87–90). Excavations here revealed evidence of craft production focused on serpentine beads, manos and metates, and especially obsidian blades. Like other Early Horizon sites in the region, most of the obsidian came from the Otumba source on the northwestern edge of the Basin. However distant sources were utilized more frequently than at other Basin of Mexico sites, and blades were unusually common, indicating that Coapexco may have been particularly engaged in their production and distribution (Tolstoy 1989a: 96).

Subtle differences in household status at Coapexco are suggested by variable proportions of slipped and painted ceramic types. Households with these types also tended to have more formally shaped manos and metates as opposed to the causal grinding stones that were more common at the site. On the other hand, ceramic vessels with Early Horizon motifs and "Olmec-style" figurines were generally present in household refuse, suggesting they were relatively unrelated to household status (Tolstoy 1989a: 98).

The eponymous Tlatilco site is located at the interface between the valley plain and the piedmont on the west side of Lake Texcoco, the largest of the lakes in the Basin of Mexico. Tlatilco was discovered in 1936 while mining clay for a brickyard, which ultimately destroyed the site. Although the site was heavily looted for its extraordinary ceramic vessels, figurines, and other artifacts, a series of excavations over the next three decades uncovered nearly 500 burials. The burials were interred over a period of 300 years (ca. 1400–1100 B.C.), which can be divided into four stages based on the seriation of associated artifacts in the grave lots (Tolstoy 1989a: 101–102, 1989b: 281–284). The first two burial stages correspond generally to the Ayotla phase and the last two to the Manantial phase in the sequence employed in this book (Niederberger 2000: Table 1). The presence of numerous bell-shaped storage and refuse pits and some clay-surfaced platforms and terraces indicate that the site was not just a cemetery, but a village of some importance (Niederberger 2000: 173; Tolstoy 1989a: 101).

Paul Tolstoy's (1989a: 101–119) careful analysis of the Tlatilco graves provides many clues to the character of Early Horizon society in the Basin of Mexico. Sets of graves form discrete clusters that suggest burial under or near residences. Most of the graves are oriented in a general east-west direction, and variation around this axis corresponds to the seasonal movement of the sun. A large minority of graves, however, are oriented north-south. Most of the burials in each cluster correspond to one or the other of these two directions, and the minority group within each cluster contains fewer grave goods than the majority. Tolstoy (1989a: 116–117) interprets these patterns as reflecting intermarriage between two social groups, with members of the in-marrying group, usually males, being accorded a lower social status. Over time, males appear to have gained higher status generally, such that males form a majority of the richer graves in the later stages of occupation (Tolstoy 1989a: 114).

The emergence of social differences is indicated in the Tlatilco burials by the quantity of grave goods, the presence of certain rare items, the depth of the interments, and the position of the body (Tolstoy 1989a: 109–112). In general, higher-status burials contained more grave goods overall and were more likely to contain iron ore mirrors, necklaces, cylinder seals, jade or greenstone objects, and ornaments of imported shell. They also were more likely to be covered with red pigment, whereas lower-status burials in declining order contained ash concentrations, or were laid on beds of sand or beds of sherds. The higher-status individuals of any particular age and sex category also tended to be laid on their backs in an extended position and to be buried in deeper graves that required more labor to dig. Though positively correlated with one another, these status distinctions do not group into discrete ranks (Tolstoy 1989a: 112). However, the fact that the graves of children and juveniles tended to contain more grave goods than those of adults suggests that status depended as much or more on its ascription at birth as on achievements later in life (Tolstoy 1989a: 115).

The intrinsic importance of these insights into Early Formative society notwithstanding, it is the presence of Early Horizon elements in the Tlatilco burials that has garnered the site its fame. As at other Early Formative sites, these elements characteristically occur on burnished black or dark gray cylindrical vessels, flat-based bowls with outleaning walls, tecomates, and bottles with tall, broad necks, which are unusually common at Tlatilco. Also represented are cylinder seals. The specific motifs include the hand-paw-wing, the St. Andrew's cross, square brackets, music brackets, flame eyebrows, U-shaped elements, gentle steps, flame eyebrows, the double scroll, and cross-hatched medallions with spiked borders (Tolstoy 1989a: 119). In Tlatilco Culture, examples of these medallions often occur on the interior bases of bowls, whereas similar medallions on San Lorenzo phase vessels from San Lorenzo appear more frequently on vessel walls (Coe and Diehl 1980a: Fig. 140b, e, f). In addition, Tlatilco has produced several hollow, white-slipped figurines. One of the most famous is actually an effigy vessel in the form of an acrobat with his feet bent over onto his head, but others are of the seated type particularly common in the Mexican highlands (Blomster 2002). As may be expected on statistical grounds alone, these relatively rare "Olmec-style" vessels and figurines occur more often in burials with many associated grave goods, but they do not show a clear statistical association with exotic high-status items and they also are found as individual items in relatively poor burials. They are, however, strongly associated with burials having an east-west orientation, especially those of females. Therefore, Early Horizon motifs at Tlatilco seem to have marked social distinctions other than rank, likely including membership in village segments based on kinship (Tolstoy 1989a: 119).

The Tlatilco culture sites of Morelos present a social picture generally similar to those of the Basin of Mexico (Grove 1996: 106–107). Most prevalent in the western two-thirds of the state, Tlatilco culture settlements included many hamlets, several small villages, and a single large village situated along the terraces of each fertile river valley (Grove 1996: 106). Though three size ranks of settlement can be identified, the administrative hierarchy seems more likely to have been organized in two tiers with each large village serving as the center of a simple chiefdom.

Evidence that the largest villages served public functions and contained individuals of higher social status comes from Chalcatzingo in eastern Morelos. At 4 to 6 ha, Chalcatzingo was the largest village in the Amatzinac river valley during the late Amate phase (ca. 1400–1150 B.C.) (Hirth 1987: 350). Two earthen platforms dating to the Amate phase were faced with stones, constituting the only such known structures of this age from Central Mexico. The largest was at least 15 m long, and by the end of the Amate phase it had been raised in two construction stages to a height of 4 m. Stone facing was confined to its lower sides and may have extended southward as a pavement (Grove 1989a: 127; Grove and Cyphers Guillén 1987: 29–31). Continued construction on top of this structure during the Middle Formative period would expand it into the site's largest civic-ceremonial platform, and it may have served such public functions already in the Amate phase (Grove 1989a: 127, 1996: 107). The smaller platform was 5.5 m long, 3 m wide, and 1.5 m high. The dimensions and stone facing of this platform suggest it may have supported an elite residence, although they also resemble the Early Formative public buildings described previously for the Valley of Oaxaca (Aviles 1995; Grove 1996: 107). A quite different sort of public construction has been reported from San Pablo in the Cuautla Valley of south-central Morelos (Grove 1970b). Several hundred meters from the main village, individuals were interred in a 30 m diameter stone-faced burial mound. This unique structure was so heavily looted in the 1960s that it is no longer possible to ascertain whether its interments were confined to high-status individuals or were drawn more broadly from the population of the village (Grove 1996: 107).

Ties between Morelos and the Basin of Mexico sites are suggested by a similar prevalence of Otumba obsidian as well as by styles of locally made pottery and figurines. As at Tlatilco, Tlapacoya, and Coapexco, pottery with Early Horizon motifs makes up less than 5% of the assemblages and were available to people of all social levels, being found in the full range of sites from hamlets to large villages (Grove 1996: 106). Although included within the Tlatilco culture sphere, Chalcatzingo's repertoire of Early Horizon motifs appears to be more impoverished than other sites, consisting mainly of St. Andrews' crosses.

This difference, however, may be a consequence of the Chalcatzingo materials coming mainly from contexts other than burials (Grove 1989a: 124).

Chalcatzingo's Amate phase ceramic assemblage also includes some imports from the Izucar de Matamoros valley about 40 km away in western Puebla (Cyphers Guillén 1987: 209). Known as "Del Prado pink" at Chalcatzingo, this ceramic type is characteristic of the "Las Bocas" style, which also includes burnished blackware bottles with carved and incised Early Horizon motifs and animal effigy vessels. So distinctive is the pottery of the Izucar de Matamoros area that it demarcates the eastern limit of the Tlatilco culture. The site of Las Bocas itself is particularly famous for its sensitively modeled hollow figurines, which represent the apogee of this Early Formative art form. Unfortunately, the history of the Las Bocas site is one of the most egregious examples of looting in the annals of Mesoamerican archaeology. By 1966 the site had been completely destroyed by illicit digging, and the continuing demand for "Las Bocas" pottery and figurines on the international antiquites market has resulted in the destruction of innumerable sites in the Izucar de Matamoros Valley and the production of many forgeries (Grove 1996: 106–107). As a result, the social contexts of the exquisite figurines and vessels is unknown. What is evident is that Las Bocas itself was a relatively minor settlement and that the number of artifacts attributed to it is implausible at best.

Guerrero

The rivers of Morelos and western Puebla flow southward into the Balsas River of the western state of Guerrero. Sheltered from coastal winds by the Sierra Madre del Sur, the river and its tributaries flow through the hot, dry basin of the Balsas-Tecaltepec Depression, occasionally revealing veins of serpentine in the metamorphic rocks that lie beneath its thin soils. In the mountains drained by its eastern tributaries, however, higher elevations produce cooler temperatures and greater rainfall. Archaeological sites in the Balsas depression and adjacent parts of eastern Guerrero have produced some of the most fascinating examples of "Olmec-style" artifacts and architecture in Mesomerica. Indeed, Guerrero has sometimes been proposed as the original heartland of Olmec culture (e.g., Covarrubias 1957: 76, 110; Gay 1973), although today there is little support for this position.

The Early Horizon is represented in Guerrero at sites like Atopula, Teopan-tecuanitlán, and Zumpango del Río (Henderson 1979; Niederberger 1996)[4] by the familiar white-slipped hollow figurines and small quantities of polished black, white-slipped, and differentially fired black-and-white pottery rendered in the forms of cylinder vessels, bottles, and flat-based bowls. The figurines and pottery from this frontier of the Early Horizon show a range of stylistic variation that encompasses examples very similar to those of Central Mexico as well as others that reinterpret the stylistic canons in local terms. Some of the

Figure 6.9. Stylized earth-monster face on balustrade, Teopantecuanitlán phase I. (Drawing based on Martínez Donjuan 1994: Fig. 1).

vessels are decorated with fields of incised cross-hatching similar to designs on Tlatilco ceramics, but excised Early Horizon motifs appear to be less common than in Central Mexico or Oaxaca (Henderson 1979: 27–32; Reyna-Robles 1996; Tolstoy 1989b: 286).

Unfortunately, many of the sites in Guerrero are known only from looted collections with no archaeological context in museums and private collections. A spectacular exception is Teopantecuanitlán, discovered only two decades ago about 8 km up the Mezcalapa River from where it joins the Amacuzac to form the Balsas (Martínez Donjuán 1994; Niederberger 1996). At the administrative and ceremonial heart of the 160 ha site a Middle Formative platform covered an earlier sunken courtyard. The earliest construction phase in this courtyard probably dates to around 1000 B.C. (cf. Martínez Donjuán 1986; Niederberger 1996: 97; Reyna Robles 1996: 132).[5] The walls and floor of this first courtyard were formed of earth covered with yellow clay. Entrance was by means of two double stairways on a small platform attached to the southern wall. At the lower ends of the ramps that divide each of the double stairways were modeled the stylized faces of felines or earth-monsters with flame eyebrows (Fig. 6.9). Four cleft elements above the eyebrows presage the headbands of monster faces carved on travertine monoliths set in the stone walls of a later phase of the courtyard.

Summary

As the foregoing tour through Mesoamerica illustrates, the social landscape of the Early Formative period was a varied and dynamic one in which diverse regions in varying degrees were tied to one another through the exchange of material goods, symbols, and ideas. In many parts of Mesoamerica, from Guerrero to Honduras, social roles were becoming more clearly differentiated. Some of this differentiation was horizontal, in the sense that groups of people of similar status specialized in their activities. Horizontal differentiation is most evident in craft production, where it is indicated by the uniformity and/or skillful execution of figurines, ceramic vessels, obsidian blades, stone monuments and other artifacts, as well as by concentrations of manufacturing debris. In some cases entire neighborhoods or villages appear to have specialized in the manufacture of particular goods, for example of iron ore mirrors in one area of San José Mogote or obsidian blades at Coapexco. This is not to say that all or even most craft specialists derived their livelihood solely from their manufactures, but that some households produced more than they required for their own use in order to exchange the surplus with other households.

Vertical social differentiation also appeared in many areas, but to varying degrees. In each of the areas we have examined, differences in house construction, artifact inventories, and/or grave lots suggest variations in household wealth. In the Soconusco, a marked difference in the size and construction of structures reasonably interpreted as residences suggests that social ranking emerged before 1500 B.C., although discrete ranks are less evident in burials. In Oaxaca, Central Mexico, and Guerrero the evidence for formal social ranking is more subtly implied by differences in mortuary practices (especially for children), body treatment, head deformation, residential construction, and the representation of apparently authoritative individuals among figurines.

At the regional scale, the widespread development of settlement hierarchies indicates the emergence of political differentiation in many Mesoamerican societies by the close of the Early Formative period. Here the evidence must be interpreted cautiously, for the simple presence of some settlements larger than others does not necessarily prove an administrative hierarchy was in place, and in some cases the arbitrary divisions in a continuum of site sizes, though useful for settlement analysis, may become reified as a settlement hierarchy. Likewise, while the identification of several functionally different classes of sites (including sites for extracting particular resources) adds a dimension of complexity to the settlement system, it need not imply greater political differentiation. A further interpretive difficulty concerns estimates of site populations, given the possibility of variations in the density of settlement within communities. In other words, although one can reasonably conclude that a settlement of one hectare is unlikely to serve as an administrative center, and one of a hundred hectares more so, there is no single limit that can be applied across regions. Rather, the judgment of the number of administrative levels in a settlement system must seek evidence for multiple modes in the distribution of site sizes or inferred populations within a region as well as evidence for the centralization of political functions within the larger sites.

That said, strong evidence indicates that precocious two-tiered settlement hierarchies suggestive of emerging centralized authority arose in the Mazatán area of the Soconusco before 1500 B.C. By 1150 B.C. two-tiered settlement hierarchies headed by large villages appeared in Oaxaca and Central Mexico. They almost certainly were present in Guerrero as well, although regional settlement data are lacking. In the Valley of Oaxaca, San José Mogote headed a strongly primate settlement system in which the regional center was ten times the size of the next largest site (Marcus and Flannery; 1996: 106; Rosenswig 2000). The political territories integrated by these head villages were quite small, however, not extending much more than 10 km from the center. Outside of Olman, only the Soconusco had a three-tiered settlement hierarchy before 1000 B.C.

How do these regions stack up against Olman? By the close of the Bajío phase at about 1450 B.C., a 20 ha village at San Lorenzo appears to have headed a two-tiered settlement hierarchy (Symonds et al. 2002: 120, Figs. 4.4, 4.5). By 1150 B.C., San Lorenzo was the largest site in Mesoamerica, covering an estimated 500 ha with 300 ha of denser occupation in its core, and it stood at the head of a settlement hierarchy that included three or perhaps four tiers (Symonds et al. 2002: 68). It is likely that the territory under the political control of San Lorenzo extended some 25 km to the secondary center of Estero Rabon (Borstein 2001: 289). In terms of scale and political complexity, Clark and Pye's (2000b: 245–246) statement that Early Horizon San Lorenzo "had no peers, only contemporaries" seems closer to the mark than "Olmec-period early Mesoamerican groups and polities had an *identical* level of sociopolitical complexity (Niederberger 1996: 97, emphasis in the original)." Moreover, the rulers of San Lorenzo lived in elaborate dwellings and controlled sufficient labor to import multi-ton monuments carved by specialized and skillful artisans over a distance of 60 km. Greater size and complexity alone, however, do not necessarily imply the domination of distant polities. It is doubtful that San Lorenzo even controlled all of Olman, and although Cantón Corralito offers evidence of an Olmec enclave in the Soconusco, further study is required to determine the degree to which the Olmecs there remained subject to Gulf Coast polities or dominated local political economies.

TABLE 6.1. *Some products exchanged interregionally in the Early and Middle Formative periods.*

Products	Sources
Highland Products	
obsidian	various sources:
	central and western Mexico
	southern Guatemala
jade	Motagua Valley, Guatemala
serpentine and other greenstones	Motagua Valley, Guatemala
	Tehuitzingo, Puebla
	Cuicatlán-Concepción Pápalo,
	Oaxaca Balsas Valley, Guerrero
iron ores (magnetite, ilmenite, specular	Oaxaca
hematite)	Central Depression of Chiapas
mica	southern Sierra Madre
Lowland Products	
marine shell	Gulf Coast
	Pacific Coast
stingray spines	Gulf Coast
	Pacific Coast
rubber	tropical lowlands
cacao	Olman Soconusco
feathers	tropical lowlands
	highland Guatemala (quetzal)
jaguar and other pelts	tropical lowlands
Highland and Lowland Products	
pottery	Coatzacoalcos Valley
	Valley of Oaxaca?
hollow ceramic figurines	Gulf Coast
	southeastern Puebla

Note: Italics indicate perishable products for which exchange is presumed or inferred indirectly from iconography.

Beyond the widespread increase in sociopolitical differentiation in Mesoamerica, the other salient characteristic of the Early Horizon – in fact, its defining characteristic – is the heightened interaction among far-flung regions indicated by the exchange of goods and the dissemination of technical and esoteric knowledge. The Early Horizon inhabitants of Mesoamerica participated in an extensive network of overlapping exchange zones for different goods (Table 6.1, Fig. 6.10). Iron ore mirrors, many made in Oaxaca, appeared in all the regions considered in this chapter. These artifacts seem associated with high status wherever they occur. Multiperforate iron ore cubes, on the other hand, are more restricted to Chiapas, where they were made, and Olman, but in the latter, at least, they are found in small, ephemeral sites and humble dwellings

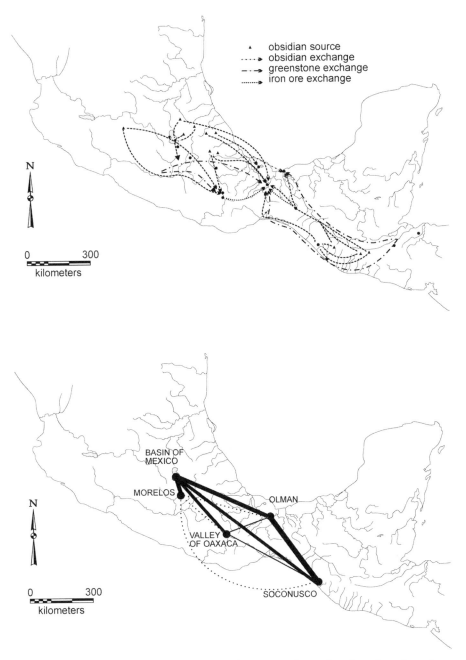

Figure 6.10. Upper map: patterns of long-distance exchange in mineral products during the early horizon. Exchange routes are approximate. Lower map: patterns of Early Horizon symbolic interaction. Thickness of line reflects number of mutually shared X-complex motifs. Some interacting regions are omitted due to lack of quantifiable data.

as well as the large elite-associated caches of San Lorenzo. Greenstone, including jade, serpentine, and other mineral varieties, was widely exchanged, although the extent of exchange from individual sources is still uncertain and, in some cases, they appear to have been available to a wider range of social statuses. Ornaments made of shell from both the Atlantic and Pacific coasts reached the inland regions of Oaxaca and Central Mexico, but in Guerrero were confined to local mussels and Pacific species. Like greenstones of the Early Horizon, shell ornaments were not confined to high status individuals (Marcus and Flannery 1996: 101–102; Tolstoy 1989a: Table 6.4).

Chemical sourcing of obsidian provides the most detailed picture of overlapping interregional exchange systems in Early Formative Mesoamerica. In broad terms, virtually all communities obtained their obsidian from multiple sources, but they differed in the presence and proportions of particular sources. Otumba obsidian was dominant in Central Mexico and perhaps Guerrero, and was a major source utilized in Oaxaca, which also imported obsidian from Guadalupe Victoria in Puebla and Zinapecuaro in Michoacan (Pires-Ferreira 1976a). Not surprisingly, only Guatemalan sources were employed in the Soconusco. From their intermediate location on the Isthmus of Tehuantepec, Olmec societies obtained obsidian both from Guatemalan and Mexican sources. Within communities, members of all social statuses had access to obsidian. Initially, individual households appear to have acquired obsidian independently from nearby trading partners in a system of down-the-line exchange, resulting in variable mixes of obsidian types among households and gradually declining amounts of obsidian as the distance from the obsidian source increased. (Pires-Ferreira 1976a). As community-wide leaders and territorial chiefs emerged in places like Oaxaca and the Soconusco, however, they began to take charge of pooling obsidian and redistributing it to their supporters and subjects. In addition, some leaders may have controlled the technology for producing obsidian blades (Clark and Salcedo 1989).

Sourcing materials is relatively straightforward, but sourcing ideas is less so. Archaeologists, of course, must rely on the physical manifestations of ideas to infer the mechanisms by which they were shared. Such inferences revolve around the analysis of artifact style, extending to the technical choices made in producing an artifact as well as the selection and execution of decoration and symbolic motifs. For the Early Horizon, the sharing of styles across regions is most evident in ceramic artifacts, and it is these that most clearly define the horizon (Fig. 6.10). Nevertheless, the accumulation of evidence indicates that the Early Horizon was not a monolithic entity, either in the symbols applied to vessels or in their social uses.

The most ubiquitous ceramic attributes of the Early Horizon relate to technology and form. They consist of black, differentially fired, and white or white-slipped cylinder vessels and open, flat-bottomed bowls. Within specific regions, however, the characteristic motifs of the horizon also may occur on tecomates, bottles, effigy vessels, and other forms, as well as on red, brown, or buff pottery. On vessels the most typical execution of the motifs is by a combination of broad, carved bars and narrow incised lines. As a ceramic technique, modeling is also widespread in the form of effigy vessels and heads decorating the rims and necks of dishes and jars, but specific themes exhibit a high degree of regionalism, for example, the blackware effigy vessels of Central Mexico. Also typical is a high degree of conventionalized abstraction in carved and excised designs. In addition, a core of specific motifs can be identified that include stylized versions of the were-jaguar and fire-serpent and the elements that represent their features such as crossed bars (the "St. Andrew's cross"), flame eyebrows, "music brackets," upside-down U-shaped elements, and V or cleft-shaped elements, the latter two of which also are represented as variants of the "double-line-break" on vessel rims. Also included among the nearly universal elements are the double-scroll, or *ilhuitl*, zones of cross-hatching, – often in the form of medallions with spiked borders – and mat-like motifs (see Tolstoy 1989a: 117 for a similar list).

On the other hand, a large number of motifs included in Grove's X-Complex and often described as "Olmec" have a more restricted spatial distribution. The Valley of Oaxaca stands out as a region where local versions of Early Horizon motifs abound. Several of the free-standing motifs identified here by Pyne (1976; Flannery and Marcus 1994) occur nowhere else, including most of the highly abstracted incised versions of the frontal were-jaguar face. Early Formative vessels from the Valley of Oaxaca also exhibit an impressive diversity of double (and triple and quadruple) line-breaks, which are shared most closely with the Basin of Mexico (Plog 1976). Although Morelos participated with the Basin of Mexico in the Tlatilco culture, its corpus of Early Horizon motifs was more restricted, and they differ overall from those shared by the Basin and Oaxaca (Flannery and Marcus 1994: 379). In the Basin of Mexico, the hand-paw-wing motif was often represented, either alone or as a component of the full-figure abstraction of the fire-serpent, and it occurs as well on ceramics and sculpture of Olman, but it is scarce or absent in other areas. The Basin of Mexico and Morelos shared the incised-and-resist representations of profile heads, but they do not seem to appear in other areas, except in the distant Soconusco during the Jocotal phase (Clark and Pye 2000b: Fig. 34; John Hodgson, personal communication, 2005). Finally, the Soconusco shares most of its Early Horizon ceramic motifs with Olman. Several parallels with the Basin of Mexico also are evident, but except for the profile heads consist mainly in the most ubiquitous of Early Horizon motifs or elements also shared between Olman and the Basin. Similarities with other areas are fewer and more tenuous (see Clark and Pye 2000b: 237–239).

Equally important as the form and execution of Early Horizon motifs are the social contexts in which they were used. These, too, varied across Mesoamerica. The most obvious variation is that they are more prevalent in societies that were

developing greater numbers of social distinctions, both horizontally, in occupations and social groups, and vertically, in the emergence of wealth and rank
distinctions. Among the participants in the Early Horizon sphere, however,
there were evident differences in how Early Horizon symbols were employed.
In Olman, they occur in social contexts that range from the humblest settings
to the "Red Palace" at the physical and social summit of San Lorenzo. In the
Soconusco, they seem to be most prevalent in chiefly centers and are likely to
have reinforced leaders' claims to authority. In the more corporately organized
Valley of Oaxaca, they were buried with men and segregated by neighborhood
and community, and in the Basin of Mexico they were preferentially buried
with the women of the numerically dominant moiety. Thus each region not
only manipulated the designs of pots, but also their social meanings.

What are these diverse and variably cross-cutting geographic and social patterns telling us about Early Horizon interaction? The most extreme poles of the
mother-culture/sister-culture debate would leave us only two choices: either
the Olmec originated the core set of Early Horizon symbols and disseminated
them to less sophisticated societies who later modified and elaborated them, or
the corpus of "pan-Mesoamerican" symbols represented on ceramics precipi-
tated from the interactions of many similarly developing societies that shared a
common heritage of belief and, perhaps, of representation in perishable media.
These positions leave ample room for a middle ground.

Much of the problem stems from the fact that the social processes that
created and disseminated the Early Horizon symbolic complex occurred more
rapidly than our chronological data are currently able to resolve. With a few
possible exceptions, the set of black and black-and-white pastes, cylindrical
vessels and flat-bottomed bowls, carved-and-incised decoration, and abstracted
motifs seem to appear simultaneously across most of Mesoamerica. Minor
variations in the first appearance of this technological and symbolic set are
more a consequence of where archaeologists decide to draw the temporal lines
between their phases than real differences in when and where they were first
manufactured. The few possible exceptions for which temporal priority can
be argued among widely disseminated ceramic elements include black-and-
white pottery in Olman, the cross-hatched spiked medallion and Tlatilco-style
profile face in Morelos and the Basin of Mexico, and the music bracket and
certain variants of double line-breaks in the Valley of Oaxaca. Another is the
report of a single white-slipped hollow baby figurine from the Bajío phase at
San Lorenzo (Blomster 2002: 176; Coe and Diehl 1980a: 261). Otherwise,
the most that can be said is that by about 1350 B.C. the core features of the
Early Horizon were integrated into ceramic assemblages from Guerrero and
the Basin of Mexico to Honduras.

On the other hand, it is unlikely that the distinctive core attributes of paste,
form, decorative technique, and conventionalized representation should have
been simultaneously combined by the individual societies participating in the

Early Horizon sphere. Whatever the specific origins of the individual attributes, it is more likely that potters sharing knowledge of technique and design within a particular culture should have created this ceramic style. Once integrated, the technological and symbolic components of the style would have been disseminated as a package that formed a model to which local elements could have been added and from which elements could have been extracted to apply to existing and developing components of the ceramic tradition. Importantly, neither the skill nor the diversity, nor the numerical dominance of vessels of the core style, necessarily determines its origin. Emulation and rapid elaboration are expected in local traditions, and the degree to which the style resonates or is useful in adoptive societies is more significant than its frequency in the region where it was combined into a coherent whole (Stark 2000: 42).

Some evidence that Olman played an important role in the dissemination of the Early Horizon ceramic style, alluded to previously, comes from chemical analysis of pottery from San Lorenzo, on the Gulf Coast, Mazatán and San Isidro in Chiapas, Laguna Zope on the southern Isthmus of Tehuantepec, the Valley of Oaxaca, Etlatongo in the western Oaxaca highlands, and the Basin of Mexico (Blomster et al. 2005; see also Neff et al. 2006a, 2006b). Blomster and colleagues' analysis indicated that each of the regions outside Olman received vessels from the San Lorenzo area, but could not confirm import into San Lorenzo from these same areas.[6] Petrographic analysis, however, raises the possibility that some vessels at San Lorenzo and in the Basin of Mexico and the Valley of Puebla came from Oaxaca (Flannery and Marcus 1994: 262–263; Stoltman et al. 2005; Sharer et al. 2006). The chemical results do not absolutely preclude the exchange of some vessels and the designs on them, between regions outside the Gulf Coast (Neff et al. 2006a: 59–60). Nor do they address the potential flow of ideas relating to pottery manufacture among multiple regions by means other than exchange of vessels. They do, however, imply that San Lorenzo was more broadly involved in the distribution of ceramic types with Early Horizon motifs than were other sites of the period.

None of this – not the size and complexity of the San Lorenzo polity, nor its broad interaction in exchange spheres, nor even its potential role in crystallizing and disseminating the complex of Early Horizon motifs – makes the Olmec the sole Mother Culture of Mesoamerica. Rather, San Lorenzo is better seen as the head of a particularly powerful and prestigious polity among many complex societies that interacted with one another to varying degrees. Its status as a prestige center would appear to have been particularly strong in the Soconusco, where rank society had an even longer history. Olmecs may even have established an enclave at Cantón Corallito, but it does not necessarily follow that San Lorenzo exerted political control over the region. More likely the leaders of Olman and the Soconusco used one another to their mutual benefit, as did other participants in the Early Horizon interaction sphere to varying degrees.

THE MIDDLE FORMATIVE PERIOD

As more societies instituted social hierarchies and came to be ruled by hereditary elites after 1000 B.C., significant shifts occurred in patterns of interregional interactions and their material expressions. Trade in jade and serpentine increased as exotic greenstones became the common symbolic currency of elite status (Garber et al. 1993: 213), and Olmec-style narrative relief carvings appeared at specific sites in the Mexican highlands and the Pacific slope of Chiapas, Guatemala, and El Salvador (Fig. 6.11). The content of these carvings suggests an increased concern with formally and publicly expressing social alliances between Olmec rulers and their foreign counterparts as well as the ideological bases for local elite power. In several sites, the appearance of Olmec sculpture appears to correlate with the initial construction of monumental public architecture, a further testament to the consolidation of hierarchical social and political institutions.

At the same time, most of the characteristic ceramic motifs of the Early Horizon were transferred to greenstone artifacts and gradually fell out of use on pottery vessels (Grove 1993: 97–98). One exception was the "double line-break," frequently executed on white, flat-bottomed bowls, which became a hallmark of the early Middle Formative period (Fig. 5.1a–c). In other respects Middle Formative social and political developments resulted in an increased regionalization of pottery and figurine styles and a division in the symbol sets used by elites and their subjects (Grove 1993: 98).

In much of Mesoamerica, changes in ceramic traditions at about 700–800 B.C. (600–700 uncalibrated B.C.) justify dividing the Middle Formative period into earlier and later portions. The earlier portion variously has been called the Intermediate Olmec Horizon (Lowe 1989), the Later Olmec Horizon (Lowe 1971, 1977), and the Olmec Whiteware Horizon (Henderson 1979), and is usually considered to correlate with the first two construction phases in Complex A at La Venta (Lowe 1989: 54), though phase II may have been constructed after 700 B.C (see Chapter 5). As Henderson's label acknowledges, it is this earlier division of the Middle Formative period that is most strongly associated with the widespread appearance of white vessels and the double-line-break motif, in addition to the expanded distribution of greenstone artifacts.

The subsequent and less extensive "Terminal Olmec Horizon" (Lowe 1989), or "Modified Olmec Horizon" (Lowe 1977), is best defined for the Greater Isthmian region of Tabasco, Chiapas, and southern Guatemala, where it is represented by the appearance of polished red-to-orange-brown pottery, often with splotchy or cloudy resist decoration. This ware resembles Usulután pottery of the Maya region and reflects increased interaction between Isthmian and Maya populations (Grove 1993: 103; Lowe 1977: 222–223, 1989: 57). Its occurrence in Olman is patchy, however, suggesting a variable pattern of external interaction and local incorporation of foreign styles. Polished orange pottery,

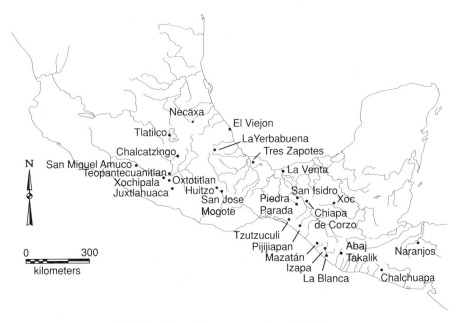

Figure 6.11. Map of Middle Formative sites mentioned in the text.

including a cloudy-resist (*"Nebulosa"*) variety, appears in Middle and Late Formative deposits at Tres Zapotes (Ortiz 1975), but is absent from San Lorenzo
(Coe and Diehl 1980a: 200). E. Wyllys Andrews V (1986) did not observe polished orange pottery in La Venta type collections, although polished "brown
lacquer" ware described by Drucker (1952b: 109–110) may be related (see also
Lowe 1989: 59), and von Nagy et al. (2002) have recently reported imported
blotchy resist Nicapa orange ware pottery in late Middle Formative deposits at
the nearby site of San Andres. Similar polished orange-slipped vessels appear
at only a handful of sites in western Mesoamerica, most notably Chalcatzingo
(Grove 1993: 99, 102–103). Elsewhere in western Mesoamerica late Middle
Formative changes in ceramic styles reflect continued development of regional
traditions more than participation in far-flung interaction systems.

These Middle Formative "Olmec Horizons" are archaeological horizons in a
loose sense only. Like the Early Horizon, they are relatively long-lived, extending over some 200–400 calendar years each. They also are based on fewer and
more generalized ceramic attributes than the Early Horizon. Defining a Terminal or Modified "Olmec Horizon" especially is questionable due to its limited
extent and, in western Mesoamerica, highly localized occurrence (Grove 1993:
103). More problematic than the "horizon" characterization, however is the
"Olmec" attribution. Although Gulf Olmec traits do occur in sculpture associated with both "horizons" (Clark and Pye 2000b; Grove 1989a; 1993), the
Gulf Coast origins of the ceramic traits that serve to define the phases are questionable (Grove 1993). In sum, the concept of two Middle Formative "Olmec
horizons" is a gross chronological tool, which adds little to our understanding

of the cultural processes that produced the spatially and chronologically variable distributions of artworks and artifacts it seeks to describe. For that understanding, we must examine in greater detail the archaeological record of particular regions that participated in Middle Formative interaction spheres.

Chiapas and the Southeastern Pacific Coast

Olman and the Soconusco form parts of the "Greater Isthmian Region" defined by Gareth Lowe (1971, 1977) as extending from northern Veracruz, through Tabasco, Chiapas, and the Pacific Coast of Guatemala to Western El Salvador. This is the area of the Initial and Early Formative Locona style zone, and it continued to be a zone of heightened interaction through the Middle Formative period, despite evidence for local cultural developments and fluctuations in interregional relations. Natural communication routes along coasts and through highland valleys facilitated exchanges of valued resources such as jade, serpentine, obsidian, and possibly cacao and contributed to the dispersion of technological and symbolic styles. Linguistic affinities probably encouraged cultural exchanges as well, since the nucleus of the Greater Isthmian Region in the southern Gulf coast, eastern Oaxaca, and Chiapas also encompasses the historical distribution of native speakers of Mije-Sokean languages.

Following the disruptions of the Jocotal phase the highlands and Pacific coast of southeastern Mesoamerica re-established close relations with Olman (Clark and Pye 2000b: 241–242). Stone monuments were carved in the narrative relief style characteristic of La Venta at a string of coastal and piedmont sites from Tiltepec, Chiapas to Chalchuapa, El Salvador (Fig. 6.12). Similar carvings are found a short distance across the mountains in the Central Grijalva Depression of Chiapas at Padre Piedra and well to the northeast in the Lacandon Forest at Xoc. Usually executed on boulders, these monuments depict richly attired individuals, probably local rulers. Their headdresses and the bundles or scepters they carry are often marked with motifs that Karl Taube (2000) interprets as symbols for maize and quetzal plumes, as well as the green color of these materials and the jade that traveled this route from the Motagua Valley of Guatemala. The Pijijiapan monument differs in that it shows an encounter or ceremony involving a man and woman. Behind the man stands another woman, perhaps his mother, and both women are served by attendants shown as smaller figures (Clark and Pye 2000b: 220, Fig. 3). The rich attire of the principal figures attests to their high social status, and it is plausible that the monument commemorates an alliance forged through marriage (Clark and Pérez 1994: 269).

Monuments are difficult to date, even under the best archaeological circumstances, because they often were reset in later times. Nevertheless, stylistic canons and scattered stratigraphic associations suggest that most of the relief boulder carvings were executed in the early Middle Formative period between about 1000 and 800 B.C. (Clark and Pye 2000b: 227–230). An exception is

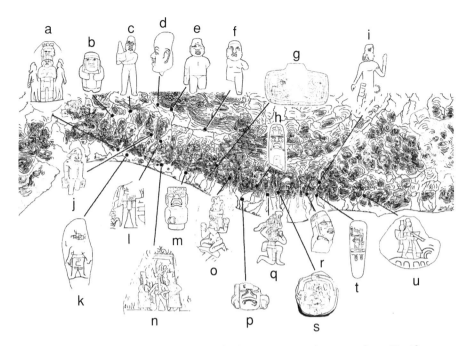

Figure 6.12. Distribution of Olmec-style the stone artworks on southeast Pacific coast: (a) Tiltepec, (b) Miramar, (c) Ocozocuautla, (d) Chiapa de Corzo, (e) Acula, (f) Laguna Francesa, (g) Motozintla, (h) San Marcos, (i) Amatitlan, (j) Villa Flores, (k) Tzutzuculi, (l) Padre Piedra, (m) Mapastepec, (n) Pijijiapan, (o) La Union, (p) La Blanca, (q) Takalik Abaj, (r) El Baul, (s) Suchitepéquez, (t) Escuintla, (u) Chalchuapa (from Clark and Pye 2000: Fig. 1) (courtesy of John E. Clark).

the probably later relief carving at Tiltepec of a central figure flanked by two smaller figures, which resembles Stela A at Tres Zapotes.

Chiapas and Guatemala also have yielded a rich assortment of stylistically Middle Formative votive axes, celts, figurines, and other items in jade and other stones. These are easier to date than monuments, when their archaeological contexts are known. Unfortunately, most are looted items now in private collections and museums. Clark and Pye (2000b) believe these, on the whole, to be later than the boulder sculptures. Nevertheless, Clark and Pye (2000b: 242) note an interesting pairing of such artifacts from the coast with artifacts and sculptures further inland on major passes into the interior, which suggests the possibility of two linked and parallel routes of communication and trade.

Settlement patterns and site plans document further changes in the political systems of the Pacific Coast in the early Middle Formative period. During the early Conchas phase (ca. 1000–900 B.C.), the site of La Blanca on the Río Naranjo in Guatemala rapidly grew to become a large and important center. Sharp population declines to the east and west in the El Mesak and Mazatán regions suggest that immigration was responsible for much of this growth (Clark and Pye 2000b: 242). In addition to containing Olmec-style sculpture, La Blanca boasted the largest construction of the time on the southeastern Pacific Coast and one of the largest in Mesoamerica, the earthen Mound 1,

which was 25 m tall and more than 100 m across at the base before its destruction in 1972 (Love 1999: 138). It should be noted that this Mound 1 at La
Blanca was nearly as broad and only five meters shorter than Mound C-1 at
La Venta, which probably achieved its final dimensions later (Gonzalez 1997:
93). Other centers in the La Blanca territory also constructed single mounds
greater than 15 m tall (Love 1999: 137). Public mound construction may have
begun about the same time at Takalik Abaj, a regional center 45 km away in
the Guatemalan piedmont, which contains many sculptures, including a niche
figure recarved from what seems to be the only Olmec-style colossal head
known outside Olman (Fig. 6.13). Soon afterward mound building prolifer-
ated across the Pacific Coast and in the interior of Chiapas, culminating in
the highly formalized, grid-like arrangement of mounds at Ujuxte, the late
Middle Formative successor to La Blanca as the regional capital on the eastern
Guatemala coast.

Much farther down the coast, Monument 12 at Chalchuapa, El Salvador,
represents the southeastern limit of Olmec-style relief sculpture. Three of the
four figures carved on the monument are standing or striding, and one wears
a stiff cape with wing-like projections (Figure 6.12u) (Anderson 1978). The
fourth figure is seated, and like two of the other figures holds a bundle with
the double-merlon motif Taube (1995) interprets as the Olmec symbol for
"green." Though clearly of Olmec derivation, the carvings on Monument 12
are more brusquely executed than are most of the more westerly examples. A
handful of clay figurines, pottery wares, and greenstone celts from Chalchuapa
bear general associations with widely distributed Middle Formative styles, but
explicit Olmec motifs are rare, and the closest affiliations are with ceramic traditions of the Chiapas and Guatemala coasts. Therefore, although Chalchuapa
has been interpreted as an Olmec trading outpost (Sharer 1978: 209, 1989a:
270–271), it seems more likely that interaction with the Olmec was indirect
via the Pacific littoral (Demarest 1989: 330).

Regardless of the precise nature of interregional interaction at Chalchuapa,
it appears to have been associated with the same kind of intensification and
social differentiation characteristic of the greater Isthmian tradition. Like La
Blanca, Takalik Abaj, Izapa, and numerous other sites, the Middle Formative
witnessed the first monumental construction at Chalchuapa, a mound (E3–1-2)
22 m tall and 60 m wide (Sharer 1989a: 251). As Michael Love (1999: 144–
146) observes, such monumental architectural efforts do not only reflect the
abilities of leaders to mobilize labor to public ends, they also serve as prominent
and durable reference points for segregating and regularizing activities in social
space. By helping shape the daily routines of individuals in reference to social
status, they contributed to the growing political power of elites.

Elsewhere in eastern Mesoamerica and lower Central America, interaction
with the Olmecs was generally indirect and probably intermittent (Demarest
1989; Sharer 1989a). The presence of apparently imported Joventud Red sherds
at La Venta suggests more direct contact with the northern Maya lowlands of

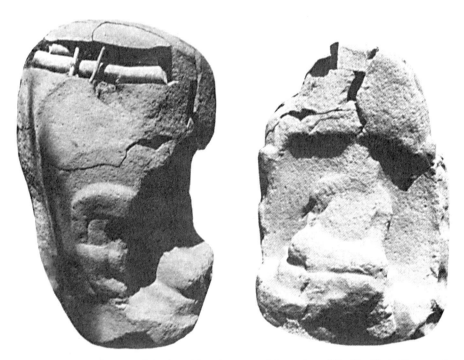

Figure 6.13. Olmec-style colossal head recarved into altar, Takalik Abaj, Guatemala (from Graham 1981: Fig. 1).

Yucatan (Andrews V 1986, 1987), but an impressive cache of jades at Chacsinkin, originally considered of Gulf Coast origin, is now thought to represent a more generalized Middle Formative tradition with no secure Olmec ties (Andrews V 1986, 1987; Garber et al. 1993: 227). Another possible exception to the general pattern of indirect Olmec contact occurs in the Ulúa Valley/Lake Yojoa region of Honduras, where monuments probably dating to the close of the Early Formative period and beginning of the Middle Formative period have been found at Puerto Escondido and Naranjos (Baudez 1971: 79; Henderson and Joyce 2000). Particularly interesting is a standing, decapitated figure from Naranjos, which by its stance and depiction of skeletal and muscular features calls to mind Middle Formative jade "transformation figures." Farther to the southeast in Costa Rica a large number of mainly unprovenienced jade artifacts have been reported. Many are of the blue-green jade favored by the Olmecs, and some exhibit strong Olmec affinities, but these latter frequently are reworked and appear to be heirloomed artifacts, which may have reached Costa Rica after the Middle Formative Period, and not necessarily from the Gulf Coast (Pohorilenko 1981).

Western Mesoamerica

West of the Isthmus of Tehuantepec, the Middle Formative period generally was a time of population growth and increasing social differentiation. In the Valley of Oaxaca, for example, population doubled to some 4,000 persons over the course of the Guadalupe (ca. 950–800 B.C.) and Rosario (ca. 800–550 B.C.) phases. New regional centers emerged in the eastern and southern arms of the valley, public buildings were enlarged, and the diversity and quality of burial goods show growing disparities in social ranking (Blanton et al. 1993: 66–69; Marcus and Flannery 1996: 111–117, 121–138; Rosenswig 2000: 436–437). These social developments were accompanied by an increase in competition among chiefdoms in the valley. Some of the story is told by ceramics. During the early Guadalupe phase there was considerable regional variation in pottery, such that the phase is difficult to define for the valley as a whole. Pottery from the village of Huitzo, for example, shows greater similarities to the Nochixtlán Valley, 50 km to the north, than with rival San José Mogote, a scant 16 km to the southeast (Marcus and Flannery 1996: 111). By 500 B.C., an intensely burned temple and a relief sculpture of a sacrificed captive (Monument 3), both at San José Mogote, attest to that site's failure and success in raids that apparently intensified in the Rosario phase (Flannery and Marcus 2003: 11802–11803, Table 1). Monument 3 also is widely regarded to contain the earliest known example of writing in Mesoamerica (cf. Pohl et al. 2002). The captive is identified by the glyph for his personal day-name, "1 Earthquake," which was taken from the 260-day sacred calendar, presaging a common practice in later Mesoamerican cultures.

Similar processes of regional integration and social differentiation proceeded, albeit more slowly, in the Valley of Mexico. Here too, Middle Formative sociopolitical developments were accompanied by substantial population growth, to an estimated 20,000 by the close of the Zacatenco phase (around 400 B.C., Niederberger 1987: 289), and the first public architecture appeared at regional centers during the Ticoman phase (ca. 400–150 B.C.) in the form of mounds some 5 m tall (Blanton et al. 1993: 114–115). In neither the Valley of Oaxaca, nor the Valley of Mexico, nor most regions of Western Mesoamerica, however, did the expansion of sociopolitical hierarchies during the Middle Formative owe much to interactions with the Olmecs or those societies with whom they were most intensively involved. Ceramics and other artifacts show greater regional variation than in the Early Horizon as well as a continuous history of local elaboration. This is not to say that the Valley of Mexico and the Valley of Oaxaca were isolated backwaters or that their inhabitants were unaware of the Olmecs and other contemporaneous societies. In the early Middle Formative period, they, too, produced white-slipped, flat-bottomed bowls with double-line-break motifs, reflecting both continuity with the early development of these motifs in the Mexican highlands and continued interaction with neighboring societies. Likewise, importation of obsidian and greenstone from sources also used by the Olmecs provides an indirect link with the Gulf Coast, as do the handful of portable Olmec-style greenstone artifacts that have been found in Oaxaca, the Valley of Mexico, and Puebla. Nevertheless, face-to-face contacts were likely rare, and the kind of direct, intensive interaction indicated by the Olmec-style relief sculptures in Chiapas and southern Guatemala is not represented.

The major exceptions to this general picture are found in a few sites in Guerrero, Morelos, and Central Veracruz, where monumental artworks attest to more intensive interaction with Olman. Even these, however, are not simple impositions of Gulf Olmec artistic canons, but adaptations of Olmec themes to local precepts (Grove 2000). We begin with the most distant of these regions, where Olmec-style monuments seem to appear early in the Middle Formative sequence.

Guerrero

Since the 1940s, extensive looting of archaeological sites in Guerrero has produced an astounding array of portable artifacts in jade and serpentine. These figurines, masks, celts, plaques, perforators, earspools, and pendants, many of them highly polished and engraved with pan-Mesoamerican motifs, include some of the most celebrated masterpieces of Middle Formative Olmec-style art. Although nearly all these isolated finds are without archaeological context, and an unknown quantity are products of a flourishing forgery industry centered on the old silver-mining town of Taxco, the still poorly understood societies of this western frontier were indisputably active participants in Middle Formative interaction spheres. Moreover, the material expressions of this participation went beyond portable artifacts to non-portable artworks. Among these is a low-relief stela at San Miguel Amuco in the Middle Balsas region, which bears a bird-masked figure holding a bundle that calls to mind bird-masked figures on the Xoc stela in distant Chiapas and Monument 2 at Chalcatzingo, Morelos (Fig. 6.14).

Guerrero has produced all but one of the painted murals known from the Early and Middle Formative periods. The most famous examples appear on cave and cliff walls at Juxtlahuaca and Oxtotitlán in east-central Guerrero (Gay 1967; Grove 1970a) (Fig. 6.15), but others have now been reported from Cacahuiziqui, Texayac, and Tepila (Villela 1989). It is notoriously difficult to ascertain the age of such paintings, but those at Juxtlahuaca appear earliest on stylistic grounds, and may date to the close of the Early Formative period. Nearly a kilometer deep in the farthest recesses of the cave, a scene in vivid colors shows a large figure wearing spotted jaguar-skin gloves and leggings, a brown cape over a red, yellow, and black-striped tunic, and a green-feathered headdress. In his left hand he holds a long, curved object, possibly a rope, which directs the viewer's attention to a small seated figure with black face and beard and red-painted body. Like Altar 4 at La Venta, the scene has been variously interpreted as an image of dominance and captivity or as indicating lineage ties and the validation of dynastic succession (Niederberger 1996: 96). Other paintings in the cave treat mythological themes involving a red-four-legged

Figure 6.14. Line drawing of Middle Formative relief on stela from San Miguel Amuco, Guerrero (left) and Xoc, Chiapas (right) (from Clark and Pye 2000: Figs. 15a and 15i) (courtesy of John Clark).

beast covered by a jaguar skin and a red serpent with a feathered headdress and crossed bands in the eye.

The Oxtotitlán murals are no less impressive (Grove 1970a). Mural 1, painted on the cliff above the cave entrance in vivid red, blue-green, yellow, and black, depicts a human dressed in a winged owl costume, his face clearly shown within the bird mask. He sits on a representation of a table-top throne adorned with the face of a zoomorphic supernatural whose maw is formed by the cave entrance in a manner parallel to the niche on La Venta Altar 4. The comma-shaped eyes, up-turned mouth corners, and outward-turned fangs of the throne image identify it as a serpent-monster (Grove 2000: 280). Other paintings show a diverse repertoire of Middle Formative symbolism, including felines (one possibly copulating with a human), serpents, human profile heads, and raindrops. One of the serpent images is accompanied by three dots that may represent an early example of Mesoamerican numerical notation.

Systematic archaeological investigation in Guerrero is relatively recent, and many finds have resulted from emergency efforts to halt looting or destruction by modern public works (Niederberger 1996: 95–96). Nevertheless, excavations at sites like Xochipala and Chilpancingo (Schmidt 1990; Reyna Robles

Figure 6.15. Murals from Guerrero: Juxtlahuaca (top) (from Niederberger 1996: Fig. 1) and Oxtotitlán (bottom) (from Clark 1994: frontispiece, painting by Ajax Moreno).

and Martínez Donjuan 1989) are providing important information on Formative chronology and life. The most spectacular finds are reserved for Teopantecuanitlán, the Early Formative occupation of which was described above.

Between 1000 and 900 B.C., or phase II in the Teopantecuanitlán construction sequence,[7] the Early Formative clay walls of the sunken courtyard
in the main ceremonial precinct were faced with blocks of cut travertine, and
a miniature stone-faced ball court was built in the courtyard's center. Four
carved stones, each weighing three to five tons and shaped like an inverted
"T," projected from the tops of the courtyard walls (Fig. 6.16). On each was
carved the face of an Olmec-style earth-monster with downturned mouth and
almond-shaped eyes, grasping a torch or feather bundle in each hand. Around
their heads they wear a band decorated with a central medallion containing
crossed bands, surmounted by three oval raindrops and four cleft elements with
double merlon designs and emerging vegetation. The crossed bars are repeated
in the medallions worn as pectorals on their chests (Martínez Donjuan 1994:
157–159). These monuments resemble the "mountain monster" faces on the
celtiform stelae erected later at the base of La Venta's Great Mound, but parallels can also be seen with the late Early Formative carved stone mask found
with an offering of greenstone axes and manufacturing debris at La Merced in
southern Veracruz.

The phase II inhabitants of Teopantecuanitlán also constructed impressive
hydraulic works (Martínez Donjuan 1994: 159–160; Niederberger 1996: 98–
99). One of these, showing parallels to San Lorenzo and La Venta, consisted
of subterranean drains formed from small U-shaped stones with flat covers
that conducted water out of the sunken platform and surrounding ceremonial
precinct. The other was a 100 m long canal lined with thick, 1–2 m tall, stone
slabs that connected with a storage dam. Apparently an irrigation canal, it is
the earliest such work known in Mesoamerica.

In phase III (ca. 900–800 B.C.) the patio and the canal were covered by
stone-faced structures. The facades of Structure 3, built over the canal, and
a similar platform identified as Structure 2, were decorated with stone slabs
arranged to form triangular niches with protruding stones in the center, an
architectural detail repeated slightly later at Chalcatzingo, Morelos (Fig. 6.16,
compare Fig. 6.18).

Beyond the central civic-ceremonial precinct, the site's Lomeríos zone has
yielded information on domestic life in Teopantecuanitlán during the Early-
Middle Formative transition (Niederberger 1986, 1996: 99–102). In addition
to regional styles of monochrome and painted vessels, ceramics from this zone
included white-slipped vessels incised with double-line-break and cleft head
elements and a modeled human effigy vessel with an incised were-jaguar design
that combines local and pan-Mesoamerican elements. Hollow white-slipped
figurines were particularly common in the Lomeríos unit. As illustrated, however, both these and solid figurines show some local reinterpretation of the

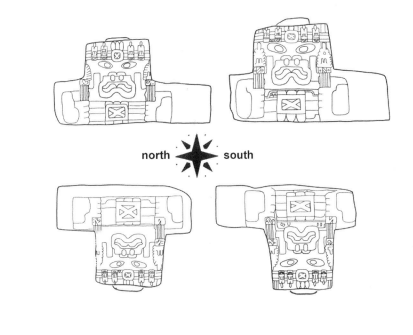

north ◆ south

Figure 6.16. Middle Formative sculpture and architecture from Teopantecuanitlán. Upper: Travertine slabs carved with earth-monster faces from sunken courtyard, Phase II (redrawn after Reilly 1994: Fig. 15.22). Compare headbands with figure 6.9. Lower: Stone slab façade, Structure 2 (redrawn after Martínez Donjuan: Fig. 9.19).

Early Horizon "baby-face" style (Niederberger 1996: 100, Figs. 4 and 5), and they are probably later. Most of the inhabitants of one excavated residential unit lived in perishable structures, including one that was built on a stone-walled foundation. Another structure, possibly a higher-status residence, was built of adobe on a low rock and rubble platform. Bell-shaped pits used for storage, refuse disposal, hearths, and craft production areas surrounding the houses attest to the varied activities of their residents. The craft activities included working a gray obsidian possibly from the Otumba source in the Basin of Mexico and producing ornaments from the nacreous shells of local mollusks and pearl oysters from the Pacific coast (Niederberger 2000: 101–102). Household members also enjoyed access to imported iron-ore mirrors, golden mica platelets, and fine earspools and other ornaments of regionally available onyx and serpentine, reflecting both status differentiation and participation in interregional exchange networks.

Circumstantial evidence suggests that the export of serpentine and other greenstones may have been an important element in the participation of

Guerrero sites in broader Formative period interaction networks (Coe 1968a: 94, 103; Griffin 1993). The Balsas River and its tributaries occasionally expose veins of serpentine as they cut through the metamorphic rocks of the region. Numerous jade artifacts attributed to the region, including fakes produced in and around the town of Taxco, have also appeared on the antiquities market over the years, and many of these are of the blue-green type also favored by the Gulf Olmecs. Geologists and archaeologists have failed to locate the source of the reputed Guerrero jade, however, and petrographic and chemical analyses together with the recent discovery of a blue jade source in Guatemala reduce the likelihood that Guerrero was a significant jade source in antiquity (Harlow 1993; Seitz et al. 2001). The issue, however, perhaps reflects an excessive modern emphasis on jade for its aesthetic qualities. Serpentine clearly was an important resource for Early and Middle Formative societies in Mesoamerica, dwarfing the amount of jade in circulation. Should no jade source ever be found in Guerrero it would do nothing to reduce the potential of the region for exchange of greenstone in the form of serpentine.

Chalcatzingo

The valleys of the Amacuzac River and its tributary, the Amatzinac, form a natural corridor connecting Teopantecuanitlan with Chalcatzingo, 100 km to the northeast. Chalcatzingo maintained its position as the largest site in the Amatzinac valley through the Barranca (ca. 1150–800 B.C.) and Cantera (ca. 800–450 B.C.) phases. During the Cantera phase the site was one of the largest in central Mexico, reaching its maximum size of 43 ha, and dominating a settlement hierarchy of villages and hamlets in the north end of the valley (Hirth 1987). The small villages and hamlets in the southern end of the valley appear to have been at least partly independent of Chalcatzingo. Although they obtained finished obsidian blades from Chalcatzingo, they also made chipped tools from local stones and used a locally made type of pottery, Carrales Coarse Gray, to a much greater extent than their northern neighbors.

   Early in the Middle Formative period the inhabitants of Chalcatzingo began to construct a series of low, broad terraces (Grove 1996: 111–112; Prindiville and Grove 1987). The uppermost terrace lay to the south at the foot of the Cerro Chalcatzingo, one of two volcanic mountains whose near-vertical slopes jut from the floor of the valley. Against this impressive backdrop the rulers of Chalcatzingo placed their residence and constructed a 70 m long ceremonial platform over the public architecture of the Early Formative period.

   Chalcatzingo is best known for its thirty or so stone carvings executed on free standing monuments, boulders, and the rock face of Cerro Chalcatzingo, nearly all of which are thought to date to the Cantera phase (Fig. 6.17). So striking are the technical and iconographic resemblances of some of the monuments to Middle Formative relief carvings in Olman that it has been suggested they were

Figure 6.17. Relief carvings from the slopes of Cerro Chalcatzingo. Top, left to right, Monuments 31, 1; center, Monument 2; Bottom, left to right, Monuments 13, 14. (Mons. 1, 14 after Angulo 1994: Figs. 14.1, 14.20 takuhón illustrations by Chappie Angulo) (Mon. 2 from Grove 1996: Fig. 9, courtesy of David C. Grove) (Mon. 13 from Grove 2000: Fig. 13, courtesy of David C. Grove) (Mon. 31 from Taube 1995: Fig. 24b, courtesy of Karl Taube.)

executed by artisans brought from La Venta (Grove 1984: 109). More recent analyses of the carvings, however, have noted stylistic links to Teopantecuanitlán and Oxtotitlán in Guerrero, as well as purely local elements (Angulo 1987; Grove 1989b, 1993: 100–102; 1996, 2000; Grove and Angulo 1987).

Chalcatzingo's monuments are organized into broad thematic groupings that served to demarcate different areas of sacred and ceremonial space (Angulo 1987; Grove 1996, 1999, 2000). To the south, on and around Cerro Chalcatzingo, the carvings depict mythico-religious themes (Fig. 6.17). High on the hillside, cloud and rain symbols are prevalent, whereas carvings on the lower slopes emphasize zoomorphic supernaturals and humans masked to resemble them, often in an aspect of domination over human figures. In contrast, monuments recovered from the terraces to the north mainly depict specific individuals and relate to themes of rulership and political alliance (Grove 1984: 49–68, 1999: 262–265).

The most famous of Chalcatzingo's monuments is "El Rey" (Monument 1) (Grove and Angulo 1987: 115–117) (Fig. 6.17). Carved on a boulder high on the mountain slope, it depicts a person seated on a rectangular "Lazy S" double scroll in a cave formed by the mouth of a zoomorphic supernatural. He or she also holds a bundle adorned with the same Lazy S motif in a manner similar to the figures holding were-jaguar babies in Gulf Olmec art. Two quetzal birds adorn the person's headdress, recalling the two quetzals above the figure on La Venta Monument 19, who is framed by the body of a crested rattlesnake. On Chalcatzingo Monument 1, the zoomorphic supernatural is also a serpent, identified by the cross in its elongated eyeball and the outward curve of its scrolled fangs as the sky-serpent (Grove 2000). The mouth/cave, shaped like a U with inset corners, is actually half of the quatrefoil motif seen on two other monuments at Chalcatzingo, Monuments 9 and 13. On Monument 1, as on the other two, vegetation springs from the corners of the quatrefoil. In addition, scroll-shaped vapors emanate from the cave/mouth and raindrops shaped like exclamation points fall from trilobed clouds above. Aside from the obvious connection to rain and fertility, these motifs link to La Venta, where vegetation appears on the edge of the cave-like niche of Altar 4, and the distinctive raindrops adorn the headdress of the niche figure on Altar 5.

A set of six closely spaced reliefs on boulders and rock faces below Monument 1 comment further upon themes of rain and agricultural fertility. The scene is most fully preserved on Monument 14, on which a curious, long-snouted animal sits on a Lazy S scroll and exhales a bifurcated scroll upward toward a sinuous tri-lobed cloud from which raindrops fall (Fig. 6.17). A clearly rendered squash plant grows toward the animal from below.

Monument 12, carved on a boulder found far to the west and lower on the hillside, depicts a human who appears to be flying, hence its nickname, "El Volador." Below him is carved a parrot, and above him two quetzals, recalling the quetzals in the headdress of the figure on Monument 1. The figure on

Monument 12 is carved in typical Olmec style with an animal headdress, a torch-like bundle in one hand, and another object, possibly a cut shell (or "knuckle duster") in the other. Wearing a thick belt and a loin cloth that covers the back of the thigh, the Volador closely resembles floating or flying figures carved on late Middle Formative stelae of Olman at La Venta (Stelae 1 and 2) (Drucker, Heizer and Squier 1959: Fig. 68; Heizer 1967) and Tres Zapotes (Stela A) (Porter 1989: Fig. 3), as well as on a boulder carving at Llano del Jícaro (Clark 2004 personal communication).

Eastward from the set of long-snouted animal monuments, along the talus slopes at the base of Cerro Chalcatzingo, a group of six boulder reliefs form a narrative sequence that may relate to Olmec creation myths and the ceremonies commemorating them. Four of the reliefs depict felines attacking humans with typical Olmec cranial deformation, (Angulo 1987: 144–148; Grove 1996: 113; Grove and Angulo 1987: 119–122) (Fig. 6.17). These call to mind the Gulf Coast "copulation" monuments in which felines also dominate humans or monkeys (Stirling 1955: 19–20). A fifth relief in this series (Monument 5) shows the sky-serpent with combined crocodilian and piscine features floating above three Lazy S motifs and devouring a human.

The subject of the sixth relief in this group (Monument 2) is a ceremony involving four humans in zoomorphic masks (Fig. 6.17). The individual on the viewer's left walks away from the others, holding a foliated staff, possibly a maize stalk, in his hands. The central two figures hold paddle-shaped staffs or clubs, and walk toward a supine, nude, human who appears to be the object of a sacrificial ritual. Another mask behind the reclining figure may be turned backwards on his head or may adorn a fifth figure holding the victim.

Monument 13 was found on a boulder below these six carvings (Fig. 6.17). The fragment that has been recovered shows a figure with the cleft, backward-curving head common in Olmec imagery seated in left profile in a quatrefoil mouth with vegetation emerging from its inset corners (Grove and Angulo 1987: 141). Though less well executed, Monument 13 mirrors and complements Monument 1.

Taken as a whole, the monuments on the slopes of Cerro Chalcatzingo present a complex cosmology that relates clouds, rain, sky-serpents, mountains, and mountain caves, places them explicitly in the celestial realm by their placement on the mountain, by reference to the Lazy S motif and through details of the sky-serpent's eyes and fangs; and links them to the fertility of earthly vegetation, felines, and the sacrifice of humans (Grove 2000, Reilly 1994, 1995). There is a further suggestion of dualism in the contrasting subjects of the eastern and western sets of relief sculptures reinforced by the right- and left-facing orientations of Monuments 1 and 13.

At the foot of Cerro Chalcatzingo, the large Cantera phase ceremonial platform on Terrace 1 marks the point of transition between the less accessible mythical space defined by the hillside monuments and the public space of the lower habitational terraces (Grove 1999: 262). Though it was long ago looted from the site, Monument 9 is thought to have originally been set on the cere-monial platform (Grove and Angulo 1987: 124) (Fig. 6.18). The monument is a large stone slab carved with an image of the earth-monster with out-turned cleft eyebrows, crossed bars in its eyes, and a quatrefoil mouth sprouting vegeta-tion from its inset corners. Most remarkably, the center of the mouth is pierced by a large cruciform hole. Wear on the lower edge of the opening suggests that people or objects may have crawled or been passed through it (Angulo 1987: 141; Grove 1984: 50). Such use would have constituted a powerful symbol of passage to or from the supernatural world (Gillespie 1993: 75).

Monuments recovered from the habitational terraces to the north of Cerro Chalcatzingo relate more to political themes of rulership and alliance. Associ-ated with low, Cantera phase platform structures on three of the lower terraces (Terraces 6, 15, and 25) were carved stelae, at least three of which depict par-ticular individuals, as opposed to generic ancestors or supernaturals. One of these, Monument 21, on Terrace 15, shows a woman (rarely identifiable as such in Middle Formative sculpture) with left breast exposed and wearing a skirt and a cape-like garment that falls down her back from her head (Grove and Angulo 1987: 126–127) (Fig. 6.18). Her high-backed sandals presage those of elites depicted in Classic Maya art. Her outstretched hands support a large column decorated with oblongs arranged between diagonal, undulating lines. Two horizontal bands with tri-lobed motifs and distinctive cleft rectangles appear to bind the diagonal elements of the bundle-like column. Both woman and column stand on a highly stylized earth-monster mask with tri-lobed flame eyebrows, large incurving fangs, and the same diagonal oblongs seen in the column (Grove 2000). Ann Cyphers suggests that the depiction of this woman may commemorate a marriage of alliance with elites of another center (Cyphers Guillén 1984). If she is correct, that center may have been Teopante-cuanitlán, for the details of the cleft rectangles on Monument 21 are repeated only on one of the four faces from the sunken patio at that site. Monument 32, recently discovered in the fill of the structure on Terrace 15, is a mirror image of Monument 21 (Aviles 1995). The personage depicted on the stela has been identified as a male, although its extended left arm obscures the chest area, and the curve of the torso above the arm hints at the presence of a breast.

A connection with Teopantecuanitlán also is indicated in the setting of Monument 22, the only table-top altar-throne known outside of Olman (Fig 6.18). Located below Terrace 15 on Terrace 25 and projecting from the south wall of a sunken patio like Teopantecuanitlán's, Monument 22 differs from the monolithic Gulf Olmec altar-thrones in being composed of many rectangular stones. Low relief carving on the stones depicts an earth-monster with the comma-shaped eyes of the serpent supernatural, but without the crossed bands that appear in the eyes of the serpent mouth-cave on Monument 1 and other Olmec-style serpent faces. The niche-cave-mouth that appears on most Olmec

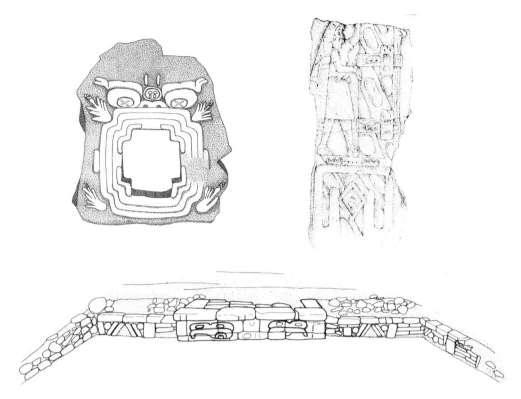

Figure 6.18. Monuments from terraces at Chalcatzingo. Clockwise from upper right, Monuments 9, 21, 22 (after Grove 2000: Figs. 10, 13, 15) (courtesy of David C. Grove).

altars is missing as well, replaced by the sunken patio, which likewise symbolizes the entrance to the underworld. The underworld association is reinforced by two Cantera phase burials of high-status adults, who were placed in stone-lined crypts within the earthen fill of the altar. A child buried in the same construction phase may represent a dedicatory sacrifice (Fash 1987). Other burials in the patio area and under the altar are of earlier and later dates.

No sunken patios have been found at Gulf Olmec sites, and they are rare in the Middle Formative period in general. The closest parallel is the sunken patio at Teopantecuanitlán. Interestingly, the cleft rectangles with double merlons on Chalcatzingo Monument 21 also appear on the earth-monster faces set in the walls of the sunken patio at Teopantecuanitlán. Interaction with Teopantecuanitlán is further reinforced by the design of the stone facing on Chalcatzingo's patio. Stone slabs were placed diagonally to form V-shaped niches like those of Structures 2 and 3 at Teopantecuanitlán, although at Chalcatzingo they are inverted and adorned with two circular stones to either side, possibly to represent the eyes and mouth of an earth-monster (Fash 1987: 82). Most datings of the Teopantecuanitlán structures would place them earlier than the Cantera phase construction of the altar and patio at Chalcatzingo (Martínez Donjuán 1986, 1994; Niederberger 1996; cf. Reyna-Robles 1996). However, some evidence suggests that the Chalcatzingo altar was originally constructed in the late Barranca phase and reassembled in the Cantera phase when the patio was expanded (Fash 1987).

In sum, the late Middle Formative relief monuments of Chalcatzingo show undeniable ties to contemporary sculpture in Olman. Those ties are most strongly seen in the body types and technical execution of "El Volador" (Monument 12) and "The Marching Olmecs" (Monument 2), but it occurs as well in the rendering of felines on Cerro Chalcatzingo and in specific shared motifs, including the exclamation-point raindrops. Similarities to Gulf Olmec mythic themes also can be discerned in the placement of "El Rey"(Monument 1) and "The Governor" (Monument 13) in caves represented by the mouth of zoomorphic "earth-monsters" and the domination of humans by feline supernaturals. The table-top altar-throne provides another remarkable point of resemblance with Gulf Olmec politico-religious practice.

On the other hand, the sculptures of Chalcatzingo are notable as well for the ways in which they differ from Gulf Olmec monuments (Grove 1994; 1999; 2000). Quatrefoils, Lazy-S scrolls, and exclamation-point motifs occur in Gulf Olmec imagery, but their meanings are more explicitly conveyed at Chalcatzingo (Grove 1984; 1989a: 132; Grove and Kann 1980). The "Marching Olmecs" are rendered in Olmec style, but their victim is not. Monument 21 and other stelae have only general resemblances to Gulf Olmec sculpture, and are better interpreted as local expressions of political and mythical themes. The external similarities that do appear on these monuments appear to be more directly connected with sites farther west in Guerrero, particularly Oxtotitlán and Teopantecuanitlán (Grove 1999: 288, 2000: 277). In other words, although the Olmec connection at Chalcatzingo is real and indisputable, it does not stand alone. Rather the monuments of Chalcatzingo show a fascinating, heterogeneous mixture of local, Gulf Olmec, and western influences. Foreign motifs and styles were reinterpreted and placed in context to make their meanings more accessible to the local inhabitants, who were neither ethnically nor linguistically Olmec (Grove 1989a: 132; Grove and Kann 1980). Interestingly, the most Olmec of Chalcatzingo's monuments are those of a religious nature or political emblems (i.e., the altar-throne) with cosmological referents, which suggests that Chalcatzingo's rulers used the imagery and mythological precepts of prestigious Gulf Olmec centers to enhance and legitimize their power locally and regionally.

The historical emphasis on Chalcatzingo's Olmec ties have cast it in the light of a "gateway community" (Hirth 1978; Grove 1987b: 439) where Olmecs oversaw the bulking and transport of exotic goods to fill the coffers (or massive offerings) of rulers at La Venta and perhaps other centers in Olman. Certainly Chalcatzingo's inhabitants prospered from the center's location at the intersection of important trade routes into Central Mexico, Oaxaca, and Guerrero, and trade with Olman was surely an important component of Chalcatzingo's

Figure 6.19. Middle Formative Olmec-style reliefs from Veracruz. Top: El Viejón. Bottom: La Yerbabuena (from Castro and Cobean 1996: Figs. 12 and 24) (Courtesy of Robert Cobean).

political economy. However, Chalcatzingo was not merely a distant outpost on the frontier of Olmec hegemony. Rather, the leaders used contacts with prestigious centers in Olman, Guerrero, and perhaps other regions to enhance their prestige and power locally. They also may have played a significant role in the exchange of ideas in both directions between Olman and Guerrero, although the chronology of interaction is not completely clear.

Central Veracruz

Two more sites from Western Mesoamerica merit special mention. These are La Yerbabuena, on the eastern slope of the Pico de Orizaba volcano, and El Viejón, on the north-central Veracruz coast. Both lie outside Olman, each has an Olmec-style monument of probable late Middle Formative date, and both may have figured in Olmec efforts to procure obsidian.

El Viejón is the more distant and earlier site (Medellín 1960: 82; Cobean 1996: 23). Its large stela shows an encounter between two personages (Fig. 6.19). One clearly is Olmec in garb and bodily proportions. He holds a foliated staff, possibly representing a corn stalk, in his right hand. The other figure is badly eroded and mutilated. In style and subject, the El Viejón monument most closely resembles Los Mangos Monument 1 and La Venta Stela 2, both from Olman. Similarities can also be noted with monuments in Chiapas, particularly in the stance of the figure on the Padre Piedra sculpture and the encounter among individuals (probably marriage participants) on Pijijiapan Monument 1. Like the Chiapas sites, the location of El Viejón suggests it played a role in interregional exchange with Olman, as it is located at a constriction in the coastal plain south of the Nautla river valley, an important access route from the Gulf Coast inland to obsidian sources at Altotonga, Zaragoza, Paredón, Pachuca, and Otumba, each of which has been identified as a significant source for obsidian in La Venta or its hinterland (Doering 2002: 97–99; Nelson and Clark 1998: 287; González, personal communication 2005; see Note 1, Chapter 5).

The stela from La Yerbabuena is carved on a piece of columnar basalt (Cobean 1996) (Fig. 6.19). The principal figure on the front of the stela wears an Olmec-style zoomorphic headdress or mask pushed back on his head and sports a beard and buccal mask. Overhead another bearded figure positioned horizontally and wearing an avian mask looks down on the first. Downward-peering figures also are known from later monuments at the Pacific Coast sites of Izapa (Stelae 4 and 7), El Baul (Stela 1), Kaminaljuyu (Stela 11), Takalik Abaj (Stela 2), and in Olman from Tres Zapotes (Stela D) (Smith 1984: 15; Quirarte 1973: Fig. 13). A specific relation between Tres Zapotes and La Yerbabuena is possible, given the fact that La Yerbabuena's ceramic assemblage dates primarily to the close of the Middle Formative period and beginning of the Late Formative period when Tres Zapotes was expanding (Cobean 1996: 18; Pool and Ohnersorgen 2003). Furthermore, La Yerbabuena lies close to the Pico de Orizaba obsidian source and appears to have specialized in the production of irregular blades from "splintered cores" (*nodulos astillados*), which are predominant in the Middle Formative obsidian assemblage at Tres Zapotes (Knight 1999, personal communication June 2003).

The differences in the El Viejón and La Yerbabuena stelae are intriguing (cf. Cobean 1996: 22, who emphasizes their similarities). Though mutilated, the El Viejón stela seems to represent an encounter between equals, shown at the same scale and, as far as can be determined, with similar dress. It quite possibly commemorates an alliance between El Viejón and an Olmec heartland site, La Venta being the most likely candidate. On the other hand, the La Yerbabuena monument, though fragmentary, appears to show only one principal individual. If the downward-peering head represents an ancestor, as it apparently did much later in Classic Maya stelae (Cobean 1996: 21; Schele and Friedel 1990: 141), a different kind of relation is implied – one that may have involved the installation of a cadet lineage, possibly originating from Tres Zapotes, to oversee the extraction, processing, and shipment of obsidian.

Summary

The material hallmarks of Middle Formative Mesoamerica – the development of increasingly distinctive regional ceramic traditions, the construction of more and larger ceremonial structures, the expanded trade in greenstone and other exotic artifacts, the widespread appearance of Olmec-style relief sculpture – all reflect the profound social and political changes of the period. Social differentiation had begun to emerge in several parts of Mesoamerica by 1000 B.C., but centralized political organization was still the exception. By the end of the Middle Formative period, formal social hierarchies with inherited status were common, and locally powerful political centers had appeared across most of Mesoamerica. The Middle Formative regionalization of pottery styles hints at a more bounded social and political landscape, as the flow of symbols and technological information among the mass of the population was increasingly restricted.

Interregional interaction among the more privileged members of society flourished, however, as elites sought out the exotic and highly crafted items that symbolized and conferred status and power. Such items included shell, pelts, feathers, and a variety of stones, but the paragon of elite paraphernalia was greenstone, and above all jade, laboriously polished and carved with the ancient symbols of supernatural power and shamanic ritual. It is unfortunate that the specific proveniences of so many of these portable items have been lost to the depredations of the international art trade. Nevertheless, their often vague attributions to locations from Northern Veracruz and Puebla, Mexico to Honduras, El Salvador, and Costa Rica attest to the extent of exchange of the objects themselves and the concepts of the Middle Formative Ceremonial Complex they materialized (see Chapter 5). Variation in the styles of these artifacts implies they were carved in different regions and probably disseminated by the leaders of various centers within and beyond Olman. It is particularly interesting that many of the most elaborately carved examples are said to come from Guerrero. Greenstone can hardly be considered an exotic good there, where serpentine (and possibly jade) outcrops naturally in the Balsas River basin. It was rather the crafting of this locally abundant material and its carving with esoteric symbols that converted greenstone into an object of ritual and power.

The Olmecs of Olman were important participants in the increasingly competitive political and economic landscape of Middle Formative Mesoamerica. The periodic demand for large quantities of greenstone in Olman, as attested in the massive offerings and numerous smaller caches at La Venta, appears to have been a critical factor in the establishment of far-flung trading relationships. The more mundane but more constant demand for obsidian in Olman also appears to have been a consideration in the formation of political and economic alliances. Those relationships are demonstrated most explicitly in the distribution of the Olmec-style relief carvings that have been the focus of the preceding discussion of the Middle Formative period. Of all the widely distributed cultural traits that have been attributed to the Olmecs, monumental stone carving, including the style of low-reliefs that appear first on Olmec altar-thrones, is the most clearly demonstrated to have originated in Olman and most convincingly argued to have been disseminated from there (Clark and Pye 2000b; Grove 1993, 1997, 2000: 277). During the Middle Formative period, Olmec-style relief monuments are strongly associated with resource zones and likely trade routes for acquiring greenstone, obsidian, and possibly other commodities. Some of these monuments, such as the El Viejón stela and Pijiapan Monument 1 show encounters and events that probably refer to the creation of alliances, in the latter case by marriage. Others, such as the Tilte-pec stela, which show important personages dressed in Olmec-style headdresses and loin cloths, could imply a subordinate relation to an Olmec center or the adoption of Olmec symbols of authority by local rulers. Still others, such as the mountainside monuments of Chalcatzingo, relate more to myth and the ideological basis for ruling authority.

This variety of themes in Olmec-style relief carvings points to a wide range of interaction with Olmec centers. Furthermore, not all of the carvings are unmitigated examples of the Olmec style. In general, relief monuments in the Greater Isthmian region, from El Viejón in the north to Padre Piedra in the south, appear to adhere more consistently to Olmec canons, possibly reflecting closer linguistic and ethnic relationships among the populations of the region. At Chalcatzingo, however, various monuments show differing degrees of "Olmecness," and Olmec elements are frequently combined with locally distinctive symbols (Grove 1996, 2000). Further, the most Olmec of the Chalcatzingo monuments express religious themes and the ideological and ritual basis for authority, whereas the more expressly political representations of elite individuals are of a more local style, suggesting different degrees of Olmec influence in religious and political realms. Farther afield, at Teopantecuanitlán and Chalchuapa, adherence to Olmec canons appears to further wane, and the relations of these centers with Olman probably were indirect via intermediaries like Chalcatzingo and the Soconusco centers.

The changing social environment of Middle Formative Mesoamerica had important repercussions for political and economic strategies in Olman. As Olmec rulers relied more heavily on exotic goods for ostentatious displays to support their authority, they also were forced to negotiate with increasingly complexly organized societies to acquire them. The formal recognition of the resulting alliances was one important factor in the increasingly historical content of Middle Formative Olmec sculpture in Olman. Ultimately, the ability of Olmec rulers to acquire the goods they so fervently desired, and indeed, required, was undercut by the success of their competitors. The La Venta polity was the most notable victim of these processes, but at least one center, Tres Zapotes, adapted to the changed political exigencies at the close of the Middle Formative period, and not only survived, but flourished.

CHAPTER 7

COLLAPSE, CONTINUITY, AND EVOLUTION: LATE FORMATIVE OLMAN

According to the standard tale, Olmec culture collapsed with the fall of La Venta, around 400 B.C. As a result, the tide of diffusion was reversed as the decadent descendants of the Olmecs became the recipients of influences from the more vigorous Izapan culture to the south. Although this story makes for good drama, ongoing research paints a more complex and more interesting picture of the Late Formative period in Olman.

It is true that by 400 B.C., intensive, direct interaction with Olman was on the wane throughout most of Mesoamerica as powerful competitors emerged in the Basin of Mexico, the Valley of Oaxaca, and the Maya region. Olmec-style relief carving disappeared in the highlands of western Mesoamerica, while the cultures of eastern Mesoamerica modified the Olmec style to develop new sculptural traditions that glorified their rulers and proclaimed their mythic origins. At the same time, the old currents that had carried information and goods to and from Olman changed course as polities across the face of Mesoamerica vied for power and renegotiated their alliances.

The whole of Olman did not become a cultural backwater, however, as some scholars dazzled by the brilliance of earlier Olmec accomplishments have declared. Although most sites in eastern Olman were abandoned, and the flow of exotic prestige goods to the southern Gulf lowlands declined, western Olman experienced a cultural and intellectual florescence in the Late and Terminal Formative periods (400 B.C.–A.D. 300), adapting ancient Olmec traditions to the requirements of a more competitive political landscape. Elements of this modified "epi-Olmec" culture, particularly its sophisticated writing system and Long Count calendar employed to record historical events, extended beyond the limits of Olman to Central Veracruz and Chiapas (Lowe 1989: 61–64; Justeson and Kaufman 1993; Pool 2000).

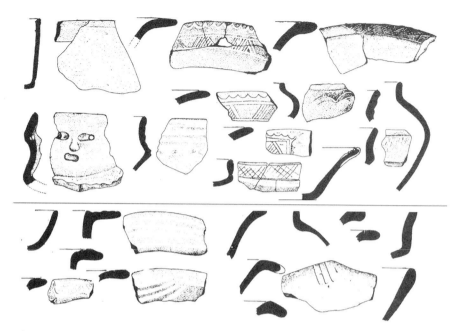

Figure 7.1. Late and Terminal Formative pottery from Tres Zapotes; lower section Polished Orange ware (after Lowe 1989: Fig. 4. from originals in Ortiz 1975: Figs. 15, 19, 32, 38, 40–44, 56, 57, 60–64).

Change, Continuity, and Regional Variation in Olman

Pottery styles provide some of the strongest evidence for variable patterns of change and continuity in Late Formative period Olman (Lowe 1989: 61–62; Stark 1997; Pool 2000) (Fig. 7.1). In Tabasco, imports and imitations of Chicanel pottery indicate interaction with the Lowland Maya region (Lowe 1989: 61; Sisson 1970). Maya influence is much less marked farther west, however, where ceramics from San Lorenzo, the central Tuxtla Mountains, and Tres Zapotes show greater continuity with Olmec technology. In particular, black wares are common, and they are often differentially fired, with white, tan, or orange rims (Coe and Diehl 1980a: 208–213; Ortiz 1975: 107–134; Pool and Britt 2000). At Tres Zapotes, polished orange pottery, which first appeared in the Middle Formative period, reached its greatest popularity in the Hueyapan phase (400 B.C.–A.D. 1), particularly in the form of dishes with grooved out-flaring rims. Coarsely tempered jars with brushed shoulders continued to be the major utilitarian type in the Tuxtla Mountains and the Tres Zapotes area throughout the Late and Terminal Formative periods. New decorative elements consisting of engraved geometric designs became especially common on black serving vessels from the Coatzacoalcos to the Papaloapan basin, and there was an important trend toward greater use of untempered pastes, which would culminate in the distinctive Fine Orange and Fine Gray wares of the Classic period (Coe and Diehl 1980a: 208–211; Pool and Britt 2000). Clay figurines continued a long trend toward less detailed and less realistic modeling,

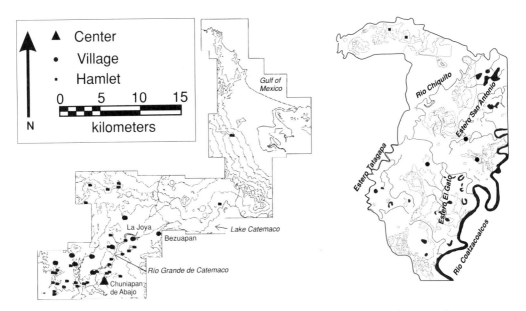

Figure 7.2. Late Formative settlement patterns from two regions in Olman. Left, central Tuxtlas; right, Middle Coatzacoalcos Basin (redrawn after Santley et al. 1997: Fig. 7.3 and Symonds et al. 2003: Fig. 4.13).

with facial features often reduced to deep perforations for pupils, nostrils, and mouth (Drucker 1943a: 76–81; Weiant 1943: 84–98).

Other significant characteristics of the Olmec to epi-Olmec transition include a marked decline in the use of exotic prestige goods and shifts in the sources and technology used for making obsidian artifacts (Nelson and Clark 1998: 292; Hester, Jack, and Heizer 1971; Santley and Arnold 1996). In western Olman, prismatic blades replaced casually fashioned flakes as the predominant obsidian artifacts. The vast majority of these were made on dark gray and black obsidian from the sources at Zaragoza and Oyameles in the Mexican state of Puebla instead of clear obsidian from nearer sources on the flanks of the Pico de Orizaba. Beads and other artifacts of greenstone occasionally appear in epi-Olmec burials and other contexts, but they are much less common than in Middle Formative contexts at La Venta or at Tres Zapotes.

Settlement Patterns

These variable changes in material culture across Olman are matched by shifting patterns of settlement (Fig. 7.2). The most dramatic change occurred in the lowlands of western Tabasco. The fall of La Venta coincides with the abandonment of sites in its hinterland (von Nagy et al. 2002). Ecological disaster and disease cannot be ruled out as causes for this demographic collapse, but it seems more likely that people abandoned the region to seek their fortunes elsewhere in response to the failure of La Venta's political system. To the west, in the

Coatzacoalcos and San Juan basins the long, gradual population decline that had begun at the end of the Early Formative period resulted in a light scatter of hamlets and villages by the beginning of the Late Formative (Borstein 2001; Symonds et al. 2002) (Fig. 7.2). In the Tuxtla Mountains, however, settlement systems faired much better. Along the southern piedmont, just a few kilometers north of Laguna de los Cerros, the number of occupied sites increased dramatically. Farther north in the central Tuxtla mountains the population dipped only slightly from a Middle Formative peak, and the first regional center appeared, at Chuniapan de Abajo (Santley et al. 1997) (Fig. 7.2). Settlement pattern studies have only recently begun on the western margin of the Tuxtlas, but the data that do exist there clearly indicate that Late Formative sites are much larger and more numerous than their Middle Formative predecessors (León 2003; Loughlin 2004). The largest and most powerful of these sites was Tres Zapotes, which not only survived the Middle to Late Formative transition, but flourished in the new, highly competitive landscape of the epi–Olmec tradition.

TRES ZAPOTES

As its frequent mention in the preceding chapters attests, the importance of Tres Zapotes lies in its long cultural sequence as well as its role in the history of Olmec studies. Among the archaeological "firsts" Tres Zapotes can claim are the first discovery of an Olmec colossal head (Melgar 1869), the first modern investigation of an Olmec center (Stirling 1943), and the first chronological sequences from Olman based on stratigraphic excavations (Drucker 1943a; Weiant 1943). Matthew Stirling's (1939) discovery of Stela C and the reconstruction of its 32 B.C. Long Count date by Marion Stirling also provided critical early support for the antiquity of Olmec culture. Renewed archaeological investigations at Tres Zapotes are now providing a much more detailed picture of its long occupation, and particularly its role in the Olmec to epi–Olmec transition (Pool 2000; Pool 2003b).

  The archaeological site of Tres Zapotes sprawls across the floodplain and terraces of the Arroyo Hueyapan, where the stream emerges from the sedimentary uplands of the Tuxtla piedmont to flow westward across the rich alluvium of the Papaloapan delta. Today, the fertile lowlands support vast fields of sugar cane, and cattle graze the denuded uplands. In the Formative period, though, the location of Tres Zapotes at the interface between these ecological zones gave its inhabitants access to a rich variety of resources. Recent excavations show that they took fish, turtles, and waterfowl from the rivers, lakes, and swamps of the Papaloapan basin, planted maize, beans, and other crops in swidden fields and household gardens, and hunted various mammals, birds, and reptiles in the fields and surrounding tropical forests (Peres et al. 2006). Clays, sandstones, and volcanic tuffs in the sedimentary uplands provided materials for pottery and mound construction, and basalt from outcrops and boulders on the slopes of nearby Cerro el Vigía was used for carving monuments and fashioning the axes and grinding stones that made it possible to plant and process maize.

The geographical position of Tres Zapotes also played an important role in its history. The Arroyo Hueyapan not only gave Tres Zapotes a means of water transport to and from the tributaries of the Papaloapan delta, but above Tres Zapotes its narrow valley provides a natural route for foot travel into the Tuxtlas across the mountain pass north of Cerro el Vigía. In its epi-Olmec heyday, Tres Zapotes easily could have controlled routes into the Tuxtlas farther north and southward around the foot of Cerro el Vigía, and possibly as far as the Río San Juan, about 20 km to the south. Such control would have been particularly important as new centers arose across the Papaloapan basin at sites such as Cerro de las Mesas, and demand increased in the Tuxtlas for prismatic blades and cores from Zaragoza-Oyameles. On the other hand, the routes into the Tuxtlas are many, and natural resources like basalt are widely distributed, so complete control over either would have been difficult for the Tres Zapotes rulers. Earlier, Tres Zapotes was at a distinct disadvantage to Laguna de los Cerros with respect to providing basalt and other upland resources to the great Olmec centers of the east (Pool 2000: 147–149) (Fig. 1.3). Thus, geography seems to have been a key factor in the political and economic history of Tres Zapotes, as its rulers sought means other than monopolizing strategic resources to establish and maintain their positions.

Settlement Organization

As described in previous chapters, the history of occupation at Tres Zapotes extends back into the Early Formative period. During the Late Formative Hueyapan phase (400 B.C.–A.D. 1), Tres Zapotes grew from 80 ha to 500 ha as the Middle Formative center and its surrounding villages expanded and coalesced (Pool and Ohnersorgen 2003). Within this area are more than 160 mounds, platforms, and habitational terraces, including four formal complexes of pyramidal mounds arranged around plazas (Groups 1, 2, 3, and the Nestepe Group) and several large isolated mounds (Fig. 7.3). Most constructions are low, residential mounds, which grew through repeated building episodes and the accumulation of refuse and debris from collapsed wattle-and-daub houses. Low platforms were constructed of earth, clay, and irregular blocks of sandstone or volcanic tuff set in a mixture of clay and sand; cut blocks of sandstone and tuff were used as pavements, retaining walls, and platform facings (Weiant 1943: 6–15). In addition, dense concentrations of refuse cover large areas of the site that contain no mounds. In some cases it is clear from old maps that the mounds have been erased by plowing, but it also is likely that much of the population lived in houses that rested directly on the ground surface. As is typical of lowland settlement in Mesoamerica, the densest settlement is concentrated in the center of the site, in an area of about

180 ha, and it gradually declines and becomes more dispersed in peripheral areas (Pool and Ohnersorgen 2003).

Formal Architecture and Epi-Olmec Political Organization

As I have argued in previous chapters, Olmec political leaders pursued mainly exclusionary strategies, seeking to monopolize economic and ideological sources of power, resulting in highly centralized governments in the largest, most influential Olmec polities. At La Venta, this political centralization was reflected by the nucleation of monumental architecture and art in the civic and ceremonial center of the site, and the clear separation of space into the restricted ceremonial plazas of Complex A and the more open public space of the great plaza of Complex B. By contrast, the forms, arrangements, and distribution of formal architecture at Tres Zapotes suggest that its leaders instituted a new, less centralized form of government in the Late Formative period, one that mediated the interests of powerful factions in a ruling assembly.

The earliest public architecture so far detected at Tres Zapotes appears to date to the end of the Middle Formative period. One of these structures formed the initial construction phase of Mound 5, at the east end of the plaza in Group 1, and consisted of a red clay platform, about 1.5 m tall (Weiant 1943: 6). On the south edge of Group 2, an altar consisting of a small, carved serpentine column set upright in a hole carved through a basalt slab was set on a low platform and surrounded by upright basalt columns, reminiscent of Tomb A at La Venta (Millet 1979). Basalt columns also ringed a 2 m high earthen platform a short distance to the south.

In the Late Formative period, the rulers of Tres Zapotes embarked on major construction programs and instituted a consistent, distinctive template for formal architecture, which they replicated in each of the site's four main mound groups (Pool 2005). The basic Late Formative plan of these mound groups consists of a large plaza, oriented approximately east–west, with a tall, pyramidal, temple mound on the west end and a lower, longer mound on the north edge. The long mounds probably supported administrative buildings, but refuse deposits behind the long mounds in the Nestepe Group and Groups 2 and 3 suggest they also were places of elite residence. In each group a low platform placed on the central axis of the plaza appears to have functioned as an altar. Other mounds that probably supported temples and residences of lesser elites and retainers were added to the east and south ends of Groups 1 and 2, and Plaza A of Group 3. The addition of Plaza B to Group 3 in the Terminal Formative period reoriented the group to a north–south axis (Sullivan 2002), but, in this and the other groups, the earlier plazas were kept clean of debris and apparently continued to be used.

The redundant forms and arrangements of architecture in the four plaza groups indicate they not only served similar ceremonial, political, and elite

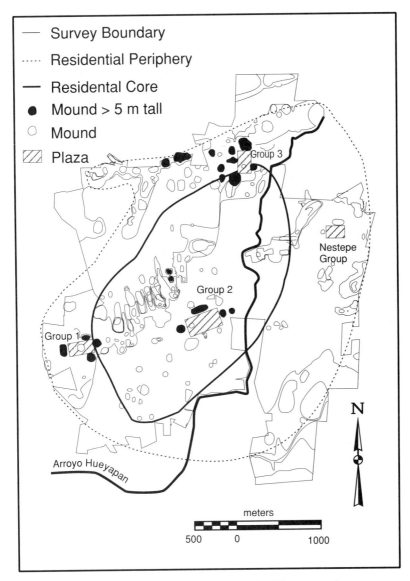

Figure 7.3. Plan of Tres Zapotes, Late Formative Hueyapan phase.

residential functions, but they also employed a common directional symbolism that associated their east-west axis with religious ceremony and the north-south axis with ruling authority. The north-south association with rulership was enhanced in Group 1 and the Nestepe Group by the incorporation of colossal heads, portraits of by-then ancient rulers, which were placed opposite to and facing the elite residential/administrative structures on the long mounds to the north.

In their final configurations, the plaza groups vary widely in scale and complexity, from the simple Nestepe group, with mounds under 3 m tall and a plaza covering about 1.5 ha, to Groups 2 and 3 with mounds up to 12 m tall, and plaza areas of some 4 ha. This variation likely reflects differences in leaders' access to labor and the duration of the groups' active use as loci of political and religious power. However, the use of the plaza groups clearly overlapped in time, and the two largest groups are comparable in the size of their mounds, total volumes of construction, and total plaza areas. Thus no single group can lay claim to overwhelming dominance of Tres Zapotes.

The spatial relationships of the plaza groups to one another and to domestic occupation also suggest a decentralized, communal form of government (Fig. 7.3). Group 2 is centrally located in the residential core of the site, but the other three plaza groups lie within the residential periphery. Moreover, they are regularly spaced at 945 to 985 m from their nearest neighbors, as measured from the centers of the plazas. At this distance, Groups 1, 2, and 3 are clearly visible to one another by observers on their taller mounds, allowing visual communication among them. The Nestepe Group is obscured from the other groups by an intervening hill, Cerro Rabon, but an observer located on the mound constructed on its summit could easily have relayed information between Nestepe and the other plaza groups (Pool 2003a; Sullivan 2002).

Formal mound construction continued in the Terminal Formative Nextepetl phase, but the area of occupation declined slightly as it withdrew from the banks of the Arroyo Hueyapan. During the Nextepetl phase a volcanic eruption deposited a thick ash over the site. The accumulation of ash in the floodplain appears to have hastened its abandonment, but occupation continued unabated on the adjoining terraces where natural erosion and human efforts removed much of the deposit.

By the opening of the Early Classic period (A.D. 300–600), Tres Zapotes was in decline. Formal mound construction continued, and the site probably still functioned as a regional center, but it never regained its Late Formative glory. By the close of the Classic period (A.D. 900), Tres Zapotes lay abandoned, only to be briefly and sparsely reoccupied a couple of centuries later in the Postclassic period. Nevertheless, the continuous occupation of Tres Zapotes for two millennia, makes it a critical site for understanding the major transitions between the Olmec, epi-Olmec, and Classic Veracruz cultures.

Stone Monuments of Tres Zapotes

Just as ceramic styles and occupational patterns document a gradual transition from Olmec to epi-Olmec culture at Tres Zapotes, so, too, do the site's 50 stone monuments (cf., Coe 1965a: 696, 1965c: 773). Scholars disagree about the ages of many sculptures from Tres Zapotes, but at least eight can be assigned to Olmec times. The earliest monuments from Tres Zapotes proper appear to be the two colossal heads, Monument A and Monument Q (also known as the Nestepe head) (Fig. 4.3). They are joined by the enormous and much cruder head from the hinterland site of Rancho Cobata, located in a mountain pass to the north of Cerro el Vigía. These three heads share squat, wide proportions, relatively simple headdresses, tapered ear plugs, and details of facial features that set them apart from most of the heads at San Lorenzo and La Venta (Clewlow et al. 1967; de la Fuente 1977: 355–356; Wicke 1971: 119–127). Together they suggest a distinctive local tradition of elite costume and sculptural representation. They also may be later than the San Lorenzo heads, for although Tres Zapotes contains an Early Formative component, it apparently did not support a major center until the Middle Formative period (Pool and Ohnersorgen 2003). At present, the best guess is that the colossal heads of Tres Zapotes and Rancho Cobata were carved around the beginning of the Middle Formative period. An early Middle Formative date also is possible for other Olmec sculptures in the round from Tres Zapotes, which include fragments of three seated figures (Monuments I, J, and M) and an elongated were-jaguar head (Monument H) (Porter 1989).

Tres Zapotes also contains two stylistically late relief stelae that share features of technique and representation with stelae from La Venta. The fragment of Stela F, discovered in 2003, preserves the left shoulder and part of the head and headdress of a high-relief figure in frontal view. A raised border around the figure recalls the stiff capes worn by personages on La Venta Stelae 2 and 3. The more complete Stela A is a massive, 5 m tall monument, which was broken in half, either intentionally or as a result of its fall (Stirling 1943: 13) (Fig. 7.4). Carved from a soft volcanic breccia, the stela has suffered a great deal of erosion, but it preserves the overall form and some details of the figures carved in relief on its front and sides. On the front of the stela a central figure carved in half-round and wearing a tall headdress stands in frontal view. To either side figures carved in low relief face the central figure. The one to the viewer's left holds a long object in his left hand and wears a broad-brimmed headdress. The flanking figure to the right may hold a trophy head by its hair or a rope (Stirling 1943: 13; Coe 1965c: 773), but the object is now so badly eroded it is difficult to tell (Porter 1989: 38). The entire scene takes place in a niche or proscenium (Porter 1989), between two monster masks. The mask below the scene has the triangular teeth of a shark, associated with the watery underworld, whereas the outcurving fangs and the crossed bands in the headdress of the upper mask mark it as the sky-serpent (see Grove 2000). Mythological themes also grace the sides of the stela. The side on the viewer's left bears a crouching feline and a serpent, while two pudgy dwarves similar to those on La Venta Stelae 2 and 3 occupy the right side, one facing upward, the other downward.

Most of the other monuments from Tres Zapotes and its environs are believed to date to the site's heyday in the Late and Terminal Formative periods. Thematic and stylistic continuity with the Olmec tradition is particularly well-illustrated in two stelae. Stela D, discovered in Group 4, a secondary center northwest of Tres Zapotes, continues the practice of depicting scenes in a niche

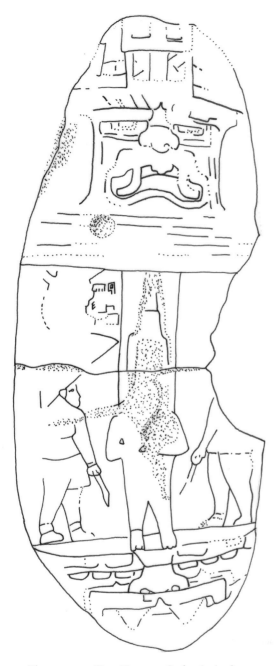

Figure 7.4. Tres Zapotes Stela A (redrawn based on Porter 1989: Fig. 1 and Plate 2 with modifications based on author's observations and photographs).

surmounted by a monster mask, thereby combining historical and mythico-religious themes (Fig. 7.5). In this case, the niche substitutes for the mouth of the monster in a manner reminiscent of niches on much earlier altar-thrones from San Lorenzo and La Venta as well as contemporary monuments from the Pacific Coast at Tiltepec and Izapa (Norman 1976: Figs. 5.26 and 5.27). On either side of the niche, a raised border contains glyph-like elements, and downward-facing serpent heads (Porter 1989: 53, Fig. 6). The latter appear frequently on stelae from Izapa, a major political and cultural center in the Pacific piedmont of Chiapas, but a more local antecedent appears in the double-serpent-headed rope held in the mouth of a jaguar on La Venta Monument 80 (Taube 1995: 93). The scene within the niche on Stela D depicts an encounter between three individuals. A figure with an elaborate headdress and stiff cape kneels before two standing figures, similarly attired, one of whom holds a long spear and a spear thrower or incense bag. A fourth, indistinct, figure, possibly an ancestor or deity, peers downward from above. Between the kneeling figure and the first standing figure is a glyphic caption, now badly effaced (Porter 1989: 54).

Stela C is the most famous of the monuments from Tres Zapotes, owing to its early inscribed Long Count date of 7.16.6.16.18 6 Etznab (14 August, 32 B.C.)[1] (John Justeson 2003, personal communication) (Fig. 2.3). Only the reconstructed date on Chiapa de Corzo Stela 2, (7.16.)3.2.13 6 Ben is earlier, falling in 36 B.C. According to

Figure 7.5. Tres Zapotes Stela D.

Justeson, Stela C appears to commemorate a lunar eclipse, which was followed two weeks later by a solar eclipse that was nearly total at Tres Zapotes. The date forms part of an inscription in two columns, now so badly eroded it cannot be read. On the opposite side of the stela is an elaborate carving that depicts a leftward-facing profile head amid radiating upward-curved lines. The profile head rests above a square medallion with triangular projections set in crossed bars, an element that appears as part of the costume of the ruler on the later Stela 6 from Cerro de las Mesas. Head and medallion appear to emerge from the cleft brow of an abstract earth-monster mask. Together the inscription and the relief carving on this remarkable epi-Olmec celtiform stela constitute a bridge between the Olmecs and the later Classic period cultures of southern Veracruz. The Olmec affinity of the mask has been defended by Coe (1965c: 756) and Porter (1989: 49–50), and the profile head recalls the profile heads on Middle Formative celts interpreted by Kent Reilly (1995: 38–39) as representations of the ruler as the *axis mundi* or world tree (see Chapter 5). As I discuss in the following, Long Count dates also appear on Terminal Formative and Classic period sculptures from southern and central Veracruz, as well as in the enormous corpus of Classic Maya inscriptions. Recalling the argument presented in Chapter 5 for La Venta, the chronological progression from Stela A, to Stela D, to Stela C at Tres Zapotes graphically reflects the continuation of the trend toward increasing historicism in Formative monuments from Olman, culminating in dated inscriptions.

Busts with rearward-projecting tenons constitute another important class of sculpture at Tres Zapotes (Fig. 7.6); the 11 known examples are the largest and most varied collection from the southern Gulf lowlands (Porter 1989: 9), and five others have been found in nearby sites. They were probably intended to be set in the sides of mounds, though none have been found in their original positions. Such sculptures are rare elsewhere, but a tenoned monkey sculpture (Monument 56) has been recovered from La Venta.

The tenoned busts from Tres Zapotes were executed in two styles, one with incised, often flat, relief, and the other with features modeled in the round or half-round with relief detailing (Porter 1989: 17–18, 20). The latter style, which includes the famous Monument F ("El Negro") and Monument G ("La Reina"), retains the Olmec concern for rounded, swelling volumes. In addition, the back-thrust head of Monument G preserves the outline of a fanged, down-turned, were-jaguar mouth, although its arms are clearly human. The tenoned monuments from the nearby sites of Providencia and Tlapacoyan also sport feline faces, and the recarved face of Tres Zapotes Monument 29 may have originally been a zoomorph (Porter 1989: 144). Therefore, accepting that they are of Late Formative age, the tenoned monuments of Tres Zapotes exhibit continuity with Olmec themes and stylistic conventions.

Other classes of monuments at Tres Zapotes include cylindrical stone basins and rectangular stone boxes. The former also are known from La Venta, and the latter may represent small sarcophagi, presaged by the large sandstone sarcophagus at La Venta (Monument 6). Three rectangular stones with carved-out borders from Tres Zapotes are of a size and shape that suggest they could have functioned as sarcophagus covers.

Figure 7.6. Tres Zapotes Monument F.

One stone box, Monument C (not to be confused with Stela C), is a masterpiece of Late Formative artwork, carved with human figures, apparently warriors, fighting amidst elaborate scrolls that cover the exterior of the box (Fig. 7.7). More than any other at Tres Zapotes, this piece evokes the cluttered narrative relief sculptures of Izapa, a major contemporary center in southeastern Chiapas (Fig. 7.8). This monument, the severed head possibly represented on Stela A, and the downward-facing head and "long-lipped" serpent heads of Stela D, constitute the evidence for the oft-cited "extensive influence" of the Izapan style on the art of Tres Zapotes. In fact, the Izapan character of the traits on these other two monuments are equivocal (Smith 1984) and, even if accepted, hardly constitute a major influence on Tres Zapotes. Rather the similarities between the two styles reflect their descent from a common ancestor, the Olmec culture, with some sharing of motifs and techniques in an evolving co-tradition.

WRITING AND CALENDARS

Although some civilizations (for example, the Inca and others of the Andes Mountains) got along quite well without writing, worldwide the invention of writing is closely associated with the emergence of states. In Mesoamerica, the Late to Terminal Formative period saw the emergence of at least three distinctive writing systems (Figs. 7.8–7.10). One of these, believed to have been written by speakers of a Zapotecan language, began to develop in Oaxaca before 500 B.C. (Flannery and Marcus 2003; cf. Pohl et al. 2002). After

Figure 7.7. Tres Zapotes Monument C (after Bernal 1969: Fig. 7).

450 B.C., another style of hieroglyphic writing appears on Izapan and early
Maya monuments from the Pacific Coast and highlands of southern Guatemala
and Chiapas. Though variable in their execution and geographic distribution,
epigraphers and linguists often lump these texts into a single Maya-Izapan
writing tradition (e.g., Justeson and Matthews 1990). Traces of glyphs in the
eroded inscription accompanying the Long Count date on Tres Zapotes Stela
C show that it belonged to a different tradition, known variously as epi-Olmec,
Isthmian and Tuxtlatec, which extended from south-central Veracruz to central Chiapas, an area that corresponds closely to the historical distribution of
the Mije-Sokean language family (Justeson and Kaufman 1993; Justeson and
Matthews 1990; Méluzin 1992; Stross 1990).[2]

   All of the Late Formative writing systems share features that suggest a common origin (Justeson and Matthews 1990). For example, they were written
in columns read from top to bottom and usually from left to right, and profile
heads used as signs for names and titles face the direction from which they were
read (typically left). Particularly indicative of common origins, because they are

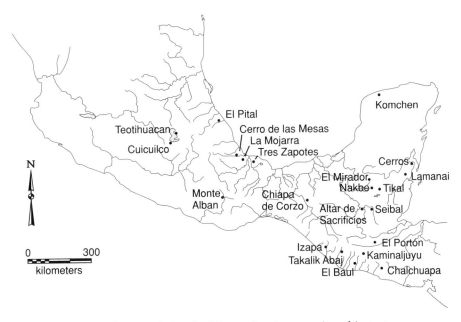

Figure 7.8. Map of Late and Terminal Formative sites mentioned in text.

arbitrary, are conventions for writing numerals and calendrical signs. Numerals for 1 through 4 were represented by dots, the numeral 5 was represented by a bar, and higher numerals up to 19 were formed by a stack of bars combined with 0 to 4 dots. Signs representing named days were usually enclosed in a cartouche. Another shared peculiarity was the practice of infixing a rectangular field at the wrist of signs depicting hands, whose characteristic gestures were employed to represent verbs, such as "to scatter" (Justeson and Matthews 1990: 104). Specific features of the epi-Olmec and Mayan-Izapan scripts suggest they are closely related and that the latter diverged from the former. Most telling is the fact that some signs in Mayan texts do not have a clear basis in Mayan languages, but are interpretable as logograms (signs representing whole words or morphemes) in Mije-Sokean languages (Justeson and Matthews 1990: 115).

The ultimate origins of these writing systems can probably be traced to Early Horizon iconography and its *pars-pro-toto* principle of representation. Closer in time, John Justeson and Peter Matthews (1990) see a common precursor in the Olmec-style incised celts that were so widely disseminated in the Middle Formative period. The symbols incised on the celts include profile heads, arms, hands, and legs, as well as weapons, vegetation, and more abstract symbols (see Chapter 5). At times, body parts appear alone or grouped with non-anatomical symbols, but even when the body parts are arranged in their approximate anatomical positions, they are not joined to one another or a depicted body. This segmentation suggests they functioned individually as symbols. In addition, the elongate form of the celts encouraged the vertical arrangement of symbols, suggesting the columnar format of later texts.

Whether the Oaxacan and southeastern Mesoamerican writing systems evolved directly from Olmec-style iconography or from a single intermediate writing system is not clear. However, some evidence from La Venta suggests that a system of writing had developed there before the site was abandoned around 400 B.C. (Fig. 5.12). La Venta Monument 13 depicts a striding individual holding what appears to be a banner before him. Behind him is a symbol representing a footprint, commonly used in later writing systems to represent a path or journey. Below the banner is a column of three symbols reasonably interpreted as glyphs. In addition, recent excavations at the neaby secondary center of San Andres uncovered a cylinder seal and fragments of greenstone plaques with symbols that bear some resemblances to later epi-Olmec and Mayan glyphs (Pohl et al. 2002). The cylinder seal depicts a bird with two long elements emanating from its beak, possibly indicating sound, which terminate in a concatenation of symbols interpreted as "King 3 Ahau." The symbols on the plaque fragments include a sign similar to the later Mayan glyph for the day "muluc" and a double merlon enclosed in a circle. All three pieces came from a stratigraphic context bracketed by radiocarbon dates of 540 ± 40 b.c. (calibrated 792–409 B.C.) and 390 ± 90 b.c. (calibrated 764–182 B.C.) and associated with ceramics of the early Franco phase (calibrated 700–500 B.C.). In other words, the San Andres finds are broadly contemporaneous with the most widely accepted age of San José Mogote Monument 3 (Flannery and Marcus 2003; Marcus 1992: 35–36; cf. Pohl et al. 2002: 1984).[3]

Calendars

Abundant ethnohistoric and epigraphic evidence shows that indigenous Mesoamerican peoples conceived of time as a set of repeating and interlocking cycles instead of the linear sequence of historical time more familiar to modern Western societies. The longest of these cycles were the repeated creations and destructions of the world described in such well-known creation stories as the Aztec "Legend of the Suns" or the Quiché Maya *Popol Vuh*. Within each creation, the progress of the seasons, the motions of the sun, moon, and planets, and the mathematical permutations of more abstract day counts defined shorter cycles with practical and supernatural import. In many cases the days, months, years, and longer periods, and even the numbers that combined with them, were believed to be animate supernaturals, which the Maya depicted as carrying units of time as burdens on their backs.

An important consequence of the cyclical conception of time was that events that took place in the past were likely to occur again on the same date in the future (with modifications dictated by historical circumstance). Moreover, specific days and day-number combinations were associated with good, bad, or indifferent fortune for the events that took place on them. It was, therefore, the task of diviners, or "calendar-priests," to select auspicious days for important activities and ceremonies – planting, harvesting, marrying, waging battle, sacrificing captives, acceding to rule, and so on – as well as to prognosticate the future. A widespread practice, reflected in some of the earliest inscriptions, was to name individuals for the day on which they were born. This calendric name and the birthday it designated was believed to affect one's fortune in life. Among the Aztecs, therefore, it was a particular function of diviners to recommend an alternative calendric name for children born on unlucky days. Such rewriting of personal history was not confined to birthdays; it also was common for rulers and others to manipulate past dates to make their actions and statuses appear pre-ordained.

All later Mesoamerican cultures recognized a 52-year "Calendar Round" formed by the combination of dates in two calendrical cycles. One was the 365-day "Vague Year," so called because it lacked a leap day to account for the accumulation of the extra quarter-day in the actual solar year. This *haab*, as it was called in Yucatec Maya, consisted of 18 months of 20 days each, plus a 5-day period added to the end of the year. Among the Maya the New Year began with day 1 in the month Pop, followed by 2 Pop, 3 Pop, etc., up to 19 Pop. Rather than having the coefficient 20, the last day of the month was represented by a sign indicating the "seating" of the following month, in accord with the idea that the influence of a particular timespan is felt before it actually begins (Coe 1993: 49).

Intermeshing with the *haab* was a 260-day "Sacred Almanac" (sometimes called by the Mayan neologism *tzolkin*) formed by the permutation of the numbers 1 through 13 with 20 named days. Among the Maya, the cycle began on the day 1 Imix, followed by 2 Ik, 3 Akbal, and so on up to 13 Ben. The numerical portion of the cycle then began again with 1 Ix, followed by 2 Cib, until the numerals and day names returned to 1 Imix. The rationale for the 260-day count is unknown, but it is attested in early epi-Olmec, Mayan-Izapan, and Oaxacan inscriptions, where it often appears as a person's name. Today, Highland Maya shamans known as calendar priests continue to use the 260-day almanac as a forecasting tool (Coe 1993: 48).

The full designation of any particular day in the Calendar Round consisted of its position in the 260-day count, followed by its poition in the Vague Year, for example, 1 Akbal, 2 Pop. The same combination could not return until 52 Vague Years (18,980 days) had passed.

The Calendar Round was the only multi-year cycle employed by the Aztecs, Zapotecs, and other cultures of highland Mexico, but it had the obvious disadvantage of being unable to place any particular day within a span greater than 52 years. One of the greatest innovations of the epi-Olmec cultures was the creation of the Long Count, literally a count of days from the beginning of the current creation, which corresponded to a Calendar Round date of 4 Ahau 8 Cumku, or 13 August 3114 B.C. in the Gregorian calendar. The Long Count employed a base-20 place system, slightly modified to accord approximately with the length of solar year. The basic unit was the day, or *kin*. Longer periods were:

20 kins =	1 uinal	= 20 days
18 uinals =	1 tun	= 360 days
20 tuns =	1 katun	= 7,200 days
20 katuns =	1 baktun	= 144,000 days

Thirteen baktuns (1,872,000 days, or slightly over 5,125 years) would return to a day 4 Ahau 8 Cumku in the Calendar Round, and the end of the present creation.

In practice, the dates were inscribed on monuments from top to bottom, followed by the calendar round date. For example, the date on Stela C was written:

7 baktuns	= 1,008,000 days
16 katuns	= 115,200 days
6 tuns	= 2,160 days
16 uinals	= 320 days
18 kins	= 18 days
6 Etznab	

a total of 1,125,698 days since the beginning of the current Great Cycle, and falling on 14 August, 32 B.C. in the Gregorian Calendar. By employing very long cycles in this manner, the epi-Olmecs and their Classic Maya successors were able to record dates unambiguously in historical time.

Epi-Olmec Texts

The epi-Olmec writing system is the best candidate for a direct descendant from heartland Olmec iconography, due to its geographical distribution, some similarity in signs, and evidence for a shared linguistic history (Campbell and Kaufman 1976; Justeson and Kaufman 1993; Justeson and Matthews 1990; Méluzin 1995; Pohl et al. 2002). The story of its decipherment begins in 1902, when a small jade statue of a shaman wearing a duck mask and dressed in a winged costume was found in a field near San Andres Tuxtla, Veracruz (Holmes 1907). The Tuxtla Statuette, as it is called, bore a long count date of 8.6.2.4.17 in A.D. 162, and an inscription of 64 signs clearly different from Maya hieroglyphics and unrelated to any other writing system known at the time. Over the succeeding eight decades another dozen or so inscriptions in the same system were discovered, but all were too short, fragmentary, or eroded to effect a decipherment of the mysterious script.

The picture changed dramatically in 1986 with the discovery of a large stela at La Mojarra, now a small village on the Acula River in the lower Papaloapan basin (Fig. 7.9). Standing over two meters tall, the four-ton stone monument depicts the life-sized image of a ruler in exquisite dress. His elaborate headdress forms the head of a hook-billed bird supernatural. A "jester god" head with buccal mask sprouts from the bird-deity's nose, and a stylized shark with serrated fin is attached to the top of the headdress, its bifurcated tail hanging down behind. Four smaller sharks swim up the main shark's rope-like notochord. Smaller bird deity masks appear below the main one and on the pectoral ornament that lies on the ruler's breast over his feathered cape. Glyphs symbolizing his exalted office adorn his arms and legs. Most astounding, the rest of the stela was covered with an inscription of some four hundred signs and two Long Count dates, one in A.D. 143 and the other in A.D. 156 (Winfield Capitaine 1988). Finally, there existed a nearly complete text of sufficient length and complexity to unlock the epi-Olmec script!

The task of decipherment still was not, easy, however, for no Rosetta stone existed with a parallel inscription in a known language, and the language of the inscription itself was not certain (Méluzin 1992, 1995). The key to decipherment turned out to be the assumption, supported by historical linguistic analysis of ancient loan words in other Mesoamerican languages, that the language of the text was a precursor to modern Sokean languages still spoken in parts of southern Veracruz and Chiapas. Starting from this linguistic basis, John Justeson and Terrence Kaufman (1993, 1997) were able to show that the epi-Olmec system combined logographic and phonetic syllabic signs. Moreover, the semantic values of logographic signs, the phonetic values of grammatical affixes, and the overall grammatical structure of the La Mojarra stela and the Tuxtla statuette were understandable in the reconstructed pre-proto-Sokean language. Justeson and Kaufman also showed that some epi-Olmec signs were adopted into the Mayan writing system, indicating a historical link between the two.

Even when the signs of an ancient text have been deciphered, and it must be noted that some scholars question whether this has truly been accomplished for epi-Olmec (e.g., Houston and Coe 2004; Méluzin 1995: ix, 123), interpreting the text's meaning requires that it be transcribed into a known language and translated for modern readers. Undoubtedly, current readings of the La Mojarra stela and other epi-Olmec texts will be revised significantly in the coming years. Kaufman and Justeson's (2001) translation of the La Mojarra stela is the most complete attempt so far; if correct, it offers important insights into political ideology and practice in the southern Gulf lowlands near the end of the Formative period. According to Kaufman and Justeson, the stela, which was erected about three years after its last Long Count date (i.e., in A.D. 161), describes the events leading up to and following the accession of Harvester Mountain Lord, the ruler depicted on the stela. Among the events described were solar

Figure 7.9. La Mojarra Stela (from Justeson and Kaufman 1992: Fig. 2) (courtesy of George Stuart).

eclipses, appearances of Venus, battles, and ceremonies. The ceremonies mentioned included Harvester Mountain Lord drawing offerings of blood from his penis and buttocks, and sacrificing his brother, an apparent rival for the throne. In an astounding coincidence, the Tuxtla statuette describes the ritual activities of a "calendar-priest," apparently Harvester Mountain Lord himself,

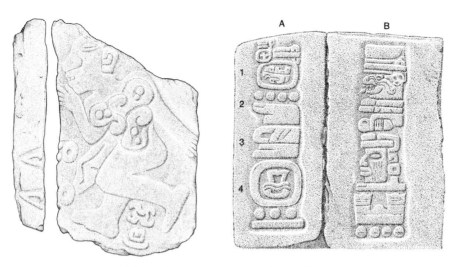

Figure 7.10. Late Middle and Late Formative sculpture from Oaxaca. Top, San Jose Mogote Monument 3; bottom, Monte Albán Stelae 12 and 13 (from Marcus 1992: Figs. 2.9 and 2.10, drawings by Mark Orsen) (courtesy of Joyce Marcus).

on the sixth anniversary of the last battle before his accession as recorded on the La Mojarra stela. These ceremonies included calling up his animal spirit companion, a shamanic practice that was maintained from Olmec times and continued among the Classic Maya and their modern descendants (Justeson and Kaufman 1993: 1703).

The La Mojarra stela and the Tuxtla statuette are particularly fine examples of the context of early writing in Mesoamerica. In essence, their message is one of political propaganda. All the common components of factional competition and exclusionary political strategy are there in their Mesoamerican particulars: the glorification of the individual ruler, the struggles with other claimants and the aid of political allies ("Coronated ones hallowed by sprinkling, noble war-leader ones, fought against succession-supporters [would-be usurpers] [Kaufman 2000]"), the use of prestige goods as symbols of authority ("His-Macaw sign, his eccentric flint, and his pectoral stone memento got brandished [Kaufman 2000]"), the manipulation of ideology through bloody autosacrifice, shamanic trance, and the timing of battles and ceremonies to celestial events.

Other Writing Systems

Such messages were not confined to epi-Olmec inscriptions. In the Valley of Oaxaca, what many consider the earliest instance of Mesoamerican writing records the defeat of an enemy. Sometime between 800 and 500 B.C. Monument 3 at San José Mogote was laid in a passage between two structures such that people walking into the ceremonial precinct trod upon the image of the captive carved on its face (Fig. 7.10). The monument is executed in the characteristic *danzante*-style, so-named because the rubbery, contorted limbs of the carved individuals reminded early scholars of the motions of dancers. In fact, however, they represent sacrificed victims, their eyes closed in death, stripped naked in humiliation, with scrolls representing blood flowing from their chests or the stumps of their severed genitals. On San José Mogote Monument 3, the victim is identified with a glyph designating his calendric name of 1 Earthquake.

Later, during phase Ia (ca. 550–300 B.C.), the rulers of the newly founded capital at Monte Albán recorded their victories with a massive display of *danzantes* on the face of Building L, and the earliest pure text (without accompanying images) in the Oaxacan writing system was carved on the paired Stelae 12 and 13 (Fig. 7.10) (Marcus 1992: 38–41). This inscription still cannot be read in its entirety, but it clearly includes both calendric and non-calendric information. Conquest slabs in a later style on building J at Monte Albán continue the practice of recording the defeat of rivals between 150 B.C. and A.D. 150, including some from beyond the Valley of Oaxaca (Marcus 1992: 391–400).

In southeastern Chiapas, the important center of Izapa also reached its height during the Late Formative period. Associated with this period at the site was a distinctive style of narrative relief sculpture, usually rendered on large stelae, which depicted deities or deity impersonators and humans engaged in various ritual acts (Fig. 7.11), including decapitation. Because Izapa has the largest concentration of these Late Formative stelae, the name "Izapan" has been extended to a diverse set of broadly similar local styles distributed through the Pacific piedmont and highlands and beyond (Smith 1984). By extension, the subgroup of related writing systems associated with these sculptures is also called Izapan, although some epigraphers consider them nothing more than early variants of Mayan writing, and glyphs are rare on monuments at Izapa itself (Justeson and Matthews 1990).

The earliest known stone monument with a Mayan inscription comes from El Porton, in the Salamá Valley in the northern highlands of southern Guatemala (Sharer 1989: 260–261; Sharer and Sedat 1973). El Porton Monument 1 was originally set on a platform built between 500 and 200 B.C. It contains a vertical glyph column with alternating numerical and non-numerical glyphs, most of which appear Mayan, but some of which appear derived from Olmec motifs. In 2006 William Saturno and colleagues reported the astounding discovery of columns of painted glyphs on the early murals of San Bartolo, in the Petén district of Guatemala. One of the glyph columns is on a mural in a construction stage securely dated to between 300 and 200 B.C. (Saturno et al. 2006). This discovery indicates that the Maya of the southern lowlands did not lag behind their neighbors to the south or west in the development of writing.

Later relief monuments from sites like Kaminaljuyu and Takalik Abaj in the southern highlands and Pacific piedmont of Guatemala also contain Late

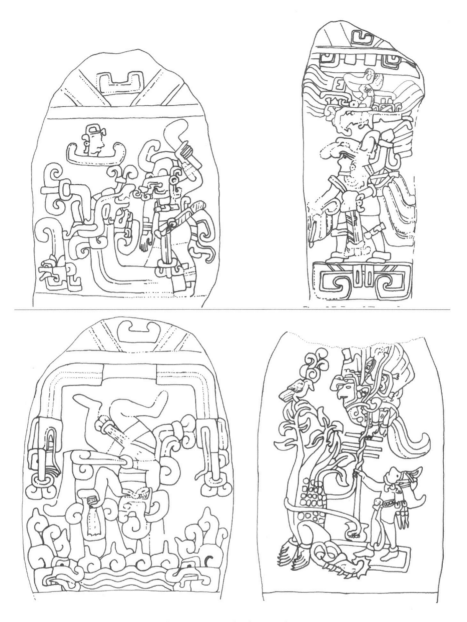

Figure 7.11. Selected stelae from Izapa; clockwise from upper left, Stela 3, Stela 4, Stela 25, Stela 23. Note sky bands with U-shaped motifs (Stelae 3,4, 23); earth band with inturned "fangs" (Stela 4); bicephalic serpent (Stela 23); feather-winged deity impersonators (Stela 4); downward-looking deity or ancestor (Stela 4, with crossed bands on wings); twinned, long-lipped, scroll-eyed heads (Stela 23); foliated crocodilian as world tree (Stela 25). (Redrawn from Norman 1978: Figs. 3.4, 3.5, 3.24, 3.26.)

Formative period glyphic inscriptions, including some in the double-column format later used by the Maya (Fig. 7.12). Takalik Abaj Stela 2 also bears a partial Long Count date beginning with 7 Baktun, and remnants of the second, katun coefficient suggest it was carved between 235 and 18 B.C. Later, but more precisely dated, is El Baul Stela 1, which has a Long Count date that can be placed confidently in A.D. 37.

The content of the Late Formative epi-Olmec, Oaxacan, Mayan, and Izapan texts and their accompanying images vary significantly. The epi-Olmec texts are the most detailed, and recount a various events, including battles, astronomical observations, and the politico-religious rituals of rulers. Early Maya texts frequently accompany depictions of rulers, whereas the Izapan scenes appear to relate more often to myth and ritual activities (Lowe et al. 1982: 317). By contrast, the terser Oaxacan texts accompany images that focus more heavily on themes of combat and sacrifice. Despite this variation, the political context of all these systems is clear. They were inscribed and displayed to convey and legitimize the power of rulers in accord with the particular beliefs and prevailing sources of power, military and/or ideological within their respective societies (see Marcus 1992). Why writing was necessary to convey this information is less clear. Surely, Late Formative rulers could have communicated military victories, rituals, and their supporting myths through images and iconography and, indeed, the graphic elements of most inscribed Late Formative monuments did exactly this. The key ingredient in the development of these early Mesoamerican writing systems was the encoding of abstract calendrical information not readily represented by iconic images. Similar to the religious specialists of later societies, it is probable that calendar priests or shamans possessed the esoteric knowledge to record and interpret the significance of dates. Moreover, it is highly likely that only they and other elites could read the inscriptions. In other words, the inscriptions were intended principally as elite discourse, accessible to the vast majority of the population only through their oral translation. The evolution of writing in Mesoamerica, therefore, had the effect of materializing the differences between noble speech, by definition sacred, profound, and true, and commoner speech – profane, trivial, and often fallacious (Marcus 1992: xviii). By incorporating writing on monuments with more widely understood iconography and images, these early Mesoamerican rulers created propaganda aimed simultaneously at their peers and their subjects.

EPI-OLMEC INTERACTION

We have already observed that the intensity of interregional interaction declined markedly across most of Mesoamerica in the Late Formative period. This is not to say that Late Formative societies existed in isolation from their

Figure 7.12. Izapan-style stelae. Top, Izapa Stela 5 (redrawn after Norman 1976: Fig 4.1); bottom, Kaminaljuyu Stela 10 (Coe 1996: Fig. 29, Courtesy of Michael D. Coe).

neighbors, but that leaders, who had previously supported their authority with
goods and symbols from distant places, and the broad social networks they
represented, now drew more heavily on their own traditions and local resources.
Utilitarian necessities not available locally were still exchanged over wide areas,
and technological styles still spread into neighboring regions. Esoteric symbols
also were diffused, sometimes widely, when they served a particular need, but
they were much more likely to be reinterpreted and recombined with local
symbolism than was the case for Middle Formative celts and monuments.

In fact, different classes of artifacts and art tell rather different stories about
interaction within and beyond the Gulf lowlands. The Gulf lowlands imported
less greenstone than before, although ornaments in burials and caches indicate
that some greenstone continued to trickle in from the highlands of Mexico
and Guatemala. In addition, recent excavations at Tres Zapotes recovered mica
flakes, apparently the waste from artifact manufacture, which probably came
from metamorphic terrains in Oaxaca or Puebla. Significantly, the costumes of
rulers shown on monuments at Tres Zapotes, El Meson, and La Mojarra appear
more elaborate than their Olmec predecessors. These are richly bedecked with
stone beads, earflares, pectorals, and feathers, and the rulers apparently wore
garments made of cloth. Indeed, Barbara Stark (2000: 44; Stark et al. 1998)
argues convincingly that cotton textiles, together with elaborate headdresses,
writing, and calendric knowledge, began to substitute for exotic prestige items
in the lower Papaloapan basin.

In contrast to greenstone, obsidian imports increased, and the sources used
provide clear evidence of interaction with the eastern altiplano. Interestingly, a
bifurcation of obsidian exchange routes apparently occurred in the Gulf lowlands. Cerro de las Mesas and other sites in south-central Veracruz continued
to receive most of their obsidian from the nearest sources, at Orizaba, Veracruz,
and Guadalupe Victoria, Puebla. Tres Zapotes, Bezuapan, and other sites in and
around the Tuxtla Mountains, however, obtained most of their obsidian from
the more distant source at Zaragoza, Puebla (Knight 1999, 2003; Pool 1997b;
Santley et al. 2001; Stark et al. 1992). The Late Formative also marks the separation of the Gulf lowlands from the exchange systems that moved Guatemalan
obsidian along the Pacific lowlands and throughout the Maya region (Nelson
and Clark 1998).

Late Formative ceramic styles tell a more nuanced and complex story of
intra- and interregional interaction (Stark 1997: 288–304). In the Late Formative period, zones of similar ceramic styles contracted across Mesoamerica.
A distinctive gray ware tradition appeared in Oaxaca, Maya ceramic spheres
became more distinctive from their neighbors, and the previously widespread
differentially fired tradition was constricted to the Isthmian region, with new
differential black-red and black-orange wares appearing in the lower Papaloapan basin and Tehuantepec. One set of motifs, often executed in a very fine line
on dry or fired vessels, was concentrated in south-central Veracruz, including

Tres Zapotes and the central Tuxtlas.[4] Other motifs that extend from south-central Veracruz westward into the Central Highlands of Mexico and southeastward into Chiapas, Tehuantepec, southern Guatemala, and western El Salvador include sets of vertical lines in a band, herringbones or chevrons, hachured or cross-hachured triangles arranged point-to-point, and hachured steps or steps on a hachured ground (Stark 1997: 293). Fine-line incision of these motifs is particularly common in Veracruz and central Chiapas (Clark and Cheetham 2002), but less so elsewhere (Stark 1997: 293). Fine-line incision also occurs in the Basin of Mexico, but the motifs differ from those found in Veracruz. Concurrently, or slightly earlier, polished red-orange pottery, sometimes with a cloudy resist decoration, made its appearance over much of eastern Mesoamerica; at Tres Zapotes it achieved its maximum popularity during the Late Formative period (Lowe 1989: 59; Ortiz 1975).

In general, and in contrast to obsidian exchange, these ceramic affinities suggest less interaction of the southern and south-central Gulf lowlands with western Mesoamerica and greater interaction along the old corridor through Chiapas and southern Guatemala. That distribution coincides reasonably well with commonalities between epi-Olmec and "Izapan" writing and sculpture noted above. Nevertheless, monuments with Izapan-related traits are relatively rare components of the diverse epi-Olmec sculptural corpus and, as noted above, significant differences distinguished regional variants in the broader Izapan sculptural style.

Interaction within the Gulf Lowlands

During the Late Formative period, the always fuzzy cultural boundary between Olman and central Veracruz blurred even more. Ceramic decoration united cultures on either side of the Papaloapan River more than they separated them. There were some notable differences in paste, with Tres Zapotes and other sites to the east employing more volcanic ash temper and experimenting early with untempered pastes, but these differences probably relate more to the localized character of ceramic production in areas of contrasting geology than to ethnic or political divisions. Sculpture remained more common to the east of the Papaloapan River in the Late Formative period, but similarities in carved basalt columns between El Meson to the east and Alvarado to the west speak to cultural sharing in a modified Olmec tradition with the addition of some Izapan-style elements. The Alvarado stela and the La Mojarra stela also document the westward extension of epi-Olmec writing in the Late and Terminal Formative periods, but it would fall to the great site of Cerro de las Mesas to carry epi-Olmec writing and the Long Count into the Early Classic period.

Cerro de las Mesas lies in the area known as the Mixtequilla, between the Río Blanco and its distributary, the Río de las Pozas, in the western Papaloapan basin. First occupied in the Middle Formative period, it became a major center with impressive earthen mounds in the Late Formative (Stark and Curet 1994). It was perhaps at that time that mound groups similar to those at Tres Zapotes, with a conical mound and a single long mound, were erected on the north end of the site's ceremonial complex (Stark, personal communication, 2003). The site continued to function as an important center well into the Classic period as regional population increased and new centers were established a short distance away. During the Terminal Formative period, elites were buried with clam shells and jade ornaments. In one particularly sumptuous burial, the deceased was covered with red cinnabar and accompanied by ceramic vessels, an Olmec-style pottery figurine (undoubtedly an heirloom), a ball-game yoke, and a turtle shell elaborately carved with a profile head surrounded by two intertwined serpents. Also possibly from the Terminal Formative period is Monument 5, a boulder carving depicting a seminude figure with a duckbill-like buccal mask, which calls to mind the Tuxtla Statuette (Miller 1991: 30).

Use of Olmec heirlooms continued in the Early Classic period, when an extraordinary cache of nearly 800 jade items, including some Olmec pieces, was buried at the foot of the large mound of the site's central group (Drucker 1943b: 11–14). It was during this period that stelae with epi-Olmec inscriptions, the latest known, were erected at the site. An Olmec heritage is likewise evident in the forms of the masks and headdresses worn by some of the individuals depicted on these stelae, particularly the half-kneeling figure on Stela 9 (Miller 1991: 30–31).

Developments in Oaxaca

Over the mountains to the south of the Gulf lowlands, major sociopolitical change was occurring in the Valley of Oaxaca (Marcus and Flannery 1996: 121–138). During the Rosario phase (ca, 800–550 B.C.), the valley appears to have been divided among three competing chiefdoms, each centered in one of the valley's major arms and separated by an unoccupied buffer zone where the arms intersect. Evidence from San José Mogote, the capital of the chiefdom in the northwestern Etla arm of the valley, reflects the growing political tensions among the chiefdoms. Late in its occupation, a wattle-and-daub temple was burned with a fire so intense that it vitrified the clay daub walls, turning them to glassy cinders. Even more graphically, the *danzante* monument was laid face up at the threshold of the narrow corridor separating two structures, so that passersby would literally and metaphorically tread upon the vanquished foe.

About 550 B.C. the settlement pattern in the Valley of Oaxaca changed radically. San José Mogote, along with most of the other communities in the Etla valley, lost most of its population (Marcus and Flannery 1996: 139–154). At the same time, populations poured into the former buffer zone, and a new capital established at the top of the 400 m tall hill known as Monte Albán became the largest site in the valley. During the next 200 years of the Monte Albán Ia phase, more than 300 danzante monuments were carved and arranged on the front of Building L, one of the major buildings on Monte Alban's main plaza. This massive display of nude, sacrificed, captives attested to the victories of the capital of the emerging Zapotec state as it consolidated its control over the valley. Later the Zapotec state would turn its attentions outside the valley to conquer other parts of Oaxaca, recording its conquests on the slabs that cover building L in the center of the plaza. Interestingly, these monuments to Monte Alban's expanding power focus on the identities of the defeated, rather than the victorious leaders.

Joyce Marcus and Kent Flannery (1996: 139–154) liken the founding of Monte Albán to the process of *synoikism* in ancient Greece, wherein new cities sometimes formed from the consolidation of many villages, either voluntarily to provide for mutual defense or through forced relocation as an act of power-building by a strong ruler. The specific scenario favored by Marcus and Flannery for Monte Albán is that San José Mogote formed a powerful confederacy of villages in the Etla region and the central valley and moved its capital to the defensive hilltop location before unifying the Tlacolula and Valle Grande chiefdoms under its control (cf. Blanton et al. 1993: 71–73).

In some ways the founding of Monte Albán and the formation of the Zapotec state parallel processes that were going on about the same time at Tres Zapotes. The details, of course, differ. Late Formative Tres Zapotes was not formed anew, but grew from a centuries-old Olmec center. It was not placed in a naturally defensible location, and its monuments do not unambiguously depict military victory (though that may be implied in Stelae A and D). In both places, though, competition appears to have been resolved through the creation of a confederacy that emphasized political cooperation over individual glorification. It also is evident that developments in Oaxaca and the Gulf Coast were largely independent. Although written texts employ some similar conventions, such as bar-and-dot numeration and cartouche-bounded day names, these seem to owe their origins to common ancestry more than intensive cross-fertilization. There also is little evidence of direct contact in ceramic styles, art, or imported materials. The Late Formative inhabitants of the Gulf Coast and Oaxaca obviously knew of one another's existence, and they probably interacted with some of the same peoples, as suggested by Gulf Coast and Oaxacan-style offerings in a burial at Chiapa de Corzo. They seem, however, to hit upon similar resolutions to their particular political challenges independently.

Southeastern Mesoamerica and the Izapan Style

The evidence of historical linguistics, pottery styles, and sculpture indicates that during most of the Formative period, southeastern Mesoamerica was divided into two broad ethnolinguistic areas along a line that ran approximately from the

Laguna de los Terminos on the Gulf Coast to just inside the western Guatemala border on the Pacific Coast (Andrews 1990; Campbell and Kaufman 1976; Lowe 1977). To the east lay speakers of Mayan languages; to the west peoples of Mije-Sokean speech.

The premier Sokean capital in central Chiapas was Chiapa de Corzo, situated astride the major communication route through the Grijalva Depression. Founded in the Middle Formative period (Lowe 2001), Chiapa de Corzo had long maintained contacts with the Gulf Coast. During the Francesa (ca. 550–300 B.C.) and Guanacaste (ca. 300–50 B.C.) phases, central Chiapas ceramics shared with Hueyapan phase pottery at Tres Zapotes finely incised geometric motifs and reddish-orange–slipped bowl forms featuring widely everted rims indicating that such interaction continued (Clark and Cheetham 2002; Lowe 1989: 59). Around 300 B.C., formal construction declined at Chiapa de Corzo and Maya Chicanel pottery was included in high-status burials and other elite contexts, possibly as the result of Mayan political expansion from El Mirador in the lowland Peten district of Guatemala (Clark et al. 2000; Lowe 1977: 230). Other sites up the Grijalva valley were abandoned, and smaller sites were founded in defensible locations, often employing Maya architectural styles and customs such as fronto-occipital cranial flattening, a mark of elite status. Whether local elites adopted Maya styles or Maya leaders were installed as rulers is not clear, but the general population apparently maintained its Soke identity, making utilitarian pottery in traditional styles. As suggested by the Sokean epi-Olmec inscription on Chiapa de Corzo Stela 2, Maya influence waned toward the end of the Late Formative period, and Chiapa de Corzo experienced an architectural resurgence, covering old platforms with large limestone blocks and stucco, though retaining elements of Maya architectural styles.

On the Pacific piedmont of the Soconusco, in the extreme southeast corner of modern Chiapas and the Mije-Sokean linguistic area, the ancient site of Izapa experienced its major florescence in the Late Formative period. Between about 300 and 50 B.C., its rulers enlarged old mounds and erected new ones in carefully laid out formal complexes, the largest mound reaching a height of 22 m (Lowe et al. 1982: 133).

Izapa is most famous for its enormous corpus of stone monuments, which includes 89 stelae, 61 altars, 3 thrones, and 68 "miscellaneous monuments" (Norman 1973, 1976) (Fig. 7.11). Twenty-six of the stelae and several altars and monuments are elaborately carved in a distinctive flat relief style with incised lines added for detail. In contrast to the placid, sculptural, "classic" lines of Olmec narrative reliefs, from which they developed, the Izapa reliefs have been described as "baroque," cluttered with great detail in more painterly compositions (Coe 1965c: 774; Miles 1965) (Fig. 7.12). With a few exceptions (Kappelman 2003), the content of the Izapa reliefs is mythico-religious and ceremonial (Lowe et al. 1982: 317). Deities or their masked impersonators perform ceremonies framed above and below by abstract representations of sky and earth or the watery underworld, which may be connected by the world tree. The deity masks, shown in profile, bear elements of feline, serpent, avian, and other zoomorphic and abstract features. Particularly characteristic is a "long-lipped" god, which appears ancestral to the long-lipped rain gods (*chacs*) of the Maya. Winged supernaturals also are common, as are individuals who gaze downward on the scene from above. The Izapa reliefs also employ a complex set of highly conventionalized symbols. Some of the most distinctive are abstract sky bands with divergent diagonal lines flanking a U-shaped element, basal bands or platforms with downward-pointing incurved scrolls (almost certainly derived from Olmec-style earth-monster masks), bicephalic serpents with heads pointing downward, and frequent scrollwork, often emphasized with an interior line. These are but a few of the numerous zoomorphic and abstract symbols that grace the reliefs (see Norman 1976; Miles 1965; Quirarte 1976; and Smith 1984 for more thorough discussions of Izapan iconography). As noted previously, occasional glyphs were carved on the reliefs. They differ from the epi-Olmec writing system, however, possibly reflecting a Mijean, rather than Sokean, language (Justeson 1986).

Although the themes of the reliefs lean strongly toward religion and ritual, their contexts and their underlying messages also are strongly political (Kappelman 2000, 2003; Lowe et al. 1982: 29–41). Set in thematic groupings at the bases of pyramidal mounds in formal architectural complexes, they conveyed the religious power of the rulers who undoubtedly commissioned them and were occasionally depicted (Kappelman 2003). Nevertheless, the scarcity of individual glorification in the Izapa stelae is notable, and contrasts with most Olmec, epi-Olmec, and Classic Maya reliefs. In Blanton et al's (1996) terms, they seem to evoke cosmic themes and renewal ceremonies tied to group interests much more than the exclusionary, individualizing themes of these other societies (Lowe 1982: 317).

The Izapa reliefs are one expression of a wider and more long-lived Izapan style. Regional variants of the Izapan style share some of their elements with the Izapa reliefs, but not all, not consistently, and not in isolation from local motifs and themes. Further, it is not clear that Izapa was the unique origin of the Izapan style. Both Michael Coe (1965c: 773) and Garth Norman (1976: 2–3) have suggested the origins of the Izapan style lay partly in the Gulf lowlands, with Norman also identifying influences from highland Guatemala.

The core area of the Izapan style transcended the Mije-Sokean–Mayan linguistic boundary, extending into the highlands and piedmont of southern Guatemala. The major sites with Izapan monuments are, from west to east, Takalik Abaj, El Baul, and Kaminaljuyu (Fig. 7.8). At Takalik Abaj, in the piedmont zone, carved stelae, plain stelae, and pot-bellied boulder sculptures were erected in association with terraces and platforms. Some of the carved stelae look more similar to later Mayan sculptures than Izapan ones, and these have more overtly political themes; several depict individual rulers, in one case with a baktun 7 Long Count date (see above) (Henderson 1997: 94; Graham et al. 1978). The latter are similar to El Baul Stela 1, which, as noted above, has an A.D. 37 Long Count date.

Kaminaljuyu is located in the same large highland valley as modern Guatemala City, whose expansion has resulted in massive destruction of the site. During the Arenal phase (ca. 300 B.C.–A.D. 100) of the Late Formative Miraflores tradition, it was a major center supported by intensive agriculture on irrigated fields and the production and exchange of fine pottery as well as implements made of obsidian from the nearby el Chayal source (Bishop 1989; Popenoe de Hatch 2001). Throughout its history the center was divided into several densely occupied neighborhoods. each of which boasted its own civic-ceremonial precinct that included temple platforms in which elites were buried in elaborate tombs (Henderson 1997: 95; Michels 1979). A particularly rich Miraflores tomb dating to the Verbena phase (ca. 400–300 B.C.) contained three victims sacrificed to accompany the principal occupant, as well as jade ornaments, pyrite-encrusted plaques, obsidian and andesite blades, animal bones, fish teeth, stingray spines, and many ceramic vessels, some with the remains of burned incense (Popenoe de Hatch 2001; Shook and Kidder 1952). The multiple mound groups and neighborhood divisions at Kaminaljuyu call to mind the factional divisons I have argued for Tres Zapotes. However, variable distributions of prestige items and architectural scale suggests a more hierarchical organization, always with one group at the apex of the political structure (Michels 1979).

The Late Formative rulers and nobles of Kaminaljuyu commissioned numerous monuments in a variety of local and regional styles. Rotund potbelly figures indicate interaction with the Pacific piedmont. Some of the relief monuments are strikingly similar to Izapa in execution and content. Others incorporate a different technique of sloping planes and double-column hieroglyphic inscriptions more similar to Classic Maya texts. The two faces of one particularly important Arenal phase stela, Monument 65, exhibit carving in two different styles. The "front," carved in a local style with slightly raised and rounded relief and recessed outlines, depicts three richly attired rulers seated on low thrones, each flanked by nude and seminude captives, their hands bound, each with a different headdress. The more eroded "back" depicts three figures, arranged to either side of and below a glyph column, all beneath a medallion with crossed bars and a band decorated with scrolls. Although the carving technique is similar to that on the front of the stela, the form and arrangement of the figures are more similar to early Mayan and Izapan monuments. It is possible that the front and back were carved at different times (Parsons 1986: 58), but Jonathan Kaplan (2000) sees them as contemporaneous exoteric and esoteric expressions of kingship respectively directed toward the public and the initiated elite.

Well to the north, in the southern Maya lowlands, other regional centers emerged in the Late Formative period at sites like Altar de Sacrificios, Seibal,

Tikal, Cerros, and Lamanai. One of the earliest was Nakbe in the Peten district of northern Guatemala. Late in the Middle Formative period, terraced platforms up to 15 m tall were set on a much larger basal platform, and construction continued in the Late Formative period, with one building reaching a height of 45 m. Stela 1, carved around the beginning of the period, shows two standing figures in a style that resembles Mayan monuments of the southern highlands more than those of Izapa. The headdress of one contains an Olmec-style profile head (Clark et al. 2000: 467, Fig. 14). Elsewhere in the Peten, the painted murals of San Bartolo, recently discovered by William Saturno, depict the Maya corn god with a virtually identical head. Painted around A.D. 100, they attest to to the persistence of this Olmec-derived motif (O'Neil 2002).

Around 300 B.C., the enormous site of El Mirador embarked on the largest construction projects ever seen in the Maya region. Just one of these, the Danta pyramid, soared 70 m over the base of its first platform (Clark et al. 2000: 469). Raised causeways extending out from El Mirador towards Nakbe and other sites reflect its status as the capital of the Mirador basin.

Epi-Olmec–Izapan Interaction

A small number of Late Formative monuments from the southern Gulf lowlands bear some resemblances to monuments from the Izapan core area (Norman 1976; Quirarte 1973; Scott 1977; Smith 1978, 1984). The most notable come from Tres Zapotes, El Meson, and Alvarado. At Tres Zapotes, the strongest parallels to monuments in the Izapan core area appear on Monument C (Figure 7.7), the stone box elaborately carved with scrolls and warrior figures in the plano–relief technique typically associated with Izapa. In addition to its technique, other Izapan elements include the form of the scrolls and the small scroll-eyed heads that connect them. Neither the theme, interpreted as "celestial combat," nor the clubs carried by the figures have parallels at Izapa, however (Coe 1965c: 773; Quirarte 1973: 31).

Tres Zapotes Stela D (Figure 7.5) also is sometimes described as Izapan. The plano-relief carving of scrolls on its sides, the representation of long-lipped serpent heads hanging from the upper jaw of the feline that frames the top of the stela's central scene, a downward-peering figure at the top of the scene, and the stiff capes worn by the human figures all have parallels in Izapan art, but the softly rounded relief of the human figures is distinctive. Moreover, as noted above, the downward-pointing suspended serpent heads are most likely derived from Olmec examples. The basal motifs of two reliefs from El Meson, about 10 km north of Tres Zapotes, and a third from Alvarado, 45 km to the northwest, suggest Izapan ties, but other elements suggest more direct derivation from Olmec antecedents (Scott 1977). Overall, this handful of monuments seems slim evidence for a major Izapan influence on Late Formative art in southern Veracruz. Rather, descent from a common Olmec relief tradition, undoubtedly facilitated by general Mije–Sokean linguistic ties, seems a better explanation for many of the artistic similarities that do exist.

TRANSMITTERS OF THE OLMEC HERITAGE

As Michael Coe (1962, 1965c, 1977) has long argued, the Izapan and epi-Olmec cultural spheres hold particular importance as historical links between the Olmecs and the Classic civilizations of the Maya and Gulf Coast regions. Both built on concepts of rulership and political practice developed by the Olmecs. Both preserved and passed on the tradition of carving narrative relief on stelas with significant modifications in execution and content. Both incorporated particular symbols and concepts derived from Middle Formative Olmec-style art in their iconography and writing and relayed them to their neighbors and successors. However, they were neither passive conduits for the transmission of Olmec traits, nor monolithic cultural entities. Both the epi-Olmec and Izapan traditions combined ancient Olmec elements and original elements in novel ways, and the Izapan tradition, in particular, exhibited signif-icant regional variation. Further, the patterns of transmission were not simply Olmec to Izapan to Maya on the one hand, and Olmec to epi-Olmec to Classic Veracruz on the other (cf. Coe 1965c: Fig. 57). Although these pathways do characterize the main courses of transmission, some direct adoption of Olmec and epi-Olmec traits by the Maya is evident, as is the adoption of some Izapan traits by the epi-Olmec tradition noted above.

Within Olman, Olmec culture did not simply collapse with the fall of La Venta. Instead, Olmec culture evolved in western Olman as their descendants, still speaking a Sokean language, drew on the symbols of their Olmec ances-tors and adapted them to the requirements of a new, more competitive political landscape. One form this adaptation took was a continuation of the Middle Formative Olmec trend toward increasing historicity in public monuments displaying the activities of rulers, sometimes under the watchful gaze of ances-tors and supernaturals. The culmination of this trend was the development of a complex logo-syllabic writing system and the development of the Long Count for recording events in historical time. Such monuments speak to heightened political competition in the Gulf lowlands, as leaders in emerging centers vied for power and sought to attract followers to their factions. At the by-then ancient center of Tres Zapotes, however, Late Formative leaders appear to have moderated the centrifugal effects of competition by instituting an assem-bly government that mediated the interests of factions seated in dispersed plaza groups. Exclusionary political strategies, however, remained dominant among other epi-Olmec centers in the Gulf lowlands, and they were likely pursued within factions at Tres Zapotes. For reasons that still are unclear, the epi-Olmec sculptural tradition was abandoned toward the end of the Terminal Formative period in the eastern Papaloapan basin, but it continued in the sculptures of Cerro de las Mesas, both in hieroglyphic texts and the insignia of rulers (Justeson and Kaufman 2004), in some cases revealing a direct link back to Olmec antecedents (Miller 1991).

Linguistic and iconographic data provide the best evidence for direct transmission from the Gulf lowlands into the emerging lowland Maya tradition. Certain Classic Maya glyphs mimic earlier epi-Olmec forms, and some Maya glyphs that have no semantic or phonological correspondence in Mayan languages do make sense in the reconstructed ancestor of Sokean languages (Justeson and Kaufman 1993: 1710). Some of these, however, may have been adopted earlier from Olmec Mije-Sokean speakers or from Mije-Sokean words and signs in the Late Formative Mayan-Izapan writing system, as well as from the epi-Olmec tradition. Some evidence also suggests a diffusion of Olmec iconography more directly into lowland Mayan art, such as the Olmec-like profile heads on Nakbe Stela 1 and the San Bartolo murals. In addition, the extensive use of the Long Count among the Maya can be traced to epi-Olmec monuments of the first century B.C. It likely passed to the lowland Maya indirectly through late "Izapan" monuments of the southern Guatemalan highlands, where a Mije–Sokean influenced Maya script was developing, although the epi-Olmec presence in the Grijalva basin may have been involved as well. One would expect bar-and-dot vigesimal notation to have diffused to the Maya by the same path, but it is ubiquitous in the early writing systems of southern Mesoamerica and so could have diffused to the lowland Maya from either of their closest neighbors.

The Izapan contribution to lowland Classic Maya art probably was greater than the epi-Olmec contribution (Coe 1965c, 1977; Lowe et al. 1982; Miles 1965; Norman 1973; Quirarte 1973, 1977) (Table 7.1). The general Olmec practice of carving reliefs on stelae had a long history in both areas, but the specific association of stelae with altars appears earlier in the Izapan sphere and was widely adopted by the Maya, suggesting a more southerly route of introduction.[5] Iconographic traits that can be traced from Olmec antecedents through the Izapan to the Classic Maya tradition include extensive use of the crossed-bar and U-shaped elements (Norman 1973: 31, 45, 312). In Izapan art they are often associated with one another in bands and panels representing sky and earth. Izapan sky bands and earth panels also retain the convention of using outcurving scrolls in sky images and incurving scrolls in earth images, both abstracted from the fangs of Olmec-style monster masks. The Maya representation of the sky as a bicephalic serpent is presaged in the Olmec Monument 80 of La Venta and Monument 37 of San Lorenzo and is particularly prevalent in Izapan monuments, although it also appears in the epi-Olmec Stela D of Tres Zapotes (Cyphers 2004: 99; Taube 1995: 93). The specific form with the two heads hanging down from a sky band or feline mouth does not appear to have been passed on to the Maya, however. Feather-winged deity impersonators in Maya art have their direct antecedents in Izapan rather than

TABLE 7.1. *Representation of stylistic traits in southeastern Mesoamerican sculptural traditions (Coe 1965b; Norman 1976; Quirarte 1973, 1977; see also Smith 1984)*

	Olmec	Epi-Olmec	Izapan	Maya
Stelae	X	X	X	X
Stela-altar complex		X	X	X
Relief carving	X	X	X	X
Rounded relief	X	X		
Plano-relief	x	x	X	X
Painterly, "baroque" style			X	X
Realistic depiction of well-fed humans	X	X	X	X
Scenes in stylized monster mouths	X	X	X	
Crossed bars	X	X	X	X
U-element	X	X	X	X
Scrollwork skies or clouds	X	X	X	
Flame-scroll brow	X	X	X	
Long-lipped profile heads	(x)	(x)	X	X
Deities descending from sky			X	X
Winged figures	x		X	X
Plumed headdresses		X	X	X
Spears		X	X	X
Clubs	X	X		X
Trophy heads	(x)		X	X
Scroll earplugs			X	X
Scroll-eyed heads		X	X	X
Scroll with emphasis line		X	X	X
Sky bands with double-opposed diagonal lines	X		X	X
Mask panels	X	X	X	X
double-opposed T			X	X
Serpent X			X	X
U in glyphs	(X)	X	X	X
U in insignia			X	X
THEMES				
Mythic Combat				
compound creature vs. serpent			X	
"War in Heaven"	X	X		
Power and Protection				
2-headed serpent	x	x	X	X
Feather-winged figures	x		X	X
Deities as Personification of Earth, Sky, Water				
compound terrestrial and celestial creatures	X	X	X	X
crocodilian-saurian-serpentine	X	X	X	X
full-bodied serpent as base line			X	

	Olmec	Epi-Olmec	Izapan	Maya
segment of terrestrial body as panel, serpent bodies extending up to frame scene			X	
croc-saurian with foliage			X	X
2-headed serpent as sky, tail-heads downward	X	X	X	
feather-winged deity impersonators	X		X	X
Twin scroll-eyed and cross-eyed profile heads			X	X

X, present; x, rare; (x) ambiguous

epi-Olmec monuments, although earlier Olmec and Olmec-style examples appear in the bird-costumed figures on La Venta Altar 4 and the Oxtotitlán mural. Furthermore, the ubiquitous long-lipped Chacs of the Classic Maya undoubtedly derive from the long-lipped profile heads so prevalent in Izapan style, and ultimately from Olmec and Olmec-style profile heads with long buccal masks. Other representations in Maya imagery with Izapan antecedents include "Serpent X" (a composite being with a U-shape above the eye) and twin profile heads with scrolled and square "cross-eyed" irises (Quirarte 1977: 276–281) (Figure 7.11).

Not all the variants of the Izapan style contributed equally to Classic Maya traditions, however. Ceramic styles indicate that the core area of the Izapan style was broken into many local zones. Sculptural styles also exhibit regional variation, though they cross-cut ceramic style zones. Plano-relief carving is far more common at Izapa than in more easterly Izapan centers or Classic Maya sculpture. Certain motifs also appear to be confined to Izapa. In addition, overtly political representations of rulers are more prevalent in the Maya segment of the Izapan core area (and epi-Olmec monuments), and are notably scarce in Izapa itself (Lowe et al. 1982: 317; cf. Kappelman 2003). The same dichotomy holds for writing, which is much less common at Izapa, and the sculptors of Izapa did not employ the Long Count. As discussed above, the linkage of these traits appears to relate to exclusionary political strategies that glorify rulers. Thus, the forerunners of the Classic Maya appear to have adopted elements of the Izapan and epi-Olmec styles from similarly organized political systems in southern Guatemala and the Gulf lowlands, rather than from the more corporately oriented polity of Izapa.

CONCLUSION

The Late and Terminal Formative periods were critical ones in the development of later Mesoamerican civilizations. During this timespan, several key areas of

Mesoamerica saw the rise of urban settlements and, at least in Oaxaca, the Valley of Mexico, and the Maya lowlands, the political institutions usually associated with states. Specific concepts of rulership and ritual were widely adopted and codified in regional art styles. In southern Mesoamerica, complex writing systems emerged from the iconographic and early glyphic systems of the Middle Formative. Art and writing were pressed into political service as leaders found new ways to glorify their exploits and justify their authority, while drawing both on widely shared art styles and local traditions of the Middle Formative. At the same time, some polities pursued corporate strategies to moderate the disruptive interests of internal factions and defend themselves from competitors. Throughout, the growing power of regional polities reshaped old interaction networks, to the detriment of some neighbors and the benefit of others. The effects of these changes were felt especially keenly in Olman as old centers in the east failed and their sustaining populations moved out, but the heirs to the Olmec heritage in western Olman adapted and flourished. It was not so much that Olmec culture regressed, but that it was equaled and, in some respects, surpassed by developments elsewhere.

The epi-Olmec developments in Olman cast the perennial question, "What is Olmec?" in a different light. As we have seen, the question has been raised primarily in the synchronic contexts of Early and Middle Formative interaction. It takes on a temporal dimension, however, when applied to Late Formative changes in Olman itself. As with the synchronic debate, the issue is whether Olmec is conceived as an art style, a culture, or something else. Those who regard Olmec principally as an art style have little difficulty declaring its demise when the canons of the style change substantially. Whether particular themes or representational elements persist is beside the point because the style has lost its coherence as a unified whole (de la Fuente 1981). The issue is more problematic when Olmec is regarded as a culture. A culture can acquire and discard traits, change its geographical distribution, or modify its institutions and beliefs without ceasing to exist. Indeed, it is precisely the ability of cultures to adapt that ensures their vitality in the face of changing conditions.

The Late Formative inhabitants of Olman were still Olmecs in the same sense that the contemporary indigenous populations of Yucatan are still Maya. They were Olmec no less than the subjects of Elizabeth I and Elizabeth II were and are English. They spoke a language directly descended from their Olmec forebears, they adapted Olmec ideological concepts, representations, and institutions to the requirements of their day, and they employed, and in some ways improved on, Olmec technology.

As John Clark and Mary Pye (2000b: 218) have argued, however, Olmec can be conceived in yet another way, parallel to the terms Roman, Byzantine, or Victorian. That is, as a particular historical constellation of cultural concepts, practices, and material representations, which has a definite temporal and spatial distribution but does not encompass the entire history of a people.

This comes close to the definition of Olmec as an art style, since it is through art, architecture, and artifact styles that the underlying concepts and practices most vividly are displayed. But it is something more, because terms such as Roman also imply a cultural commitment to specific ideals beyond the form and content of their material markers. As we have seen, the epi-Olmec cultural configuration did differ in recognizable ways from its Olmec progenitor. That said, it did not replace it with something completely new, but evolved from it, preserving significant elements of its Olmec heritage.

CHAPTER 8

THE OLMECS AND THEIR LEGACY

What have we learned about the Olmecs and their contributions to later
Mesoamerican civilizations? The first lesson is that there never was a single,
unitary "Olmec society." From the moment the Olmecs of San Lorenzo created a system of hereditary inequality and extended their control over nearby
settlements, the sociopolitical landscape of Olman was a diverse one. It included
egalitarian societies whose largest political unit may have been a single village,
as well as centralized regional polities with marked differences in social status
that divided rulers from their subjects. While Early Formative Olmecs in the
Coatzacoalcos and San Juan river valleys were building large enduring centers, Olmecs in the Tuxtla Mountains lived in small settlements and moved
frequently (Arnold 2000). Moreover, contemporaneous variation in procurement networks, as well as styles of monuments and artifacts, suggest that no
Olmec polity ever managed to rule all of Olman (see Chapters 5 and 6). Rather,
these polities established their own exchange networks, obtaining obsidian and
other exotic goods from overlapping sets of sources in varying proportions.

The sizes of the territories under direct control of Olmec capitals remain
uncertain. Earlier applications of central-place and peer-polity models arrived
at estimates of about 20 to 25 km for the radius of Olmec polities (Bove 1978;
Gómez Rueda 1996; cf. Earle 1976: Figure 7.9). These estimates, however,
do not take into account differences in the size and relative power of capitals
in different periods. Although a radius of 25 km seems a reasonable average,
it is likely that more powerful polities had larger territories than less powerful
but autonomous contemporaries. Furthermore, alliances between some capitals
may have been unequal, as in the case of San Lorenzo and Laguna de los Cerros
(cf. Borstein 2001), and Olmecs may have occasionally established colonies or
diaspora communities beyond Olman, as appears to have occurred at Cantón
Corralito (Cheetham 2005).

What tied the societies of Olman together was a shared set of beliefs and practices expressed in iconography and craft technology, the widespread adoption of
which attests to the openness of communication among Olmec societies. Even

shared styles of artifacts and art show local variation, however. Distinctive, temporally overlapping "schools" of monumental sculpture, can be distinguished for San Lorenzo, Laguna de los Cerros, and possibly La Venta in the Early Formative, and among La Venta, Laguna de los Cerros, and Tres Zapotes in the Middle Formative (de la Fuente 2000; cf. Clewlow 1974). Likewise, Early Formative pottery motifs and figurines from La Joya differ in several respects from those of San Lorenzo, and some show greater similarity with artifact styles in the Mexican highlands, suggesting different patterns of interregional interaction in eastern and western Olman (Arnold 2001; Arnold and Follensbee 2003).

Olmec society and culture also were dynamic. Major and minor Olmec centers rose and fell, settlement hierarchies expanded and contracted, and regional populations grew and declined in a veritable kaleidoscope of developmental sequences across Olman. Monumental art, although perpetuating particular elements of iconography and themes of rulership and cosmology, changed over the centuries in form and content, increasingly emphasizing narrative reliefs and historical events. In Olman, as elsewhere, portable art in exotic stone increasingly shouldered the burden of iconographic representation previously expressed in pottery, promoting more restricted access to the symbols of earth, sky, and the *axis mundi* that legitimized ruling authority. At the same time, the character of Olmec interaction with societies beyond Olman changed, becoming more targeted and more explicitly defined in terms of elite alliances.

The diversity and dynamism of Olmec societies have profound implications for understanding their development. Most importantly, processes that responded to specific local conditions cannot be generalized to the development of Olmec culture as a whole. Control over river levees and riverine transportation nodes may have contributed to the emergence of social hierarchies at San Lorenzo and La Venta, but they are unlikely to have been important in the more upland settings of Laguna de los Cerros and Tres Zapotes. Granted, if San Lorenzo had extended its dominion over all of Olman, as Monte Alban later did over the Valley of Oaxaca, then explaining its unique development might constitute a sufficient explanation for the evolution of Olmec society, but the evidence simply does not support such a scenario.

Neither can the emergence of hierarchies elsewhere in Olman simply be explained as a response to a powerful competitor at San Lorenzo; the timing of events is too variable. Before the San Lorenzo phase, when San Lorenzo was still a large village of about 20 ha (Symonds et al. 2002: 56), Estero Rabón was already substantially larger than nearby sites, covering 60 to 80 ha (Borstein 2001: 151). Politically, the two sites were, at least, evenly matched at this time – if Estero Rabón did not, in fact, hold the upper hand. Later, Laguna de los Cerros may have reached its Formative period height at the same time as San Lorenzo, but La Venta and Tres Zapotes experienced their major florescences after San

Lorenzo's decline. Meanwhile, other Olmec societies failed or declined to develop social ranks at all.

The variable ecological conditions detailed in Chapter 3 surely contributed to the diversity of Olmec sociopolitical organization. The abundance of wild resources, the agricultural productivity of soils, and the kinds and severity of risks (from floods, fluctuations in rainfall, and volcanic eruptions) varied unevenly across Olman. The riverine and estuarine environments of the Coatzacoalcos and Tonalá drainages provided a particularly abundant and stable resource base for the mixed subsistence economy that began to be established in the Late Archaic period. These areas may have had an early advantage in attracting foragers and incipient horticulturalists, and they were capable of generating large subsistence surpluses to support the political activities of Olmec leaders. It is not clear why similar environments in the Papaloapan delta do not appear to have been settled as early or to have supported large Early and Middle Formative centers, although more severe and less predictable flooding may have been a factor. Settlement patterns in the San Juan drainage suggest an early focus on the river floodplain, with gradual expansion into piedmont zones more dependent on rainfall agriculture (Borstein 2001). Maize was introduced to the Tuxtla Mountains by 2880 B.C. and became an important subsistence item in the Early Formative period, and fish, turtles, snails, and other aquatic resources were available in the region's lakes and rivers (Goman 1998; VanDerwarker 2006). In general, however, the forests that covered the Tuxtlas are less attractive for foragers, and they require greater expenditures of labor in field clearance. Aquatic resources also are less abundant and less widely distributed than in the large lowland river basins, and the Early Formative inhabitants of La Joya relied more heavily on wild terrestrial fauna than did their contemporaries at San Lorenzo. In addition, volcanic eruptions add an unpredictable component to agricultural risk in the Tuxtlas. Thus, several characteristics of the Tuxtlas environment may have helped delay the development of permanent settlement and the emergence of large centers.

Despite these variations in productivity and risk, however, it is important to recognize that the environment of Olman provided relatively abundant resources for the mixed subsistence economy adopted by the Olmecs. Further, populations appear to have remained well within the carrying capacity of the environment, except possibly for a restricted portion of the hinterland immediately surrounding San Lorenzo during that site's apogee (Symonds et al. 2002: 75–79). Neither do the Coatzacoalcos basin or other parts of Olman appear to have been highly circumscribed by the natural or social environment. Therefore, population pressure and competition over subsistence resources do not provide convincing explanations for the rise of Olmec sociopolitical hierarchies (cf. Sanders and Webster 1978; Coe 1981).

As I have argued throughout this book, variation in Formative sociopolitical organization in Olman is most fully understood in terms of the strategies

employed by political actors operating within specific environmental and historical contexts. Political leaders typically draw on multiple sources of power
to attract and retain followers and to attain and keep their positions in society
(Blanton et al. 1996; Earle 1997: 4–10; Mann 1986). Those sources of power
may include social relationships, control over economic resources, military
might, or ideological precepts that support claims to authority (Earle 1997:
4–10).

Economic power is based on the ability to grant or withhold resources
that are needed for existence or desired for the material or social advantages
they provide (Earle 1997: 6–7; Hirth 1996). Economic strategies focus on the
accumulation of resources that can be expended to secure loyalty, either through
direct disbursements or in civic and ceremonial projects perceived to benefit
the group as a whole. Leaders and political institutions may seek direct com-
pensation for their services, lay claim to the surplus production of foodstuffs
and crafts, or control the distribution of resources and the networks through
which they flow (Hirth 1996: 209).

Military might is another obvious source of political power, and it is one
which frequently provides economic benefits (Carneiro 1970). Directed outward, military raids offer a means of accumulating wealth, and conquests secure
tribute, labor, and land. Directed toward subordinates and potential competitors within a society, threats of violent force, selectively applied, allow military
leaders to coerce compliance On the other hand, the use of military power to
enforce demands carries substantial risks of treachery, usurpation, and rebellion
(Earle 1997: 8).

Social relationships define rights and obligations among individuals, including those concerned with property, inheritance, cooperation, defense, privilege, and authority. They include relationships of kinship (consanguineal, affi-
nal, and "fictive"), peer relationships among friends, sodality members, and
exchange partners, and unequal relationships between patron and client, ruler
and ruled, commander and warrior. In other words, political and economic
relationships are fundamentally social relationships, and the manipulation of
social relationships beyond those that are explicitly political and economic is
one source of power for political actors.

Leaders in a broad range of societies can expand their power through strategic
and multiple marriages and adoptions, or the extension of kin-like relationships
to non-kin (Earle 1997: 5). However, such relationships also place reciprocal
obligations on heads of household, lineage, clan, and faction, and social mores
limit the exercise of power with respect to different classes of kin and associates.
Moreover, each person in a society is at the center of a network of kindred
and associates on whom they may draw support. Therefore, although political
leaders must employ and cultivate social relationships to lead effectively, claims
to power based on social relationships tend to be widely distributed and multi-
centered (Earle 1997: 6). Ultimately, rights to control the power derived from

social relationships lie in the ethics attending that relationship, and relationships beyond those of consanguineal kin more often than not must be validated by economic exchanges of goods or labor.

The ideas shared by the members of a society about the structure of the cosmos, the nature of supernatural forces and beings, and the proper relationship of humans to these and to one another are sources of order and legitimacy in all societies (Baines and Yoffee 2000). As applied to structure and practice in social, political, and economic systems these "cognitive codes" (Blanton et al. 1996) constitute ideology. In complex societies, ideologies legitimize the rights of individuals and groups to accumulate and allocate resources and to exercise force – they also specify how and when resources and force must be used toward the benefit of the collective. Ideologies, however, are rarely so monolithic that they cannot be used toward different, even diametrically opposed, ends – witness the use of Biblical scripture in the history of Western countries to argue for and against slavery, monarchy, capital punishment, and war. Thus, there is ample opportunity for political actors to manipulate ideologies: (1) by emphasizing those existing concepts that suit their agendas, (2) by extending existing concepts (e.g., regarding kinship and patrimony) through analogy and metaphor to legitimate emerging statuses and institutions, (3) by importing new concepts and melding them with old ones or restricting them to specific contexts, or (4) by promulgating new ideologies (whether imported or of their own making) when the old ones no longer seem to work.

In addition to legitimizing the use of economic, military, or social sources of power, ideological concepts can also be a source of power in their own right, as when religious specialists draw on belief in their abilities to communicate with the spirit world to persuade or coerce others into meeting their demands. To be most effective as a source of political power, however, ideology must be materialized in physical symbols and ceremonies, the creation, use, and performance of which can be controlled by political actors (DeMarrais et al. 1996). By controlling the labor, materials, and knowledge employed in the processes of creation and display, elites can also control the meanings of symbolic objects and acts. Because the recipients of symbolic communication also participate in the construction of its meaning, however, elite control is not absolute. Subjects and members of other, interacting, cultures can alter the meanings of symbols, and such reinterpretation often becomes a tool of resistance.

Thus, political power derives from control over resources in economic, social (including military), or ideological domains, and combinations thereof. These domains constitute sources of power, and identifying their relative significance (and the significance of the specific resources they encompass) in constructing power relationships in particular societies is an important component of politico-economic analysis. Control in this context refers to the ability to restrict access to resources and to direct others toward particular ends (cf. Earle 1997: 4). The ways in which control over material and ideological resources is achieved and used to enhance and extend power constitute political strategies, as do the ways in which power itself is employed.

Critical issues in the analysis of political strategies include the extent to which leaders can gain exclusive rights to obtain and exercise power or must share power with others, and the degree to which power is directed toward self-aggrandizement or providing for the common good (Blanton et al. 1996; Blanton 1998; Feinman 2000). Of course, the latter practice need not be entirely selfless, as expending one's own economic and social resources in communal activities is a common way to enhance personal prestige, build trust, and encourage others to cede authority. Indeed, it is this pursuit of enlightened self-interest, together with the benefits to weaker factions of demanding a voice in governance, that makes strategies of practices termed "collective" (Kolb 1996: 59), "communal" (Stark 2000: 37), or "corporate" (Blanton et al. 1996: 2). What is most important for the succeeding discussion is to recognize that the sets of strategies broadly glossed as exclusionary and corporate are complementary means to acquire and retain power, potentially available to leaders in all societies, which may be employed alternately with respect to different contexts and circumstances, or for that matter simultaneously with respect to different social and political scales, even if one appears dominant at a particular scale (cf. Blanton et al. 1996: 7).

Olmec archaeology offers ample evidence of political leaders manipulating multiple sources of power and of their employing them toward individualizing aggrandizement as well as communal projects with collective themes (Stark 2000: 36–37). In the lowland river valleys and the Tuxtlas piedmont, powerful early rulers erected monumental portraits and depicted themselves as cosmic mediators on their altar-thrones. At San Lorenzo, they lived in elaborate residences, accumulated vast quantities of exotic iron-ore artifacts, and at times may have controlled the distribution of basalt for utilitarian implements. On the other hand, numerous sculptures of felines and other animals at San Lorenzo are not obviously individualized representations of rulers, whereas earlier and contemporaneous celt offerings in the spring at El Manatí and at La Merced suggest collective themes of fertility and renewal. As the Middle Formative period progressed, rulers at La Venta and Tres Zapotes glorified their activities on low-relief stelae. At La Venta rulers had themselves interred in elaborate tombs and imported thousands of tons of serpentine and jade, but they expended much of these resources in massive buried offerings and pavements that express cosmological themes. Meanwhile, Early and Middle Formative settlements in the central Tuxtla Mountains do not exhibit great discrepancies in household or mortuary wealth (Santley et al. 1997; McCormack 2002). Therefore, although a household might acquire the occasional ilmenite cube or greenstone bead, group leadership in the Tuxtlas probably emphasized reciprocal obligations and equitable distributions of exotic utilitarian goods such as obsidian.

Competition among leaders for control over sources of power helps explain variation in Olmec sociopolitical organization, and provides a framework for integrating environmental, economic, and political factors in its historical development. Differing degrees of social hierarchy and political integration are to be expected as a consequence of the variable success leaders had in controlling local and extraregional sources of power and attracting local followers. In large part, variable success can be attributed to differences in the social and political skills of individual leaders and their ability to build on the successes of their predecessors. Failure to retain followers, whether due to local political mismanagement, environmental disaster, or disruptions in prestige-good exchange systems, results in the cycling fortunes of early complex polities. Such cycling is exemplified dramatically by the asynchronous abandonment of Olmec centers and the collapse of their sustaining populations. On a regional scale, this cycling contributed greatly to the persistent variation in Olmec sociopolitical organization.

In addition, environmental variation within Olman offered different sources of material power to aspiring leaders, with variable potential for mobilizing surplus production, controlling local distribution networks, and extracting resources for exchange to the leaders of other polities. In particular, the complementary distributions of resources such as basalt in the Tuxtlas piedmont; red ochre (hematite), fine kaolin pottery clay, salt, and bitumen in the middle Coatzacoalcos basin; and cacao, marine shell, salt, and bitumen in the Tabasco lowlands, gave the leaders of Laguna de los Cerros, San Lorenzo, and La Venta differential access to exchange goods not universally available across Olman (Grove 1994). Although some materials – basalt, salt, and bitumen – had utilitarian uses, basalt also served as a prestige good in its use for monuments. It is also likely that the receivers of massive basalt stones were responsible for their transport. The important point, however, is that the differential distribution of resources in Olman encouraged the development of social networks by aspiring leaders to acquire locally unavailable prestige goods as well as critical materials for utilitarian artifacts (cf. Rathje 1972). The individual efforts by local leaders to establish long-distance exchange partnerships also accounts for contemporaneous variation in obsidian sources at different sites.

Patterns of difference and similarity in art and artifact styles within Olman also are consistent with politico-economic strategies based in competition to monopolize sources of power locally and to establish networks for the acquisition of strategic non-local goods. Political leaders monopolizing ideological sources of power must employ a symbolic vocabulary broadly understood by their followers and allies. In the Olmec case, leaders drew upon a common and ancient cosmology that favored specific ideas regarding the source of legitimate power, including the ability of shamans to communicate between the earth and sky realms and between the human and supernatural worlds (Furst 1995; Reilly 1995; Schele 1995; Taube 1995). Leaders shaped that ideology to

their own political ends and built upon it over successive generations, insert-
ing themselves in the shamanic role as supreme and exclusive mediators. In
doing so, they imprinted their own vision on symbolic representations of
their authority, which along with the transmission of technical knowledge
by artisans, created the subtle variations in artistic traditions that de la Fuente
identifies as "schools" of Olmec monumental art. Likewise, variable contacts
with specific regions beyond Olman contributed to the differences observed
in Early Formative pottery and figurine styles between the Tuxtla Mountains
and the middle Coatzacoalcos basin. On the other hand, networks of social
and economic interaction within Olman spread technical, political, and esoteric knowledge, which in combination with a common substrate of beliefs
and their iconographic representation, created the underlying unity of a Gulf
Olmec art style.

THE OLMEC LEGACY

How did the Olmecs contribute to the development of Mesoamerican civilization? The origins of the Classic civilizations of Teotihuacan, Monte Alban,
Veracruz, the Maya, and others lie in the practices, institutions, and ideologies
that evolved over the course of the Formative period. The Olmecs were important participants in the Early and Middle Formative networks of social and economic interaction that fostered the rise of social and political hierarchies and
diffused elements of symbolism, ritual, and belief across Mesoamerica. In this
sense, there can be no dispute that the Olmecs did contribute to the development of specific Mesoamerican civilizations and to Mesoamerican civilization
in general. If these interaction spheres, as reflected in pan-Mesoamerican styles
of art and iconography, are what are conceived as "Olmec," then the argument
ends there. That is not what lies at the heart of the debate between Mother
Culture adherents and their detractors, but rather the degree to which the Gulf
Olmecs shaped the course of Mesoamerican history through their influence
on their contemporaries and their specific contributions to their successors.

Although there was great diversity in the cultural expressions and sociopolitical arrangements of Classic Mesoamerican civilizations, they also shared
many features. Among them were the social stratification, hierarchical integration of territories, and populous centers that are generally characteristic
of civilizations. More specifically, Mesoamerican were shared religious concepts and practices that included the division of the cosmos into vertical tiers;
common deity complexes that represented forces of creation, nature, and destiny; a cyclical concept of time that included multiple creations and destructions and that was incorporated into a common calendrical system based on
the permutation of 260- and 365-day periods; and rituals that included the
sacred rubber ball game, human sacrifice and blood offerings, and ceremonial
precincts with plazas and temple pyramids, often laid out with astronomical and

cosmological referents (Kirchoff 1943; see also Joyce 2004; Matos 2000). In addition, Mesoamerica was the only area of the New World that developed indigenous writing systems.

The Classic period cultural traits commonly attributed to an Olmec legacy span the interrelated realms of economy; society and government; and art, iconography, and ritual (e.g., Clark 1997; Diehl and Coe 1995; cf. Flannery and Marcus 2000). In the economic realm the Olmecs are credited with the creation of extensive trade networks that moved large quantities of exotic materials long distances and the assignment of high value to greenstone, iron ore, shell, and other, more perishable, materials (Diehl and Coe 1995: 23). In the sociopolitical arena they are argued to have developed the first stratified societies with exalted hereditary rulers, or kings (Clark 1997), who ruled large territories through multitiered, hierarchical settlement systems (Diehl and Coe 1995: 23). The largest category of traits attributed to Olmec origins concern art, iconography, and ritual. As enumerated by Diehl and Coe (1995: 23) these include: special sites of sacred ritual at springs, caves, and mountaintops; cosmological town plans; a sophisticated symbol system expressed in a coherent art style; monumental stone sculpture; the ball game and ritual use of rubber; and infant sacrifice in water-related rituals.

How can one evaluate claims for the specific cultural origin of a trait? Temporal priority is the first and most basic consideration, but it alone is not enough, for later cultures may hit upon similar ideas independently. This is less likely if the trait in question is highly specific, arbitrary, and/or complex; that is, if it is not determined by functional requirements, not grounded in a shared history of meaningful associations or universal cognitive structures, and not so simple as to be obvious or easily accomplished without training. This second criterion of specificity is most readily appreciated with respect to elements of artifact style and iconography, but it may be extended to architectural layouts, ceremonial practices, technology, and even sociopolitical institutions.

The third consideration is the demonstration of cultural transmission, either through space (diffusion or interaction) or time (continuity). These are linked in that traits diffused in one era may persist, often with modifications, in subsequent eras. Cultural continuity does not mean lack of change but, rather, the demonstration of direct historical linkages through time. Furthermore, demonstrating the diffusion of traits through cultural interaction is not a simple matter of observing that those traits are shared by contemporaneous cultures. First, traits may be shared as a consequence of descent from a common specific origin, or they may derive from more general antecedent conditions, such as ancient, widely held, beliefs (e.g., Grove 1993: 91). Second, demonstrating the direction of transmission is often difficult owing to the imprecision of archaeological dating and the fact that horizon styles, by definition, are disseminated rapidly over wide areas. Third, diffusion is a multivariate phenomenon, which may reflect direct or indirect interaction, and may result from the imposition of foreign styles or their emulation and adaptation to local circumstances. The diffusion may involve migrations of people, exchange of goods, transmission of ideas, or reactions to interregional political and economic competition (e.g., Schortman and Urban 1992; Stark 2000: 40–43). The succeeding discussion focuses first on evidence regarding the temporal priority, specificity, and coeval diffusion of traits then turns to questions of continuity.

Priority, Specificity, and Diffusion

Everyone involved in the debate recognizes that Olmec societies were not the first in Mesoamerica to engage in long-distance exchange. Obsidian was already exchanged widely in Mesoamerica in the Archaic period, most likely through a series of short, "down-the-line" hops, and inland villages in places like the Valley of Oaxaca acquired small amounts of marine shell from the coasts. By the Early Formative period, communities throughout Mesoamerica were participating in the exchange networks that moved these items and modest amounts of pottery, greenstone, and other minerals over substantial distances. Where the Early Formative Olmecs *do* stand out is in the variety and breadth of their interregional exchange contacts. For example, whereas most Early Formative villages obtained their obsidian from five or fewer sources, the San Lorenzo Olmecs used obsidian from eight or more sources, distributed from Michoacan to Guatemala (Cobean et al. 1971; Nelson and Clark 1998: Table 1; Pires-Ferreira 1976: Table 10.4). Chemical sourcing also documents the export of pottery from the San Lorenzo area to regions ranging from the Valley of Mexico to the Soconusco (Blomster et al. 2004).

Estimating the volume of exchange in these and other materials is much more difficult than specifying their sources. It stands to reason that a site the size of San Lorenzo would have consumed more obsidian overall than its smaller contemporaries, but per capita obsidian consumption rates are difficult to compare using the published data (Cobean et al. 1972; Coe and Diehl 1980a), With the exception of the tons of ilmenite cubes that were imported by San Lorenzo, it is not clear that the Early Formative Olmecs were unusual in the quantity of prestige goods they acquired from beyond their region. They did move impressive quantities of basalt over the landscape, but this has no bearing on long-distance exchange. The recovery of numerous greenstone celts in Early Formative offerings at El Manatí also is notable, but it is hard to assess the overall volume of greenstone imports based on this very specific context or to compare it with assemblages from other parts of Mesoamerica.

The volume of Olmec prestige-good exchange increases dramatically after about 800 B.C. when the rulers of La Venta started to bury hundreds – and, ultimately, thousands – of tons of greenstone in massive offerings, which surpass anything known from elsewhere in Middle Formative Mesoamerica. The means by which the Middle Formative Olmec rulers acquired exotic prestige

goods also appear to have become more directed, exclusive, and centrally organized than their neighbors or predecessors, and in this they may have contributed to the evolution of Mesoamerican exchange systems, although the
Late Formative evidence suggests significant disruption and regionalization of
exchange networks with increasing competition from rival centers. Neither do
the Olmecs appear to have been unique in assigning early value to the goods
that were widely exchanged, this having more to do with the intrinsic qualities of the materials, their local scarcity, and the symbolic associations of goods
from distant lands (e.g., Helms 1993). Furthermore, extensive trade in exotic
materials is a fundamental characteristic of exclusionary (network) politico-
economic strategies, and is therefore better understood as a consequence of
the internal social dynamics of later political systems than as an Olmec legacy.

The Olmecs also were not the first in Mesoamerica to develop centralized
political systems and ranked social statuses. Currently that honor goes to the
Locona phase societies in the Mazatán region (Chapter 6). San Lorenzo, however, soon surpassed its contemporaries in the hierarchical differentiation of
its sociopolitical system. No other Early Formative center was as large, and
among other regions, only Mazatán is known to have developed a three-tiered
settlement hierarchy before 1000 B.C. (Clark 1997: Figure 3 [corrected to calibrated dates]; Marcus and Flannery 1994: 106–107; cf. Symonds et al. 2002).
Determining the scale of Olmec political territories is not a simple matter, as
they rely on debatable interpretations of the temporal and political relationships
among Olmec centers and often incomplete information on hinterland settlement. A typical diameter of about 40 to 50 km is a reasonable guess (Bove 1978;
Earle 1976; Gómez Rueda 1996; 116–119), but rulers of larger, more powerful
centers probably consolidated larger territories under their administration and
may have extended their influence yet farther through assymetrical alliances.
That said, the ease with which ideas and materials flowed across Olman, despite
subregional variation, suggests territories were not strongly bounded. By comparison, Tlatilco, Chalcatzingo, San José Mogote, and Cantón Corralito all
appear to have controlled territories less than about 15 km across. La Blanca's
early Middle Formative political territory may have been on a par with the
Olmec estimates, if it encompassed Izapa, over 30 km away (Love 1999: 132).
In sum, the territories controlled by Olmec capitals do appear to have been
in the upper range for Early and Middle Formative polities, although some
others may have been comparable after about 1000 B.C.

By all indications, the Olmec rulers of San Lorenzo were precocious in
the degree to which they asserted their elevated social status and political
authority. Although some leaders elsewhere, most notably at Paso de la Amada,
also lived in large, elaborate residences, no Early Formative leaders outside of
Olman mobilized the amount of labor expressed in the transport of scores of
impressively heavy basalt monuments over 60 km to San Lorenzo. Nor did they
express their exalted positions as explicitly in colossal portraits and thrones as

did the Olmec rulers. Olmec leaders undoubtedly controlled access to prestige goods, as did some of their counterparts elsewhere. Whether they also achieved the control over access to basic resources that underlies social stratification (Fried 1960: 186) is still an open question Systems of land tenure are difficult to document archaeologically, and there is no evidence for large storage facilities of any kind. If their identification is correct, the strongest evidence for control over utilitarian goods are the monument recycling workshops of San Lorenzo (Cyphers 1996: 66; 1997b: 181–184; cf. Clark 1996: 193), but we simply do not know to what extent nonelites may have independently acquired basalt and worked it into grinding stones. It seems likely that Olmec rulers controlled the acquisition of obsidian and its distribution to their subjects. They also may have controlled the specialized technology for prismatic blade production, accounting for the greater occurrence of blades in centers (Clark 1987), but they do not appear to have restricted access to obsidian in general or the technology for making it into flake tools.

Was interaction with the Olmecs specifically responsible for the development of similar sociopolitical institutions in other Mesoamerican societies? Categories of social and political systems are not specific enough, in and of themselves, to resolve the question. Paramount chiefdoms, stratified societies, and states are all general kinds of sociopolitical systems that have developed time and again around the world. Moreover, population increases, the practices of aspiring local leaders, and competition with societies other than the Olmecs all were probable factors in the development of complex Formative societies. In other words, the simple conclusion that the Olmecs were the first does not guarantee they were the cause of similar developments elsewhere in Mesoamerica.

What *is* specific to the Olmec case are the particular forms in which political authority was expressed. Therefore, an argument for Olmec influence on sociopolitical developments is strengthened when such forms of expression can be demonstrated. For the Early Formative period, the case is strongest for the Mazatán region where Olmec-style stone monuments have been found, and reorganization of settlement hierarchies appears to have occurred in concert with a period of specifically Olmec contacts (Cheetham 2005; Clark 1990b, 1997; Clark and Pye 2000b). Elsewhere, Early Formative Olmec interaction seems to have been more a consequence than a cause of increasing sociopolitical complexity.

During the Middle Formative period, Olmec-style relief sculptures with themes of rulership and alliance are widely distributed and generally associated with centers, suggesting that Olmec principles of rulership had wider influence. At Chalcatzingo, especially, rulers adopted Olmec politico-religious iconography and practice into their legitimizing programs. However, increasing sociopolitical complexity was already a well-established trend in all these regions, and emerging centers had closer competitors and allies. Meanwhile, other regions, including the Basin of Mexico and the Valley of Oaxaca, pursued their own paths toward increasing sociopolitical complexity with little or no direct Olmec contact in the Middle Formative period.

Turning to the ideological realm, the claim for temporal priority of Olmec cosmological town plans is ambiguous (cf. Diehl and Coe 1995: 23). Clark (2004) argues that the earlier Mazatán site of Paso de la Amada was planned and constructed as a ceremonial center by the Locona phase (1650–1500 B.C.) using regular arrangements of spatial modules based on a native measurement unit (1.666 m) combined in multiples and simple fractions of 13, 20, 52, 260, and 365 (Clark 2004: 59). These numbers also define cycles in later Mesoamerican calendar counts, suggesting that the builders of Paso de la Amada may have encoded cosmological cyles of time in the layout of their center.

Later, in Olman, the distribution of monuments in the elite precinct at the summit of the San Lorenzo plateau suggests they were placed with respect to directional symbolism. Colossal heads and altars tend to cluster along two parallel north-south axes, whereas other monuments cluster to the west of these axes and are themselves concentrated along two parallel east-west axes that intersect the first pair in the site center. Grove (1994: 282) suggests an association of north with ancestors based on the location of two heads recarved from thrones, presuming they were carved after the death of the rulers they represent. There is also a hint of modular spatial units here, but with unequal north-south and east-west dimentions.

The most obvious example of a cosmological town plan in Olman is La Venta (Reilly 1999; Tate 1999). As discussed in Chapter 5, monument styles and some excavated materials suggest temporal overlap with Early Formative San Lorenzo. The basic orientation of the site to 8° W of north was probably established by early in the Middle Formative period, ca. 900 B.C. (Clark and Hansen 2001: 3; Drucker et al. 1959). The identical orientation of public architecture in the Valley of Oaxaca was long thought to have derived from contact with La Venta, but it is now known to have been established earlier (Flannery and Marcus 1994: 31). Several elements of La Venta's public architecture (especially Complexes B, C, and the northern part of Complex D) are shared by Middle Formative sites in Chiapas, including Chiapa de Corzo (Clark and Hansen 2001). These include a central plaza measuring about 160 × 320 m and oriented north-south, with the tallest mound at the north, a low central mound at about the midpoint, a broad "acropolis" (probably an elite residential compound) to the east, other low mounds to the west, and at the south end a pairing of a long mound flanked by a conical mound or pyramid on the west, which resembles later Maya "E-Groups" (named for Group E at Uaxactun) (Clark and Hansen 2001: 4). The Chiapas sites lack a complex at the north end comporable to Complex A at La Venta (though a similar arrangement is seen in the long platforms extending south from Mound 17 in the center of the plaza at Chiapa de Corzo), and there are other variations in the precise orientations and mound dimensions in each. Nevertheless, the specificity and overall arrangements of architectural elements at these sites rather strongly suggests diffusion through a network of interaction. La Venta may well have provided the model for some or all of the elements, as Clark and Hansen (2001) argue, but some of the relevant construction at Chiapa de Corzo dates to the Chiapa II phase (ca. 1000–800 B.C.) (Clark and Hansen, pp. 6–8). The construction sequences in Complexes B and C and the "E-Group" at La Venta are still too poorly known to rule out mutual borrowings between these two sites.

Large temple mounds also can be thought of as a kind of cosmogram, in that they connect earth and sky realms. By all indications, however, La Venta's mound C-1 was preceded by large earthen mounds at La Blanca and other Pacific Coast sites in Chiapas and Guatemala. The Early and Middle Formative site plans of other Gulf Olmec centers are too poorly known to assess whether they were also laid out as cosmograms. In any event, the division of the cosmos into vertical layers and of the earth's surface into a center and four quadrants with associated directional symbolism are widespread and apparently ancient concepts in Mesoamerican thought; site plans that reflect these concepts in a general fashion cannot conclusively be attributed to Olmec contact.

The Olmecs did view springs, mountains, and caves as sacred places from early times (Diehl and Coe 1995: 23), but so do most cultures. The kinds and arrangements of offerings made at Olmec sacred locales are more distinctive. El Manatí contains the earliest known non-burial offerings of polished greenstone celts, dated to about 1700 B.C. Between 1500 and 1200 B.C., celts were being placed carefully in the spring in bundles, flower-shaped arrangements, north-south and east-west lines, and a rough quincunx. These seem clearly ancestral to the celt offerings of La Venta and of San Isidro in the Central Depression of Chiapas. The waterlogged El Manatí offerings of 1700 B.C. and later also contain the earliest rubber balls known from Mesoamerica. Rubber is a tropical lowland product, and is unlikely to have been first used in the Mesoamerican highlands. Moreover, although rubber trees are common throughout the Mesoamerican lowlands, mixing morning glory sap with raw latex to enhance its elasticity is not an obvious technological innovation (Hosler et al. 1999). Thus, although Paso de la Amada may have the earliest formal ballcourt (Hill et al. 1998), until earlier balls and courts are found, the Olmecs have a reasonable claim to having initiated the ball game and to having been the first to use rubber in a ritual context (Diehl and Coe 1995: 23; cf. Flannery and Marcus 2000: 8).

The sacrificed infants offered in the El Manatí spring are the earliest known example of the association of water and infant sacrifice in Mesoamerica. Although it may not be "earth-shattering" that inhabitants of the humid coastal lowlands used a spring for such sacrifices (Flannery and Marcus 2000: 8), springs also exist in the highlands, and water scarcity is a greater concern there. More tellingly, the Aztecs explained the association by reference to the tears of the infants, which were taken as a good omen for rain (Carrasco 1999: 85). Thus, while the specific water-infant sacrifice association at El Manatí is suggestive, other cultures may have hit upon the same idea independently of an Olmec legacy.

The most serious claim for a pervasive Olmec legacy in Mesoamerica is the contention that the Olmecs created the "oldest, fully elaborated system of conventionalized symbols and symbol complexes" (Diehl and Coe 1995: 23), that the Olmecs disseminated this system widely through their art style, and that elements of these symbolic representations and their referential meanings persisted among the descendants of the Olmecs and the Formative cultures with which they interacted (Coe 1989). The dissemination of this style is usually conceived as occurring in two waves, the earlier one attributed to the Early Formative influence of San Lorenzo, and the later one (often divided chronologically into "Modified Olmec" and "Terminal Olmec" Horizons, see Chapter 6) attributed to Middle Formative La Venta (Diehl and Coe 1995: 23). Many of the symbols and motifs of the "Middle Formative Ceremonial Complex" (Chapter 5) first appear on Early Horizon ceramics, however, so most attention has focused on the Early Formative period.

Most of the motifs that define the Early Horizon are conventionalized, abstract, and complex. It is therefore unlikely that different societies across Mesoamerica independently developed the full set of symbols at about the same time. That does not, however, mean that the entire set of Early Horizon motifs necessarily had a single origin, just that once developed they were rapidly adopted by other societies. For the most part, archaeological dating techniques do not provide the resolution necessary to specify where particular Early Horizon motifs first developed. The exceptions include music brackets and certain varieties of the double-line-break in Oaxaca (Flannery and Marcus 1994), Tlatilco-style profile heads and cross-hatched spiked medallions in central Mexico (Niederberger 1986), and possibly one style of hollow, white-slipped baby figurines in Olman (Blomster 2002). These exceptions strongly suggest that some of the Early Horizon symbols did have diverse origins. In addition, variants of the Early Horizon developed in different regions, apparently rapidly, as shared motifs, and concepts were elaborated and adapted to local technological traditions, social circumstances, and ideologies.

The most widely disseminated Early Formative pottery style consisted of white-and-black to gray vessels with boldly carved, abstract, and conventionalized representations of composite zoomorphs ("sky-serpents" and "earth-monsters"). Consistent elements of these representations include cleft heads, flame eyebrows, inverted U-shaped gum brackets, crossed bands, and the paw-wing motif. This particular constellation of motifs and technology is so distinctive and complex that it is unlikely to have had multiple origins. Where it first appeared is more difficult to say, however. Black wares have a longer history, and were more prevalent, in the transisthmian lowlands (including Olman) and central Chiapas. It is therefore possible that the technological style incorporating carved designs on black pottery developed within this zone. It also is interesting that the most naturalistic Early Formative representations of the supernatural beings abstracted on pottery appear on carved Olmec monuments, but these monuments are no earlier than the ceramics. Chemical evidence documents the exchange of pottery with Early Horizon motifs from Olman to other regions, suggesting a prominent role for the Olmec in disseminating the pottery style (Blomster et al. 2005), but each of these areas also produced black or gray pottery with Early Horizon motifs, both carved and incised, locally, and the possibility of some exchange of pottery (and diffusion of pottery motifs) among regions outside of Olman remains. In highland Mexico, the variety of motifs was greater than in Olman, and in Oaxaca pottery with all varieties of Early Horizon motifs make up a slightly larger proportion of the assemblage (Flannery and Marcus 2000; Stark 2004).[1] Whether these highland expressions of the carved black ware style represent elaborations of a Gulf Olmec tradition, or the Gulf Olmec tradition a simplification of a style acquired from elsewhere, simply cannot be resolved with current evidence.

The degree to which the Olmecs were responsible for the spread of Middle Formative symbols also is uncertain. Many of the symbols and forms that constitute the material expression of the Middle Formative Ceremonial Complex derive from Early Horizon motifs that were already widely disseminated, and the shared ceramic motifs of the early Middle Formative, particularly the double-line-break, originated outside Olman. The other symbols are most frequently found on portable items of jade, serpentine, and other stones that were widely traded from their sources, also outside Olman. Some of the traded items probably were carved by Olmecs, but regional stylistic variations indicate that many were not.

Some elements of the Middle Formative Ceremonial Complex do, however, appear to have a Gulf Olmec inspiration. For example, more-or-less naturalistic representations of were-jaguars (Joralemon's "God IV"), such as those seen in Middle Formative votive axes, appear first in Early Formative Olmec monumental art (e.g., San Lorenzo Monuments 10 and 52). "Transformation figures" generally adhere to Gulf Olmec sculptural conventions of rounded volumes and swelling masses, and they are presaged by Early Formative Olmec sculptures of humans with feline attributes and felines with human attributes. Most are also claimed to have been found on the Gulf Coast (Furst 1995: Figures 1, 2, 3, 7, 9; Guthrie and Benson 1995: pp. 168–172). The Olmecs of La Venta also were involved to an unusual extent in the acquisition of exotic greenstones from widely dispersed sources, and it is reasonable to conclude that they had a greater role in disseminating Middle Formative symbol complexes than areas that participated in more restricted exchange networks.

The Gulf Olmecs also made early steps toward writing, as seen in the glyphlike elements on La Venta Monument 13 and on the cylinder seal and plaque fragments from San Andres (see also Note 3, Chapter 7). These are almost certainly ancestral to the epi-Olmec writing system of the southern Gulf lowlands and Chiapas, and probably to the closely related Izapan-Mayan writing system. The Olmecs were not the only ones experimenting with writing in the Late Middle Formative period, however, because the first inscriptions in the very different Zapotec writing system appear at essentially the same time (Flannery and Marcus 2003; cf. Pohl et al. 2002).

The Olmecs were the first in Mesoamerica to carve stone sculptures on a monumental scale (cf. Graham 1981, 1989). The full-round and relief styles of carving that developed in Olman also are so distinctive that they convincingly demonstrate Olmec influence in other regions, particularly along the Pacific slope of southeastern Mesoamerica and in a fairly narrow zone across the Mexican highlands to Guerrero. Furthermore, the Olmecs were the first to use this medium to express the authority of individual rulers and its legitimation grounded in myth, cosmology, descent, and ceremony. Although its historical links to later sculptural traditions of the Mexican highlands are tenuous, Olmec monumental art laid the foundation for epi-Olmec, Izapan, and Maya sculpture. Consequently, it is in the creation of this art form and its specific uses that the Olmecs have the greatest claim to an enduring legacy in Mesoamerica.

Continuity

Ultimately, the argument for an Olmec legacy in later Mesoamerican civilizations hinges on demonstrating cultural continuity from a time of Olmec influence in the Middle or Early Formative period. As noted earlier in this chapter, continuity does not mean lack of change in form, meaning, or practice. Rather, it is better conceived as "descent with modification," to borrow a term from evolutionary biology. Neither does continuity necessarily imply gradual change; rates of cultural change can and do vary over time and with respect to different realms of material culture, social practice, and ideology. Although it is easier to infer continuity where changes were gradual, the key issue is the demonstration of historical linkages through time regardless of how rapidly change occurred.

The idea of continuity has a long history in studies of Olmec iconography (Coe 1989: 71). It constituted the foundation for Marshall Saville's (1929a, 1929b) argument that the Olmec were-jaguar was the forerunner of the Aztec god Tezcatlipoca, who was often represented as a jaguar. Miguel Covarrubias (1957) later employed a version of the "continuity hypothesis" to argue that all Classic and Postclassic representations of Mesoamerican rain gods were derived from Olmec were-jaguar images. More recently, Karl Taube (1995) has expanded upon Covarrubias's reconstruction to argue for a derivation of later Mesoamerican rain gods and "avian serpents" from Olmec representations in a symbolic complex associated with maize and agricultural fertility. Taube (2000) also extends his argument to an ultimate Olmec origin of maize symbolism in the form of celts and feathered maize fetishes among the Maya, the Aztecs, and the indigenous peoples of the southwestern United States. Each of these authors takes a broad, stylistic, view of what constitutes Olmec, incorporating examples from oustide Olman, though Taube explicitly attributes the origin of the style to the Gulf Olmec. Epistemologically what these examples also share is the use of similarity in form and meaningful associations to infer historical continuities, although Taube's vastly more detailed analysis of specific representational elements through time more strongly argues for historical linkages, particularly in eastern Mesoamerica.

All of the regions discussed in this book contain cultural traditions that can be traced back in an unbroken line to the Middle Formative period or earlier. Each region also participated in Middle and/or Early Formative interaction spheres that included the Gulf Olmecs. In a general sense, then, the Olmecs contributed to the development of interregional networks of interaction and competition that laid the basis for an emerging Mesoamerican cultural tradition. They also contributed some specific elements to that tradition, especially in monumental sculpture and its political uses. However, they were not the only contributors to the development of Mesoamerican civilization, nor was their influence homogeneous across Mesoamerica.

Not surprisingly, the case for cultural continuity is strongest in the Gulf lowlands. As polities and populations declined in eastern Olman, Tres Zapotes and other settlements grew in western Olman and carried the Olmec tradition forward, with modifications, in their ceramic technology and monumental art. Among their most impressive accomplishments was their development, along with their related contemporaries in central Chiapas, of the Long Count calendar and a sophisticated writing system derived from Olmec iconography. Both were passed along to the Early Classic period capital at Cerro de las Mesas (Kaufman and Justeson 2001: 2.2), and echoes of epi-Olmec symbolic systems can be discerned in later iconography from central Veracruz (e.g., Miller 1991). The Olmecs also initiated a long-standing tradition of exclusionary political strategies on the Gulf Coast, although some polities, like Late Formative Tres Zapotes, appear to have experimented with more collective forms of governance.

There is also a strong argument for continuity in southern Chiapas and Guatemala. The Soconusco and Pacific slope of Guatemala had a long, though fluctuating, history of contact with Olman from the Early Formative period. The proliferation of Olmec-style narrative relief monuments in the region during the Middle Formative period laid the foundation for the development of Late Formative Izapan and highland Maya monumental art, which incorporated not only the narrative relief style, but specific iconographic elements with convincing antecedents in Olmec sculpture. Late Formative Mayan and Izapan writing systems also share specific characteristics with epi-Olmec writing, such as the vertical arrangement of glyphs, bar-and-dot numerical notation, and the Long Count, which suggest a common origin, if not coeval borrowing.

The lowland Maya region did not share the Soconusco's history of intensive interaction with Olman. Early Horizon ceramic attributes and sculpture in Honduras were probably adopted from the Pacific coast, and the few Middle Formative jades that trickled into the region may not have come from Olman. Some Olmec trade or emulation of Maya ceramics also occurred, but contact in general appears to have been light and sporadic, at least until the late Middle Formative period. Nevertheless, Late Formative lowland Maya elites evidently adopted the practice of erecting relief stelae to glorify individual rulers, as well as some elements of their iconography and calendrical systems, from their late Olmec, epi-Olmec, Izapan, and highland Maya neighbors, as detailed in Chapter 7.[2] Some of these elements have specific Middle Formative Olmec antecedents, and they persisted and were elaborated in the Classic period. Thus, while the Olmecs did not exert strong, direct influence on the lowland Maya, a significant Olmec legacy is evident in the practices of the Formative Mayas' Classic period descendants.

The argument for continuity in traits of specifically Olmec derivation in western Mesoamerica is much less convincing. The Valley of Oaxaca seems to have all but ceased contact with Olman following the Early Horizon and, while later Zapotec images of sky and earth, and the spiritual concepts they embody, may derive from Early Horizon motifs, their Olmec origins are still unresolved. Some authors see an Olmec heritage in the carved images of Late Formative danzantes in Oaxaca (e.g., Bernal 1969: 154–156; Coe 1965c: 772; Covarrubias 1957: 148), but they differ substantially from Olmec, epi-Olmec, and Izapan monuments in technique, subject, and formal qualities. The Basin of Mexico continued to participate in interaction spheres that included the Olmecs in the Middle Formative period, and were-jaguar imagery on central Mexican greenstone artifacts may have originated in Olman. On the other hand, monumental sculpture does not appear in the Basin of Mexico until centuries later, and other Middle Formative horizon elements there are not specifically Olmec. The strongest Middle Formative Olmec influence (albeit with reinterpretation and mixing with locally developed styles) is seen in sculpture and murals along the "greenstone route" through Morelos and Guerrero. However, nothing that is specifically Olmec persists in the Late Formative period in the Basin of Mexico, Morelos, or Guerrero. If feathered serpent and rain god images from Classic period Teotihuacan owe anything to an Olmec legacy, as is often claimed, it was only indirectly through their later contacts with Late Formative and Classic period societies in the Gulf of Mexico.[3]

CONCLUSION

In the end, Mesoamerican civilizations seem less the offspring of a single Mother Culture than the progeny of a promiscuous horde. Olmec culture was a particularly prolific father, but by no means the only one, and its involvement with its children, borne and nurtured by many mothers, was selective and inconstant. Yes, the Olmecs left a legacy to Classic and Postclassic Mesoamerica, and that legacy was particularly strong in eastern Mesoamerica, but everywhere Formative cultures shaped their own distinctive traditions and shared them to varying degrees with their neighbors.

This understanding should not diminish our appreciation of the Olmecs. They were the first in the New World to form highly differentiated, hierarchical societies. From the raw material of ancient Native American shamanic beliefs and practices, their leaders crafted an ideology of rulership that continued to support Maya kings two thousand years later. To express that ideology, they created Mesoamerica's first monumental art, the scale, technical skill, and beauty of which was never equaled in their time. Furthermore, to acquire the exotic materials that embodied sacred power and enabled the mundane tasks of day-to-day life, they established an exchange network that eventually stretched 1,000 km from end to end, spreading the Olmec monument style as they did so.

These were not the feats of a single Olmec Alexander, or even a line of Olmec Caesars expanding their empire to the corners of the Mesoamerican world. There was never even a single, unified, Olmec state that ruled all of Olman. Instead Olmec sociopolitical complexity emerged from competition and cooperation among many local leaders, and Olmec symbolic systems proved flexible enough to serve egalitarian villagers as well as rulers of powerful hierarchical polities. That conclusion, as much as their impressive monuments and their precocious political developments, makes the Olmec a fascinating case in the evolution of the world's complex societies, worthy of the efforts of the many *olmequistas* who have gone before and the many who are to come.

NOTES

1. Introduction

1. All dates in this book are expressed in calendar (sidereal) years rather than radiocarbon years. For most times and places in Middle America aside from the Classic period in the Maya lowlands, the beginning and ending dates for periods and their subdivisions have been established by radiocarbon dating of organic materials found in archaeological contexts and most authors have reported their dates using the Libby half-life of 5,568 years for Carbon-14. However, comparisons with the highly precise chronology provided by sequences of tree rings have shown that, in general, radiocarbon dates become progressively younger than actual calendar dates as one goes farther back in time. Moreover, variations in the amount of C14 in the atmosphere over time have produced significant fluctuations superimposed upon the general trend. The tree ring studies have yielded calibration curves that allow radiocarbon dates to be adjusted to calendar years. For this study I have calibrated dates using the Calib Rev 4.4.2 computer program and the intcal98 calibration curve (Stuiver et al. 1998), recalculating radiocarbon dates with the 5,568 half-life when necessary. Figure 1.4 shows beginning and ending dates of chronological divisions of the Formative period both in radiocarbon and calendar years for comparison.

2. Formerly known in the archaeological literature as Abaj Takalik, a Spanish-style inversion of the Maya name, which means "standing stones" (Tarpy 2004: 72).

3. Flannery and Marcus (2003: 6) interpret this structure, the "Red Palace," as a public building rather than an elite residence.

4. Flannery has since revised his 1968 model (Flannery and Marcus 1994: 389; 2000). See discussion in Chapter 6.

5. Blanton et al. (1996: 7) identify Dynastic-period China as one such case. In Mesoamerica, they identify some elements of an exclusionary strategy in the Early Postclassic Maya polity of Chichén Itza (1996: 12) and hint at their existence in the Aztec Triple Alliance (1996: 11), but emphasize evidence for corporate strategies in both cases.

6. Stark (personal communication, 2003) now doubts that these do represent communal themes, but I think her original observation is valid.

2. "Great Stone Faces of the Mexican Jungle"

1. See Chapter 7 for a discussion of Long Count notation. Subsequently, even earlier Long Count dates were discovered. The two earliest are at Tres Zapotes (Stela C, 7.16.6.16.18, 14 August 32 B.C.) (Stirling 1943: 14) and Chiapa de Corzo (Stela 2, (7.16).3.2.13, 9 December 36 B.C.) (Lee 1969: 105–106). Fragments of a Long Count date on Takalik Abaj Stela 2 suggest a date between 235 and 18 B.C. (Graham et al. 1978:6–8).

2. This is equivalent to 917–528 b.c. using the 5,568-year half-life of carbon-14, or ca. 1040–580 calibrated B.C.

3. John Clark (personal communication 2004) has recently examined this monument, which until recently was reburied. He disputes its identification as a recarved colossal head, and suggests that what appears to be a human ear on one side may be a vine like that on the similar Monument 2 ("El León") from Izapa.

4. This figure does not include stone drains, drain lids, blocks, slabs, and small carved figures, included among the 129 currently numbered monuments of San Lorenzo (see Cyphers 2004: Figure 9).

4. Olmec Beginnings

1. Coe and Diehl's argument for an exogenous origin of Olmec culture at San Lorenzo was based on the appearance of a new suite of ceramic types in the Chicharras phase (ca. 1450–1400 B.C. [1250–1150 uncalibrated B.C.]) (1980a: 150–151) and of distinctive carved and incised decoration in the San Lorenzo phase (ca. 1400–1000 B.C. [1150–900 uncalibrated B.C.) (1980a: 159). However, sherd counts were recorded for only four excavations, only one of these (Stratigraphic Pit II) penetrated to the pre-Olmec Bajío phase (ca. 1550 – 1450 B.C. [1350 – 1250 uncalibrated B.C.]), and nearly half (45.6%) of the sherds from this pit were too badly eroded to be classified (Coe and Diehl 1980a: 133). The claim of discontinuity at San Lorenzo is therefore difficult to assess quantitatively. Coe and Diehl (1980a: 150) acknowledge the persistence from pre-Olmec phases of the utilitarian type, Camaño Coarse (usually rendered as tecomates with brushed decoration) and Achiotal Gray (polished fine sand-tempered tecomates and bowls, some with incised decoration). Some decorative modes and forms transcend the pre-Olmec to Olmec transition as well. An Ojochi phase (ca. 1750 – 1550 B.C. [1500 – 1350 uncalibrated B.C.]) sherd has incised zoned crosshatching similar to that which appears on the Chicharras phase type, Tatagapa Red, and some of the curvilinear incised designs that frame zones of punctuation in the Bajío phase type, Embarcadero Zoned presage designs of San Lorenzo phase Limón Carved-Incised.

Support for cultural continuity is found in the excavation of a stratigraphic series of floors at the site of Las Galeras in the "outer hinterland" of San Lorenzo, which document the persistence of types defined primarily on the basis of paste characteristics and surface treatments (O'Rourke 2002: Table 6.1) as well as vessel forms (O'Rourke 2002: Tables 6.2 and 6.3) from "pre-Olmec" to Olmec levels. Changes are observed primarily in decoration (Tables 6.4 and 6.5) and in the addition of new types and forms to the "pre-Olmec" inventory. At El Manatí, 17 km southeast of San Lorenzo, ceramic types assigned to the Manatí phase (ca. 1700 – 1400 B.C. [ca. 1450–1200 uncalibrated B.C.]), includes types referable to those of the Ojochi, Bajío, and Chicharras phases at San Lorenzo, but without internal chronological subdivisions. Black and differentially fired types that continue in the succeeding Macayal phase (ca. 1400 – 1000 B.C.) show new modes of decoration and increasing control over firing conditions. The ceramic sequences from both of these sites suggest the elaboration of existing ceramic traditions more than sudden replacement by new traditions. As described later in this chapter, the sequence of offerings of greenstone celts and other materials at El Manatí further indicates the gradual development of Olmec ritual practices from 1700 B.C. onward.

The claim that monumental sculpture appears suddenly and fully developed at San Lorenzo also merits critical assessment. Most of the site's 80+ stone sculptures lack stratigraphic provenience, but Coe and Diehl (1980a: 295) report stratigraphic associations of eighteen monuments and one possible monument fragment from Chicharras phase deposits. Three of these (Monuments 21, 42, and 51) are reported to have been associated with deposits of the San Lorenzo A phase, and the rest with the San Lorenzo B phase. The Chicharras phase fragment, only 5.4 cm long, is carved to resemble two parallel ropes, as also appear in the headdress of some colossal heads, but could be from a smaller artifact. Monument 51 is a plain stone slab with many gouges on its upper surface. The other two monuments assigned to the San Lorenzo A phase are executed simply, without the sophistication typical of later monuments. However, the dating of Monument 21 is equivocal; it overlay a cache with San Lorenzo A phase pottery and serpentine celts, but carbon from beneath the monument yielded a date of 1620 ± 120 B.P., and one of the sherds in the cache was possibly of the Villa Alta phase (Coe and Diehl 1989a: 100–103; Graham 1989: 244–246). If Monuments 21 and 42 were executed early, it could suggest some chronological development of sculptural techniques and aesthetic canons over the 400 (calibrated)-year San Lorenzo phase.

2. Symonds et al. (2002) employ a slightly different chronology for their survey data. In some cases they have lumped phases that are difficult to distinguish with surface materials, which are

often eroded. More significant revisions include an expansion of the Late Preclassic (or Late Formative) period Remplás phase and refinement of the Classic period sequence, after the period with which this chapter is concerned. Their phase designations and (uncalibrated) dates are: Early Preclassic, Ojochi and Bajío phases (1500–1200 B.C.), Early Preclassic, Chicharras and San Lorenzo phases (1200–900/800 B.C.), Middle Preclassic (900/800–600 B.C.), Late Preclassic (Remplás phase, 600 B.C.–A.D. 200), Early and Middle Classic (A.D. 200–600), Ortices phase (A.D. 600–700), early Villa Alta phase (A.D. 700–800), late Villa Alta phase (A.D. 800–1000).

3. Symonds et al. (2002) lump Potrero Nuevo with Loma del Zapote, although the area between these two localities apparently was less intensively occupied.

4. Evidence for an Early Formative occupation at La Venta is reported by Hallinan et al. (1968) and Rust and Sharer (1988: 103). Hallinan et al. (1968: 164–165) recovered Early Formative pottery in the lower levels of their test pit 8 in a depression to the west of Mound C-1, "considerably below the point" from which a carbon sample (UCLA-1253) was collected that produced a date reported as 1110 B.C. in radiocarbon years, or ca. 1340 B.C. in calendar years. Tecomates accounted for 18% to 55.5% of vessel shapes recovered from levels below 130 cm, corroborating a date before 800 B.C., after which tecomates drop to less than 2% of vessels in assemblages from the western Tabasco plain (von Nagy 2003: 820). Michael Coe is reported to have identified two tecomate rims with a coarse red paste and bright red slip as characteristic of the San Lorenzo phase (Hallinan 1968: 165), which suggests they were equivalent to the Early Formative San Lorenzo type, Tatagapa Red (Coe and Diehl 1980a: 187). Hallinan et al. (1968: 161, 163, 167) also report similar pottery from mound fill in pits 2 and 7 south of Mound C-1 (i.e., Complex B) and at depths of 360–420 cm in a deep sounding in the Stirling Group. Squier (1968) also reports a date (UCLA 1276b) of 2930 ± 80 B.P. (980 ± 80 uncalibrated B.C., 2σ 1375–919 calibrated. B.C.) from pit C, which, as van Nagy (2003: 813) observes, "may indicate an early occupation coeval with that of Isla Alor" (i.e., Palacios phase). Rust and Sharer (1988: 103) state that "Early Preclassic (1400 – 1150 B.C.)" occupational evidence was recovered from Complex E at La Venta, and report a radiocarbon date

of 3020 ± 100 B.P. (1070 ± 100 uncalibrated B.C., 1495 – 944 calibrated B.C.) from Complex G. These reports suggest an Early Formative occupation at La Venta distributed over an area on the order of 20 ha or more. There is no evidence that this occupation is associated with the construction of civic-ceremonial mounds at La Venta, but the same is true of the San Lorenzo phase at San Lorenzo.

5. Olmec Transformations: The Middle Formative Period

1. Previous identifications of Altotonga (Hester et al. 1973: 167 footnote 1; Nelson and Clark 1998: Table 1) as the major source at La Venta designated "Type B" by Hester et al. (1971) have been called into question by recent studies (Cobean 2002). The Altotonga source is part of the Jaltipán ignimbrite, which also includes the compositionally similar source complex Zaragoza-Oyameles, Puebla (Cobean et al. 1991: Table 5; Ferriz 1985; cf. Jiménez-Reyes 2001: 470). The Paredón source is not part of the Xaltipán ignimbrite, but also is similar to Altotonga with respect to the elements originally analyzed by Hester and colleagues using X-ray fluorescence spectrometry. Artifacts previously assigned to the Altotonga source are currently considered to be from Zaragoza-Oyameles (Cobean 2002) or Paredón. That said, the Type B compositions prevalent at La Venta differ consistently in their strontium levels from the Type D (Zaragoza) compositions prevalent at Tres Zapotes (Hester et al. 1971: Figures 8 and 9). Whether different sources or different components of the same source, the critical point, that Middle Formative inhabitants of La Venta and Tres Zapotes established independent obsidian procurement networks, is supported by the evidence.

6. The Olmecs and Mesoamerica

1. Clark and Cheetham (2002) (see also Clark et al. 2004) currently view the Cherla phase as coeval with the Chicharras phase at San Lorenzo, that is, 1250–1150 uncal. B.C. (ca. 1450–1400 cal. B.C.). If correct, this would require a modification of the Olmecization model. The acquisition of goods and emulation of styles from Olman could still have conferred prestige on Mazatán leaders, but as a result of their exotic origin

and the difficulty in acquiring them rather than their association with a more complexly organized society.

2. In a critique of Marcus' (1989, 1998; Flannery and Marcus 1994: 136–139) model, Clark (2001) correctly observes that Flannery and Marcus (1994: Figure 12.2) use the naturalistic frontal image from a probable Middle Formative votive axe as the model from which more abstract Early Formative were-jaguar images were derived. The axe in question is unprovenanced, but said to be from Oaxaca (Joralemon 1971: Figure 165), which I surmise is why Flannery and Marcus chose to illustrate it. I take Flannery and Marcus's illustration as a formal model of the process of abstraction, rather than a historical sequence. The profile view Clark equates with the image on the votive axe is from a Tlatilco vessel, which Niederberger (1987: 528) attributes to the Early Formative Ayotla phase.

3. Marcus Winter (1994: 135; see also Clark 2001) has suggested that the differential distributions of these motifs may result from chronological differences in the emphasis given each. The long span of the San José phase makes this possible, but the chronological explanation is difficult to evaluate at present, since the published radiocarbon dates from the San José phase in the Valley of Oaxaca fall relatively late in the phase, and they all come from areas in which "fire-serpent" motifs predominate (Drennan 1983; Flannery and Marcus 1994: 382–383).

It is also possible that some pottery from the Valley of Oaxaca represents frontal and profile views on the same vessel in the form of cleft motifs and double-line-breaks on plate rims. Grove (1993) has suggested that the double-line-break represents the gum-line of Olmec supernaturals, which usually appears in profile views. In contrast, Flannery and Marcus (1994) argue that the double-line-break derives from the cleft head of the frontal view, based on examples from the Valley of Oaxaca in which a cleft motif appears between line-breaks. Interestingly, a Manantial phase vessel from Tlapacoya, which Flannery and Marcus (1994: Figure 19.2) use to bolster their argument, has a clear representation of a frontal cleft head flanked by a profile view below a double-line-break.

4. Archaeological excavation has failed to find an Early Horizon component at Xochipala (Schmidt 1990), although looted artifacts of Early Horizon style have been attributed to the Xochipala area.

5. The Phase I patio construction at Teopantecuanitlan is bracketed by a date of 1390 ± 120 B.C. (1948–1374 cal. B.C., p = .947, median = 1635 B.C.) below the yellow floor and dates of 844 ± 58 (1054–826 cal. B.C., p = .901, median = 945 B.C.) and 822 ± 117 B.C. (1051–804 cal. B.C., p = .943, median = 956 B.C.) associated with the stone architecture of Phase II (Niederberger 1996: 97; Stuiver and Reimer 2004). Ceramics from strata below and immediately above the yellow clay floor are similar in form, surface treatments, and decoration to those of the Manantial (ca. 1150–900 cal. B.C.), Barranca (ca. 1150–800 cal. B.C.), San Lorenzo (ca. 1400–1000 cal. B.C.), and Jocotal (ca. 1150–1000 cal. B.C.) phases (Reyna Robles 1996). A few sherds from below the yellow clay floor also resemble types from the Middle Formative Tejas phase of nearby Xochipala (Reyna Robles 1996: 129). The single radiocarbon date for the Tejas phase of 585 ± 370 B.C. (1524 cal. B.C. – cal. A.D. 240, p = .954, median = 655 B.C.) reported by Schmidt (1990: 221) does not preclude a ca. 1000 B.C. date for the phase I materials at Tepoantecuanitlan. Scarce sherds similar to types of the Ayotla (ca. 1400–1150 cal. B.C.), Amate (ca. 1650–1150 cal. B.C.), and Cuadros (ca. 1400–1100 cal. B.C.) can be attributed to re-deposition from earlier deposits in the vicinity.

6. The additional claim of Blomster et al. (2005: 1071) that regions outside of Olman did not export pottery with Early Horizon motifs to one another or San Lorenzo relies on a multivariate statistical analysis conservatively designed so as not to erroneously identify locally made vessels as imports, but which leaves the source of many specimens unassigned (Blomster et al. 2005: 1070). There is always the possibility that a sample has missed infrequent classes of phenomena, including, in this case, rare imports. Nevertheless, the authors of Blomster et al. and their colleagues (Neff et al. 2006a; 2006b) have effectively countered a less conservative "discriminant function" analysis of the same data by Stoltman et al. (2005: 11215-11216) that attemtpte to show that more exchange existed among regions and suggested that Etlatongo (or the broader Mixteca Alta region) was an important exporter (Stoltman et al. 2005: 11215–11216). The reader is directed to the original article by Blomster et al. (2005) in the journal and the vociferous debate it prompted in the *Proceedings of the National Academy of Sciences* (Stoltman et al. 2005; Flannery et al. 2005)

and an equally animated exchange in *Latin American Antiquity* (Neff et al. 2006a, 2006b; Sharer et al. 2006) for a through discussion of these and other issues.

7. See note 5 on the dating of patio construction phases at Teopantecuanitlán.

7. Collapse, Continuity, and Evolution: Late Formative Olman

1. The 14 August date is 20 days earlier than the usually reported date of 3 September. This derives from Kaufman and Justeson's identification of a solar eclipse on the epi-Olmec La Mojarra Stela recorded as occurring 20 days (one "month") before its corresponding date in the Maya vague year. Both dates are backward-projected Gregorian dates, not Julian dates (Justeson, personal communication 2006).

2. A recently reported, but unprovenienced, stone mask of Teotihuacan style with an epi-Olmec inscription carved on the interior surface (Houston and Coe 2003) is clearly of the Classic period, and so later than the inscriptions discussed here.

3. As this book went to press, a possibly earlier inscription was reported from the site of Cascajal, Veracruz, near San Lorenzo (Rodríguez et al. 2006). Unfortunately, the serpentine block was not in archaeological context when first shown to archaeologists, so its age is uncertain. The authors of the study favor a date of ca. 900 uncalibrated b.c. (ca. 1000 calibrated B.C.), but the possibility that the block was associated with late Middle Formative Palangana phase deposits at the site cannot be ruled out. Unlike known Late Formative Mesoamerican scripts, the 62 symbols on the block are arranged horizontally. The authors note that the Cascajal script bears no secure links to other Mesoamerican writing systems.

4. Stark (1997: 289) lists these as hachured and fringed triangles, fringed lines, clumped herringbones or chevrons, "abacus" ticks (offset groups of ticked lines in registers), slanted bands or lines with hachured triangles, and entwined boxes.

5. An earlier stela (Monument 26) and circular altar (Monument 25) pairing was discovered in Terrace 6 at Chalcatzingo, Morelos. These apparently date to the Middle Formative Cantera phase.

8. The Olmecs and Their Legacy

1. Relative frequencies of pottery with carved motifs are roughly the same in Oaxaca and San Lorenzo, however (Stark 2005).

2. The recent evidence from San Bartolo (Saturno et al. 2006), it should be noted, also accords a significant role to the lowland Maya in the elaboration of writing systems; they may have incorporated some epi-Olmec and highland Maya elements in their wirting, but they may also have contributed elements to the other systems.

3. Kaufman and Justeson (2006), however, suggest that a version of Mije-Sokean was spoken by some residents at Teotihuacan.

REFERENCES CITED

Agrinier, P. 1984. *The Early Olmec Horizon at Mirador, Chiapas, Mexico*, Papers of the New World Archaeological Foundation. Provo, UT.

Anderson, D. 1978. 'Monuments', in R.J. Sharer (ed.), *The Prehistory of Chalchuapa, El Salvador, Vol. 1*, pp. 155–180. Philadelphia, PA: University of Pennsylvania Press.

Anderson, D.G. 1994a. 'Factional competition and the political evolution of Mississippian chiefdoms in the southeastern United States,' in E.M. Brumfiel and J.W. Fox (eds.), *Factional Competition and Political Development in the New World*, pp. 61–76. Cambridge: Cambridge University Press.

Anderson, D.G. 1994b. *The Savannah River Chiefdoms*. Tuscaloosa: University of Alabama Press.

Anderson, D.G. 1996a. 'Chiefly cycling and large-scale abandonments as viewed from the Savannah River Basin,' in J.F. Scarry (ed.), *Political Structure and Change in the Prehistoric Southeastern United States*, pp. 150–191. Gainesville: The University Press of Florida.

Anderson, D.G. 1996b. 'Fluctuations between simple and complex chiefdoms: cycling in the Late Prehistoric Southeast,' in J.F. Scarry (ed.), *Political Structure and Change in the Prehistoric Southeastern United States*, pp. 231–252. Gainesville: The University Press of Florida.

Andrews, E.W., V 1986. 'Olmec jades from Chacsinkin, Yucatán, and Maya ceramics from La Venta, Tabasco,' in E.W. Andrews, V (ed.), *Research and Reflections in Archaeology and History*, Middle American Research Institute Publication 57, pp. 11–49. New Orleans: Tulane University.

Andrews, E.W., V 1987. 'Cache of early jades from Chacsinkin, Yucatan.' *Mexicon* 9: 78–85.

Andrews, E.W., V 1990. 'The early ceramic history of the lowland Maya,' in F.S. Clancy and P.D. Harrison (eds.), *Vision and Revision in Maya Studies*, pp. 1–19. Albuquerque: University of New Mexico Press.

Angulo V., J. 1987. 'The Chalcatzingo reliefs: an iconographic analysis,' in D.C. Grove (ed.), *Ancient Chalcatzingo*, pp. 132–158. Austin, TX: University of Texas.

Armillas, P. 1948. 'Sequence of cultural development in Meso-America,' in W.C. Bennet (ed.), *A Reappraisal of Peruvian archaeology*, Memoir 4, pp. 105–111. Menasha: Society for American Archaeology.

Arnold, P.J., III 1994. 'An overview of southern Veracruz archaeology.' *Ancient Mesoamerica* 5: 215–21.

Arnold, P.J., III 1996. 'Craft specialization and social change along the southern Gulf Coast of Mexico,' in B. Wailes (ed.), *Craft Specialization and Social Evolution: In Memory of V. Gordon Childe*, pp. 201–207. Philadelphia: The University of Pennsylvania Museum of Archaeology and Anthropology.

Arnold, P.J., III 1999. 'Tecomates, residential mobility, and early Formative occupation in coastal lowland Mesoamerica,' in J.M. Skibo and G.M. Feinman (eds.), *Pottery and People*, pp. 157–170. Salt Lake City: University of Utah Press.

Arnold, P.J., III 2000. 'Sociopolitical complexity and the Gulf Olmecs: a view from the Tuxtla Mountains, Veracruz, Mexico,' in J.E. Clark and M.E. Pye (eds.), *Olmec Art and Archaeology in Mesoamerica*, pp. 117–135. Washington, DC: National Gallery of Art.

Arnold, P.J., III 2001. Singin' the Gulf Olmec interaction blues: Olman River, Olmec Donald, and other Early Formative ditties Paper presented at the 66th annual meeting of the Society for American Archaeology, New Orleans.

Arnold, P.J., III 2003. 'Early Formative pottery from the Tuxtla Mountains and implications for Gulf Olmec origins.' *Latin American Antiquity* 14: 29–46.

Arnold, P.J., III 2005. 'Gulf Olmec variation and implications for interaction,' in T. Powis (ed.), *Bridging Formative Mesoamerican Cultures*, pp. 73–82. London: BAR International Series.

Arnold, P.J., III and Follensbee, B.J.A. 2003. 'Early Formative figurines from La Joya: Implications for Gulf Olmec regional variation,' in C. Kolb and C. Otis-Charlton (eds.), *Figurines in Mesoamerica*. Philadelphia: University of Pennsylvania Museum Press. In press.

Arnold, P.J., III, Pool, C.A., Kneebone, R.R., and Santley, R.S. 1993. 'Intensive ceramic production and Classic period political economy in the Sierra de los Tuxtlas, Veracruz, Mexico.' *Ancient Mesoamerica* 4: 175–191.

Aviles, M. 1995. The archaeology of Early Formative Chalcatzingo, Morelos, Mexico, 1995. Report submitted to the Foundation for the Advancement of Mesoamerican Studies, Inc., Coral Gables, FL, http://www.famsi.org/reports/aviles/aviles.htlm. Downloaded 26 July 2001.

Balser, C. 1959. 'Los "baby-faces" olmecas de Costa Rica.' *Actas del XXXII Congreso Internacional de Americanistas* 2: 280–285. San José, Costa Rica.

Barba Pingarrón, L.A. 1988. 'Trabajos de prospección realizados en el sitio arqueológico La Venta, Tabasco.' *Arqueología* 4: 167–218.

Barth, F. 1950. 'Ecologic adaptation and cultural change in archaeology.' *American Antiquity* 15: 338–9.

Baudez, C.F. 1971. 'Commentary on "Inventory of some Preclassic traits in the highlands and Pacific Guatemala and adjacent areas.' *Contributions of the University of California Archaeological Research Facility* 11: 78–84.

Benson, E.P. (ed.) 1968. *Dumbarton Oaks Conference on the Olmec.* Washington DC: Dumbarton Oaks.

Benson, E.P. 1981a. *The Olmec and their Neighbors: Essays in Memory of Matthew W. Stirling.* Washington, DC: Dumbarton Oaks.

Benson, E.P. 1981b. 'Some Olmec objects in the Robert Woods Bliss Collection at Dumbarton Oaks,' in E.P. Benson (ed.), *The Olmec and Their Neighbors*, pp. 95–108. Washington, DC: Dumbarton Oaks.

Benson, E.P. (ed.) 1996. 'History of Olmec investigations,' in E.P. Benson and B. de la Fuente (eds.), *Olmec Art of Ancient Mexico*, pp. 17–27. Washington, DC: National Gallery of Art.

Benson, E.P. and de la Fuente, B. (eds.) 1996. *Olmec Art of Ancient Mexico.* Washington, DC: National Gallery of Art.

Berger, R., Graham, J.A., and Heizer, R.F. 1967. 'Reconsideration of the age of the La Venta site.' *Contributions of the University of California Archaeological Research Facility* 3: 1–24.

Bernal, I. 1968a. *El mundo olmeca.* Mexico City: Editorial Porrúa, S.A.

Bernal, I. 1968b. 'Views of Olmec culture,' in E.P. Benson (ed.), *Dumbarton Oaks Conference on the Olmec*, pp. 135–142. Washington, DC: Dumbarton Oaks.

Bernal, I. 1969. *The Olmec World.* Berkeley: University of California Press.

Beverido Pereau, F. 1987. 'Breve historia de la arqueología olmeca.' *La palabra y el hombre* 64: 161–194.

Beyer, H. 1927. '*Tribes and Temples* (Review).' *El Mexico Antiguo* 2: 11–12.

Blake, M. 1991. 'An emerging Early Formative chiefdom at Paso de la Amada, Chiapas, Mexico,' in W.R. Fowler (ed.), *The Formation of Complex Society in Southeastern Mesoamerica*, pp. 27–46. Boca Raton, FL: CRC Press.

Blake, M., Clark, J.E., Voorhies, B., Love, M.W., and Chisholm, B.S. 1992. 'Prehistoric subsistence in the Soconusco region.' *Current Anthropology* 33: 83–94.

Blake, M., Clark, J.E., Voorhies, B., Michaels, G., Love, M.W., Pye, M.E., Demarest, A.A., and Arroyo, B. 1995. 'Radiocarbon chronology for the Late Archaic and Formative periods on the Pacific coast of southeastern Mesoamerica.' *Ancient Mesoamerica* 6: 161–183.

Blanton, R. 1998. 'Beyond centralization: steps toward a theory of egalitarian behavior in archaic states,' in G.M. Feinman and J. Marcus (eds.), *Archaic States*, pp. 135–172. Santa Fe: School of American Research.

Blanton, R., Feinman, G.M., Kowalewski, S.A., and Finsten, L.M. 1993. *Ancient Mesoamerica: A Comparison of Change in Three Regions.* Cambridge: Cambridge University Press.

Blanton, R., Feinman, G.M., Kowalewski, S.A., and Peregrine, P.N. 1996. 'A dual-processual theory for the evolution of Mesoamerican civilization.' *Current Anthropology* 37: 1–14.

Blom, F. and La Farge, O. 1926. *Tribes and Temples*, Middle American Research Series No. 1. New Orleans: Tulane University.

Blomster, J.P. 1998. 'Context, cult, and Early Formative Public Ritual in the Mixteca Alta: analysis of a Hollow Baby figurine from Etlatongo, Oaxaca.' *Ancient Mesoamerica* 9: 309–326.

Blomster, J.P. 2002. 'What and where is Olmec style? Regional perspectives on hollow figurines in Early Formative Mesoamerica.' *Ancient Mesoamerica* 13: 171–195.

Blomster, J.P. 2004. *Etlatongo: Social Complexity, Interaction, and Village Life in the Mixteca Alta of Oaxaca, Mexico*, Case Studies in Archaeology. Belmont, CA: Thomson Wadsworth.

Blomster, J.P., Neff, H., and Glascock, M.D. 2005. 'Olmec pottery production and export in ancient Mexico determined through elemental analysis.' *Science* 307 (1068–1072).

Boggs, S.H. 1950. *"Olmec" Pictographs in the Las Victorias Group, Chalchuapa Archaeological Zone*, Notes on Middle American Archaeology and Ethnology 99. Washington, DC: Carnegie Institution of Washington.

Borstein, J.P. 2001. *Tripping over Colossal Heads: Settlement Patterns and Population Development in the Upland Olmec Heartland*. Ph.D. dissertation, Department of Anthropology, Pennsylvania State University, State College. Ann Arbor: UMI.

Bove, F.J. 1978. 'Laguna de los Cerros: an Olmec central place.' *Journal of New World Archaeology* 2: 1–56.

Braniff, B. 1989. 'Oscilación de la frontera norte mesoamericana: un nuevo ensayo.' *Arqueología* 1: 89–114.

Brüggemann, J.K. and Harris, M. 1970. 'Aplicación del magnetómetro en San Lorenzo Tenochtitlan.' *Boletín del Instituto Nacional de Antropología e Historia* 39: 26–29.

Brüggemann, J.K. and Hers, M.-A. 1970. 'Exploraciones arqueológicas en San Lorenzo.' *Boletín del Instituto Nacional de Antropología e Historia* 39: 18–23.

Brumfiel, E.M. 1992. 'Distinguished lecture in archeology: breaking and entering the ecosystem: gender, class and faction steal the show.' *American Anthropologist* 94: 551–567.

Brumfiel, E.M. 1994. 'Factional competition and political development in the New World: an introduction,' in E. Brumfiel and J.W. Fox (eds.), *Factional Competition and Political Development in the New World*, pp. 3–13. Cambridge: Cambridge University Press.

Brumfiel, E.M. and Earle, T.K. 1987. 'Specialization, exchange and complex societies: an introduction,' in E. Brumfiel and T.K. Earle (eds.), *Specialization, Exchange and Complex Societies*, pp. 1–9. Cambridge: Cambridge University Press.

Campbell, L.R. and Kaufman, T.S. 1976. 'A linguistic look at the Olmecs.' *American Antiquity* 41(1): 80–89.

Carneiro, R.L. 1970. 'A theory on the origin of the state.' *Science* 169: 733–738.

Carneiro, R.L. 1981. 'The chiefdom: precursor to the state,' in G. Jones and R. Kautz (eds.), *The Transition to Statehood in the New World*, pp. 37–75. Cambridge: Cambridge University Press.

Carneiro, R.L. 1998. 'What happened at the flashpoint? Conjectures on chiefdom formation at the very moment of conception,' in *Chiefdoms and Chieftancy in the Americas*, pp. 18–42. Gainesville: University Press of Florida.

Carrasco, D. 1999. *City of Sacrifice: The Aztec Empire and the Role of Violence in Civilization*. Boston: Beacon Press.

Caso, A. 1938. *Exploraciones en Oaxaca, quinta y sexta temporadas, 1937–1937*. Tacubaya: Pan American Institute of Geography and History.

Caso, A. 1942. 'Definición y extensión del complejo "olmeca".' *Mayas y Olmecas, segunda reunión de mesa redonda*, pp. 43–46. Mexico City: Sociedad Mexicana de Antropología.

Caso, A. 1965. 'Existió un imperio olmeca?.' *Memoria del Colegio Nacional* 5(3): 30–52.

Ceja Tenorio, J.F. 1981. 'Ixtlahuehue: la salina vieja de los Tuxtlas.' *Revista mexicana de estudios antropológicos* 28: 41–47.

Ceja Tenorio, J.F. 1998. 'Ixtlahuehue, la "Salina Vieja" de los Tuxtlas.' *La Sal en México II*. Colima, Mexico: Universidad de Colima.

Chavero, A. 1988. 'Historia antigua y de la conquista,' in V.R. Palacio (ed.), *México a través de los siglos*, Vol. 1. Barcelona.

Cheetham, D. 2005. 'Cunil: A pre-Mamom horizon in the southern Maya lowlands,' in T. Powis (ed.), *Bridging Formative Mesoamerican Cultures*, pp. 27–38. London: BAR International Series.

Cheetham, D. 2005. Recent investigations at Cantón Corralito: a possible Olmec Enclave on the Pacific Coast of Chiapas, Mexico. Paper presented at the 70th annual meeting of the Society for American Archaeology, Salt Lake City.

Childe, V.G. 1950. *Prehistoric Migrations in Europe*. Cambridge, MA: Harvard University Press.

Christaller, W. 1966. *Central Places in Southern Germany*. Englewood Cliffs: Prentice Hall.

Clark, J.E. 1987. 'Politics, prismatic blades, and Mesoamerican civilization,' in J.K. Johnson and C.A. Marrow (eds.), *The Organization of Core Technology*, pp. 259–284. Boulder, CO: Westview Press.

Clark, J.E. 1990a. 'La cultura mokaya: una civilización pre-olmeca del Soconusco. Tuxtla Gutierrez, Mexico.' *Primer foro de arqueología de Chiapas: cazadores-recolectores-pescadores*, Serie Memorias, Vol. 4, pp. 63–74. Tuxtla Gutiérrez, Chiapas: Gobierno del Estado de Chiapas.

Clark, J.E. 1990b. 'Olmecas, olmequismo y olmequización en Mesoamérica.' *Arqueología* (3): 49–56.

Clark, J.E. 1991. 'Beginnings of Mesoamerica: apologia for the Soconusco Early Formative,' in W.R. Fowler (ed.), *The Formation of Complex Society in Southeastern Mesoamerica*, pp. 13–26. Boca Raton: CRC Press.

Clark, J.E. 1993. 'Quienes fueron los olmecas.' *Segundo y Tercer Foro de Arqueología de Chiapas*, pp. 45–55. Tuxtla Gutiérrez, Chiapas: Gobierno del Estado de Chiapas.

Clark, J.E. 1994a. 'Antecedentes de la cultura olmeca,' in J.E. Clark (ed.), *Los olmecas en Mesoamérica*, pp. 31–43. Mexico City: Citibank.

Clark, J.E. 1994b. *The Development of Early Formative Rank Societies in the Soconusco, Chiapas, Mexico*. Ph.D. dissertation, Department of Anthropology, University of Michigan, Ann Arbor.

Clark, J.E. 1994c. 'El sistema económico de los primeros olmecas,' in J.E. Clark (ed.), *Los olmecas en Mesoamérica*, pp. 189–201. Mexico City: Citibank.

Clark, J.E. 1996. 'Craft specialization and Olmec civilization,' in B. Wailes (ed.), *Craft Specialization and Social Evolution: In Memory of V. Gordon Childe*, University Museum Symposium Series, Vol. VI, pp. 187–199.

Philadelphia: University Museum, University of Pennsylvania.

Clark, J.E. 1997. 'The arts of government in early Mesoamerica.' *Annual Review of Anthropology* 26: 211–34.

Clark, J.E. 2001. Olmec supernaturals and scholarly muddles: gods, totems, cults, or clans? Paper presented at the 66th annual meeting of the Society for American Archaeology, New Orleans.

Clark, J.E. 2004. 'Mesoamerica goes public: early ceremonial centers, leaders, and communities,' in R.A. Joyce and J.A. Hendon (eds.), *Mesoamerican Archaeology*, pp. 43–72. Oxford: Blackwell Publishing.

Clark, J.E. 2005. 'The birth of Mesoamerican metaphysics: sedentism, engagement, and moral superiority,' in E. De Marrais, C. Gosden and C. Renfrew (eds.), *Rethinking Materiality: The Engagment of Mind with the Material World*, pp. 205–224. Cambridge: McDonald Institute for Archaeological Research.

Clark, J.E. and Blake, M. 1989a. 'Investigaciones del Formativo Temprano del litoral chiapaneco.' *Boletín del Instituto Nacional de Antropología e Historia* 1989: 21–24.

Clark, J.E. and Blake, M. 1989b. 'El origen de la civilización en Mesoamérica: los olmecas y mokaya del Soconusco de Chiapas, México,' in M. Carmona Macias (ed.), *El Preclásico o Formativo: avances y perspectivas*, pp. 385–403. Mexico City: Museo Nacional de Antropología.

Clark, J.E. and Blake, M. 1994. 'The power of prestige: competitive generosity and the emergence of rank in lowland Mesoamerica,' in E.M. Brumfiel and J.W. Fox (eds.), *Factional Competition and Political Development in the New World*, pp. 17–30. Cambridge: Cambridge University Press.

Clark, J.E. and Cheetham, D. 2002. *Cerámica Formativo de Chiapas* (unpublished typescript). New World Archaeological Foundation, Provo, UT.

Clark, J.E., Gibson, J.L. and Zeidler, J.A. 2004. *First towns in the Americas: searching for agriculture and other enabling conditions*. Unpublished typescript, Department of Anthropology, Brigham Young University, Provo, Utah.

Clark, J.E. and Gosser, D. 1995. 'Reinventing Mesoamerica's first pottery,' in W.K. Barnett and J.W. Hoopes (eds.), *The Emergence of Pottery: Technology and Innovation in*

Ancient Societies, pp. 209–221. Washington, DC: Smithsonian Institution.

Clark, J.E. and Hansen, R.D. 2001. 'The architecture of early kingship: Comparative perspectives on the origins of the Maya royal court,' in T. Inomata (ed.), *Houston, Stephen D.*, pp. 1–45. Boulder, CO: Westview.

Clark, J.E., Hansen, R.D., and Pérez Suárez, T. 2000. 'La zona maya en el preclásico,' in L. Manzanilla and L. López Luján (eds.), *Historia antigua de México, volumen I: el México antiguo, sus áreas culturales, los orígenes y el horizonte preclásico*, pp. 437–510. Mexico City: Instituto Nacional de Antropología e Historia and Universidad Nacional Autónoma de México.

Clark, J.E. and Parry, W.J. 1990. 'Craft specialization and cultural complexity.' *Research in Economic Anthropology* 12: 289–346.

Clark, J.E. and Pérez-Suárez, T. 1994. 'Los olmecas y el primer milenio de Mesoamérica,' in J.E. Clark (ed.), *Los olmecas en Mesoamérica*, pp. 261–75. Mexico City: Citibank.

Clark, J.E. and Pye, M.E. (eds.) 2000a. *Olmec Art and Archaeology in Mesoamerica*. Washington, DC: National Gallery of Art.

Clark, J.E. and Pye, M.E. 2000b. 'The Pacific Coast and the Olmec Question,' in J.E. Clark and M.E. Pye (eds.), *Olmec Art and Archaeology in Mesoamerica*, pp. 217–251. Washington, DC: National Gallery of Art.

Clark, J.E. and Salcedo Romero, T. 1989. 'Ocós obsidian distribution in Chiapas, Mexico,' in F.J. Bove and L. Heller (eds.), *New Frontiers in the Archaeology of the Pacific Coast of Southern Mesoamerica*, pp. 15–24. Tempe: Arizona State University.

Clewlow, C.W., Jr. 1974. *A Stylistic and Chronological Study of Olmec Monumental Sculpture*, Contributions of the University of California Archaeological Research Facility, No. 19. Berkeley: University of California.

Clewlow, C.W., Cowan, R.A., O'Connell, J.F., and Beneman, C. 1967. *Colossal Heads of the Olmec Culture*, Contributions of the University of California Archaeological Research Facility, No. 4. Berkeley: University of California.

Cobean, R. 1996. 'La Oaxaqueña, Veracruz: un centro olmeca menor en su contexto regional,' in A.G. Mastache, J. Parsons, R.S. Santley, and M.C. Serradr Puche (eds.), *Arqueología Mesoamericana: Homenaje a William T. Sanders, Tomo II*. Mexico City: INAH.

Cobean, R.H., Coe, M.D., Perry, E.A., Jr., Turekian, K.K., and Kharkar, D.P. 1971. 'Obsidian trade at San Lorenzo Tenochtitlan, Mexico.' *Science* 174: 666–671.

Cobean, R.H., Vogt, J.R., Glascock, M.D., and Stocker, T.L. 1991. 'High-precision trace-element characterization of major Mesoamerican obsidian sources and further analyses of artifacts from San Lorenzo Tenochtitlan, Mexico.' *Latin American Antiquity* 2: 69–91.

Coe, M.D. 1962. *Mexico*. London: Thames and Hudson.

Coe, M.D. 1965a. 'Archaeological synthesis of Southern Veracruz and Tabasco,' in R. Wauchope (ed.), *Archaeology of Southern Mesoamerica, Part 2*, Handbook of Middle American Indians, Vol. 3, pp. 679–715. Austin: University of Texas Press.

Coe, M.D. 1965b. *The Jaguar's Children: Pre-classic central Mexico*. New York: Museum of Primitive Art.

Coe, M.D. 1965c. 'The Olmec style and its distributions,' in R. Wauchope (ed.), *Archaeology of Southern Mesoamerica, Part 2*, Handbook of Middle American Indians, Vol. 3, pp. 739–75. Austin: University of Texas Press.

Coe, M.D. 1968a. *America's First Civilization: Discovering the Olmec*. New York: American Heritage Publishing Co., Inc.

Coe, M.D. 1968b. 'San Lorenzo and the Olmec civilization,' in E.P. Benson (ed.), *Dumbarton Oaks Conference on the Olmec*, pp. 41–78. Washington, DC: Dumbarton Oaks.

Coe, M.D. 1970a. 'The archaeological sequence at San Lorenzo Tenochtitlan, Veracruz, Mexico.' *Contributions of the University of California Archaeological Research Facility* 8: 21–40.

Coe, M.D. 1970b. 'Olmec man and Olmec land.' *Discovery* 5(2): 69–78.

Coe, M.D. 1974. 'Photogrammetry and the ecology of Olmec civilization,' in E.Z. Vogt (ed.), *Aerial Photography in Anthropological Field Research*, pp. 1–13. Cambridge, MA: Harvard University Press.

Coe, M.D. 1977. 'Olmec and Maya: a study in relationships,' in R.E.W. Adams (ed.), *The Origins of Maya Civilization*, pp. 183–195. Albuquerque: University of New Mexico Press.

Coe, M.D. 1981. 'Gift of the river: ecology of the San Lorenzo Olmec,' in E.P. Benson (ed.), *The Olmec and Their Neighbors: Essays in Memory of Matthew W. Stirling*, pp. 15–19. Washington,

DC: Dumbarton Oaks Research Library and Collections.

Coe, M.D. 1989. 'The Olmec heartland: evolution of ideology,' in R.J. Sharer and D.C. Grove (eds.), *Regional Perspectives on the Olmec*, pp. 68–82. Cambridge: Cambridge University Press.

Coe, M.D. 1993. *The Maya*. London: Thames and Hudson.

Coe, M.D. 1994. *Mexico: From the Olmecs to the Aztecs*. London: Thames and Hudson.

Coe, M.D. and Diehl, R.A. 1980a. *In the Land of the Olmec, Vol. 1, The Archaeology of San Lorenzo Tenochtitlán*. Austin: University of Texas Press.

Coe, M.D. and Diehl, R.A. 1980b. *In the Land of the Olmec, Vol. 2, The People of the River*. Austin: University of Texas Press.

Coe, M.D., Diehl, R.A., and Stuiver, M. 1967a. 'La civilización olmeca de Veracruz. Fechas para la fase San Lorenzo.' *La palabra y el hombre* 43: 517–524.

Coe, M.D. and Diehl, R.A. 1967b. 'Olmec civilization, Veracruz, Mexico: dating of the San Lorenzo phase.' *Science* 155: 1399–1401.

Coe, M.D. and Flannery, K.V. 1964. 'Microenvironments and Mesoamerican preshistory.' *Science* 143: 650–654.

Coe, M.D. and Diehl, R.A. 1967. *Early Cultures and Human Ecology in South Coastal Guatemala*, Smithsonian Institution Contributions to Anthropology, Vol. 3. Washington, DC: Smithsonian Institution.

Coe, M.D. and Koontz, R. 2002. *Mexico: From the Olmecs to the Aztecs*. New York: Thames and Hudson.

Coe, W.R. and Stuckenrath, R. 1964. 'A review of La Venta, Tabasco and its relevance to the Olmec problem.' *Kroeber Anthropological Society Papers* 31: 1–43.

Covarrubias, M. 1946. 'El arte "olmeca" o de La Venta.' *Cuadernos americanos* 4: 153–179.

Covarrubias, M. 1957. *Indian Art of Mexico and Central America*. New York: Alfred A. Knopf.

Cowgill, G.L. 1993. 'Distinguished lecture in archeology: beyond criticizing new archeology.' *American Anthropologist* 95: 551–573.

Crumley, C.L. 1979. 'Three locational models: an epistemological assessment of anthropology and archaeology,' in M.B. Schiffer (ed.), *Advances in Archaeological Method and Theory*, Vol. 2, pp. 141–173. New York: Academic Press.

Crumley, C.L. 1995. 'Heterarchy and the analysis of complex societies,' in R.M. Ehrenreich,

C.L. Crumley, and J.E. Levy (eds.), *Heterarchy and the Analysis of Complex Societies*, Archaeological Papers of the American Anthropological Association, No. 6, pp. 1–5. Arlington, VA: American Anthropological Association.

Curtis, G.H. 1959. 'Appendix 4. The petrology of artifacts and architectural stone at La Venta,' in P. Drucker, R.F. Heizer. and R.H. Squier (eds.), *Excavations at La Venta, Tabasco, 1955*, Bureau of American Ethnology, Bulletin 170, pp. 284–289. Washington, DC: Smithsonian Institution.

Cyphers, A. 1995. 'Las cabezas colosales.' *Arqueología Mexicana* 2(12): 43–47.

Cyphers, A. 1996. 'Reconstructing Olmec Life at San Lorenzo,' in E.P. Benson and B. de ladr Fuente (eds.), *Olmec Art of Ancient Mexico*, pp. 61–71. Washington, DC: National Gallery of Art.

Cyphers, A 1997a. 'La arquitectura olmeca en San Lorenzo Tenochtitlán,' in A. Cyphers (ed.), *Población, subsistencia y medio ambiente en San Lorenzo Tenochtitlán*, pp. 91–117. México City: Universidad Nacional Autónoma de México.

Cyphers, A. 1997b. 'El contexto social de monumentos en San Lorenzo,' in A. Cyphers (ed.), *Población, subsistencia y medio ambiente en San Lorenzo Tenochtitlán*, pp. 163–194. México City: Universidad Nacional Autónoma de México.

Cyphers, A. 1997c. 'Crecimiento y desarrollo de San Lorenzo,' in A. Cyphers (ed.), *Población, subsistencia y medio ambiente en San Lorenzo Tenochtitlán*, pp. 255–274. México City: Universidad Nacional Autónoma de México.

Cyphers, A. 1997d. 'Los felinos de San Lorenzo,' in A. Cyphers (ed.), *Población, subsistencia y medio ambiente en San Lorenzo Tenochtitlán*, pp. 195–225. México City: Universidad Nacional Autónoma de México.

Cyphers, A. 1997e. 'La gobernatura en San Lorenzo: inferencias del arte y patron de asentamiento,' in A. Cyphers (ed.), *Población, subsistencia y medio ambiente en San Lorenzo Tenochtitlán*, pp. 227–242. México City: Universidad Nacional Autónoma de México.

Cyphers, A. 1997f. 'Olmec architecture at San Lorenzo,' in B.L. Stark and P.J. Arnold, III (eds.), *Olmec to Aztec: Settlement Patterns in the Ancient Gulf Lowlands*, pp. 96–114. Tucson, Arizona: The University of Arizona Press.

Cyphers, A. 1997g. *Población, subsistencia y medio ambiente en San Lorenzo Tenochtitlán*. México

City: Universidad Nacional Autónoma de México.

Cyphers, A. 1999. 'From stone to symbols: Olmec art in social context at San Lorenzo Tenochtitlán,' in D.C. Grove and R.A. Joyce (eds.), *Social Patterns in Pre-Classic Mesoamerica*, pp. 155–181. Washington, DC: Dumbarton Oaks Research Library and Collection.

Cyphers, A. 2004. *Escultura Olmeca de San Lorenzo Tenochtitlán*. Mexico City: Universidad Nacional Autónoma de México.

Cyphers, A. and Di Castro Stringher, A. 1996. 'Los artefactos multiperforados de ilmenita en San Lorenzo.' *Arqueología* 16: 3–14.

Cyphers Guillén, A. 1984. 'The possible role of a woman in Formative exchange,' in K.G. Hirth (ed.), *Trade and Exchange in Early Mesoamerica*, pp. 115–123. Albuquerque: Universtiy of New Mexico.

Cyphers Guillén, A. 1987. 'Ceramics,' in D.C. Grove (ed.), *Ancient Chalcatzingo*, pp. 200–251. Austin: University of Texas Press.

Cyphers Guillén, A. 1990. 'Espacios domésticos olmecas en San Lorenzo Tenochtitlán, Veracruz.' *Boletín del Consejo de Arqueología* 1989: 284–289.

Cyphers Guillén, A. 1994. 'San Lorenzo Tenochtitlan,' in J.E. Clark (ed.), *Los olmecas en Mesoamérica*, pp. 43–67. Mexico City: Citibank.

de la Fuente, B. 1973. *Escultura monumental olmeca: catálogo*. Mexico City: Instituto de Invesigaciones Estéticas, Universidad Nacional Autónoma de México.

de la Fuente, B. 1977. *Los hombres de piedra: escultura olmeca*. Mexico City: Universidad Nacional Autónoma de México.

de la Fuente, B. 1981. 'Toward a conception of monumental Olmec art,' in E.P. Benson (ed.), *The Olmec and their Neighbors*, pp. 83–94. Washington, DC: Dumbarton Oaks.

de la Fuente, B. 1994. 'Arte monumental olmeca,' in J.E. Clark (ed.), *Los olmecas en Mesoamérica*, pp. 203–221. Mexico City: Citibank.

de la Fuente, B. 1996. 'Homocentrism in Olmec art,' in E.P. Benson and B. de la Fuente (eds.), *Olmec Art of Ancient Mexico*, pp. 41–49. Washington, DC: National Gallery of Art.

de la Fuente, B. 2000. 'Olmec sculpture: the first mesoamerican art,' in J.E. Clark and M.E. Pye (eds.), *Olmec Art and Archaeology in Mesoamerica*, pp. 253–263. Washington, DC: National Gallery of Art.

de Montmollin, O. 1989. *The Archaeology of Political Structure: Settlement Analysis in a Classic Maya Polity*. Cambridge: Cambridge University Press.

del Paso y Troncoso, F. 1892. *Catálogo de la sección de México*. Madrid: Exposición Histórico-Americana de Madrid.

Demarest, A.A. 1989. 'The Olmec and the rise of civilization in eastern Mesoamerica,' in R.J. Sharer and D.C. Grove (eds.), *Regional Perspectives on the Olmec*, pp. 303–344. Cambridge: Cambridge University Press.

Di Castro Stringher, A. 1997. 'Los bloques de ilmenita de San Lorenzo,' in A. Cyphers (ed.), *Población, subsistencia y medio ambiente en San Lorenzo Tenochtitlán*, pp. 153–160. México City: Universidad Nacional Autónoma de México.

Diehl, R.A. 1973. 'Political evolution and the Formative period of Mesoamerica,' *Occasional Papers in Anthropology*, Vol. 8, pp. 1–92. University Park: Pennsylvania State University.

Diehl, R.A. 1981. 'Olmec architecture: a comparison of San Lorenzo and La Venta,' in E.P. Benson (ed.), *The Olmec and their Neighbors*, pp. 69–81. Washington, DC: Dumbarton Oaks.

Diehl, R.A. 1989. 'Olmec archaeology: what we know and what we wish we knew,' in R.J. Sharer and D.C. Grove (eds.), *Regional Perspectives on the Olmec*, pp. 17–32. Cambridge: Cambridge University Press.

Diehl, R.A. 2004. *The Olmecs: America's First Civilization*. London: Thames and Hudson, Ltd.

Diehl, R.A. and Coe, M.D. 1995. 'Olmec archaeology,' in J. Guthrie and E.P. Benson (eds.), *The Olmec World: Ritual and Rulership*, pp. 11–25. Princeton, NJ: The Art Museum, Princeton University.

Dillehay, T.D. 1989. *Monte Verde: A Late Pleistocene Settlement in Chile, Volume 1, Paleoenvironment and Site Context*. Washington, DC: Smithsonian Institution Press.

Dillehay, T.D. 1992. 'Keeping outsiders out: public ceremony, resource rights, and hierarchy in historic and contemporary Mapuche society,' in F.W. Lange (ed.), *Wealth and Hierarchy in the Intermediate Area*, pp. 379–422. Washington, DC: Dumbarton Oaks.

Dillehay, T.D. 1997. *Monte Verde: A Late Pleistocene Settlement in Chile, Vol 2, The Archaeological Context and Interpretation*. Washington, DC: Smithsonian Institution Press.

Doering, T. 2002. *Obsidian artifacts from San Andrés, La Venta, Tabasco, Mexico*. Unpublished M.S. thesis, Department of Anthropology, Florida State University, Tallahassee.

Drennan, R.D. 1976. *Fábrica San José and Middle Formative society in the Valley of Oaxaca*, Prehistory and Human Ecology of the Valley of Oaxaca 4, Memoirs of the University of Michigan Museum of Anthropology 8. Ann Arbor.

Drennan, R.D. 1991. 'Pre-Hispanic chiefdom trajectories in Mesoamerica, Central America, and northern South America,' in T. Earle (ed.), *Chiefdoms: Power, Economy, and Ideology*, pp. 263–287. Cambridge: Cambridge University Press.

Drennan, R.D. 2000. 'Games, players, rules, and circumstances,' in G.M. Feinman and Manzanilla (eds.), *Cultural Evolution: Contemporary Viewpoints*, pp. 177–196. New York: Kluwer Academic/Plenum Publishers.

Drucker, P. 1943a. *Ceramic Sequences at Tres Zapotes, Veracruz, Mexico*, Bureau of American Ethnology Bulletin 140. Washington DC: Smithsonian Institution.

Drucker, P. 1943b. *Ceramic Stratigraphy at Cerro de las Mesas Veracruz, Mexico*, Bureau of American Ethnology Bulletin 141. Washington, DC: Smithsonian Institution.

Drucker, P. 1947. *Some implications of the Ceramic Complex of La Venta*, Smithsonian Miscellaneous Collections 107, No. 8. Washington, DC: Smithsonian Institution.

Drucker, P. 1952a. *La Venta, Tabasco: A Study of Olmec Ceramics and Art*, Bureau of American Ethnology Bulletin 153. Washington, DC: Smithsonian Institution.

Drucker, P. 1952b. 'Middle Tres Zapotes pottery and the Pre-Classic ceramic sequence.' *American Antiquity*: 258–260.

Drucker, P. 1961. 'The La Venta Olmec support area.' *Kroeber Anthropological Society Papers* 25: 59–72.

Drucker, P. 1981. 'On the nature of Olmec polity,' in E.P. Benson (ed.), *The Olmec and their Neighbors*, pp. 49–68. Washington, DC: Dumbarton Oaks.

Drucker, P. and Contreras, E. 1953. 'Site patterns in the eastern part of the Olmec territory.' *Journal of the Washington Academy of Sciences* 43: 389–396.

Drucker, P. and Heizer, R.F. 1960. 'A study of the milpa system of La Venta island and its archaeological implications.' *Southwestern Journal of Anthropology* 16: 36–45.

Drucker, P. and Heizer, R.F. 1965. 'Commentary on W. R. Coe and Robert Stuckenrath's review of *Excavations at La Venta Tabasco, 1955*.' *Kroeber Anthropological Society Papers* 33: 37–70.

Drucker, P., Heizer, R.F., and Squier, R.H. 1959. *Excavations at La Venta, Tabasco*, Bureau of American Ethnology Bulletin 170. Washington DC: Smithsonian Institution.

Dunnell, R.C. 1980. 'Evolutionary theory and archaeology.' *Advances in Archaeological Method and Theory* 3: 38–99.

Earle, T.K. 1976. 'A nearest-neighbor analysis of two Formative settlement systems,' in K.V. Flannery (ed.), *The Early Mesoamerican Village*, pp. 196–223. New York: Academic Press.

Earle, T.K. 1991. 'The evolution of chiefdoms,' in T.K. Earle (ed.), *Chiefdoms: Power, Economy, and Ideology*, pp. 1–15. Cambridge: Cambridge University Press.

Earle, T.K. 1997. *How Chiefs Come to Power: The Political Economy in Prehistory*. Stanford, CA: Stanford University Press.

Easton, D. 1959. 'Political anthropology.' *Biennial Review of Anthropology* 1959: 210–262.

Ekholm, G.F. 1945. '*An Introduction to the Ceramics of Tres Zapotes, Veracruz, Mexico; Ceramic Sequences at Tres Zapotes, Veracruz, Mexico; Ceramic Stratigraphy at Cerro de las Mesas, Veracruz, Mexico* (Review).' *American Antiquity* 11: 63–64.

Ekholm-Miller, S. 1969. *Mound 30a and the Early Preclassic Ceramic Sequence of Izapa, Chiapas, Mexico*, Papers of the New World Archaeological Foundation, No. 25. Provo, UT.

Ekholm-Miller, S. 1973. *The Olmec Rock Carving at Xoc, Chiapas, Mexico*, Papers of the New World Archaeological Foundation, No. 32. Provo, UT.

Eliade, M. 1964. *Shamanism: Archaic Techniques of Ecstasy*. New York: Bollingen Foundation/Pantheon.

Evans, S.T. 2004. *Ancient Mexico and Central America: Archaeology and Culture History*. London: Thames and Hudson.

Fash, W., Jr. 1987. 'The altar and associated features,' in D.C. Grove (ed.), *Ancient Chalcatzingo*, pp. 82–94. Austin: University of Texas Press.

Fash, W.L. 1991. *Scribes, Warriors and Kings*. London: Thames and Hudson.

Feinman, G.M. 2001. 'Mesoamerican political complexity,' in J. Haas (ed.), *From Leaders to Rulers*, pp. 151–175. New York: Kluwer/Plenum Publishers.

Fields, V.M. 1989. *The Origins of Kingship among the Lowland Classic Maya.* Unpublished Ph.D. dissertation, Department of Art History, University of Texas, Austin.

Fields, V.M. 1991. 'The iconographic heritage of the Maya jester god,' in V.M. Fields (ed.), *Sixth Palenque Round Table, 1986.* Norman, OK.

Flannery, K.V. 1968a. 'Archaeological Systems Theory and early Mesoamerica,' in B.J. Meggers (ed.), *Anthropological Archaeology in the Americas,* pp. 67–87. Washington, DC: Anthropological Society of Washington.

Flannery, K.V. 1968b. 'The Olmec and the Valley of Oaxaca: a model for interregional interaction in Formative times,' in E.P. Benson (ed.), *Dumbarton Oaks Conference on the Olmec,* pp. 79–110. Washington, DC: Dumbarton Oaks.

Flannery, K.V. 1976. *The Early Mesoamerican Village.* New York: Academic Press.

Flannery, K.V. 1986. *Guilá Naquitz.* New York: Academic Press.

Flannery, K.V. 1998. 'The ground plans of archaic states,' in G.M. Feinman and J. Marcus (eds.), *Archaic States,* pp. 15–57. Santa Fe: School of American Research Press.

Flannery, K.V. 1999. 'Process and agency in early state formation.' *Cambridge Archaeological Journal* 9: 3–21.

Flannery, K.V., Balkansky, A.K., Feinman, G.M., Grove, D.C., Marcus, J., Redmond, E.M., Reynolds, R.G., Sharer, R.J., Spencer, C.S., and Yaeger, J. 2005. 'Implications of new petrographic analysis for the Olmec "mother culture" model.' *Proceedings of the National Academy of Sciences* 102 (11219–11213).

Flannery, K.V. and Marcus, J. 1993. 'Cognitive archaeology.' *Cambridge Archaeological Journal* 3: 260–267.

Flannery, K.V. and Marcus, J. 1994. *Early Formative Pottery of the Valley of Oaxaca, Mexico.* Ann Arbor: University of Michigan.

Flannery, K.V. and Marcus, J. 2000. 'Formative Mexican chiefdoms and the myth of the "Mother Culture".' *Journal of Anthropological Archaeology* 19: 1–37.

Flannery, K.V. and Marcus, J. 2003. 'The origin of war: new ^{14}C dates from ancient Mexico.' *Proceedings of the National Academy of Sciences* 100: 11803–11805.

Fried, M.H. 1960. 'On the evolution of social stratification and the state,' in S. Diamond (ed.), *Culture in History: Essays in Honor of Paul Radin,* pp. 713–731. New York: Columbia University Press.

Fried, M.H. 1967. *The Evolution of Political Society.* Clinton, MA: The Colonial Press.

Friedel, D.A., Schele, L. and Parker, J. 1993. *Maya Cosmos: 3,000 Years on the Shaman's Path.* New York: William Morrow and Company, Inc.

Friedlander, I. and Sonder, R.A. 1923. 'Uber das vulkangebiet von San Martin Tuxtla in Mexico.' *Zeitschrift fur Vulkanologie* VII: 3–42.

Fuentes Mata, P. and Pérez, E. 1997. 'Peces de agua dulce y estuarinos,' in E. González Soriano, R. Dirzo, and R.C. Vogt (eds.), *Historia natural de Los Tuxtlas,* pp. 457–471. Mexico: Universidad Nacional Autónoma de México.

Furst, P.T. 1968. 'The Olmec were-jaguar motif in the light of ethnographic reality,' in E.P. Benson (ed.), *Dumbarton Oaks Conference on the Olmec,* pp. 143–178. Washington, DC: Dumbarton Oaks.

Furst, P.T. 1981. 'Jaguar baby or toad mother: A new look at an old problem in Olmec iconography,' in E.P. Benson (ed.), *The Olmec and Their Neighbors: Essays in Memory of Matthew W. Stirling,* pp. 149–162. Washington, DC: Dumbarton Oaks.

Furst, P.T. 1995. 'Shamanism, transformation, and Olmec art,' in J. Guthrie and E.P. Benson (eds.), *The Olmec World: Ritual and Rulership,* pp. 69–81. Princeton, New Jersey: The Art Museum, Princeton University.

Gallegos Gómora, M.J. 1990. 'Excavaciones en la estructura D-7 en La Venta, Tabasco.' *Arqueología* (3): 17–24.

Gamio, M. 1913. 'Arqueología de Atzcapotzalco,' *Proceedings, Eighteenth International Congress of Americanists,* pp. 180–187. London.

Garber, J.F., Hirth, K.G., Hoopes, J.W., and Grove, D.C. 1993. 'Jade use in portions of Mexico and Central America: Olmec, Maya, Costa Rica, and Honduras: a summary,' in F.W. Lange (ed.), *Precolumbian Jade: New Geological and Cultural Interpretations,* pp. 211–231. Salt Lake City: University of Utah Press.

Gay, C.T.E. 1967. 'Oldest paintings of the New World.' *Natural History* 76: 28–35.

Gay, C.T.E. 1973. 'Olmec hieroglyphic writing.' *Archaeology* 26: 278–288.

Gay, C.T.E. 1973. *Xochipala: The Beginnings of Olmec Art.* Princeton, NJ: The Art Museum, Princeton University.

Gillespie, S.D. 1993. 'Power, pathways, and appropriations in Mesoamerican art,' in D. Whitten and N. Whitten, Jr (eds.), *Image and Creativity: Ethnoaesthetics and Art Worlds in the Americas*. Tucson: University of Arizona Press.

Gillespie, S.D. 1994. 'Llano del Jícaro: an Olmec monument workshop.' *Ancient Mesoamerica* 5: 231–242.

Gillespie, S.D. 1999. 'Olmec thrones as ancestral altars: the two sides of power,' in J.E. Robb (ed.), *Material Symbols: Culture and Economy in Prehistory*, Center for Archaeological Investigations, Occasional Paper No. 26, pp. 224–253. Carbondale: Southern Illinois University.

Gillespie, S.D. 2000. 'The monuments of Laguna de los Cerros and its hinterland,' in J.E. Clark and M.E. Pye (eds.), *Olmec Art and Archaeology in Mesoamerica*, pp. 95–115. Washington, DC: National Gallery of Art.

Girard, R. 1968. *La misteriosa cultura olmeca*. Guatemala: Empresa Eléctrica de Guatemala, S.A.

Goman, M. 1992. *Paleoecological Evidence for Prehistoric Agriculture and Tropical Forest Clearance in the Sierra de los Tuxtlas, Veracruz, Mexico*. Unpublished M.A. thesis, Department of Geography, University of California, Berkeley.

Goman, M. 1998. 'A 5000-year record of agriculture and tropical forest clearance in the Tuxtlas, Veracruz, Mexico.' *The Holocene* 8: 83–98.

Gómez Rueda, H. 1996. *Las Limas, Veracruz, y otros asentamientos prehispánicos de la región olmeca*, Colección Científica No. 324. Mexico City: INAH.

Gómez-Pompa, A. 1973. 'Ecology of the vegetation of Veracruz,' in A. Graham (ed.), *Vegetation and Vegetational History of Northern Latin America*, pp. 73–148. Amsterdam: Elsevier.

González Lauck, R. 1985. *The 1984 Archaeological Investigations at La Venta, Tabasco, Mexico*. Ph.D. dissertation, Department of Anthropology, University of California, Berkeley, Berkeley.

González Lauck, R. 1988. 'Proyecto arqueológico La Venta.' *Arqueología* 4: 121–165.

González Lauck, R. 1996. 'La Venta: An Olmec capital,' in E.P. Benson and B. de la Fuente (eds.), *Olmec Art of Ancient Mexico*, pp. 73–81. Washington, DC: National Gallery of Art.

González Lauck, R. 1997. 'Acerca de pirámides de tierra y seres sobrenaturales: observaciones

preliminares en torno al Edificio C-1, La Venta, Tabasco.' *Arqueología* 17: 79–97.

González Lauck, R. 1998. 'Prospección arqueológica con equipo moderno en La Venta.' *Arqueología Mexicana* 5(30): 49.

González Lauck, R. 2000. 'La zona del Golfo en el Preclásico: la etapa olmeca,' in L. Manzanilla and L. López Luján (eds.), *Historia Antigua de México, Volúmen I: El México antiguo, sus areas culturales, los orígenes y el horizonte Preclásico*, pp. 363–406. Mexico City: INAH, UNAM.

González Lauck, R. and Solis Olguín, F. 1996. 'Olmec collections in the museums of Tabasco: a century of protecting a millenial civilization (1896–1996),' in E.P. Benson and B. de la Fuente (eds.), *Olmec Art of Ancient Mexico*, pp. 145–152. Washington, DC: National Gallery of Art.

González Soriano, E., Dirzo, R., and Vogt, R.C. (eds.) 1997. *Historia natural de los Tuxtlas*. Mexico City: Universidad Nacional Autónoma de México.

Gossen, G.H. 1996. 'The religious traditions of Mesoamerica,' in R.M. Carmack, J. Gasco, and G.H. Gossen (eds.), *The Legacy of Mesoamerica: History and Culture of a Native American Civilization*, pp. 290–319. Englewood Cliffs, NJ: Prentice-Hall.

Graham, J.A. 1981. 'Abaj Takalik: the Olmec style and its antecedents in Pacific Guatemala,, in J.A. Graham (ed.), *Ancient Mesoamerica: Selected Readings*, pp. 163–176. Palo Alto, CA: Peek Publications.

Graham, J.A. 1989. 'Olmec diffusion: a sculptural view from Pacific Guatemala,' in R.J. Sharer and D. Grove (eds.), *Regional Perspectives on the Olmec*, pp. 227–246. Cambridge: Cambridge University Press.

Graham, J.A., Heizer, R.F., and Shook, E.M. 1978. 'Abaj Takalik 1976: exploratory investigations.' *Contributions of the University of California Archaeological Research Facility* 36: 85–109.

Green, D.F. and Lowe, G.W. 1967. *Altamira and Padre Piedra, Early Preclassic Sites in Chiapas, Mexico*, Papers of the New World Archaeological Foundation, No. 20. Provo, UT: Brigham Young University.

Griffin, G.G. 1981. 'Olmec forms and materials found in central Guerrero,' in E.P. Benson (ed.), *The Olmec and Their Neighbors: Essays in Memory of Matthew W. Stirling*, pp. 209–222. Washington, DC: Dumbarton Oaks.

Griffin, G.G. 1993. 'Formative Guerrero and its jade,' in F.W. Lange (ed.) *Precolumbian Jade: New Geological and Cultural Interpretations*, pp. 203–210.

Grove, D.C. 1969. 'Olmec cave paintings: discovery from Guerrero, Mexico.' *Science* 172: 421–423.

Grove, D.C. 1970a. *The Olmec Paintings of Oxtotitlan Cave, Guerrero, Mexico*, Studies in Pre-Columbian Art and Archaeology, No. 6. Washington, DC: Dumbarton Oaks.

Grove, D.C. 1970b. 'The San Pablo pantheon mound: a Middle Preclassic site in Morelos, Mexico.' *American Antiquity* 35: 62–73.

Grove, D.C. 1973. 'Olmec altars and myths.' *Archaeology* 26: 128–135.

Grove, D.C. 1974. 'The highland Olmec manifestation: a consideration of what it is and isn't,' in N. Hammond (ed.), *Mesoamerican Archaeology: New Approaches*, pp. 109–128. Austin: University of Texas Press.

Grove, D.C. 1981a. 'The Formative period and the evolution of complex culture,' in J.A. Sabloff (ed.), *Archaeology: Supplement to the Handbook of Middle American Indians, Vol 1*, pp. 373–391. Austin: University of Texas Press.

Grove, D.C. 1981b. 'Olmec monuments: mutilation as a clue to meaning,' in E.P. Benson (ed.), *The Olmec and Their Neighbors: Essays in Memory of Matthew W. Stirling*, pp. 48–68. Washington, DC: Dumbarton Oaks.

Grove, D.C. 1984. *Chalcatzingo: Excavations on the Olmec Frontier*. London: Thames and Hudson.

Grove, D.C. ed. 1987a. *Ancient Chalcatzingo*. Austin: University of Texas Press.

Grove, D.C. 1987b. 'Chalcatzingo in a broader perspective,' in D.C. Grove (ed.), *Ancient Chalcatzingo*, pp. 434–442. Austin: University of Texas Press.

Grove, D.C. 1987c. 'Torches, knuckle dusters, and the legitimation of Formative period rulership.' *Mexicon* 9: 60–66.

Grove, D.C. 1989a. 'Chalcatzingo and its Olmec connection,' in R.J. Sharer and D.C. Grove (eds.), *Regional Perspectives on the Olmec*, pp. 122–147. Cambridge: Cambridge University Press.

Grove, D.C. 1989b. 'Olmec: what's in a name?,' in R.J. Sharer and D.C. Grove (eds.), *Regional Perspectives on the Olmec*, pp. 8–14. Cambridge: Cambridge University Press.

Grove, D.C. 1993. '"Olmec" horizons in Formative Period Mesoamerica: diffusion or social evolution?,' in D.S. Rice (ed.), *Latin American Horizons*, pp. 83–111. Washington, DC: Dumbarton Oaks Research Library and Collections.

Grove, D.C. 1994. 'La Isla, Veracruz, 1991: A preliminary report, with comments on the Olmec uplands.' *Ancient Mesoamerica* 5: 223–230.

Grove, D.C. 1996. 'Archaeological contexts of olmec art outside of the Gulf Coast,' in E.P. Benson and B. de la Fuente (eds.), *Olmec Art of Ancient Mexico*, pp. 105–117. Washington, DC: National Gallery of Art.

Grove, D.C. 1997. 'Olmec archaeology: a half century of research and its accomplishments.' *Journal of World Prehistory* 11: 51–101.

Grove, D.C. 1999. 'Public monuments and sacred mountains: observations on three Formative period sacred landscapes,' in D.C. Grove and R.A. Joyce (eds.), *Social Patterns in Pre-Classic Mesoamerica*, pp. 255–295. Washington, DC: Dumbarton Oaks Research Library and Collections.

Grove, D.C. 2000. 'Faces of the earth at Chalcatzingo, Mexico: Serpents, caves and mountains in Middle Formative period iconography,' in J.E. Clark and M.E. Pye (eds.), *Olmec Art and Archaeology in Mesoamerica*, pp. 277–295. Washington, DC: National Gallery of Art.

Grove, D.C. and Angulo, V.J. 1987. 'A catalog and description of Chalcatzingo's monuments,' in D.C. Grove (ed.), *Ancient Chalcatzingo*, pp. 114–131. Austin: University of Texas Press.

Grove, D.C. and Cyphers Guillén, A. 1987. 'Chronology and cultural phases at Chalcatzingo,' in D.C. Grove (ed.), *Ancient Chalcatzingo*, pp. 56–61. Austin: University of Texas Press.

Grove, D.C. and Joyce, R.A. (eds.) 1999. *Social Patterns in Pre-Classic Mesoamerica*. Washington, DC: Dumbarton Oaks.

Grove, D.C. and Kann, V. 1980. Olmec monumental art: heartland and frontier. Paper presented at the 79th Annual Meeting of the American Anthropological Society, Washington, DC.

Grove, D.C., Ortiz, C.P., Hayton, M., and Gillespie, S.D. 1993. 'Five Olmec monuments from the Laguna de los Cerros hinterland.' *Mexicon* 15: 91–95.

Grove, D.C. and Paradis, L.I. 1971. 'An Olmec stela from San Miguel Amuco, Guerrero.' *American Antiquity* 36: 95–102.

Guthrie, J. and Benson, E.P. (eds.) 1995. *The Olmec World: Ritual and Rulership*. Princeton, NJ: The Art Museum, Princeton University.

Haas, J. 1982. *The Evolution of the Prehistoric State*. New York: Columbia University Press.

Hallinan, P.S., Ambro, R.D., and O'Connell, J.F. 1968. 'Appendix I: La Venta Ceramics, 1968,' in R.F. Heizer, J.A. Graham, and J.K. Napton (eds.), *The 1968 Investigations at La Venta*, Contributions of the University of California Archaeological Research Facility, Vol. 11, pp. 155–170. Berkeley.

Halstead, P. and O'Shea, J. 1989. 'Introduction: cultural responses to risk and uncertainty,' in P. Halstead and J. O'Shea (eds.), *Bad Year Economics: Cultural Responses to Risk and Uncertainty*, pp. 1–7. Cambridge: Cambridge University Press.

Hammond, N. 1989. 'Cultura Hermana: reappraising the Olmec.' *Quarterly Review of Archaeology* 9(4): 1–4.

Hammond, N. 2001. 'The Cobata colossal head: An unfinished Olmec monument?.' *Antiquity* 75: 21–22.

Harlow, G.E. 1993. 'Middle American jade: Geologic and petrologic perspectives on variability and source,' in F.W. Lange (ed.), *Precolumbian Jade: New Geologic and Cultural Interpretations*, pp. 9–29. Salt Lake City: University of Utah Press.

Harlow, G.E. 1995. 'Rocks and minerals employed by the Olmec as carvings,' in J. Guthrie and E.P. Benson (eds.), *The Olmec World: Ritual and Rulership*, pp. 123–129. Princeton, New Jersey: The Art Museum, Princeton University.

Haslip-Viera, G., Ortiz de Montellano, B., and Barbour, W. 1997. 'Robbing Native American cultures.' *Current Anthropology* 38: 419–441.

Hassig, R. 1985. *Trade, Tribute, and Transportation: The Sixteenth Century Political Economy of the Valley of Mexico*. Norman: University of Oklahoma Press.

Hassig, R. 1988. *Aztec Warfare*. Norman: University of Oklahoma Press.

Hayden, B. 1986. 'Resource models of interassemblage variability.' *Lithic Technology* 15(3): 82–89.

Hayden, B. 1987. 'Traditional metate manufacturing in Guatemala using chipped stone tools,' in B. Hayden (ed.), *Lithic Studies among the Contemporary Highland Maya*, pp. 8–119. Tucson: University of Arizona Press.

Heizer, R.F. 1960. 'Agriculture and the theocratic state in lowland southeastern Mexico.' *American Antiquity* 26: 215–222.

Heizer, R.F. 1964. 'Some interim remarks on the Coe-Stuckenrath review.' *Kroeber Anthropological Society Papers* 31: 45–50.

Heizer, R.F. 1967. 'Analysis of two low relief sculptures from La Venta.' *Contributions of the University of Califronia Archaeological Research Facility* 3: 25–55.

Heizer, R.F. 1968. 'New observations on La Venta,' in E.P. Benson (ed.), *Dumbarton Oaks Conference on the Olmec*, pp. 9–40. Washington, DC: Dumbarton Oaks.

Heizer, R.F., Drucker, P. and Graham, J.A. 1968a. 'Investigaciones de 1967 y 1968 en La Venta.' *Boletín del Instituto Nacional de Antropología e Historia* 33: 21–28.

Heizer, R.F., Drucker, P., and Graham, J.A. 1968b. 'Investigations at La Venta, 1967.' *Contributions of the University of California Archaeological Research Facility* 5: 1–33.

Helms, M.W. 1993. *Craft and the Kingly Ideal*. Austin: University of Texas Press.

Henderson, J.S. 1979. *Atopula, Guerrero, and Olmec Horizons in Mesoamerica*, Yale University Publications in Anthropology, No. 77. New Haven: Department of Anthropology, Yale University.

Henderson, J.S. 1997. *The World of the Ancient Maya*. Ithaca: Cornell University Press.

Henderson, J.S. and Joyce, R.A. 2000. Puerto Escondido: exploraciones preliminares del formativo temprano. Unpublished ms. on file, Department of Anthropology, Cornell University, Ithaca, NY.

Hester, T.R., Heizer, R.F., and Jack, R.N. 1971. 'Technology and geologic sources of obsidian from Cerro de las Mesas, Veracruz, Mexico, with observations on Olmec trade.' *Contributions of the University of California Archaeological Research Facility* 13: 133–141.

Hester, T.R., Jack, R.N., and Heizer, R.F. 1971. 'The obsidian of Tres Zapotes, Veracruz, Mexico.' *Contributions of the University of California Archaeological Research Facility* 13: 65–131.

Hill, W.D., Blake, M., and Clark, J.E. 1998. 'Ball court design dates back 3,400 years.' *Nature* 392: 878–879.

Hirth, K.G. 1978. 'Interregional trade and the formation of prehistoric gateway cities.' *American Antiquity* 43: 35–45.

Hirth, K.G. 1987. 'Formative period settlement patterns in the Río Amatzinac Valley,' in D.C. Grove (ed.), *Ancient Chalcatzingo*, pp. 343–367. Austin: University of Texas Press.

Hirth, K.G. 1992. 'Interregional exchange as elite behavior: an evolutionary perspective,' in D.Z. Chase and A.F. Chase (eds.), *Mesoamerican Elites: an Archaeological Assessment*, pp. 18–29. Norman: University of Oklahoma Press.

Hirth, K.G. 1996. 'Political economy and archaeology: perspectives on exchange and production.' *Journal of Archaeological Research* 4: 203–239.

Holmes, W.H. 1907. 'On a nephrite statuette from San Andres Tuxtla, Veracruz, Mexico.' *American Anthropologist* 9: 691–701.

Hosler, D., Burkett, S.L. and Tarkanian, M.J. 1999. 'Prehistoric polymers: Rubber processing in ancient Mesoamerica.' *Science* 284: 1988–1991.

Houston, S. and Coe, M.D. 2003. 'Has Isthmian writing been deciphered?.' *Mexicon* XXV: 151–161.

Humboldt, A.v. 1810. *Vues des Cordillères et Monuments des Peuples Indigènes de l'Amérique*. Paris.

Ibarra-Manríquez, G., Martínez-Ramos, M., Dirzo, R., and Núñez-Farfán 1997. 'La vegetación,' in E. González Soriano, R. Dirzo and R.C. Vogt (eds.), *Historia natural de los Tuxtlas*, pp. 61–85. Mexico: Universidad Nacional Autónoma de México.

INEGI 1984a. *Carta Uso de Suelo y Vegetación Coatzacoalcos E15-1-4*. Mexico City: Instituto Nacional de Estadísitica, Geografía e Informática.

INEGI 1984b. *Carta Uso de Suelo y Vegetación Minatitlan E15–7*. Mexico City: Instituto Nacional de Estadística, Geografía e Informática.

INEGI 1993. *Carta Edafológica Minatitlan E15–7*. Mexico City: Instituto Nacional de Estadística, Geografía e Informática.

Jaime Riverón, O. 2003. *El hacha olmeca: biografía y paisaje*. Unpublished Maestría thesis, Instituto de Investigaciones Antropológicas, Universidad Autónoma de México, Mexico City.

Jiménez Salas, O.H. 1990. 'Geomorfología de la región de La Venta, Tabasco: un sistema fluvio-lagunar costero del cuaternario.' *Arqueología* 3: 3–16.

Joesink-Mandeville, L.R.V. and Méluzin, S. 1976. 'Olmec-Maya relationships: Olmec influence in Yucatan.' *UCLA Latin American Studies Series* 31: 87–105.

Jones, S. 1998. *The Archaeology of Ethnicity: Constructing Identities in the Past and Present*. London: Routledge.

Joralemon, P.D. 1971. *A Study of Olmec Iconography*, Studies in Pre-Columbian Art and Archaeology, No. 7. Washington, DC: Dumbarton Oaks.

Joralemon, P.D. 1976. 'The Olmec dragon: a study in Pre-columbian iconography.' *UCLA Latin American Studies Series* 31: 27–71.

Joralemon, P.D. 1996. 'In search of the Olmec cosmos: reconstructing the world view of Mexico's first civilization,' in E.P. Benson and B. de la Fuente (eds.), *Olmec Art of Ancient Mexico*, pp. 51–59. Washington, DC: National Gallery of Art.

Joyce, R.A. 2004. 'Mesoamerica: a working model,' in J.A. Hendon and R.A. Joyce (eds.), *Mesoamerican Archaeology*, pp. 1–42. Oxford: Blackwell Publishing.

Joyce, R.A., Edging, R., Lorenz, K., and Gillespie, S.D. 1991. 'Olmec bloodletting: an iconographic study,' in V.M. Fields (ed.), *Sixth Palenque Round Table, 1986*, pp. 143–150. Norman, OK.

Joyce, R.A. and Henderson, J.S. 2001. 'Beginnings of village life in eastern Mesoamerica.' *Latin American Antiquity* 12: 5–23.

Justeson, J.S. 1986. 'The origins of writing: Preclassic Mesoamerica.' *World Archaeology* 17: 437–458.

Justeson, J.S. and Kaufman, T. 1993. 'A decipherment of epi-Olmec hieroglyphic writing.' *Science* 259: 1703–1711.

Justeson, J.S. and Kaufman, T. 1997. 'A newly discovered column in the hieroglyphic text on La Mojarra Stela 1: a test of the epi-Olmec decipherment.' *Science* 277: 207–210.

Justeson, J.S. and Kaufman, T. 2006. 'The epi-Olmec tradition at Cerro de las Mesas in the Classic period,' in P.J. Arnold and C.A. Pool (eds.), *Cultural Currents in Classic Veracruz*. Washington, DC: Dumbarton Oaks. In press.

Justeson, J.S. and Matthews, P. 1990. 'Evolutionary trends in Mesoamerican hieroglyphic writing.' *Visible Language* 24: 38–61.

Kaplan, J. 2000. 'Monument 65: a great emblematic depiction of throned rule and royal sacrifice at Late Preclassic Kaminaljuyu.' *Ancient Mesoamerica* 11: 185–198.

Kappelman, J.G. 2000. 'Late Formative toad altars as ritual stages.' *Mexicon* XXII: 80–84.

Kappelman, J.G. 2003. 'Reassessing the Late Preclassic Pacific slope: the role of sculpture.' *Mexicon* XXV: 39–42.

Kaufman, T. 2000. Running Translation of the La Mojarra Stela. http://www.pitt.edu/~pittanth/kaufman.htm. Downloaded 1 Sept. 2002.

Kaufman, T. and Justeson, J.S. 2001. *Epi-Olmec Hieroglyphic Writing and Texts*. Austin: Texas Workshop Foundation.

Kaufman, T., and Justson, J.S. 2006. 'The Epi-Olmec Language and its Neighbors,' in P.J. Arnold and C.A. Pool (eds.), *Cultural Currents in Classic Veracruz*. Washington, DC: Dumbarton Oaks. In press.

Killion, T.W. 1987. *Agriculture and Residential Site Structure among Campesinos in Southern Veracruz, Mexico: A Foundation for Archaeological Inference*. Unpublished Ph.D. dissertation, Department of Anthropology, University of New Mexico, Albuquerque.

Killion, T.W. 1990. 'Cultivation intensity and residential site structure: an ethnoarchaeological examination of peasant agriculture in the Sierra de los Tuxtlas, Veracruz, Mexico.' *Latin American Antiquity* 1: 191–215.

Killion, T.W. and Urcíd, J. 2001. 'The Olmec legacy: Cultural continuity in Mexico's southern Gulf Coast lowlands.' *Journal of Field Archaeology* 28: 3–25.

Kirchoff, P. 1943. 'Mesoamerica: its geographical limits, ethnic composition, and cultural characteristics.' *Acta Americana* 1: 92–107.

Klein, C.F., Guzmán, E., Mandell, E.C., and Stanfield-Mazzi, M. 2002. 'The role of shamanism in Mesoamerican art.' *Current Anthropology* 43: 383–418.

Kluckhohn, C. 1940. 'The conceptual structure in Middle American studies,' in C.L. Hay (ed.), *The Maya and their Neighbors*, pp. 4–51. New York: Appleton-Century.

Knight, C. 1999. *The Late Formative to Classic Period Obsidian Economy at Palo Errado, Veracruz, Mexico*. Ph.D. dissertation, University of Pittsburgh.

Knight, C. 2003. 'Obsidian production, consumption, and distribution at Tres Zapotes: piecing together political economy,' in C.A. Pool (ed.), *Settlement Archaeology and Political Economy at Tres Zapotes, Veracruz, Mexico*, Monograph 50, pp. 69–89. Los Angeles: Cotsen Institute of Archaeology, University of California.

Kowalewski, S.A., Feinman, G.M., Finsten, L., Blanton, R., and Nicholas, L. 1989. *Monte Alban's Hinterland, Part II: The Prehispanic Settlement Patterns in Tlacolula, Etla, and Ocotlán, the Valley of Oaxaca, Mexico*, Museum of Anthropology Memoir 23. University of Michigan, Ann Arbor.

Kruger, R.P. 1996. *An Archaeological Survey in the Region of the Olmec: Veracruz, Mexico*. Ph.D. dissertation, Department of Anthropology, University of Pittsburgh, Pittsburgh.

Kruger, R.P. 1997. 'Reconocimiento arqueológico en la región de los Olmecas,' in S. Ladrón de Guevara and S. Vásquez Zárate (eds.), *Memoria del Coloquio Arqueología del Centro y Sur de Veracruz*, pp. 141–161. Xalapa, Veracruz, México: Universidad Veracruzana.

Kruger, R.P. 1999. Investigations of a rural Olmec settlement in southern Veracruz. Paper presented at the 64th Annual Meeting of the Society for American Archaeology, Chicago, Illinois.

Kruszczynski, M.A.R. 2001. *Prehistoric Basalt Exploitation and Core-Periphery Relations Observed from the Cerro el Vigía Hinterland of Tres Zapotes, Veracruz, Mexico*. Ph.D. dissertation, Department of Anthropology, University of Pittsburgh.

Kubler, G. 1962. *The Art and Architecture of Ancient America*. Baltimore: Penguin Books.

Kunz, G.F. 1890. *Gems and Precious Stones of North America*. New York: Scientific Publishing.

Ladrón de Guevara, S. and Vásquez, Z.S. (eds.) 1997. *Memoria del coloquio Arqueología del Centro y Sur de Veracruz*. Xalapa, Veracruz: Universidad Veracruzana.

León Pérez, I. 2003. Rescate arqueológico realizado en estudios sismológicos. Report submitted to the Instituto Nacional de Antropología e Historia, Veracruz, Veracruz, Mexico.

Lesure, R.G. 1997. 'Early Formative platforms at Paso de la Amada, Chiapas, Mexico.' *Latin American Antiquity* 8: 217–235.

Lesure, R.G. 2000. 'Animal imagery, cultural unities, and ideologies of inequality in Early Formative Mesoamerica,' in J.E. Clark and M.E. Pye (eds.), *Olmec Art and Archaeology in Mesoamerica*, pp. 193–215. Washington, DC: National Gallery of Art.

Lesure, R.G. 2004. 'Shared art styles and long-distance contact in early Mesoamerica,' in R.A. Joyce and J.A. Hendon (eds.), *Mesoamerican Archaeology*, pp. 73–96. Oxford: Blackwell Publishing.

Lesure, R.G. and Blake, M. 2002. 'Interpretive challenges in the study of early complexity: economy, ritual, and architecture at Paso de la Amada, Mexico.' *Journal of Anthropological Archaeology* 21: 1–24.

Lorenzo, J.L. 1976. *La arqueología mexicana y los arqueólogos norteamericanos*, Cuadernos de Trabajo, No. 14. Mexico City: Departamento de Prehistoria, Instituto Nacional de Antropología e Historia.

Lorenzo, J.L. 1981. 'Archaeology south of the Río Grande.' *World Archaeology* 13: 190–208.

Lösch, A. 1954. *The Economics of Location*. New Haven: Yale University Press.

Loughlin, M. 2004. El Mesón Regional Survey, Veracruz, Mexico. Report submitted to the Foundation for the Advancement of Mesoamerican Studies, Inc., Coral Gables, FL.

Love, M.W. 1999. 'Ideology, material culture, and daily practice in Pre-Classic Mesoamerica: a Pacific Coast perspective,' in D.C. Grove and R.A. Joyce (eds.), *Social Patterns in Pre-Classic Mesoamerica*, pp. 127–153. Washington, DC: Dumbarton Oaks.

Lowe, G.W. 1971. 'The civilizational consequences of varying degrees of agricultural and ceramic dependence within the basic ecosystems of Mesoamerica,' *Contributions of the University of California Archaeological Research Facility* 11(11): 212–248.

Lowe, G.W. 1975. 'La cultura Barra de la costa del Pacífico de Chiapas: un resumen y nuevos datos.' *Sociedad Mexicana de Antropología. Mesa redonda* 2: 11–20.

Lowe, G.W. 1977. 'The Mixe-Zoque as competing neighbors of the early lowland Maya,' in R.E.W. Adams (ed.), *Origins of Maya Civilization*, pp. 197–248. Albuquerque: University of New Mexico Press.

Lowe, G.W. 1981. 'Olmec horizons defined in Mound 20, San Isidro, Chiapas,' in E.P. Benson (ed.), *In The Olmec and their Neighbors*, pp. 231–255. Washington, DC: Dumbarton Oaks.

Lowe, G.W. 1989. 'Heartland Olmec: evolution of material culture,' in R.J. Sharer and D.C. Grove (eds.), *Regional Perspectives on the Olmec*, pp. 33–67. Cambridge: Cambridge University Press.

Lowe, G.W. 1998. *Los olmecas de San Isidro en Malpaso, Chiapas*, Serie Arqueología. Mexico City: Consejo Nacional para la Cultura y las Artes/Instituto Nacional de Antropología e Historia.

Lowe, G.W. 2001. 'Chiapa de Corzo (Chiapas, Mexico),' in S.T. Evans and D.L. Webster (eds.), *Archaeology of Ancient Mexico and Central America: an Encyclopedia*, pp. 122–123. New York: Garland Publishing, Inc.

Lowe, G.W., Lee, T.A., and Martínez Espinosa, E. 1982. *Izapa: An Introduction to the Ruins and Monuments*, Papers of the New World Archaeological Foundation, No. 31. Provo, UT: New World Archaeological Foundation.

Lowie, R.H. 1963 (1954). *Indians of the Plains*. Garden City: Natural History Press.

Lunagómez, R. 1995. *Patron de asentamiento en el hinterland interior de San Lorenzo Tenochtitlán, Veracruz*. Unpublished Licenciatura thesis, Department of Anthropology, Universidad Veracruzana, Xalapa.

MacNeish, R.S. 1958. 'Preliminary archaeological investigations in the Sierra de Tamaulipas, Mexico.' *Transactions of the American Philosophical Society* 48: 1–209.

MacNeish, R.S. 1967. 'An interdisciplinary approach to an archaeological problem,' in D.S. Byers (ed.), *Prehistory of the Tehuacan Valley, Vol. 1: Environment and Subsistence*, pp. 14–24. Austin: University of Texas Press.

MacNeish, R.S. 1971. 'Ancient Mesoamerican civilization,' in S. Streuver (ed.), *Prehistoric Agriculture*, pp. 143–156. Garden City, NY: Natural History Press, 1971.

Mann, M. 1986. *The Sources of Social Power, Vol. 1, A History of Power from the Beginning to A.D. 1760*. Cambridge: Cambridge University Press.

Manzanilla, L. and López Luján, L. (eds.) 2000. *Historia antigua de México, volumen I: el México antiguo, sus áreas culturales, los orígenes y el horizonte preclásico*. Mexico City: Instituto Nacional de Antropología e Historia and Universidad Nacional Autónoma de México.

Marcus, J. 1989. 'Zapotec chiefdoms and the nature of Formative religions,' in R.J. Sharer and D.C. Grove (eds.), *Regional Perspectives on the Olmec*, pp. 148–197. Cambridge: Cambridge University Press.

Marcus, J. 1992. *Mesoamerican Writing Systems.* Princeton, NJ: Princeton University Press.

Marcus, J. 1998. 'The peaks and valleys of ancient states,' in J. Marcus and G.M. Feinman (eds.), *Archaic States*, pp. 59–94. Santa Fe: School of American Research.

Marcus, J. 1999. 'Men's and Women's Ritual in Formative Oaxaca,' in D. Grove and R.A. Joyce (eds.), *Social Patterns in Pre-Classic Mesoamerica*, pp. 67–96. Washington, DC: Dumbarton Oaks.

Marcus, J. and Feinman, G.M. 1998. 'Introduction,' in G.M. Feinman and J. Marcus (eds.), *Archaic States*, pp. 3–13. Santa Fe: School of American Research Press.

Marcus, J. and Flannery, K. 1996. *Zapotec Civilization: How Urban Society Evolved in Mexico's Oaxaca Valley*. London: Thames & Hudson.

Martín-Del Pozzo, A.L. 1997. 'Geología,' in E. González Soriano, R. Dirzo and R.C. Vogt (eds.), *Historia natural de los Tuxtlas*, pp. 25–31. Mexico: Universidad Nacional Autónoma de México.

Martínez Donjuán, G. 1986. 'Teopantecuanitlán,' *Primer coloquio de arqueología y etnohistoria del estado de Guerrero*, pp. 55–80. Mexico City: Instituto Nacional de Antropología e Historia.

Martínez Donjuán, G. 1994. 'Los olmecas en el estado de Guerrero,' in J.E. Clark (ed.), *Los olmecas en mesoamerica*, pp. 143–163. Mexico City: Citibank.

Martínez-Gallardo, R. and Sánchez-Cordero, V. 1997. 'Lista de mamíferos terrestres,' in E. González Soriano, R. Dirzo and R.C. Vogt (eds.), *Historia natural de los Tuxtlas*, pp. 625–628. Mexico: Universidad Nacional Autónoma de México.

Matos Moctezuma, E. 2000. 'Mesoamérica,' in L. Manzanilla and L. Lópezdr Luján (eds.), *Historia antigua de México*, Vol. 1: El México antiguo, sus áreas culturales, los orígenes y el horizonte Preclásico, pp. 92–119. Mexico City: Consejo Nacional para la Cultural y las Artes/Instituto Nacional de Antropología e Historia.

McCormack, V.J. 2003. *Sedentism, Site Occupation and Settlement Organization at La Joya, A Formative Village in the Sierra de los Tuxtlas, Veracruz, Mexico*. Ph.D. dissertation, Department of Anthropology, University of Pittsburgh, Pittsburgh.

McDonald, A.J. 1977. 'Two Middle Preclassic engraved monuments at Tzutzuculi on the Chiapas coast of Mexico.' *American Antiquity* 42: 560–567.

Medellín Zenil, A. 1960. 'Nopiloa. Un sitio clásico del Veracruz Central.' *La palabra y el hombre*: 37–48.

Melgar, J.M. 1869. 'Antiguedades Mexicanos.' *Boletin de la Sociedad Mexicana de Geografia y Estadistica*, 2 ep. 1: 292–297.

Melgar, J.M. 1871. 'Estudio sobre la antiguedad y el origen de la cabeza colosal de tipo etiópico que existe en Hueyapán, del Canton de los Tuxtlas.' *Boletin de la Sociedad Mexicana de Geografia y Estadistica*, 2 ep. 3: 104–109.

Méluzin, S. 1992. 'The Tuxtla script: Steps toward decipherment based on La Mojarra Stela 1.' *Latin American Antiquity* 3: 283–297.

Méluzin, S. 1995. *Further Investigations of the Tuxtla script: An Inscribed Mask and La Mojarra Stela 1*, Papers of the New World Archaeological Foundation, No. 65. Provo, Utah: New World Archaeological Foundation.

Methner, B. 2000. *Ceramic Raw Material and Pottery Variability from La Venta, Tabasco, Mexico: A Test For Zonal Complementarity*. Unpublished M.A. thesis, Department of Anthropology, University of Kansas, Lawrence.

Michels, J.W. 1979. *The Kaminaljuyu Chiefdom*, Monograph Series on Kaminaljuyu. State College, PA: The Pennsylvania State University Press.

Milbrath, S. 1979. *A Study of Olmec Sculptural Chronology*, Studies in Pre-Columbian Art and Archaeology, No. 23. Washington, DC: Dumbarton Oaks.

Miles, S. 1965. 'Sculpture of the Guatemala-Chiapas highlands and Pacific slopes and associated hieroglyphs,' in G.R. Willey (ed.), *Archaeology of Southern Mesoamerica, Part I*, Handbook of Middle American Indians, Vol. 2, pp. 237–275. Austin: University of Texas Press.

Miller, M.E. 1991. 'Rethinking the Classic sculptures of Cerro de las Mesas, Veracruz,' in B.L. Stark (ed.), *Settlement Archaeology of Cerro de las Mesas, Veracruz, Mexico*, Monograph 34, pp. 26–38. Los Angeles: Institute of Archaeology, University of California, Los Angeles.

Miller, M.E. and Taube, K.A. 1993. *An Illustrated Dictionary of the Gods and Symbols of Ancient Mexico and the Maya*. London: Thames and Hudson, Ltd.

Millet Camara, L.A. 1979. *Rescate arqueológico en la región de Tres Zapotes, Ver.* Unpublished Licenciatura thesis in anthropology, Escuela Nacional de Antropología e Historia, Mexico City.

Mirambell Silva, L. 2000. 'Los primeros pobladores del actual territorio mexicano,' in L. Manzanilla and L. Lópezdr Luján (eds.), *Historia antigua de México, volumen 1: El México antiguo, sus áreas culturales, los orígenes y el horizonte preclásico*, pp. 223–254. Mexico City: Instituto Nacional de Antropología e Historia, Universidad Nacional Autónoma de México.

Morley, S.G. 1946. *The Ancient Maya*. Stanford University, CA: Stanford University Press.

Moziño, J. 1870. 'La erupción del volcán de San Martín Tuxtla (Veracruz) ocurida en el año de 1793.' *Boletin de la Sociedad Mexicana de Geografía y Estadística 2 ep.* 2: 62–70.

Navarrete, C. 1974. *The Olmec rock carvings at Pijijiapan, Chiapas, Mexico and other Olmec pieces from Chiapas and Guatemala*, Papers of the New World Archaeological Foundation 35. Provo, UT: Brigham Young University.

Neff, H., Blomster, J., Glascock, M.D., Bishop, R.L., Blackman, M.J., Coe, M.D., Cowgill, G.L., Diehl, R.A., Houston, S., Joyce, A.A., Lipo, C.P., Stark, B.L., and Winter, M. 2006a. 'Methodological issues in the provenance investigation of Early Formative Mesoamerican ceramics.' *Latin American Antiquity* 17: 54–76.

Neff, H., Blomster, J., Glascock, M.D., Bishop, R.L., Blackman, M.J., Coe, M.D., Cowgill, G.L., Cyphers, A., Diehl, R.A., Houston, S., Joyce, A.A., Lipo, C.P., and Winter, M. 2006b. 'Smokescreens in the provenance investigation of Early Formative Mesoamerican ceramics.' *Latin American Antiquity* 17: 104–118.

Neff, H. and Glascock, M.D. 2002. Instrumental Neutron Activation Analysis of Olmec Pottery. Ms. on file, University of Missouri-Columbia Research Reactor Center, Columbia, Missouri.

Nelson, B. 1995. 'Complexity, hierarchy, and scale: a controlled comparison between Chaco Canyon, New Mexico and La Quemada, Zacatecas.' *American Antiquity* 60: 597–618.

Nelson, F.W. and Clark, J.E. 1998. 'Obsidian production and exchange in eastern Mesoamerica,' in E.C. Rattray (ed.), *Rutas de intercambio en Mesoamérica*, III Coloquio Pedro Bosch Gimpera, pp. 277–333. Mexico City: Universidad Nacional Autónoma de México.

Nicholas, L.M. 1989. 'Land use in prehispanic Oaxaca,' in S.A. Kowalewski, G.M. Feinman, L. Finsten, R.E. Blanton, and L.M. Nicholas (eds.), *Monte Alban's Hinterland, Part II: The Prehispanic Settlement Patterns in Tlacolutla, Etla and Ocotlán, the Valley of Oaxaca, Mexico*, Museum of Anthropology Memoir 23, pp. 449–505. University of Michigan, Ann Arbor.

Nicholson, H.B. 1971. 'Religion in pre-Hispanic central Mexico,' *Handbook of Middle American Indians*, Vol. 10, pp. 395–446. Austin: University of Texas Press.

Niederberger, C. 1976. *Zohapilco: Cinco milenios de ocupación humana en un sitio lacustre de la Cuenca de México*. Mexico City: Instituto Nacional de Antropología e Historia.

Niederberger, C. 1986. 'Excavaciones de un área de habitación doméstica en la capital 'olmeca' de Tlalcozotitlán,' *Primer coloquio arqueología y etnohistoria del estado de Guerrero*, pp. 81–103. Mexico City: Instituto Nacional de Antropología e Historia.

Niederberger, C. 1987. *Paléopaysages et archéologie pré-urbaine du Bassin de Mexico.* Mexico City: CEMCA.

Niederberger, C. 1996. 'Olmec horizon Guerrero,' in E.P. Benson and B. de la Fuente (eds.), *Olmec Art of Ancient Mexico*, pp. 95–103. Washington, DC: National Gallery of Art.

Niederberger, C. 2000. 'Ranked Societies, Iconographic Complexity, and Economic Wealth in the Basin of Mexico toward 1200 B.C.,' in J.E. Clark and M.E. Pye (eds.), *Olmec Art and Archaeology in Mesoamerica*, pp. 169–191. Washington, DC: National Gallery of Art.

Norman, V.G. 1973. *Izapa Sculpture, Part 1: Album*, Papers of the New World Archaeological Foundation, No. 30. Provo, UT: New World Archaeological Foundation.

Norman, V.G. 1976. *Izapa Sculpture, Part 2: Text*, Papers of the New World Archaeological Foundation, No. 30. Provo, UT.

O'Brien, M.J. (ed.) 1996. *Evolutionary Archaeology: Theory and Application*. Salt Lake City: University of Utah Press.

O'Neil, T. 2002. 'Uncovering a Maya Mural'. *National Geographic* 201(4): 70–75.

Ortiz Ceballos, P. 1975. *La cerámica de los Tuxtlas.* Unpublished Maestría thesis in archaeology, Universidad Veracruzana, Jalapa.

Ortiz Ceballos, P. 1988. 'La arqueología en Veracruz,' in M. Mejía Sánchez (ed.), *La antropología en México, panorama histórico 13. La antropología en el occidente, el Bajío, la Huasteca y el oriente de México,* pp. 395–465. Mexico City: Instituto Nacional de Antropología e Historia.

Ortiz Ceballos, P. and Rodríguez, M.d.C. 1989. 'Proyecto Manatí 1989.' *Arqueología* 1: 23–52.

Ortiz Ceballos, P. and Rodríguez, M.d.C. 1997. 'Las ofrendas de El Manatí, Ver. ¿Religión o magia?,' in S. Ladrón de Guevara and S. Vásquez Z. (eds.), *Memoria del Coloquio Arqueología del centro y sur de Veracruz,* pp. 223–244. Xalapa, Veracruz, México: Universidad Veracruzana.

Ortiz Ceballos, P. and Rodríguez, M.d.C. 2000. 'The sacred hill of El Manatí: a preliminary discussion of the site's ritual paraphernalia,' in J.E. Clark and M.E. Pye (eds.), *Olmec Art and Archaeology in Mesoamerica,* pp. 75–93. Washington, DC: National Gallery of Art.

Ortiz Ceballos, P., Rodríguez, M.d.C., and Delgado, A. 1997. *Las Investigaciones arqueológicas en el cerro sagrado Manatí.* Xalapa, Veracruz, México: Universidad Veracruzana.

Ortiz Ceballos, P., Schmidt, P., and Rodríguez, M.d.C. 1988. 'Proyecto Manatí, temporada 1988: informe preliminar.' *Arqueología* 3: 141–154.

Ortiz de Montellano, B., Haslip-Viera, G., and Barbour, W. 1997. 'They were not here before Columbus: Afrocentric hyperdiffusionism in the 1990's.' *Ethnohistory* 44: 199–234.

Ortiz Pérez, M.A. and Cyphers, A. 1997. 'La geomorfología y las evidencias arqueológicas en la región de San Lorenzo Tenochtitlán, Veracruz,' in A. Cyphers (ed.), *Población, subsistencia y medio ambiente en San Lorenzo Tenochtitlán,* pp. 31–53. Mexico City: Universidad Nacional Autónoma de México.

Paradis, L.I. 1990. 'Revisión del fenómeno olmeca.' *Arqueología* 3: 33–40.

Parsons, L.A. 1986. *The Origins of Maya Art: Monumental Stone Sculpture of Kaminaljuyu, Guatemala and the Southern Pacific Coast,* Studies in Pre-Columbian Art and Archaeology No. 28. Washington, DC: Dumbarton Oaks.

Peres, T.M., VanDerwarker, A.M., and Pool, C.A. 2006. The farmed and the hunted: integrating floral and faunal data from Tres Zapotes, Veracruz. Paper presented at the 71st Annual Meeting of the Society for American Archaeology, San Juan, Puerto Rico.

Piña Chán, R. 1955. *Las culturas preclásicas de la cuenca de México.* Mexico City: Fonda de Cultura Económica.

Piña Chán, R. 1989. *The Olmec: Mother Culture of Mesoamerica.* New York: Rizzoli.

Piña Chán, R. and Covarrubias, L. 1964. *El pueblo del jaguar.* Mexico City: Museo Nacional de Antropología.

Pires-Ferreira, J.C.W. 1975. *Formative Mesoamerican Exchange Networks, with Special Reference to the Valley of Oaxaca,* Museum of Anthropology Memoir 7. Ann Arbor: University of Michigan.

Pires-Ferreira, J.C.W. 1976a. 'Obsidian exchange in Formative Mesoamerica,' in K.V. Flannery (ed.), *The Early Mesoamerican Village,* pp. 292–306. New York: Academic Press.

Pires-Ferreira, J.C.W. 1976b. 'Shell and iron-ore mirror exchange in formative Mesoamerica, with comments on other commodities,' in K.V. Flannery (ed.), *The Early Mesoamerican village,* pp. 311–326. New York: Academic Press.

Plog, S. 1976. 'Measurement of prehistoric interaction between communities,' in K.V. Flannery (ed.), *The Early Mesoamerican Village,* pp. 255–272. New York: Academic Press.

Pohl, M.D., Pope, K.O. and von Nagy, C.L. 2002. 'Olmec origins of Mesoamerican writing.' *Science* 298: 1984–1987.

Pohorilenko, A. 1981. 'The Olmec style and Costa Rican archaeology,' in E.P. Benson (ed.), *The Olmec and their Neighbors,* pp. 309–327. Washington, DC: Dumbarton Oaks.

Pohorilenko, A. 1996. 'Portable Carvings in the Olmec Style,' in E.P. Benson and B. de la Fuente (eds.), *Olmec Art of Ancient Mexico,* pp. 119–131. Washington, DC: National Gallery of Art.

Pompa y Padilla, J.A. and Serrano Carreto, E. 2001. 'Los más antiguos americanos.' *Arqueología Mexicana* 9(52): 36–41.

Pool, C.A. 1990. *Ceramic Production, Resource Procurement, and Exchange at Matacapan, Veracruz, Mexico.* Ph.D. disseratation, Department of Anthropology, Tulane University, New Orleans.

Pool, C.A. 1992. 'Strangers in a strange land: ethnicity and ideology at an enclave community in Middle Classic Mesoamerica,' in A.S. Goldsmith (ed.), *Ancient Images, Ancient Thought: the Archaeology of Ideology*, pp. 41–55. Calgary: University of Calgary.

Pool, C.A. 1997a. 'Proyecto arqueológico Tres Zapotes,' in S. Ladrón de Guevara and S. Vásquez Z. (eds.), *Memoria del Coloquio Arqueología del centro y sur de Veracruz*, pp. 169–176. Xalapa, Veracruz, México: Universidad Veracruzana.

Pool, C.A. 1997b. 'The Spatial Structure of Formative Houselots at Bezuapan,' in B.L. Stark and P.J. Arnold, III (eds.), *Olmec to Aztec: Settlement Patterns in the Ancient Gulf Lowlands*, pp. 40–67. Tucson, Arizona: The University of Arizona Press.

Pool, C.A. 2000. 'From Olmec to Epi-Olmec at Tres Zapotes, Veracruz, Mexico,' in J.E. Clark and M.E. Pye (eds.), *Olmec Art and Archaeology in Mesoamerica*, pp. 137–153. Washington, DC: National Gallery of Art.

Pool, C.A. 2003a. 'Centers and peripheries: Urbanization and political economy at Tres Zapotes,' in C.A. Pool (ed.), *Settlement Archaeology and Political Economy at Tres Zapotes, Veracruz, Mexico*, Monograph 50, pp. 90–98. Los Angeles: Cotsen Institute of Archaeology, University of California.

Pool, C.A. ed. 2003b. *Settlement Archaeology and Political Economy at Tres Zapotes, Veracruz, Mexico*, Monograph 50. Los Angeles: Cotsen Institute of Archaeology, University of California.

Pool, C.A. 2005. 'Architectural plans, factionalism, and the Protoclassic-Classic transition at Tres Zapotes,' in P.J. Arnold and C.A. Pool (eds.), *Cultural Currents in Classic Veracruz*. Washington, DC: Dumbarton Oaks. In press.

Pool, C.A. and Britt, G.M. 2000. 'A ceramic perspective on the Formative to Classic transition in southern Veracruz, Mexico.' *Latin American Antiquity* 11: 139–161.

Pool, C.A., King, B.C. and Ettensohn, F.R. 2001. 'Volcanic Ash-Tempered "Fine Paste" Pottery at Tres Zapotes, Veracruz.' *La Tinaja* 13(1): 7–8.

Pool, C.A. and Ohnersorgen, M.A. 2003. 'Archaeological survey and settlement at Tres Zapotes,' in C.A. Pool (ed.), *Settlement Archaeology and Political Economy at Tres Zapotes, Veracruz, Mexico*, Monograph 50, pp. 7–31.

Los Angeles: Cotsen Institute of Archaeology, University of California.

Pool, C.A. and Santley, R.S. 1992. 'Middle Classic pottery economics in the Tuxtla Mountains, Southern Veracruz, Mexico,' in G.J. Bey, III and C.A. Pool (eds.), *Ceramic Production and Distribution: An Integrated Approach*, pp. 205–234. Boulder, Colorado: Westview Press.

Pope, K.O., Pohl, M.D., Jones, J.G., Lentz, D.L., von Nagy, C.L., Vega, F.J., and Quitmyer, I.R. 2001. 'Origin and environmental setting of ancient agriculture in the lowlands of Mesoamerica.' *Science* 292: 1370–1373.

Popenoe de Hatch, M. 2001. 'Kaminaljuyu (Guatemala, Guatemala),' in S.T. Evans and D.L. Webster (eds.), *Archaeology of Ancient Mexico and Central America: an Encyclopedia*, pp. 387–390. New York: Garland Publishing, Inc.

Porter, J.B. 1989. *The Monuments and Hieroglyphs of Tres Zapotes, Veracruz, Mexico*. Unpublished Ph.D. dissertation, Department of Anthropology, University of California, Berkeley.

Porter, J.B. 1990. 'Cabezas colosales olmecas como altares reesculpidos: "mutilación," revolución y reesculpido.' *Arqueología* 3: 91–97.

Porter, J.B. 1992. '"Estelas celtiformes": un nuevo tipo de estructura olmeca y sus implicaciones para los epigrafistas.' *Arqueología* 8: 3–13.

Prindiville, M. and Grove, D.C. 1987. 'The settlement and its architecture,' in D.C. Grove (ed.), *Ancient Chalcatzingo*, pp. 63–81. Austin: University of Texas.

Proskouriakoff, T. 1974. *Jades from the Cenote of Sacrifice, Chichén Itzá, Yucatán*, Peabody Museum Memoirs, Vol. 10, No. 1. Cambridge, MA: Harvard University.

Pugh, M.S. 1981. 'An intimate view of archaeological exploration,' in E.P. Benson (ed.), *The Olmec and their Neighbors*, pp. 1–13. Washington, DC: Dumbarton Oaks.

Quirarte, J. 1973. *Izapan-Style Art: A Study of its Form and Meaning*, Studies in Pre-Columbian Art and Archaeology, No. 10. Washington, DC: Dumbarton Oaks.

Quirarte, J. 1976. 'The relationship of Izapan-style art to Olmec and Maya art: a review,' in H.B. Nicholson (ed.), *Origins of Religious Art and Iconography in Preclassic Mesoamerica*, UCLA Latin American Studies Series 31, pp. 73–86: Los Angeles.

Quirarte, J. 1977. 'Early art styles of Mesoamerica and Early Classic Maya art,' in R.E.W. Adams (ed.), *The Origins of Maya Civilization*, pp. 249–283. Albuquerque: University of New Mexico.

Raab, M.L., Boxt, M.A., Bradford, K., Stokes, B.A., and González Lauck, R. 2000. 'Testing at Isla Alor in the La Venta Olmec hinterland.' *Journal of Field Archaeology* 27: 257–270.

Rambo, A.T. 1991. 'The study of cultural evolution.' *Profiles in Cultural Evolution*: 23–109.

Ramírez-Bautista, A. and Nieto-Montes de Oca, A. 1997. 'Ecogeografía de anfibios y reptiles,' in E. González Soriano, R. Dirzo, and R.C. Vogt (eds.), *Historia natural de los Tuxtlas*, pp. 523–532. Mexico: Universidad Nacional Autónoma de México.

Rathje, W.L. 1972. 'Praise the gods and pass the metates: a hypothesis of the development of lowland rainforest civilizations in Mesoamerica,' in M. Leone (ed.), *Contemporary Archaeology*, pp. 365–392. Carbondale, Illinois: Southern Illinois University Press.

Rathje, W.L., Sabloff, J.A., and Gregory, D.A. 1973. 'El descubrimeinto de un jade olmeca en la isla de Cozumel, Quintana Roo, México.' *Estudios de Cultura Maya* 9: 85–91.

Record, P. 1969. *Tropical Frontier*. New York: Alfred A. Knopf.

Reilly, F.K., III 1991. 'Olmec iconographic influences on the symbols of Maya rulership: an examination of possible sources.' in V. M. Fields (ed.), *Sixth Palenque Round Table, 1986*, pp. 151–174. Norman, Oklahoma.

Reilly, F.K., III 1994. 'Enclosed ritual spaces and the watery underworld in Formative period architecture: new observations on the function of La Venta Complex A,' in M.G. Robertson and V.M. Fields (eds.), *Seventh Palenque Round Table, 1989*, pp. 125–135. San Francisco: Pre-Columbian Art Research Institute.

Reilly, F.K., III 1995. 'Art, Ritual, and Rulership in the Olmec World,' in J. Guthrie and E.P. Benson (eds.), *The Olmec World: Ritual and Rulership*, pp. 27–45. Princeton, New Jersey: The Art Museum, Princeton University.

Reilly, F.K., III 1999. 'Mountains of creation and underworld portals: the ritual function of Olmec architecture at La Venta, Tabasco,' in J.K. Kowalski (ed.), *Mesoamerican Architecture as Cultural Symbol*, pp. 14–39. New York and Oxford: Oxford University Press.

Reinhardt, B.K. 1991. *Volcanology of the Younger Volcanic Sequence and Volcanic Hazards Study of the Tuxtla Volcanic Field, Veracruz, Mexico.* Unpublished M.A. thesis, Tulane University, New Orleans.

Renfrew, C. 1974. 'Beyond a subsistence economy: the evolution of social organization in prehistoric Europe,' in C.B. Moore (ed.), *Reconstructing Complex Societies: An Archaeological Colloquium*, Supplement to the Bulletin of the American Schools of Oriental Research 20, pp. 69–95. Cambridge, MA.

Reyna Robles, R.M. 1996. *Cerámica de época olmeca en Teopantecuanitlán, Guerrero*, Colección Científica, No. 316. Mexico City: Instituto Nacional de Antropología e Historia.

Reyna Robles, R.M. and Martínez Donjuán, G. 1989. 'Hallazgos funerarios de la época olmeca en Chilpancingo, Guerrero.' *Arqueología* 1: 13–22.

Ricketson, O.G.J. and Ricketson, E.B. 1937. *Uaxactun, Guatemala, Group E: 1926–1931*, Carnegie Institution of Washington, Publication 447. Washington DC.

Ríos Macbeth, F. 1952. 'Estudio geológico de la región de los Tuxtlas.' 4: 324–376.

Rodríguez, M.d.C. and Ortiz, C.P. 2005. Los asentamientos olmecas y preolmecas de la cuenca baja del Río Coatzacoalcos, Ver. Paper presented at the Mesa Redonda Olmeca: Balance y Perspectivas, Mexico City.

Rodríguez, M.d.C. and Ortíz Ceballos, P. 1997. 'Olmec Ritual and Sacred Geography at Manatí,' in B.L. Stark and P.J. Arnold, III (eds.), *Olmec to Aztec: Settlement Patterns in the Ancient Gulf Lowlands*, pp. 68–95. Tucson, Arizona: The University of Arizona Press.

Rodríguez, M.d.C. and Ortíz Ceballos, P. 2000. 'A Massive Offering of Axes at La Merced, Hidalgotitlán, Veracruz, Mexico,' in J.E. Clark and M.E. Pye (eds.), *Olmec Art and Archaeology in Mesoamerica*, pp. 155–167. Washington, DC: National Gallery of Art.

Rodríguez, M.L., Aguirre, R., and González, J. 1997. 'Producción campesina del maíz en San Lorenzo Tenochtlán,' in A. Cyphers (ed.), *Población, subsistencia y medio ambiente en San Lorenzo Tenochtitlán*, pp. 55–73. Mexico City: Universidad Nacional Autónoma de México.

Rodríguez Martínez, M.d.C., Ortíz Ceballos, P., Coe, M.D, Diehl, R.A., Houston, S.D.,

Taube, K.A. and Delgado Calderón, A. 2006. Oldest Writing in the New World. *Science*, 313: 1610–1614.

Rojas Chávez, J.M. 1990. 'Análisis preliminar de la industria de la lítica tallada en La Venta, Tabasco.' *Arqueología* 3: 25–32.

Romano, A. 1962. 'Exploraciones en Tlatilco, México.' *Boletín del INAH* 10: 1–2.

Romano, A. 1963. 'Exploraciones en Tlatilco, México.' *Boletín del INAH* 14: 11–3.

Romano, A. 1967. 'Tlatilco.' *Boletín del INAH* 30: 38–42.

Rosenswig, R.M. 2000. 'Some political processes of ranked societies'. *Journal of Anthropological Archaeology* 19: 413–460.

Rust, W.F., III 1992. 'New ceremonial and settlement evidence at La Venta, and its relations to Preclassic Maya cultures,' in N. Hammond (ed.), *New Theories on the Ancient Maya*, pp. 123–129. Philadelphia: University Museum of Archaeology and Anthropology, University of Pennsylvania.

Rust, W.F. and Leyden, B.W. 1994. 'Evidence of maize use at Early and Middle Preclassic La Venta Olmec sites,' in S. Johannessen and C.A. Hastorf (eds.), *Corn and Culture in the Prehistoric New World*, pp. 181–201. Boulder, Colorado: Westview Press.

Rust, W.F. and Sharer, R.J. 1988. 'Olmec settlement data from La Venta, Tabasco, Mexico.' *Science* 242: 102–104.

Sahlins, M.D. 1958. *Social Stratification in Polynesia*. Seattle: University of Washington Press.

Sahlins, M.D. and Service, E.R. (eds.) 1960. *Evolution and Culture*. Ann Arbor: University of Michigan Press.

Sanders, W.T. 1953. 'The anthropogeography of Central Veracruz.' *Revista mexicana de estudios antropológicos*: 27–78.

Sanders, W.T. 1956. 'The Central Mexican symbiotic region: a study in prehistoric settlement patterns,' in G.R. Willey (ed.), *Prehistoric Settlement Patterns in the New World*, pp. 115–127: New York, 1956.

Sanders, W.T. 1965. *The Cultural Ecology of the Teotihuacan Valley*. University Park: Pennsylvania State University.

Sanders, W.T. 1981. 'Ecological adaptation in the basin of Mexico: 23,000 B.C. to the present,' in J.A. Sabloff (ed.), *Archaeology*, Supplement to the Handbook of Middle American Indians, No. 1, pp. 147–197. Austin: University of Texas Press.

Sanders, W.T., Parsons, J., and Santley, R.S. 1979. *The Basin of Mexico: Ecological Processes in the Evolution of a Civilization*. New York: Academic Press.

Sanders, W.T. and Price, B.J. 1968. *Mesoamerica: The Evolution of a Civilization*. New York: Random House.

Sanders, W.T. and Webster, D. 1978. 'Unilinealism, multilinealism, and the evolution of complex societies,' in C. Redman, M.J. Berman, E. Curtin, W. Langhorne, Jr., N. Versaggi, and J. Wanser (eds.), *Social Archaeology: Beyond Subsistence and Dating*, pp. 249–302. New York: Academic Press.

Santley, R.S. 1992. 'A consideration of the Olmec phenomenon in the Tuxtlas: Early Formative settlement pattern, land use, and refuse disposal at Matacapan, Veracruz, Mexico,' in T.W. Killion (ed.), *Gardens of Prehistory: The Archaeology of Settlement Agriculture in Greater Mesoamerica*, pp. 150–183. Tuscaloosa: University of Alabama Press.

Santley, R.S. 1994. 'The Economy of Ancient Matacapan.' *Ancient Mesoamerica* 5: 243–266.

Santley, R.S. 2004. 'Prehistoric salt production at El Salado, Veracruz, Mexico.' *Latin American Antiquity* 15: 199–221.

Santley, R.S. and Arnold, P.J., III 1996. 'Prehispanic settlement patterns in the Tuxtla Mountains, southern Veracruz, Mexico.' *Journal of Field Archaeology* 23: 225–249.

Santley, R.S., Arnold, P.J., III, and Barrett, T.P. 1997. 'Formative period settlement patterns in the Tuxtla Mountains,' in B.L. Stark and P.J. Arnold, III (eds.), *Olmec to Aztec: Settlement Patterns in the Ancient Gulf Lowlands*, pp. 174–205. Tucson, Arizona: The University of Arizona Press.

Santley, R.S., Barrett, T.P., Glascock, M.D., and Neff, H. 2001. 'Pre-Hispanic obsidian procurement in the Tuxtla Mountains, southern Veracruz, Mexico.' *Ancient Mesoamerica* 12: 49–63.

Santley, R.S., Nelson, S.A., Reinhardt, B.K., Pool, C.A., and Arnold, P.J., III 2000. 'When day turned to night: volcanism and the archaeological record from the Tuxtla Mountains, southern Veracruz, Mexico,' in G. Bawden and R.M. Reycraft (eds.), *Environmental Disaster and the Archaeology of Human Response*, pp. 143–161. Albuquerque, New Mexico: Maxwell Museum of Anthropology.

Santley, R.S., Ortiz Ceballos, P., Arnold, P.J., Kneebone, R.R., Smyth, M.P., Kerley, J.M., Berman, M., Hall, B.A., Kann, V., Pool, C.A., Salazar Buenrostro, Z., and Yarborough, C. 1985. Final Field Report, Matacapan Project: 1984 Season. Report submitted to the Instituto Nacional de Antropologia e Historia, Mexico City.

Santley, R.S., Ortiz Ceballos, P., Arnold, P.J.I., Kneebone, R.R., Smyth, M.P., and Kerley, J.M. 1984. Final Field Report, Matacapan Project: 1983 Season. Report submitted to the Instituto Nacional de Antropologia e Historia, Mexico City.

Santley, R.S., Ortiz Ceballos, P., and Kludt, T.J. 1988. Prehistoric Salt Production at El Salado. Report submitted to the Heinz Trust of the Pittsburgh Foundation, Pittsburgh.

Santley, R.S., Ortíz Ceballos, P., and Pool, C.A. 1987. 'Recent Archaeological Research at Matacapan, Veracruz: A Summary of the Results of the 1982 to 1986 Field Seasons.' *Mexicon* 9(2): 41–48.

Santley, R.S., Yarborough, C., and Hall, B.A. 1987. 'Enclaves, ethnicity, and the archaeological record at Matacapan,' in R. Auger, M.F. Glass, S. MecEachern, and P.H. McCartney (eds.), *Ethnicity and Culture*, pp. 85–100. Calgary: Archaeological Association, University of Clagary.

Saturno, W.A., Stuart, D., and Beltrán, B. 2006. Early Maya Writing at San Bartolo, Guatemala. *Science* 311:1281–1283.

Saville, M.H. 1900. 'A votive adze of jadeite from Mexico.' *Monumental Records* 1: 138–140.

Saville, M.H. 1929a. 'Votive axes from ancient Mexico.' *Indian Notes* 6: 266–299.

Saville, M.H. 1929b. 'Votive axes from ancient Mexico II.' *Indian Notes* 6: 335–342.

Schaldach, W.J., Jr. and Escalante-Pliego, B.P. 1997. 'Lista de aves,' in E. González Soriano, R. Dirzo, and R.C. Vogt (eds.), *Historia natural de los Tuxtlas*, pp. 571–588. Mexico: Universidad Nacional Autónoma de México.

Schele, L. 1995. 'The Olmec Mountain and the Tree of Creation in Mesoamerican Cosmology,' in J. Guthrie and E.P. Benson (eds.), *The Olmec World: Ritual and Rulership*, pp. 105–117. Princeton, New Jersey: The Art Museum, Princeton University.

Schele, L. and Friedel, D.A. 1990. *A Forest of Kings: The Untold Story of the Ancient Maya.* New York: William Morrow and Company, Inc.

Schmidt, P.S. 1990. *Arqueología de Xochipala, Guerrero.* Mexico City: Universidad Nacional Autónoma de México.

Schortman, E.M. and Urban, P.A. 1992. 'The place of interaction studies in archaeological thought,' in E.M. Schortman and P.A. Urban (eds.), *Resources, Power, and Interregional Interaction*, pp. 3–15. New York: Plenum Press.

Scott, J.F. 1977. 'El Mesón, Veracruz, and its monolithic reliefs.' *Baessler-Archiv* 25: 83–138.

Seitz, R., Harlow, G.E., Sisson, V.B., and Taube, K.E. 2001. '"Olmec Blue' and Formative jade sources: New discoveries in Guatemala.' *Antiquity* 75: 687–688.

Seler-Sachs, C.F. 1922. 'Altertümer des Kanton Tuxtla im Staate Vera-cruz,' in W. Lehmann (ed.), *Festschrift Eduard Seler*, pp. 543–556. Stuttgart.

Service, E.R. 1962. *Primitive Social Organization: An Evolutionary Perspective.* New York: Random House.

Service, E.R. 1971. *Primitive Social Organization: An Evolutionary Perspective.* New York: Random House.

Service, E.R. 1975. *Origins of the State and Civilization: The Process of Cultural Evolution.* New York: Norton.

Sharer, R.J. 1978. *The Prehistory of Chalchuapa, El Salvador, Vol. 3, Pottery and Conclusions.* Philadelphia: University of Pennsylvania Press.

Sharer, R.J. 1989a. 'The Olmec and the southeast periphery of Mesoamerica,' in R.J. Sharer and D.C. Grove (eds.), *Regional Perspectives on the Olmec*, pp. 247–271. Cambridge: Cambridge University Press.

Sharer, R.J. 1989b. 'Olmec studies: a status report,' in R.J. Sharer and D.C. Grove (eds.), *Regional Perspectives on the Olmec*, pp. 3–7. Cambridge: Cambridge University Press.

Sharer, R.J., Balkansky, A.K., Burton, J.H., Feinman, G.M., Flannery, K.V., Grove, D.C., Marcus, J., Moyle, R.G., Price, T.D., Redmond, E. M., Reynolds, R.G., Rice, P.M., Spencer, C.S., Stoltman, J.B., and Yaeger, J. 2006. 'On the logic of archaeological inference: Early Formative Pottery and the Evolution of Mesoamerican Societies.' *Latin American Antiquity* 17: 90–103.

Sharer, R.J. and Grove, D.C. (eds.) 1989. *Regional Perspectives on the Olmec.* Cambridge: University of Cambridge Press.

Sharer, R.J. and Sedat, D.W. 1973. 'Monument 1, El Portón, Guatemala, and the development of Maya calendrical and writing systems.' *Contributions of the University of California Archaeological Research Facility* 18: 177–194.

Shepard, A. 1952. 'Technological Analysis,' in P. Drucker, *La Venta, Tabasco: A Study of Olmec Ceramics and Art,* pp. 234–240. Bureau of American Ethnology Bulletin 153. Washington, DC: Smithsonian Institution.

Shook, E.M. 1956. 'An Olmec sculpture from Guatemala.' *Archaeology* 9: 260–262.

Shook, E.M. and Kidder, A.V. 1952. *Mound E-III-3, Kaminaljuyu, Guatemala,* Contributions to American Anthropology and History 53. Washington, DC: Carnegie Institution of Washington.

Siemens, A.H. 1998. *A Favored Place: San Juan River Wetlands, Central Veracruz, A.D. 500 to the Present.* Austin: University of Texas Press.

Sisson, E.B. 1970. 'Settlement patterns and land use in the northwestern Chontalpa, Tabasco, Mexico: a progress report.' *Cerámica de cultura Maya* 6: 41–65.

Sisson, E.B. 1976. *Survey and Excavation in the Northwestern Chontalpa, Tabasco, Mexico.* Unpublished Ph.D. dissertation, Department of Anthropology, Harvard University, Cambridge, MA.

Smith, A.T. 2003. *The Political Landscape: Constellations of Authority in Early Complex Politics.* Berkeley: University of California Press.

Smith, B.D. 1997. 'Reconsidering the Ocampo caves and the era of incipient cultivation in Mesoamerica.' *Latin American Antiquity* 8: 342–83.

Smith, B.D. 2000. 'Guilá Naquitz revisited: agricultural origins in Oaxaca, Mexico,' in G.M. Feinman and L. Manzanilla (eds.), *Cultural Evolution: Contemporary Viewpoints,* pp. 15–60. New York: Kluwer Academic/Plenum Press.

Smith, R.E. 1936a. *Ceramics of Uaxactun: A Preliminary Analysis of Decorative Techniques and Designs,* Special Publications of the Carnegie Institution. Washington DC.

Smith, R.E. 1936b. *Preliminary Shape Analysis of Uaxactun Pottery,* Special Publications of the Carnegie Institution. Washington DC.

Smith, V.G. 1978. *An Analysis of Izapan-Style Art: Its Form, Content, Rules of Design and Role in Mesoamerican Art History and Archaeology.* Unpublished M.A. thesis, Department of Anthropology, University of Kentucky, Lexington.

Smith, V.G. 1984. *Izapa Relief Carving: Form, Content, Rules for Design, and Role in Mesoamerican Art History and Archaeology,* Studies in Pre-Columbian Art and Archaeology, No. 27. Washington, DC: Dumbarton Oaks.

Sociedad Mexicana de Antropología 1943. *Mayas y Olmecas, Segunda Reunión de Mesa Redonda.* Mexico City: Sociedad Mexicana de Antropología.

Soto, M. and Gama, L. 1997. 'Climas,' in E. González Soriano, R. Dirzo, and R.C. Vogt (eds.), *Historia natural de los Tuxtlas,* pp. 7–23. Mexico: Universidad Nacional Autónoma de México.

Spencer, C.S. 1993. 'Human agency, biased transmission, and the cultural evolution of chiefly authority.' *Journal of Anthropological Archaeology* 12: 41–74.

Spinden, H.J. 1928. *Ancient Civilizations of Mexico and Central America,* American Museum of Natural History Handbook Series, no. 3. New York.

Stark, B.L. 1974. 'Geography and economic specialization in the Lower Papaloapan, Veracruz, Mexico.' *Ethnohistory* 21: 199–221.

Stark, B.L. 1981. 'The rise of sedentary life,' in J.A. Sabloff (ed.), *Archaeology: Supplement to the Handbook of Middle American Indians, Vol. 1,* pp. 345–372. Austin: University of Texas Press.

Stark, B.L. 1991. *Settlement Archaeology of Cerro de Las Mesas, Veracruz, Mexico,* Monograph 34. Los Angeles: Institute of Archaeology, University of California.

Stark, B.L. 1992. 'Ceramic production in prehistoric La Mixtequilla, south-central Veracruz, Mexico,' in G.J. Bey, III and C.A. Pool (eds.), *Ceramic Production and Distribution: An Integrated Approach,* pp. 175–204. Boulder, Colorado: Westview Press.

Stark, B.L. 1997. 'Gulf lowland ceramic styles and political geography in ancient Veracruz,' in B.L. Stark and P.J. Arnold, III (eds.), *Olmec to Aztec: Settlement Patterns in the Ancient Gulf Lowlands,* pp. 278–309. Tucson: The University of Arizona Press.

Stark, B.L. 2000. 'Framing the Gulf Olmecs,' in J.E. Clark and M.E. Pye (eds.), *Olmec Art and Archaeology in Mesoamerica,* pp. 31–53. Washington, DC: National Gallery of Art.

Stark, B.L. 2004. 'Out of Olmec,' in V. Scarborough and J.E. Clark (eds.), *The Early Mesoamerican State*: In preparation.

Stark, B.L. and Arnold, P.J., III 1997a. 'Introduction to the archaeology of the Gulf Lowlands', in B.L. Stark and P.J. Arnold, III (eds.), *Olmec to Aztec: Settlement Patterns in the Ancient Gulf Lowlands*, pp. 3–32. Tucson, Arizona: The University of Arizona Press.

Stark, B.L. eds. 1997b. *Olmec to Aztec: Settlement Patterns in the Ancient Gulf Lowlands*. Tucson, Arizona: The University of Arizona Press.

Stark, B.L. and Curet, L.A. 1994. 'The development of the Classic-period Mixtequilla in south-central Veracruz, Mexico.' *Ancient Mesoamerica* 5: 267–287.

Stark, B.L. and Heller, L. 1991. 'Residential dispersal in the environs of Cerro de las Mesas,' in B.L. Stark (ed.), *Settlement Archaeology of Cerro de las Mesas, Veracruz, Mexico*, Monograph 34, pp. 49–58. Los Angeles: Instute of Archaeology, University of California.

Stark, B.L., Heller, L., Glascock, M.D., Elam, M.J., and Neff, H. 1992. 'Obsidian artifact source analysis for the Mixtequilla region, south-central Veracruz, México'. *Latin American Antiquity* 3: 221–239.

Stark, B.L., Heller, L., and Ohnersorgen, M.A. 1998. 'People with cloth: Mesoamerican economic change from the perspective of cotton in south-central Veracruz.' *Latin American Antiquity* 9: 7–36.

Stark, M.T. (ed.) 1998. *The Archaeology of Social Boundaries*. Washington, DC: Smithsonian Institution Press.

Stephens, J.L. 1841. *Incidents of Travel in Central America, Chiapas, and Yucatan*. New York: Harper.

Stephens, J.L. 1843. *Incidents of Travel in Yucatan*. New York: Harper.

Steward, J.H. 1949. 'Cultural causality and law: a trial formulation of the development of early civilizations.' *American anthropologist* 51: 1–27.

Stirling, M. 1941. 'Jungle housekeeping for a Geographic expedition.' *National Geographic Magazine* 80: 303–327.

Stirling, M.W. 1939. 'Discovering the New World's oldest dated work of man.' *National Geographic Magazine* 76: 183–218.

Stirling, M.W. 1940. 'Great stone faces of the Mexican jungle.' *National Geographic Magazine* 78: 309–334.

Stirling, M.W. 1942. 'Recientes hallazgos en La Venta,' *Mayas y Olmecas, segunda reunión de mesa redonda*, pp. 56–58. Mexico City: Sociedad Mexicana de Antropología.

Stirling, M.W. 1943. *Stone Monuments of Southern Mexico*, Bureau of American Ethnology, Bulletin 138. Washington DC.

Stirling, M.W. 1947. 'On the trail of La Venta man.' *National Geographic Magazine* 91: 137–172.

Stirling, M.W. 1955. 'Stone monuments of the Rio Chiquito, Veracruz, Mexico.' *Anthropological Papers, No. 43*, Bureau of American Ethnology Bulletin 157, pp. 1–23. Washington, DC: Smithsonian Institution.

Stirling, M.W. 1965. 'Monumental sculpture of southern Veracruz and Tabasco,' in G.R. Willey (ed.), *Archaeology of Southern Mesoamerica, Part 2*, Handbook of Middle American Indians, Vol. 3, pp. 716–738: Austin, 1965.

Stirling, M.W. 1968. 'Early history of the Olmec problem,' in E.P. Benson (ed.), *Dumbarton Oaks Conference on the Olmec*, pp. 1–8. Washington, DC: Dumbarton Oaks.

Stirling, M.W. and Stirling, M. 1942. 'Finding jewels of jade in a Mexican swamp.' *National Geographic Magazine* 82: 635–661.

Stocker, T.L., Meltzhoff, S., and Armsey, S. 1980. 'Crocodilians and Olmecs: further interpretations of Formative period iconography.' *American Antiquity* 45: 740–758.

Stoltman, J.B., Marcus, J., Flannery, K.V., Burton, J.H., and Moyle, R.G. 2005. 'Petrographic evidence shows that pottery exchange between the Olmec and their neighbors was two-way.' *Proceedings of the National Academy of Sciences* 102: 11213–11218.

Stross, B. 1990. 'Mesoamerican writing at the crossroads: the Late Formative.' *Visible Language* 24: 38–61.

Stuiver, M., Reimer, P.J., Bard, E., Beck, J.W., Burr, G.S., Hughen, K.A., Kromer, B., McCormac, F.G., Plicht, J.v.d., and Spurk, M. 1998. 'INTCAL98 radiocarbon age calibration, 24,000–0 cal. BP'. *Radiocarbon* 40: 1041–83.

Sullivan, T.D. 2002. *Landscape of Power: A Spatial Analysis of Civic-Ceremonial Architecture at Tres Zapotes, Veracruz, Mexico*. Unpublished M.A. thesis, Department of Anthropology, Southern Ilinois University, Carbondale.

Symonds, S. 1995. *Settlement Distribution and the Development of Cultural Complexity in the*

Lower Coatzacoalcos Drainage, Veracruz, Mexico: An Archaeological Survey at San Lorenzo. Ph.D. dissertation, Department of Anthropology, Vanderbilt University, Nashville. Ann Arbor: UMI.

Symonds, S. 2000. 'The ancient landscape at San Lorenzo Tenochtitlán, Veracruz, México: settlement and nature,' in J.E. Clark and M.E. Pye (eds.), *Olmec Art and Archaeology in Mesoamerica*, pp. 55–73. Washington, DC: National Gallery of Art.

Symonds, S., Cyphers, A. and Lunagómez, R. 2002. *Asentamiento prehispánico en San Lorenzo Tenochtitlán.* Mexico City: Universidad Nacional Autónoma de México.

Symonds, S. and Lunagómez, R. 1997a. 'Settlement system and population development at San Lorenzo,' in B.L. Stark and P.J. Arnold, III (eds.), *Olmec to Aztec: Settlement Patterns in the Ancient Gulf Lowlands*, pp. 144–173. Tucson, Arizona: The University of Arizona Press.

Symonds, S. and Lunagómez, R. 1997b. 'El sistema de asentamientos y el desarrollo de poblaciones en San Lorenzo Tenochtitlán, Veracruz,' in A. Cyphers (ed.), *Población, subsistencia y medio ambiente en San Lorenzo Tenochtitlán*, pp. 119–152. Mexico City: Universidad Nacional Autónoma de México.

Tarpy, C. 2004. 'Place of the Standing Stones: Unearthing a King from the Dawn of the Maya.' *National Geographic Magazine* 205(5): 66–78.

Tate, C.E. 1995. 'Art in Olmec culture,' in J. Guthrie and E.P. Benson (eds.), *The Olmec World: Ritual and Rulership*, pp. 47–67. Princeton, New Jersey: The Art Museum, Princeton University.

Tate, C.E. 1999. 'Patrons of shamanic power: La Venta's supernatural entities in light of Mixe beliefs.' *Ancient Mesoamerica* 10: 169–188.

Taube, K.A. 1995. 'The rainmakers: the Olmec and their contribution to Mesoamerican belief and ritual,' in J. Guthrie and E.P. Benson (eds.), *The Olmec World: Ritual and Rulership*, pp. 83–103. Princeton, New Jersey: The Art Museum, Princeton University.

Taube, K.A. 2000. 'Lightning celts and corn fetishes: the Formative Olmec and the development of maize symbolism in Mesoamerica and the American Southwest,' in J.E. Clark and M.E. Pye (eds.), *Olmec Art and Archaeology in Mesoamerica*, pp. 297–337. Washington, DC: National Gallery of Art.

Taylor, W.W., Jr. 1948. *A Study of Archaeology*, Memoir Series of the American Anthropological Association, No. 69. Menasha.

Thompson, J.E.S. 1941. *Dating of Certain Inscriptions of Non-Maya origin*, Theoretical Approaches to Problems, No. 1. Cambridge: Division of Historical Research, Carnegie Institution of Washington.

Thorpe, R.S. 1977. 'Tectonic significance of alkaline volcanism in eastern Mexico.' *Tectonophysics* 40: T19–T28.

Tolstoy, P. 1989a. 'Coapexco and Tlatilco: sites with Olmec materials in the Basin of Mexico,' in R.J. Sharer and D.C. Grove (eds.), *Regional Perspectives on the Olmec*, pp. 85–121. Cambridge: Cambridge University Press.

Tolstoy, P. 1989b. 'Western Mesoamerica and the Olmec,' in R.J. Sharer and D.C. Grove (eds.), *Regional Perspectives on the Olmec*, pp. 275–302. Cambridge: Cambridge University Press.

Tolstoy, P. and Paradis, L.I. 1970. 'Early and Middle Preclassic culture in the Basin of Mexico,' *Science* 167(3917): 344–351.

Tolstoy, P. and Paradis, L.I. 1971. 'Early and Middle Preclassic culture in the Basin of Mexico.' *Contributions of the University of California Archaeological Research Facility* 11: 7–28.

Vaillant, G. 1930. *Excavations at Zacatenco*, Anthropological Papers of the American Museum of Natural History. New York.

Vaillant, G. 1931. *Excavations at Ticomam*, Anthropological Papers of the American Museum of Natural History. New York.

Vaillant, G. 1932. 'A precolumbian jade.' *Natural History* 32: 512–520.

Vaillant, G. 1935. 'Chronology and stratigraphy in the Maya area.' *Maya Research*, Vol. 2, no 2, pp. 119–143. New Orleans: Middle American Research Institute, Tulane University.

Vaillant, G.C. 1941. *Aztecs of Mexico*. Garden City: Garden City Press.

VanDerwarker, A.M. 2003. *Agricultural Intensification and the Emergence of Political Complexity in the Formative Sierra de los Tuxtlas, Southern Veracruz, Mexico.* Ph.D. dissertation, Department of Anthropology, University of North Carolina, Chapel Hill, NC. Ann Arbor: UMI.

VanDerwarker, A.M. 2006. *Farming, Hunting, and Fishing in the Olmec World*. Austin: University of Texas Press.

Villela, S.F. 1989. 'Nuevo testimonio rupestre en el oriente de Guerrero.' *Arqueología* 2: 37–48.

Vivó-Escoto 1964. 'Weather and climate of Mexico and Central America,' in R. West (ed.), *Natural Environment and Early Cultures*, Handbook of Middle American Indians, Vol. 3, pp. 187–215. Austin: University of Texas Press.

von Nagy, C.L. 1997. 'The geoarchaeology of settlement in the Grijalva delta,' in B.L. Stark and P.J. Arnold, III (eds.), *Olmec to Aztec: Settlement Patterns in the Ancient Gulf Lowlands*, pp. 253–277. Tucson, Arizona: The University of Arizona Press.

von Nagy, C.L. 2003. *Of Meandering Rivers and Shifting Towns: Landscape Evolution and Community within the Grijalva delta*. Ph.D. dissertation, Department of Anthropology, Tulane University, New Orleans.

von Nagy, C.L., Pohl, M.D., and Pope, K.O. 2002. Ceramic chronology of the La Venta Olmec polity: the view from San Andrés, Tabasco. Paper presented at the 67th Annual Meeting of the Society for American Archaeology, Denver, Colorado.

Voorhies, B. 1976. *The Chantuto People: An Archaic Period Society of the Chiapas Littoral, Mexico*, Papers of the New World Archaeological Foundation, No. 41. Provo, Utah: New World Archaeological Foundation.

Voorhies, B. 1996. 'The transformation from foraging to farming in the lowlands of Mesoamerica,' in S. Fedick (ed.), *The Managed Mosaic: Ancient Maya Agriculture and Resource Use*, pp. 17–29. Salt Lake City: University of Utah Press.

Voorhies, B. and Kennett, D.J. 1995. 'Buried sites on the Soconusco coastal plain, Chiapas, Mexico.' *Journal of Field Archaeology* 22: 65–79.

Wauchope, R. 1950. 'A tentative sequence of Pre-Classic ceramics in Middle America.' *Middle American Research Records* 1(14): 211–250.

Weaver, M.P. 1993. *The Aztecs, Maya, and Their Predecessors: Archaeology of Mesoamerica*, 3rd edition. New York: Academic Press.

Wedel, W.R. 1952. 'Structural investigations in 1943,' in P. Drucker (ed.), *La Venta, Tabasco, a Study of Olmec Ceramics and Art*, Bureau of American Ethnology Bulletin 153, pp. 34–79. Washington, DC: Smithsonian Institution.

Weiant, C.W. 1943. *An Introduction to the Ceramics of Tres Zapotes, Veracruz, Mexico*, Bureau of American Ethnology Bulletin 139. Washington DC: Smithsonian Institution.

Weiant, C.W. 1952. 'Reply to "Middle Tres Zapotes and the Preclassic ceramic sequence."' *American Antiquity* 18: 57–59.

Wendt, C.J. 2003. 'Buried occupational deposits at Tres Zapotes: the results from an auger testing program,' in C.A. Pool (ed.), *Settlement Archaeology and Political Economy at Tres Zapotes, Veracruz, Mexico*, Monograph 50, pp. 32–46. Los Angeles: Cotsen Institute of Archaeology, University of California.

Wendt, C.J. and Lu, Shan-Tan 2006. 'Sourcing archaeological bitumen in the Olmec region.' *Journal of Archaeological Science* 33: 89–97.

Werner, D. 1983. 'Why do the Mekranoti trek?,' in R. Hames and W. Vickers (eds.), *Adaptive Responses of Native Amazonians*, pp. 225–238. New York: Academic Press.

West, R.C., Psuty, N.P., and Thom, B.G. 1969. *The Tabasco Lowlands of Southeastern Mexico*, Coastal Studies Series 27. Baton Rouge: Louisiana State University.

Weyerstall, A. 1932. *Some Observations on Indian Mounds, Idols, and Pottery in the Lower Papaloapan Basin, State of Veracruz, Mexico*. Middle American Research Series, No. 4. New Orleans: Middle American Research Institute, Tulane University.

Whitecotton, J.W. 1977. *The Zapotecs: Princes, Priests, and Peasants*. Norman: University of Oklahoma Press.

Wicke, C.R. 1971. *Olmec: An Early Art Style of Precolumbian Mexico*. Tucson: University of Arizona Press.

Wilkerson, S.J.K. 1981. 'The northern Olmec and pre-Olmec frontier on the Gulf Coast,' in E.P. Benson (ed.), *The Olmec and their Neighbors*, pp. 181–194. Washington, DC: Dumbarton Oaks.

Willey, G.R. 1978. 'Artifacts,' in G.R. Willey (ed.), *Excavations at Seibal, Department of Petén, Guatemala*, Memoirs of the Peabody Museum of American Archaeology and Ethnology, Vol. 14, No. 1, pp. 1–189. Cambridge, MA: Harvard University.

Willey, G.R., Bullard, W.R., Glass, J.B., and Gifford, J.C. 1965. *Prehistoric Settlement Patterns in the Belize Valley*, Peabody Museum of Archaeology and Ethnology Papers, Vol. 54. Cambridge, MA: Harvard University.

Willey, G.R. and Phillips, P. 1955. 'Method and theory in American archeology, II: historical-developmental interpretation'. *American Anthropologist* 57: 723–819.

Willey, G.R. and Phillips, P. 1958. *Method and Theory in American Archaeology*. Chicago: University of Chicago Press.

Willey, G.R. and Sabloff, J.A. 1993. *A History of American Archaeology*. New York: W. H. Freeman and Co.

Williams, H. and Heizer, R.F. 1965. 'Sources of stones used in prehistoric Mesoamerican sites.' *Contributions of the University of California Archaeological Research Facility* 1: 1–39.

Winfield Capitaine, F. 1988. *La estela 1 de La Mojarra, Veracruz, México*, Research Reports on Ancient Maya Writing, No. 16. Washington, DC: Center for Maya Research.

Wing, E.S. 1980. 'Aquatic fauna and reptiles from the Atlantic and Pacific sites,' in M.D. Coe and R.A. Diehl (eds.), *In the Land of the Olmec, Vol. 1, The Archaeology of San Lorenzo Tenochtitlán*, pp. 375–386. Austin: University of Texas Press.

Wing, E.S. 1981. 'A comparison of Olmec and Maya food ways,' in E.P. Benson (ed.), *The Olmec and their Neighbors*, pp. 20–28. Washington, DC: Dumbarton Oaks.

Winker, K. 1997. 'Introducción a las aves de los Tuxtlas,' in E. González Soriano, R. Dirzo, and R.C. Vogt (eds.), *Historia natural de los Tuxtlas*, pp. 535–543. Mexico: Universidad Nacional Autónoma de México.

Winter, M. 1994. 'Los Altos de Oaxaca y los olmecas,' in J.E. Clark (ed.), *Los olmecas en Mesoamerica*, pp. 119–141. Mexico City: Citibank.

Wright, H.T. 1984. 'Prestate political formations,' in T. Earle (ed.), *On the evolution of complex societies: essays in honor of Harry Hoijer 1982*, pp. 41–77. Malibu: Undena Publications.

Wright, H.T. and Johnson, G.A. 1975. 'Population, exchange, and early state formation in southwestern Iran,' *American Anthropologist* 77(2): 267–289.

Wyllie, C.E. 2004. 'Children of the Cultura Madre: continuity and change in Late Classic southern Veracruz art, hieroglyphs, and relgion,' in P.J. Arnold and C.A. Pool (eds.), *Cultural Currents in Classic Veracruz*. Washington, DC: Dumbarton Oaks. In press.

Yadéun Angulo, J. 1983. 'Arqueología del tiempo y el espacio de las notaciones en piedra,' *Antropología e historia de los Mixe-Zoques y Mayas. México*, pp. 131–146. Mexico City: Universidad Nacional Autónoma de México, Centro de Estudios Mayas.

Yoffee, N. 1993. 'Too many chiefs? (or safe texts for the '90s),' in N. Yoffee and A. Sherrat (eds.), *Archaeological Theory: Who Sets the Agenda?*, pp. 60–78. Cambridge: Cambridge University Press.

Yoffee, N. 2005. *Myths of the Archaic State*. Cambridge: Cambridge University Press.

Zurita Noguera, J. 1997. 'Los fitolitos: indicaciones sobre dieta y vivienda en San Lorenzo,' in A. Cyphers (ed.), *Población, subsistencia y medio ambiente en San Lorenzo Tenochtitlán*, pp. 75–87. Mexico City: Universidad Nacional Autónoma de México.

INDEX

Abasolo, 202
acropolis, 122, 127, 294
adapatationist strategy, 134–135, 137–138
aggrandizer strategy, 135–136, 287
   agriculture, subsistence, 3, 26, 51, 64, 73, 81, 82,
      84, 85, 94, 145–146, 155, 246. *See also* maize
      agriculture; soils
altars, 57, 106, 110, 116, 127, 139, 166, 174, 177
Altotonga, 240
Alvarado, 275
Alvarado stela, 269
Alvaro Obregón, 194
Amate phase, 209
"The Ambassador", 169. *See also* La Venta, Monument
      13
andesite, 148
Andrews V., E. Wyllys, 221
Angulo V., Jorge, 57
anthropomorphic axe, 97
anthropomorphic supernatural
   feline figure, 122, 144
   shark/fish monster, 117. *See also* were-jaguar
archaeobotanical studies, 64
archaeological cultures, 12, 14
archaeological sites. *See* specific site
archaeologist. *See* specific person
Archaic Horizon, 45
Archaic period, 6, 39, 46
   estuarine resources during, 94
   maize cultivation during, 64, 93
   subsistence agriculture during, 94
archaic state, 143, 176
Arenal phase, 274
Armillas, Pedro, 7
Arnold III, Philip J., 24, 60–61, 95, 131
Arroyo Pesquero, 172, 174
Arroyo Sonso "wrestler", 111
art/iconography, political influence on, 65. *See also*
      monumental art/iconography/power
asphalt, natural, 78, 90
atomic mass spectrometry, 73

Atopula, Guerrero, 57, 210–212
   a vocados, 64, 75, 196
axes
   anthropomorphic, 97
   greenstone, 96, 230
   greenstone, polished, 97
   stone, 247
   stone, polished, 96, 192
   votive, 35–36, 38, 58, 108–109, 116, 223. *See also*
      celts
axis mundi (world tree), 123, 143, 172
Ayotla phase, 9, 181, 206, 207
Aztecs
   calendric names and, 259
   creation story of, 258
   myth of the Five Suns, 114
   name for land of Olman, 4–5
   name for people of Olman, 5
   sacred drink of, 85–86, 184
Azuzul acropolis, 122. *See also* El Azuzul, acropolis
      at

baby-face sculpture, Early Horizon, 38, 231
badges of office, 140
Bajío phase, 98, 125, 189
ballcourt, 186, 187, 230
ball game
   importance in Mesoamerican cultures, 96
   sacrifice associated with, 114
balls, rubber, 62, 95, 96, 97
bar-and-dot numerical notation, 27, 271, 277,
      299
bar-and-four-dots motif, 112
Barranca phase, 232, 238
Barth, Fredrik, 50
basalt
   elite control over, 65
   source of, 1, 68, 78, 103, 129, 130, 141, 148,
      246–247
   uses for, 64, 78, 90, 146
   uses for, utilitarian *vs.* prestige, 140–141

San Lorenzo, 98–105
    aquatic resources at, 77
    basalt at, 1, 10
    beans, appearance at, 73
    ceremonial bars/scepters, 139
    civic/ceremonial precinct at, 1, 11
    clay-paved floors at, 78
    colossal head 2, 121
    colossal head 7, 121
    colossal head processional arrangement at, 122–123
    craft specialization, 103–105
        elite control over, 105
        ilmenite cubes, 104–105
        obsidian working, 105
        prestige/public display articles, 104
        "workshops", 104
    decline of, 148, 151–152, 156
    drains at, 100
    elite control of resources at, 64
    elite residential complex at, 62
    Group A mounds, 100
    Group D workshop, 62, 121, 141
    Group E, monument display at, 122
    hierarchical differentiation in, 292
    hierarchical differentiation in Early Formative, 11
    human ecology project at, 51–52
    hydraulic works at, 52, 230
    landscape/architecture change at, 98–102
        causeways/dikes, 102
        residences, 100–102
        ritual, 100
        terraces, 102
    lithic industry at, 64
    maize cultivation at, 73
    Mounument 10, 119, 195
    Mounument 14, 110, 116, 139, 177
    Mounument 18, 174
    Monument 20, 116
    Monument 52, 116, 119, 195
    Monument 77, 120
    Monument 78, 139
    Monument 83, 139
    Monument 91, 139
    Monument 107, 110
    Monument 112, 139
    multidisciplinary project at, 62–63
    mutilation/resculpting of monuments at, 121, 156
    obsidian source for, 148, 150
    occupational phases, 98
    Palangana plaza, 100
    political organization of, 23
    power vacuum in, 195
    predominance of profile view pottery at Early
        Horizon, 202
    prestige good exchange at, 10–11
    production/exchange at, 102–105
        greenstone, 103
    production/exchange, materials/sources, 102–103

    basalt,
    clay, 102–103
    ilmenite, 103
    natural petroleum seeps, 103
    obsidian, 103
    salt, 103
    stone, 103
    wood, 102
    riverine trade at, 62, 64
    size/population of site, 62
    source of obsidian at, 131
    stone monuments at, 52, 62–63
    utilitarian use of basalt at, 141
    weapon depictions at, 139
    workshop, monument recycling, 62, 121, 141. *See
        also* Lower Coatzacoalcos River Basin
San Lorenzo Horizon, 181
San Lorenzo phase, 98, 129, 136–137, 142
    San Lorenzo A phase, 129–130
    San Lorenzo B phase, 129, 130, 195
San Lorenzo series soil, 81
San Lorenzo Tenochtitlán. *See* San Lorenzo
San Martín Jilotepeque,
San Martín Pajapan monument, 38, 118, 122, 123,
    143
San Miguel Amuco, 57, 227
San Pablo, Morelas, 209
Santley, Robert S., 60–61
sarcophagus, 110, 177, 254
Saturno, William, 275
Saville, Marshall, 12, 36, 38, 58, 298
Schele, Linda, 122, 123
schist, 108–109, 148, 166
School of American Research (S.A.R.) Advanced
    Seminar, 59–60
scroll motif
    bounded, 204
    ilhuitl (double scroll), 181, 208, 217, 234, 235
sculpture-in-the-round, 194, 251
Seler, Eduard, 36
Seler-Sachs, Caecilie, 36
serpentine
    exchange of, 9, 216, 220, 222
    La Venta figurine, 163–164, 165
    mosaic pavements of, 46
    source of, 11, 142, 231–232
    uses of, 1–2, 48, 97, 108–109, 177–178
    in Veracruz, 54. *See also* greenstone
serpentine beads, 207
Serpent X, 279
Service, Elman R., 19, 180
shaman-chief figurines, 188
shamanic transformation, 56, 120, 173–174
shamanic were-jaguar, 56
shamans, 118–119, 144, 172–174
Sharer, Robert J., 60
shark/fish monster, 117
shark teeth, 78, 141, 164